THE BRITISH
DIPLOMATIC SERVICE
1689–1789

Oxford University Press, Amen House, London E.C.4

GLASGOW   NEW YORK   TORONTO   MELBOURNE   WELLINGTON
BOMBAY   CALCUTTA   MADRAS   KARACHI   KUALA LUMPUR
CAPE TOWN   IBADAN   NAIROBI   ACCRA

The British Diplomatic Service

1689-1789

BY

D. B. HORN, D.Litt.

PROFESSOR OF MODERN HISTORY IN THE
UNIVERSITY OF EDINBURGH

OXFORD
AT THE CLARENDON PRESS
1961

TO MY WIFE

ACKNOWLEDGEMENTS

I wish to place on record my deep and abiding sense of gratitude to the authorities and staffs of the various archives and libraries in which I have worked, and especially to the Public Record Office, the British Museum, the National Library of Scotland, the National Central Library, and, above all, the Library of the University of Edinburgh. The University of Edinburgh made possible the speedy completion of a book for which I had long been collecting material by giving me leave of absence for the autumn term of 1958. The Carnegie Trust for the Universities of Scotland offered me a generous grant in aid of publication. The Clarendon Press not only undertook publication, but have guided me with unobtrusive and unerring skill through the labyrinths which lie between any manuscript, no matter how carefully prepared, and the printed book.

Certain parts of this book have already appeared, textually or in substance, in print. I am grateful to the editors and publishers of the *English Historical Review* and of *History* for allowing me to reprint such material. The Council of the Royal Historical Society has granted me permission to reprint Chapter III, most of which had already appeared in their *Transactions*, 5th Series, Volume 9. The Historical Association allowed me to incorporate parts of a pamphlet on *Scottish Diplomatists 1689–1789*, which originally appeared under their auspices in 1944.

The Controller of H.M. Stationery Office gave permission to reproduce a long extract from Volume IV of the Historical Manuscripts Commission Report on the Manuscripts of the Rt. Hon. Lord Polwarth, C.B.E., and also two other lengthy passages, one from the Portland Manuscripts, Volume V, the other from the Downshire Manuscripts, Volume I. These quotations will be found below on pp. 171–2, 198–200 and 209–10, respectively. Many short quotations have also been made from these and other volumes published by the Commission.

It is fitting that I should acknowledge here the constant inspiration I have received in the thirty years during which I have been intermittently engaged in writing this book from the precepts and example of Sir Richard Lodge, who first introduced me

to the pleasures and tribulations of historical composition. Nor
can I omit to mention my indebtedness to my friend and former
pupil, Dr. Matthew Anderson, of the London School of Economics, for help, always generously and promptly given. On the
subject matter of Chapter XIII, I have corresponded with Sir
Godfrey Fisher and have benefited greatly from this exchange of
views, although the conclusions presented in this chapter are
entirely my own. My chief indebtedness is acknowledged in-
adequately in another place.

D. B. HORN

Edinburgh, July 1960

CONTENTS

LIST OF ABBREVIATIONS

A.E.	Archives du Ministère des Affaires Étrangères
Add. MSS.	British Museum, Additional Manuscripts
Adm.	Admiralty
B.M.	British Museum
C.O.	Colonial Office
F.O.	Public Record Office, Foreign Office Papers
H.C., or H. of C.	House of Commons
H.M.C.	Publications of the Historical Manuscripts Commission
N.L.S.	National Library of Scotland
P.C.	Privy Council
P.P.	*Parliamentary Papers*
P.R.O.	Public Record Office
S.P.	State Papers Foreign (at Public Record Office)
T.	Treasury

Note. Titles of books and periodicals given in abbreviated form will be found *infra* on p. xiii.

LIST OF BOOKS AND PERIODICALS
REGULARLY REFERRED TO UNDER
SHORT TITLES

The initials or words preceding the colon are those under which the work is cited. The full title follows.

A.H.R.: *American Historical Review*

Auckland Journal: *Journal and Correspondence of William, Lord Auckland, with a Preface and Introduction by the Bishop of Bath and Wells* (4 vols., London, 1861–2)

B.D.R.: *British Diplomatic Representatives 1689–1789*, ed. for the Royal Historical Society by D. B. Horn (London, 1932)

Bedford Corresp.: *Correspondence of John, Fourth Duke of Bedford, selected from the Originals at Woburn Abbey with an Introduction by Lord John Russell* (3 vols., London, 1842–6)

Bolingbroke Corresp.: *Letters and Correspondence of Viscount Bolingbroke*, ed. G. Parke (2 vols., London, 1798)

Buckinghamshire Desp.: *The Despatches and Correspondence of John, Second Earl of Buckinghamshire, Ambassador to the Court of Catherine II of Russia*, ed. for the Royal Historical Society by Adelaide D'A. Collyer (2 vols., London, 1900–2)

Bull. Inst. Hist. Research: *Bulletin of the Institute of Historical Research*

Cal. H.O. Papers: *Calendar of Home Office Papers*

Chatham Corresp.: *Correspondence of William Pitt, Earl of Chatham*, ed. W. S. Taylor and J. H. Pringle (4 vols., London, 1838–40)

Chesterfield, Letters: *Letters of Philip Dormer Stanhope, Earl of Chesterfield, with the Characters*, ed. J. Bradshaw (3 vols., London, 1892)

C.J.: *Journals of the House of Commons*, &c. (London n.d.)

Clark, Trumbull: Ruth Clark, *Sir William Trumbull in Paris 1685–1686* (Cambridge, 1938)

Cole, Memoirs: Christian Cole, *Historical and Political Memoirs containing Letters written by Sovereign Princes, State Ministers, Admirals, and General Officers etc. from almost all the Courts of Europe* [1697–1708] (London, 1735)

Coxe, Lord Walpole Memoirs: William Coxe, *Memoirs of Horatio, Lord Walpole, selected from his Correspondence and Papers* (2 vols., London, 1808)

Coxe, Walpole Memoirs: William Coxe, *Memoirs of the Life and Administration of Sir Robert Walpole, Earl of Orford, with Original Correspondence and Authentic Papers* (3 vols. London, 1798)

C.T.B.: *Calendar of Treasury Books*

C.T.B. & P.: *Calendar of Treasury Books and Papers*

C.T.P.: *Calendar of Treasury Papers*

D.N.B.: *Dictionary of National Biography*

E.H.R.: *English Historical Review*

Elliot Memoir: *A Memoir of the Rt. Hon. Hugh Elliot by the Countess of Minto* (Edinburgh, 1868)

Fraser, *Intelligence*: Peter Fraser, *The Intelligence of the Secretaries of State and their Monopoly of Licensed News 1660–88* (Cambridge, 1956)

George III Corresp.: *The Correspondence of King George the Third from 1760 to December 1783*, ed. Sir John Fortescue (6 vols., London, 1927–8)

Grenville Papers: *The Grenville Papers: being the Correspondence of Richard Grenville, Earl Temple, and the Rt. Hon. George Grenville*, ed. W. J. Smith (4 vols., London 1852–3)

Hervey Memoirs: *Some Materials towards Memoirs of the Reign of King George II by John Lord Hervey . . .*, ed. R. Sedgwick (3 vols., London, 1931)

Honest Diplomat: *An Honest Diplomat at The Hague*, ed. J. J. Murray (Indiana Univ. Publications, 1955)

Keene Corresp.: *The Private Correspondence of Sir Benjamin Keene*, ed. Sir R. Lodge (Cambridge, 1933)

Keith Memoir: *Memoirs and Correspondence (Official and Familiar) of Sir Robert Murray Keith*, ed. Mrs. Gillespie Smyth (2 vols., London, 1849)

Larpent: *Turkey; its History and Progress from the Journals and Correspondence of Sir James Porter by Sir George Larpent* (2 vols., London, 1854)

Last Journals: *Journal of the Reign of King George the Third from the year 1771 to 1783 by Horace Walpole*, ed. Dr. Doran (2 vols., London, 1859)

L.J.: *Journals of the House of Lords*, &c. (London, n.d.)

Malmesbury Diaries: *Diaries and Correspondence of James Harris, First Earl of Malmesbury, edited by his grandson, the Third Earl* (4 vols., London, 1844)

Manchester, *Court and Society*: The Duke of Manchester, *Court and Society from Elizabeth to Anne* (2 vols., London, 1864)

Marchmont Papers: *A Selection from the Papers of the Earls of Marchmont in the possession of the Rt. Hon. Sir George Henry Rose* (3 vols., London, 1831)

P.H.: *Parliamentary History*

Stair Annals: *Annals and Correspondence of the Viscount and the First and Second Earls of Stair by J. M. Graham* (2 vols., Edinburgh and London, 1875)

Sutton Desp.: *The Despatches of Sir Robert Sutton, Ambassador in Con-stantinople (1710–1714)*, ed. for the Royal Historical Society by A. N. Kurat (London, 1953)

Trans. R. Hist. Soc.: *Transactions of the Royal Historical Society*

Wood, *Levant Co.*: A. C. Wood, *A History of the Levant Company* (London, 1935)

Note. Titles of other works quoted are given at sufficient length for easy identification.

CHAPTER I

Foreign Policy and the Diplomatic Service

IN the history of international relations in the modern European state system two landmarks stand out—the establishment of regular diplomatic representation in place of occasional and special missions and the concentration of the handling of all inter-state relations in each country by a specialized ministry of foreign affairs. Whereas the first of these developments occurred in Western Europe in the second half of the fifteenth century[1] the second did not become the general rule in Europe until the eighteenth century and many of the embryo foreign offices still retained responsibility for certain domestic affairs, while other state departments in most countries controlled business which would now be automatically assigned to the foreign office.

In Britain the decisive date is 1782, when in place of the time-honoured distribution of foreign affairs between the secretaries of state for the northern and southern departments, each of them responsible also for some domestic business, the Home and Foreign Offices were created. The reasons why this change, which was certainly in line with the general tendency of eighteenth-century European administrative development, was made at this precise point have never been examined; but it is clear that George III was personally concerned. He had proposed the change—for a special reason—in 1771[2] and claimed then, quite wrongly, that this division of duties was already 'the case in every other court'.[3] In 1781 he again proposed that one of his secretaries of state, Stormont, should conduct the correspondence with all the European courts.[4]

Although the creation of the Foreign Office was much the most important administrative change in the sphere of foreign policy during the eighteenth century, its immediate effects were less

---

[1] P. Renouvin, *Histoire des relations internationales*, vol. ii, seems to doubt whether permanent embassies were really a sign of progress in international affairs.

[2] *Infra*, p. 8.

[3] *George III Corresp.* ii. 205.   [4] Ibid. v. 326–7; cf. vi. 70.

epoch-making than might have been expected. In the years following immediately upon the Revolution of 1688 the sovereign
was sufficiently powerful to give a reasonable measure of coherence
and unified direction to our foreign policy. Under Anne, Marlborough and Godolphin worked in close concert down to 1710.
These desirable objectives were fairly well attained under the
Hanoverians by the tendency for one of the secretaries to take the
lead and impose his own views upon his junior or less forceful
colleagues. Foreign policy continued to be formulated in discussions between the sovereign and his most influential advisers: it
continued also to be occasionally approved, or much more rarely
disapproved, by a parliamentary majority.

Proposals for a more radical alteration of the mode of conducting foreign affairs were made from time to time. In 1701, during
the discussions on the partition treaties, the House of Lords suggested that the king should establish a council of his trustworthy
natural-born subjects to discuss all affairs of importance both at
home and abroad. The implication, of course, was that he should
no longer depend for advice in conducting foreign policy on Ben-
tincks and Keppels.[5]

A few years later, for rather different reasons, Abraham Stanyan
proposed the setting up of an *ad hoc* council[6] to advise the king on
foreign affairs and suggested that this council should be exclusively composed of professional diplomatists who had served
abroad for at least seven years before becoming members
of it.[7]

In practice, however, foreign affairs continued to be dealt with
formally in the Privy Council, and less formally in the various
forms assumed by the Cabinet during the eighteenth century.
These bodies formulated foreign policy, so far as it ever was
formulated in eighteenth-century Britain, and took executive
decisions, or, more often, made recommendations to the king.
Once these recommendations had been approved by the king, it
was the task of the diplomatic service to do its best to carry them
out. Few diplomatists would have claimed more than this, al-

[5] 16 *L.J.* under date 20 Mar. 1701, quoted Ogg, *England in the Reigns of
James II and William III*, pp. 497–8.
[6] See his 'Reflections upon the Management of our Foreign Affairs' [April
1712] in S.P. 96. 15.
[7] M. Meier, *Die diplomatische Vertretung Englands in der Schweiz im 18. Jahrhundert*, pp. 11–12.

though Sir James Harris, while envoy at The Hague,[8] argued that 'our *Principals* at home are too much occupied with the House of Commons to attend to what passes on the Continent; and, if any good is ever done there, it must be effected through the King's ministers abroad, and not by those about his person. Long experience has taught me this; and I never yet received an instruction that was worth reading.'[9] Harris was writing to a junior colleague in the diplomatic service and overstates his case: he would have been the last man to express this point of view in a letter to the secretary of state.

Earlier in the seventeenth century it was not unusual for diplomatists to correspond directly with the king, as French diplomatists continued to do as long as the *ancien régime* lasted. For example, Lord Preston sent private advices to the king from Paris and instructed his messenger 'to deliver the enclosed with as much secrecy as you can to the King and choose your time when neither of the Secretaries are by'.[10] After the Glorious Revolution direct correspondence between the Sovereign and 'his' agents abroad became quite unusual.[11] Prior, after the accession of George I, wrote a series of letters from Paris, trying to curry favour with the new sovereign. On at least one occasion Walpole suspected George II of conveying a hint to the British minister at Vienna, possibly 'by a juggle through some German hand', with the result that Robinson's reply to his official orders 'was certainly, for the purpose it was to serve, extremely well-drawn; that is, it was impossible more plausibly to defeat what his public orders were to promote . . .'.[12] But such instances are very rare.

George III showed a slight tendency to revert to earlier practice in this respect. He corresponded directly with Sir Joseph Yorke at The Hague, mostly about affairs which were not the concern of the British government, such as the appointment of the hereditary prince of Brunswick to a post in the Dutch service.[13] But in the course of this exchange of letters he expressly asked Yorke to send him accounts of 'any little occurrences that may delineate the

---

[8] The diplomatic careers of diplomatic agents mentioned in the text are summarized in *B.D.R.* Fuller treatment of many of them will be found in *D.N.B.*

[9] *Malmesbury Diaries*, ii. 112–13. [10] H.M.C., *Report VII App.*, pp. 325–6.

[11] H.M.C., *Downshire MSS.* i. 114.

[12] *Hervey Memoirs*, ii. 393–4. Walpole later averred that Robinson 'deserved hanging for his conduct in that affair' (ibid.).

[13] *George III Corresp.* i. 207–9, 228–31, 240–4, 248.

character of the Prince of Orange that you may think improper to be conveyed in a ministerial dispatch'.[14] In later correspondence Yorke dealt with other topics, such as the proposed Orange–Hohenzollern marriage alliance, which were definitely of interest to the British government.[15] It appears that the Hanoverian Resident at The Hague acted as a go-between between Yorke and the king.[16] In Sweden in 1723 the secret committee of the Diet had strictly limited the right of the king to correspond with diplomatic agents abroad;[17] but this restriction, of course, disappeared after Gustavus III's *coup d'état* in 1772, when the king once again became his own minister for foreign affairs. No such law was ever passed in Britain; but the king, in corresponding personally with Yorke, was certainly breaking an established convention of the constitution.

All British diplomatists received instructions to follow the orders sent to them by the secretaries and to correspond regularly with the secretaries; and, after 1689, it became increasingly rare for the crown to use any other channel. The lowest point in the position of the Secretariat of State as the sole authorized means of communication with the ministers abroad came at the end of William III's reign. In 1698 Vernon, secretary of state for the northern department, wrote to Prior:

I approve very well of your method of writing everything to my Lord Portland at large, and you are very kind in sending me an extract of what you think proper for the Office; I would by no means have you do it otherwise. On all accounts the correspondence ought to be directly with my Lord Portland and he is the fittest person to receive and transmit His Majesty's directions upon all emergencies. You must very shortly write to him in Holland, but I hope you will spare us a sketch from time to time, that I may be able to inform the Lords Justices how affairs go.[18]

Even under Anne the secretaries were occasionally by-passed. Imperative instructions were sent by Marlborough to Raby at Berlin.[19] On another occasion, about the same time, Lord Treasurer

---

[14] *George III Corresp.* i. 248.   [15] Ibid. i. 335, 357, 362–6, &c.

[16] Ibid. i. 397, ii. 110. Cf. Namier, *Additions and Corrections*, p. 44.

[17] *Histoire de l'administration des affaires étrangères de Suède*, ed. Tunberg and others, p. 247.

[18] H.M.C., *Bath MSS.* iii. 237.

[19] *Infra*, Chapter VIII, p. 149.

Godolphin, in the absence of both secretaries, sent from Windsor instructions, written in his own hand, to the duke of Manchester, the British ambassador at Venice. Manchester was instructed to propose that the Republic of St. Mark should immediately join the Grand Alliance and conclude with Britain a treaty of subsidy. On the advice of his secretary, Cole, that he should 'do nothing in it: but rather to get plainer and safer instructions', Manchester replied that he could not act in a matter of such consequence until after his public entry as ambassador, and begged for further directions.[20] When Sunderland, secretary of state for the south, repeated the instructions, though in a less imperative and specific manner, Manchester was already doing what he could to carry them out.[21]

Under George II, Newcastle, as the leading minister from 1754 to 1756, not infrequently sent what were in effect instructions to British diplomatists abroad; but he usually guarded himself carefully. Thus in writing to Andrew Mitchell at Berlin in 1756 he stated:

My Lord Holdernesse's letters will I dare say be a sufficient instruction to you, but I had not a mind that you should be ignorant of my ideas and the use I made of them here. I trust to your honour and friendship that you will not mention to any one creature your having received this paper; for I should be most unhappy if Lord Holdernesse should know it who might imagine that I was sending you orders when I only mean to give you a notion of my own way of thinking.[22]

If the secretaries of state had become by this time almost the only link between the men who formulated foreign policy at London and the men whose job it was to execute the agreed policy at foreign courts, it should be remembered that the secretaries could also communicate with foreign governments through the diplomatic agents at London. Throughout our period the secretaries had frequent discussions with the foreign ministers accredited to the court of St. James and sometimes preferred to do business with them. This method had the incidental advantage that it enabled the secretaries by means of intercepted dispatches to read the reports sent home by the foreign ministers and the instructions which they received. On the other hand, the secretaries could only be certain that their point of view was accurately and vigorously

[20] Cole, *Memoirs*, pp. 473, 478–9.   [21] Ibid., p. 483.
[22] B.M. Add. MS. 32866, fo. 98.

impressed upon foreign governments by sending appropriate instructions to our own agents abroad. One disadvantage of doing business through diplomatic agents abroad was that it exposed the instructions sent to them to the danger of interception and deciphering by the foreign government with a consequent strengthening of its negotiating power.

Lord Auckland, at the end of the eighteenth century, writing to his brother who had just been appointed to Berlin, summed up what had undoubtedly been the normal practice throughout the century:

A new plan was adopted by Schulemberg [one of the Prussian ministers] which you must gradually supersede, and which Lord Grenville [the Foreign Secretary] will assist you in breaking through. Schulemberg said that Prussia should adopt the English plan and execute its foreign businesses by its own ministers resident in the foreign courts. That idea was not discouraged here [London] at the moment, because it was wished to take the business out of Ewart [British minister at Berlin]'s hands, which were too feverish to hold it; but now it must be gradually changed to the old channel, which in truth is necessary; for our constitution as well as our habits require that the English minister in the foreign court should execute the business there. In any other mode the Secretary of State has no document to refer to for the rectitude of his own conduct, and he becomes personally responsible for measures which ought to rest on written instructions. By degrees you will get all this into a right shape.[23]

A good example of the difficulties which might arise when a secretary decided to negotiate personally with the diplomatic agent of a foreign power at London is offered by Carteret's negotiation with the Prussian Minister Andrié. Subsequently Andrié claimed that Carteret had assured him that during the Franco-British War Prussian ships would not be molested, unless they carried contraband of war. Carteret added, according to Andrié, that 'it was not the usage in England under such circumstances to give declarations in writing to a neutral power' and that he hoped 'Frederick [II] would be satisfied with what [sic] declaration he had just made by word of mouth in the name of the King, his master'.[24] After Carteret's fall Frederick founded his claims for compensation on this assurance, only to be informed by Bedford,

---

[23] *Auckland Journal*, ii. 394–5.
[24] Satow, *Silesian Loan and Frederick the Great*, pp. 12–13.

the new secretary of state, that he was 'entirely ignorant of any such verbal declaration having passed between the earl of Granville and Monsieur Andrié, having never heard any mention made of it 'till he [Andrié] some time ago informed me of it himself, and having never seen a copy of it 'till this he now delivered to me'.[25] Bedford then challenged the accuracy of Andrié's statement on the ground that 'the judge of the Court of Admiralty could [not] possibly take any cognizance in his court of such a verbal declaration, even though it had been transmitted to him by the Secretary of State (which I could not find to have been the case)'.[26]

In answer to Bedford the British Minister at Berlin was compelled to point out that a Prussian or other foreign minister

must take it for granted that the declaration of the Secretary of State is conformable to law, and contains no more than can be and will be made good; for, if the contrary is supposed, there is an end of all the confidence, and consequently of all intercourse between His Majesty's ministers and those of foreign powers. I am afraid if we were to plead at any foreign court the insufficiency (according to the laws of England) of a declaration made by the Secretary of State, the answer would be that it is matter of domestic consideration for ourselves, and that if they have been led into an error by a declaration which had no validity, the person who made it ought to pay the damage and not those who have acted upon it.[27]

The British government was not impressed by these arguments and a later British diplomatist, setting out for Berlin, was informed that 'nothing sure was so trifling or extraordinary as to pretend that matters of right should be decided upon a pretended representation of M. Andrié of what had passed in verbal conferences between him and the Secretaries of State which may have been misunderstood and most probably misrepresented'.[28]

There were, therefore, sound reasons, both theoretical and practical, why the secretaries of state normally made use of their own agents abroad rather than depended upon their own contacts with the foreign diplomatists at London. There was, however, another reason which is worth some examination. Secretaries of state could rarely speak or even understand any foreign language except French. Some of them could not even understand French. When

[25] Ibid., p. 231. [26] Ibid., p. 232.
[27] Ibid., pp. 233-4.
[28] Secretary of state to Hanbury Williams, 7 Dec. 1750, in S.P. 88. 71.

George III in 1771 was anxious to appoint Suffolk as secretary of
state, Suffolk confessed that 'he was a very bad frenchman'.
George III held that ability to speak French 'is an absolute requisite for one who is to treat with foreign ministers' and therefore
proposed to divide the secretaries' duties between a home and a
foreign secretary. In replying to the king, Lord North seems to
have thought that French was more essential for the northern
than for the southern department—unless he was accepting the
king's proposal to set up a specialized foreign office and intended
to transform the southern into the home department.[29]

Suffolk was not the only poor French scholar in George III's
cabinets. When the Foreign Secretary, Carmarthen, began to read
certain papers to a Cabinet Meeting in 1787 he was soon stopped,
and 'as they were in French, it was agreed they had better circu-
late'.[30] And Horace Walpole's tribute to Charles James Fox when
he became Foreign Secretary in 1782 is a sad reflection on his predecessors: 'The foreign ministers were in admiration of him. They
had found few who understood foreign affairs or who attended to
them, and no man who spoke French so well or could explain himself in so few words.'[31] As late as 1815 the British delegation at the
Congress of Vienna had to employ Gentz to translate some of
Castlereagh's papers into French.[32] Since foreign diplomats at
London were often poorly equipped to converse in English, the
secretaries of state had a special reason for preferring to act, as a
general rule, through our own agents abroad.

One other possible complication should perhaps be briefly mentioned. In the reigns of William and Mary and of Anne until 1707,
the sovereign might have maintained a separate Scottish diplomatic service side by side with the English and, up to 1702, the
Dutch services. This, however, did not happen in practice. When
specifically Scottish problems arose, such as the vaunted special
privileges of Scottish merchants in France, instructions were
normally given by the crown to the British diplomatic representatives. Thus the plenipotentiaries at Ryswick received special
orders to try to secure confirmation and restitution of privileges
and lands formerly held in France by William III's subjects
in Scotland.[33] In practice, therefore, such claims came to be

[29] *George III Corresp.* ii. 205–6.   [30] *Malmesbury Diaries*, ii. 306.
[31] *Last Journals*, ii. 542–3.   [32] Webster, *Castlereagh*, i. 331.
[33] H.M.C., *Bath MSS.* iii. 118.

overshadowed by what both William III and his agents regarded as major objectives—the extreme case being the conduct of William III and his foreign ministers in regard to the Darien Scheme. On the other hand, when the Scots complained of the activities of the Barbary pirates, at least once orders were sent to the Admiral commanding the English fleet in the Mediterranean to 'procure them what security you can'.[34]

Neither William III nor Anne seems to have sent any official Scottish missions between 1689 and 1707, but there are occasional traces of semi-official activity to secure Scottish interests. At the end of William III's reign Alexander Cunningham claims that he was sent to France to try to secure justice there for Scottish subjects, but Torcy refused to treat with him unless he produced evidence that he had been sent with the consent and authority of the king.[35] Even less official was the mission of Lord Polwarth in 1712 when 'having obtained leave of Queen Anne to drink the waters of Spa he proceeded to Hanover, at the desire of his friends in Scotland, in order to ascertain the truth of a report, eagerly circulated, that the Electoral family was altogether indifferent to the succession to the Crown'.[36] The last trace of a separate Scottish diplomatic service was presumably the continuance at Campvere of the Conservator of the Privileges of the Scots Nation, who is also sometimes described as Resident there for the affairs of Scotland.[37]

There is perhaps slightly more evidence for attempts by foreign powers, especially Louis XIV when at war with England, to send emissaries to Scotland. At least one of the French spies, Le Moyne de Brie, arrested when Harley was secretary of state, claimed that he travelled to Scotland as the accredited agent of the King of France; but this did not prevent the English government from ordering his arrest 'as being an alien enemy and spy'.[38]

After the accession of George I, separate British and Hanoverian diplomatic services did in fact exist for, on his accession, George I had a considerable *corps diplomatique* of his own. Within the Empire he had Hanoverian agents of differing ranks at Augsburg,

[34] H.M.C., *Buccleuch MSS.* ii. 181.
[35] A. Cunningham, *History of Great Britain*, i. 238; H.M.C., *Portland MSS.* viii. 376; *Carstares State Papers*, pp. 710–12.
[36] *Marchmont Papers*, i. xxxix–xl.
[37] *Cal. H.O. Papers 1760–65*, nos. 764, 1173.
[38] H.M.C., *Portland MSS.* iv. 174.

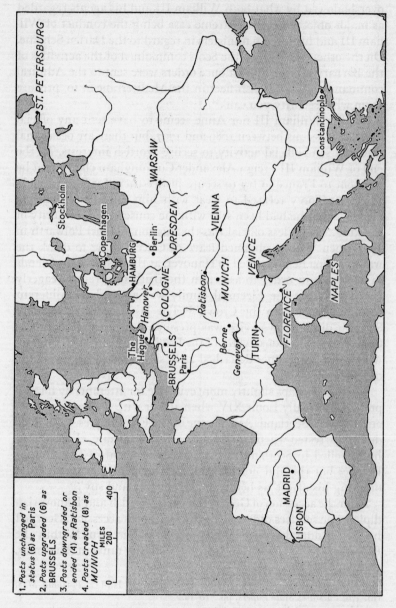

BRITISH DIPLOMATIC MISSIONS ABROAD, 1689–1789

Bremen, Vienna, Ratisbon, Frankfurt-on-Main, Hamburg, Lübeck, the Palatinate, and Berlin. Elsewhere he was represented at the courts of Denmark, France, United Provinces, Austrian Netherlands, Russia, and Venice. But regular Hanoverian representation soon ceased at certain courts, e.g. Lübeck in 1716 and Brussels in 1722. The process was accelerated in the reign of George II and within a few years of his accession regular representation was limited to Augsburg, Bremen, Vienna, Ratisbon, Frankfurt-on-Main, and Hamburg within the Empire. Outside of the Empire, Hanover after 1735 maintained regular diplomatic intercourse only with Denmark, the United Provinces, and Venice. George II clearly preferred to cut down 'overheads' and when a particular problem arose send a special mission to a particular court. Therefore at least after 1730 Hanoverian ministers were few in number and only three of them were to be found outside of the Holy Roman Empire. Several of those who survived held the rank of Agent which by this time marked them off as personal agents of the Elector for the transaction of miscellaneous business rather than genuine diplomatic representatives.[39]

Neither George I nor George II ever seriously considered the idea of pursuing two distinct foreign policies, one as king and the other as elector. They preferred, therefore, as a rule to entrust occasional Hanoverian jobs to the British diplomatic representatives at courts where there was no resident Hanoverian minister. This saved both time and money and no doubt gave the elector a delicious feeling that he was, for once, getting something for nothing out of his close-fisted and cantankerous British subjects.

[39] This paragraph is based on *Repertorium der diplomatischen Vertreter aller Länder*, ii. 173–9.

CHAPTER II

The Anatomy of the Diplomatic Service

ONE of the most marked and until recently least regarded features of eighteenth-century British history is the growth of a civil service, increasing in numbers and more closely articulated, serving the developing departments of state and organized under departmental chiefs, who were responsible to a minister appointed by the king but holding office only so long as he was supported, or at least tolerated, by the House of Commons. In no sphere of government was this growth clearer than in diplomacy, but it is dangerous to exaggerate its extent.

Looking back upon the eighteenth century, nineteenth-century politicians and diplomatists were impressed by the absence of a regular diplomatic service. This, they believed, was essentially the creation of the period after 1815. The more candid witnesses before the Select Committee of 1861 did indeed confess their almost complete ignorance of eighteenth-century conditions. In spite of the fact that his father had been an under-secretary of state in George III's reign, Sir E. Hammond's evidence in 1861 showed that the traditions and character of the eighteenth-century service had been almost entirely forgotten even in the Foreign Office.[1] Stratford de Redcliffe, one of the best known nineteenth-century British diplomatists, asserted that 'the diplomatic service, when I went into it [in 1807] was no profession at all',[2] and later stated: 'I partake the opinion expressed by many, that our diplomacy, taken [in comparison with that of other states], has not been remarkably successful. The nation may be said to have made its way to an increase of power and glory less by negotiation than by force of arms and commercial enterprise.'[3] Lord John Russell, too, opined that 'there was not such a regular diplomatic service before the war of 1793 as there has been since 1815'. Here he was on firmer ground than the other witnesses as also in his suggestion

---

[1] *Report from the Select Committee on Diplomatic Salaries H. of C. Session 1861*, vol. vi *passim*. Similar ignorance is shown in Sir Edward Hertslet, *Recollections of the Old Foreign Office*. [2] Ibid., question 1658.

[3] Ibid., question 1749.

that the unpaid *attachés* originated in the custom of persons being attached to a foreign minister without being considered members of the profession.[4] The Committee, convinced by this consensus of opinion, drew a highly idealized and in many respects false picture of the British eighteenth-century diplomatic service:

The most prominent witnesses are agreed that the Diplomatic Service has of late years acquired a more formal and professional character than it possessed in previous times, when it was so organized as to combine, as far as possible, the satisfactory maintenance of international relations with the social convenience and advantage of the upper classes of the community. In its higher branches it was then liberally remunerated in proportion to the prices of the period; and the chance of attaining its social and political distinctions was a sufficient inducement to young men of rank and fortune to enter a service which united the benefits of foreign travel with the comforts and confidences of a home. Even at the larger missions the staff was not too numerous for the arrangements of domestic life, and their attention was almost exclusively directed to matters of public and political interest. Gratuitous employment was readily accepted where it could be resigned as soon as it became burdensome, and the minister had no scruple in imposing labour which he repaid by friendship, hospitality and protection. He had, besides, by custom, if not the choice, at least a veto on the appointment of his attachés, and the claims of British residents or travellers on his time or his table were few and far between.[5]

In later chapters some of these wild assertions will be discussed: meantime I wish merely to suggest that there had been a marked development of professionalism in the British diplomatic service between 1660 and 1789. It would indeed be surprising if such a development, parallel to changes in the civil service at home, had not taken place. A regular hierarchy of ranks was organized and stabilized. Salaries and allowances and methods of paying them were regulated. There was a substantial increase in the openings available abroad: promotion from grade to grade became possible, if not always rapid and regular enough to satisfy aspirants. Under George III retiring allowances were introduced by administrative action and regulated by statute. Men began to talk not about accepting a temporary offer of employment abroad but of going in for the foreign minister line. Whereas Horace Walpole's diplomatic career depended on his brother's continuation in power at home, Malmesbury came to be regarded as a specialist in diplomacy who was employed abroad by successive governments. One diplomatist, Alexander Cunningham,[6] early in the eighteenth century actually used the phrase 'the foreign service', but it does not gain currency until much later.

It would be generally agreed that in the years after 1689 foreign policy became more important than it had been since the end of the Elizabethan war with Spain in 1604. William III and the first two Georges, if not Anne and George III, were more closely connected with continental politics than any of their Stuart predecessors, while it was often argued that our commercial interests required an active continental policy, not only to maintain and further our trade with, for example, Germany and the Mediterranean and the Baltic countries, but also to enable us to check France in the colonies. Colonial conquests would hardly be long maintained if France were allowed to dominate Europe and use its resources against us in America or India. The maintenance of a real balance of power in Europe might well be the essential basis for an expanding commercial and colonial empire beyond Europe. There was also still surviving, though now strictly subordinate, the idea that it was Britain's duty to defend the Protestant interest in Europe, partly from anti-Papist prejudice but partly also because an alliance of Protestant, or at least non-Catholic, powers might still give support to the idea of a political balance of power in Europe.

Taken together, these factors contributed to a considerable extension of the area covered by British diplomacy between 1689 and 1789 and also to an intensification of our diplomatic efforts within the area already covered in 1689.[7]

This was not at first apparent because a number of states which had maintained diplomatic relations with the Stuarts, such as France and Poland, continued to regard James II as the legitimate sovereign of England and refused to recognize the *de facto* government established under William and Mary.[8] Not until armed opposition to the new régime had been suppressed in Ireland and

---

[6] '. . . the Queen's Minister who methinks is one of the best bred gentlemen in the foreign service . . .' (H.M.C. *Portland MSS*. v. 100).

[7] See map, p. 10.

[8] Not until 1692 did the King of Poland formally recognize William III as King of Great Britain (Przezdiecki, *Diplomatic Ventures and Adventures*, pp. 150–1).

Scotland and English fleets had shown the flag in the Mediterranean did most of the Italian states recognize William III and
re-establish diplomatic relations with England. Thus Blathwayt
wrote to Shrewsbury in 1694: 'His Majesty has at the same time
received a letter of respect from the Great Duke of Tuscany, which
seems to be intended as a forerunner of the acknowledgement of
their Majesties, which may be soon expected, as well as from the
other Princes and States of Italy, upon the stay of our Fleet in the
Spanish seas.'[9] And Admiral Russell about 1694, after describing
his interferences in the Genoese trade, remarked to Shrewsbury:
'I have brought them to be very humble, having laid three of their
captains by the heels. I do not remember that State [Genoa] has
ever sent to acknowledge his Majesty as king of England. Why
should not the town be visited by the Fleet the next summer? The
sight of some bomb-vessels would make them say, do or give anything.'[10]

In fact, although Genoa and Venice had recognized William III
in 1695, it was not until 1697 that British diplomatic representatives appeared at those courts. The Grand Duke of Tuscany
refused to receive, in 1690, the new government's envoy, but
allowed him to reside at Leghorn in a consular capacity. Not until
1698 were full diplomatic relations restored with the Tuscan court
at Florence. The only Italian state with which diplomatic relations were maintained in this period was Savoy, one of William III's
allies in the war against Louis XIV. Similarly in Germany, English diplomatic representation was almost confined at first to the
mainly Protestant states which were supporting the Emperor in
the war of the League of Augsburg. It may have been partly the
shortage of posts rather than a determination not to employ
agents used by his predecessor that caused the marked change in
the *personnel* of the diplomatic service after 1688. One or two
reappeared later in the new reign. This abnormal period came to
an end with the grudging recognition accorded to William III by
Louis XIV in the treaty of Ryswick.

What were really new posts were created at Munich, Cologne,
Dresden, Naples, Florence, Venice, Warsaw, and St. Petersburg.
Other posts already in existence in 1689 were up-graded. These
were Brussels, Vienna, Hanse Towns, Lisbon, Turin, and Madrid.
With the accession of the House of Hanover, envoys ceased to be

---

[9] H.M.C., *Buccleuch MSS.* ii. 151.   [10] Ibid. ii. 158.

sent to Brunswick-Lüneburg. The only other post with a regular existence to be ended was Geneva; but the secretary to the Ratisbon Diet was replaced (as the Empire declined) by a titular minister who stayed at Munich and rarely appeared at Ratisbon and the Swiss envoyship came to be held by a mere *chargé d'affaires*. The other missions which had existed in 1689 at Copenhagen, Berlin, Stockholm, Paris, The Hague, and Constantinople remained essentially unchanged in 1789. Summing up these changes, we may say that Britain came to be regularly represented in northeastern Europe and developed for the first time an adequate network of missions in central Europe, especially Italy and Germany. There was also some increase in the number and importance of British consulates, chiefly in the Mediterranean countries but also to a less extent in the north of Europe.

While continuous diplomatic representation had been established with all the major and many of the minor European powers, there were as yet no buildings at the various capitals permanently occupied by British diplomatic agents. The usual practice was for each successive minister to make his own arrangements. He hired a house suitable to his personal requirements, furnished it as best he could, and lived in it with his family, allocating certain rooms for the transaction of official business. Externally the building was distinguished from its neighbours by the mounting of the royal arms over the door.[11] In the case of the Paris embassy this process is most fully explained by Dr. Joan Evans in a recent article,[12] while there are interesting details about the material background of the Lisbon mission at the time of Lord Tyrawley in the Buccleuch MSS.[13] published by the *Historical Manuscripts Commission*. Views of the embassy at Madrid in Keene's time have been published in Sir Richard Lodge's edition of Keene's private correspondence.[14] Keith reported from Vienna in 1773:

my new *hotel* has precisely thirty-four rooms, besides passages and entries. These rooms I intend to furnish handsomely, with my two dozen and a half of chairs (ten of which you know have damask

---

[11] e.g. Cole, *Memoirs*, p. 550. Tyrawley wrote from Lisbon in 1739 of the king's arms hanging over his gate 'placed there at the very beginning of Mr Methuen's Ambassy and are grown so old and decayed that they are no longer repairable' (S.P. 89. 40, dispatch of 14 Feb. 1739).

[12] 'The Embassy of the Fourth Duke of Bedford to Paris 1762–1763' in *Archaeological Journal*, cxiii. 137–56.

[13] i. 381–7.   [14] Opposite p. 127.

bottoms), one settee, six *tabourets*, and three card tables! Well, sir! I have stabling for sixteen stout saddle and coach horses and stout ones they shall be! and three of them (my stalls) are actually filled with *live* horses, my own property. I have but three kitchens and two ice-houses, and yet I defy any man to guess *which* is *which*, for ice or fire *have I none*![15]

Throughout the period after the resumption of diplomatic relations with France in 1697, the British ambassador at Paris was regarded by contemporaries as holding the most important post in the whole service. At first awkward incidents were likely to arise as long as France maintained diplomatic relations with both kings of England. Thus Jersey in 1698 reported to the secretary of state: 'The same day I saw the King [Louis XIV] King James with his Queen made a visit at Versailles, and had I stayed a quarter of an hour longer I might have seen them, which I shall not be able always to avoid, unless this Court changes its manner of proceeding, or that his Majesty [William III] commands me never to go in places where they are, which I suppose he will not do.'[16] Jersey's secretary, Prior, was less punctilious and describes his meeting with the Old Pretender. The difficulties inherent in this situation were not removed until Louis XIV undertook by the treaty of Utrecht to remove the rival sovereign from his court. Indeed long after this British diplomatists found themselves in difficulties. After the collapse of the '45 Lord George Murray appeared at Dresden. The British envoy there was invited to a great supper at the Saxon Prime Minister's 'but, finding that rebel was to sup there, I retired. I wish I had orders and instructions upon that head.'[17] The situation was even more embarrassing when the Jacobite noble was not merely a passing visitor, but a duly accredited diplomatic agent from the French or Prussian government.

Great nobles who would have contemptuously rejected the offer of any other post abroad regularly filled the Paris embassy. It was so near home that even in the primitive conditions of eighteenth-century travel it could be reached in a few days from London, unless the Channel was exceptionally unkind. Exile abroad could be alleviated by frequent trips home on one pretext or another. If one was a family man it was relatively easy to remove one's whole

---

[15] *Keith Memoir*, i. 417.   [16] H.M.C., *Buccleuch MSS*. ii. 614–15.
[17] Hanbury Williams to secretary of state, 6 Mar. 1748, S.P. 88. 69.

household to Paris, whereas this could only be done with difficulty and ruinous cost if the appointment held was in eastern Europe. And even Francophobe noblemen admitted that Parisian society was not without its attractions. Indeed, eighteenth-century secretaries of state must have noticed, as Palmerston did later, that 'no climate agrees with an English diplomatist, excepting that of Paris, Florence or Naples'.[18]

Changes of personnel were so frequent and so many of the ambassadors were mere playboys that it proved difficult to build up a sound tradition of service at this post. Although Newcastle in 1751 believed that it was 'very unnecessary to have an ambassador and a minister of the second order at the same time in France',[19] the regular appointment of the secretary of embassy to be also minister plenipotentiary in the latter part of the eighteenth century was at once an indication of failure of the older arrangement and an attempt to remedy it.[20] Wars frequently caused the breaking off of our diplomatic relations with France. Then an ambassador would be sent to negotiate peace, as for example Portland in 1697 and Bedford in 1762. There would be a period of great diplomatic activity, dotting i's and crossing t's of the peace settlement and trying to convince the French government that we were negotiating from strength. Then hopes of a permanent settlement of differences would fade. The old points of friction would become acute and new ones probably be added to them while the British diplomats at Paris sought to paper over the cracks. Before long diplomatic relations would again be broken off.

If Paris was the nerve centre of British diplomacy, the main artery passed through The Hague. British diplomatists attached throughout the period an importance to maintaining good relations with the United Provinces which was not justified by the material strength and political ineffectiveness of the Dutch. In the elder Horace Walpole's view 'the situation and conduct of the States [General] is of that consequence to England, and to the balance of power in Europe, that this place [The Hague] cannot

[18] Guedalla, *Palmerston*, p. 337.
[19] B.M. Add. MS. 32828, fo. 248.
[20] See, for example, Carmarthen's appeal to Hailes: 'My dear Sir, for Heaven's sake have pity upon the Department, and either prevail upon our friend the Duke [of Dorset] to write something worth our Master's perusal or else suppose your principal absent, and let your own zeal and abilities have fair play' (H.M.C., *Leeds MSS.* 54).

be without an able and agreeable minister from England'.[21] Protests were made from time to time. Bedford compared our alliance with the Dutch to tying ourselves fast to a dead corpse and calling it our ally,[22] but his views failed to find much acceptance. Even after the Dutch had taken part against us in the War of American Independence, James Harris, later first earl of Malmesbury, was sent to try to recover the alliance of the United Provinces[23] and his success, short lived though it proved to be, was not without repercussions on British foreign policy in the nineteenth century.

But the diplomatic mission to the United Provinces was not important merely because it was responsible for maintaining good relations with the power which down to 1756, at least, was usually regarded as our closest ally. Our agents to other countries in northern and eastern Europe usually passed through The Hague on their journeys to and from their posts. Couriers were for ever arriving on their post-haste journeys with highly confidential dispatches. Often these dispatches were sent under flying seal so that they could be read by the British agents at The Hague[24] and the intelligence they contained might be communicated to our own agents at other courts or, in confidence, to foreign governments. When Harley, after the election of 1710, drew up his 'Plan of Administration' he wrote: 'The Hague is the centre of business and intelligence, and is first to be taken care of.'[25] In 1778 George III referred to Sir Joseph Yorke, our envoy to the United Provinces, as 'immured in the post of foreign political watchman at The Hague'.[26] It was an essential part of a diplomatist's job in the United Provinces to keep abreast with, sift, and pass on to his own government all the gossip which inevitably arose from all this diplomatic coming and going.[27]

One thing made this easier than it might otherwise have been. The federal and provincial organization of the United Provinces rendered it almost impossible to keep secret any information

---

[21] Coxe, *Walpole Memoirs*, iii. 535.   [22] *Bedford Corresp.* i. 336.
[23] *Malmesbury Diaries*, ii, *passim*; A. Cobban, *Ambassadors and Secret Agents, passim*.
[24] This practice was a general one, but was particularly important at The Hague.
[25] Quoted from D. Coombs, *The Conduct of the Dutch*, p. 230.
[26] *George III Corresp.* iv. 20.
[27] Details of the communications between The Hague and London are given in Ragnhild Hatton, *Diplomatic Relations between Great Britain and the Dutch Republic 1714–1721*, pp. 28–29.

which had for any reason to be communicated to Their High Mightinesses the States General. Certain decisions had to be referred not merely to the seven provinces but even to the individual towns in the province of Holland.[28] For this purpose, we are told, the deputies for foreign affairs in the provinces 'usually repair [to their respective towns] on Saturdays and return again to the Assembly on Tuesday morning'.[29] This system gave innumerable opportunities to the numerous members of the diplomatic corps and their still more numerous hangers-on. The British diplomatists were continually being approached by dubious characters anxious to sell them real or imaginary pieces of information. Earlier in our period a good deal of this information found its way into the newsletters of the time, from which it was often transferred to the *London Gazette*.[30] Later on, the various *Gazettes* published in the United Provinces became notorious for their extensive, if unreliable, information on the politics of Europe. Unscrupulous propagandists did not hesitate to use them to set into circulation entirely false rumours.[31] The Hague in the eighteenth century has been well described as the whispering gallery of Europe.

Yielding only to Paris in dignity and to The Hague in importance was the Madrid embassy, at least in the second half of the eighteenth century. Here, as at Paris, the regular flow of diplomatic relations was much interrupted by wars and rumours of war. Anglo-Spanish relations were closest and most satisfactory in the reign of Ferdinand VI, for most of which Sir Benjamin Keene resided at Madrid as the British diplomatic representative.[32] At other times Spain was too easily persuaded by France to join in a Bourbon league against Britain, only to find at the end of each war that France had no intention of securing the objects for which Spain was really fighting.[33] While in the earlier half of the

---

[28] *Honest Diplomat*, pp. 169 n. and 184 n.; Mrs. Hatton, op. cit., pp. 21–28.

[29] *Honest Diplomat*, p. 184 n.   [30] Fraser, *Intelligence*, *passim*.

[31] Frederick the Great was much addicted to this, but he was not the only one. On the Gazettes published in French see E. Hatin, *Les Gazettes de Hollande* (Paris, 1865).

[32] *Keene Corresp.*, *passim*. Opposite p. 12 of this work will be found two views of the embassy in Keene's time which help to explain why Keene's successor, Bristol, who took over Keene's house, kept near a hundred domestics (Clarke, *Letters Concerning the Spanish Nation*, pp. 342–4).

[33] See Stetson Conn, *Gibraltar in British Diplomacy*, *passim*, for the development of this point so far as the recovery of Gibraltar is concerned.

period envoys were normal and ambassadors exceptional, from 1746 there was at Madrid a succession of ambassadors with short breaks due mainly to wars. English noblemen, however, found residence at Madrid much less attractive than at Paris. It proved so difficult to get a peer to go that George III in 1767 had to appoint a commoner, Sir James Gray, 'a person of an ancient family and most respectable character', who had the additional advantage of having gained Charles III's personal approbation while serving as envoy at Naples.[34] And William Eden, who readily changed his political allegiance to secure appointment to Paris, only agreed to go to Spain with reluctance and kept referring to it in his letters as 'that horrid Siberia'.[35]

With the neighbouring kingdom of Portugal, close relations were maintained from 1692 onwards. Usually envoys, often promoted envoy extraordinary and plenipotentiary, were appointed to Lisbon, but there were occasional special embassies. Three of these occurred during the Spanish Succession War when Portuguese co-operation was vital to the success of British armies in Spain. The fourth—that of the earl of Kinnoull in 1760—was sent to apologize for British violation of Portuguese territorial waters during the naval battle of Lagos.[36] One peculiarity of the Portuguese legation was the practice of appointing to it (sometimes) the British consul at Lisbon.

The increasing importance attached to relations with Russia is shown when we consider that William III found it unnecessary to have any diplomatic agent in Russia until 1699 and that relations could be entirely broken off from 1719 to 1730, whereas after 1740 the British diplomatic representative at St. Petersburg was often an ambassador[37] and always at least envoy extraordinary and minister plenipotentiary. The only ambassador between 1689 and 1743 was Whitworth, who was specially commissioned in this character to apologize for the insult to the Russian ambassador at London which led to the passing of the Act 7 Anne, cap. 12.

Britain and Russia both benefited from trading with each other

---

[34] S.P. 94. 175.   [35] *Auckland Journal*, i. 446.

[36] See the interesting letter from Hardwicke, who was consulted by Pitt on the legal problems involved, with a reference to Bynkershoek's *Questiones Juris Publici*, 'a book of the best authority', in *Chatham Corresp.* ii. 16–17.

[37] Catherine II was believed to have declared, early in her reign, against having ambassadors at her court (*Chatham Corresp.* iii. 173); but ambassadors continued to be sent.

and this trade increased markedly in the eighteenth century. The numerous attempts to secure effective political co-operation between them, especially in the middle years of the century, all failed; but mutual economic interests helped to avert an actual rupture of diplomatic relations. While there is no reason to doubt that British sympathies lay with Russia in Catherine II's Turkish wars, British attempts to evade promising support against Turkey was one reason why a political alliance was not reached.[38] The Ochakov incident immediately after 1789 foreshadowed the transition from friendly, if not particularly close, relations to the overt hostility and latent suspicion which have characterized Anglo-Russian relations in the nineteenth and twentieth centuries.[39] Competition for the Petersburg post was rarely keen. When it was suggested that Joseph Yorke might be moved from The Hague to Petersburg in 1754, he wrote: 'I am not good for much, but I am really too good for that country.'[40]

Our relations with Austria were much closer than with Russia down to 1756, but ambassadors were rarely sent to the Imperial court. This was partly due to ceremonial difficulties, especially when for a time the stiff-necked Hapsburgs refused to give the title of Majesty in Latin letters to their English ally in the Spanish Succession War.[41] Even after this was settled, the normal rank of the British diplomatic agent at Vienna was that of envoy or even minister plenipotentiary. These men had a thankless task trying to hold together the 'old system' of alliances based on the union of the Maritime Powers with Austria. Neither Charles VI nor Maria Theresa had much reason to trust the British government and did not hesitate to explain their attitude and the reasons for it to the British agents, Robinson and Keith, at Vienna. On the other hand, Robinson's and Keith's superiors at London blamed them for not standing up to the Austrians.[42] Bolingbroke, as early as Anne's reign, had written 'That house of Austria has been

---

[38] Anglo-Russian relations during Harris's mission to St. Petersburg (1777–83) are discussed by Isabel de Madariaga (Mrs. Schapiro) in an unpublished thesis submitted for the Ph.D. degree of the University of London in 1959.

[39] M. S. Anderson, *Britain's Discovery of Russia 1553–1815* gives an admirable account of the basic problems of Anglo-Russian relations in the eighteenth century.   [40] B.M. Add. MS. 35356, fo. 235.

[41] H.M.C., *Portland MSS.* iv. 96; ibid. ix. 282.

[42] Walpole described Robinson as 'as obstinate a German and as servile an Imperialist as Hatolf [the Hanoverian minister in England]' (*Hervey Memoirs*, p. 394; cf. the Prince of Wales's comments in *Marchmont Papers*, i. 216–17).

the evil genius of Britain. I never think of the conduct of that family without recollecting the image of a man braiding a rope of hay whilst his ass bites it off at the other end.'[43] Practically every successive secretary of state said something like this for the next half century, yet no sooner was the alliance with Austria broken off than some secretaries made equally misguided and ineffective attempts to restore it. Bute's hankering for the old alliance contributed to his famous quarrel with Frederick the Great; and it is perhaps significant that one of the four ambassadors sent by Britain to Austria in 100 years was Lord Stormont at the end of the Seven Years War. When he was recalled, the post reverted to a legation, occupied for twenty years by the elder Keith's son, Sir Robert Murray Keith.

With Prussia, after 1740 clearly the second power in Germany, our relations were no more satisfactory.[44] Great Britain was regularly represented at Berlin from 1689 to 1730, though there were some gaps, partially filled by special missions, including one embassy.[45] The unsatisfactory nature of our relations with Prussia is clearly indicated in the second quarter of the eighteenth century by Hervey's story that George II had sent, or would have sent if not prevented by Townshend, a challenge to his Prussian Majesty to engage in single combat.[46] It is also indicated by the fact that from 1730 to 1747 we maintained a mere secretary at Berlin and supplemented his activity by short and usually unsuccessful special missions. One of these envoys, before taking up his post, wrote of the great difficulties which attended the negotiating with the present court of Berlin,[47] while Chesterfield believed in 1747 that whoever was sent to Berlin 'must be a very unhappy man between the two courts'.[48] From 1756 Britain was continuously represented at a high level, usually by an envoy extraordinary, but it was currently accepted 'that Berlin was a disagreeable post for an English minister'.[49]

Much the most successful of our diplomatists at the Prussian

[43] *Bolingbroke Corresp.* i. 36–37.

[44] See Sir Richard Lodge, *Great Britain and Prussia, passim.*

[45] The father of our envoy to Copenhagen in 1706 vainly tried to secure a transfer to Berlin for his son because the air and way of living at Berlin were much better than at Copenhagen (H.M.C., *Portland MSS.* iv. 333).

[46] *Hervey Memoirs*, p. 103.

[47] Hanbury Williams to secretary of state, 16 Apr. 1749, in S.P. 88. 70.

[48] *Marchmont Papers*, i. 239.

[49] *Malmesbury Diaries*, i. 95.

court was Andrew Mitchell,[50] who resided there from 1756 to 1764 and again from 1766 to 1771. He was the only British diplomatist that Frederick the Great ever trusted, but even he was unable to restore the Anglo-Prussian alliance which had been broken off at the end of the Seven Years War. In the late eighties, with the death of Frederick and the emergence of what was, up to a point, a common interest between Britain and Prussia in resisting French domination of the United Provinces, Joseph Ewart and James Harris succeeded in restoring the Anglo-Prussian alliance, but their triumph was short lived.

Britain was also represented continuously at Ratisbon, the seat of the Imperial Diet. These agents varied in rank. The first of them was one of the few diplomatists who remained in office after the Glorious Revolution of 1688. William III thought there was not enough for an English minister to do at Ratisbon[51] and left the post vacant for some years while one of his secretaries of state, Vernon, remarked acidly of two English ministers who had served at Ratisbon before the Glorious Revolution: 'I have heard how two of your predecessors spent their time there, Mr. Pooley in making love to the fräuleins and Sir George Etheredge in making lampoons upon them.'[52] The succession of secretaries, residents, and ministers plenipotentiary gave way after 1725 to a regular succession of 'ministers' until an ill-fated attempt was made in 1763 to appoint Chesterfield's son, Philip Stanhope, as envoy extraordinary. This soon foundered on ceremonial difficulties and Stanhope was never formally received. When Stanhope's successor Gordon was appointed an experienced diplomatist wrote to him: 'Your post at R[atisbon] is full of ceremony. You cannot spit out of the window without offending the head or paraphernalia of an *Excellence*. You are all so, that Ceremonial there is looked on as essential and subject to contests.'[53] After 1765 the post at Ratisbon was combined with the representation of Britain at Munich, which became the normal place of residence of the titular agent to the Diet. This, in itself, indicates the decline during the century of the political importance of the empire and the imperial title in British eyes.

Considering the lesser states of the Empire, our relations were

[50] On whom see A. Bisset, *Memoirs and Papers of Sir A. Mitchell.*
[51] H.M.C., *Bath MSS.* iii. 61.   [52] Ibid. iii. 52.
[53] H.M.C., *Report XII, App.* 9, 339 (Aitken MSS.).

at first closest and most continuous with Hanover. After the Saxon elector became also King of Poland more importance came to be attached to Saxony, to which William III had merely sent occasional missions. Thereafter the British diplomatist at Dresden was also normally accredited to the king and/or the Republic of Poland until the final separation of the electorate and the kingdom in 1763. Subsequently the British government continued to be regularly represented at Dresden by envoys extraordinary. At this time the post was 'a pleasant and respectable situation, and the expenses are not unequal to the pay'.[54] There was no regular British representation in Bavaria before the appointment of Onslow Burrish in 1746. After Burrish's death at Munich in 1758 there is another gap, but from 1766 onwards the Munich and Ratisbon posts were combined and the holder resided regularly at Munich until the union of Bavaria and the Palatinate in 1780. Thereafter the holder of the combined posts resided with the court either at Munich or Mannheim or (occasionally) Düsseldorf. Until 1778, when a series of appointments begins, Britain had rarely sent any diplomatic agent to the Electors Palatine.

At one other German electoral court we were regularly represented after 1745—Cologne, except when the electorate was in French occupation during the Seven Years War. The holder of this post often transacted British business with the neighbouring ecclesiastical electors of Mainz and Trier. The only other German courts with which regular representation was maintained were the Hanse Towns. Ministers, normally residents, but occasionally promoted to the rank of envoy, were separately accredited to Hamburg, Bremen, and Lübeck. Usually they resided at Hamburg, visiting the other towns only to present credentials, take leave, or when business required their presence. In the second half of the century the practice developed of accrediting the resident at Hamburg as minister plenipotentiary to the circle of Lower Saxony.

British missions to the other courts in Germany were merely occasional. Frequently British diplomatists would be sent to Hesse Cassel to hire troops or conclude subsidy treaties. During the War of American Independence Major-General William Faucitt was sent to many German courts with which we had no regular diplomatic representation to raise German mercenaries to take part in the war. There were many other occasional missions throughout the century, such as Garter missions to invest a German prince with the order of the Garter, and missions of compliment on the accession of a new elector or of condolence on the death of a prince. Unique in this period was the mission of Earl Harcourt in 1761 to conclude a treaty of marriage between George III and the Princess Charlotte of Mecklenburg Strelitz. Of very few British diplomatic representatives in Germany could it be said, as it was of George Stepney, that 'no Englishman ever understood the affairs of Germany so well, and few Germans better'.[55]

The regular network of British missions to the German courts, thus established, did not escape criticism. In the earlier part of the century it was often regarded as one of many indications of excessive regard for Hanover. When this ceased to be a specious line of attack at least one 'angry young man' wrote of 'the petty envoys at the secondary courts (who are little better than gentlemen ushers to English fools, who squander their fortunes in foreign countries) like the jay in the fable, are adorned with this wreath of the soldier [the Order of the Bath]'.[56] Most of these posts forcibly disappeared with the extension of the Napoleonic influence in central Europe, only to be restored in 1815.

English diplomatic contacts had probably been closer in the seventeenth century with the Italian than with the German courts, and at the end of Anne's reign Peterborough was given a commission to all the princes and states of Italy. This did not become a precedent, though one or two similar appointments appear to have been made in the following decade. Down to the 1750's, from the political point of view at least, Savoy-Sardinia was much the most important of the Italian states to Britain. This was inevitable as long as Britain was the enemy of France and the ally of Austria since Savoy's geographical position made it either a bulwark of Italy against French penetration of the Lombard plain or a French bridgehead for the subjection of northern Italy. Moreover, with the acquisition of Sardinia and the status of a kingdom, Piedmont became important and powerful enough to play the risky role of buffer state between France and Austria.

[55] Macky, *Characters*, p. 142. These are said to be the work of Bishop Burnet (cf. Chapter VI, p. 115, n. 15).
[56] *Observations on the Prevailing Abuses in the British Army* (no author: ? Thomas Erskine, London, 1775), p. 40.

British statesmen in the first half of the eighteenth century consistently encouraged Savoy. Bolingbroke meant to check Austrian
power in Italy by raising up Savoy and the addition of Sicily to
Savoy-Piedmont by the treaty of Utrecht was deliberately intended to make Britain a Mediterranean power. 'May I not add',
Bolingbroke continued, 'that there arises a prospect of changing
the scene of future wars, and removing them to a greater distance
from our Island, to a part of the world where we cannot well inter-
vene, unless by our fleets, instead of running into the extravagant,
ruinous scheme of maintaining armies on the Continent?'[57] Again
in the 1730's Savoy was able to bring pressure on Britain by
threatening to join with France in an attack on Austria; and when
Britain failed to secure adequate concessions from Austria to
Savoy, Charles Emanuel III did in fact fight on the French side in
the War of the Polish Succession. In the next war the treaty of
Worms by which Carteret secured Sardinian assistance for Maria
Theresa (at a price) was hailed as his greatest triumph and did in
fact contribute to the preservation of most of Austria's Italian
lands. Soon afterwards, the end of active Bourbon–Hapsburg conflict in Italy by the treaty of Aranjuez cut the ground from under
Sardinia's feet and greatly reduced, in Britain's eyes, her political
value. Yet at the beginning of the Seven Years War Pitt wrote of
the court of Turin 'from a situation and connection so essential to
any plan that concerns Italy' and mentioned the King of Sardinia
as 'a firm and affectionate ally' with a part to play in the future
system of Europe.[58]

It should be noted that throughout the period Britain attached
commercial value to her good relations with Sardinia. British naval
vessels made some use of Villefranche and Sardinia attempted to
develop it as a free port. What Sardinia really needed for commercial development, however, was control of the port of Genoa.
Britain was prepared to support Sardinian claims to Finale if not
to Genoa itself, with the inevitable result that the Genoese were
driven into the French camp and the island of Corsica which was
held by Genoa gradually passed under the control of France—a
change which was completed in 1768 and was regarded by many
contemporaries as an alteration of the Mediterranean balance of
power which might well prove disastrous to Britain.

The British mission to Savoy-Sardinia was regularly maintained

[57] *Bolingbroke Corresp.* i. 583.   [58] *Chatham Corresp.* i. 253–4.

from 1691 to 1789 with a gap from 1714 to 1720. The heads of
this mission varied in rank from secretaries and residents to
envoys; but there is an unbroken succession of envoys or envoys
and plenipotentiaries in the concluding forty years to 1789. The
higher rank indicates rather that residence at Turin had become
not unattractive to peers and influential politicians than that
business was increasing.

At Genoa we were diplomatically represented intermittently
from 1697 to 1722. Thereafter, apart from two eccentric appointments of naval officers as ministers in the sixties, such business as
we had at Genoa was dealt with by the resident consuls. On the
contrary, with Tuscany Britain maintained fairly regular representation. At first there were attempts to combine the missions to
Genoa and Tuscany, but after 1722 there was usually an envoy at
Florence, though in the middle period down to 1765 residents were
common. There was also a British consul at the free port of Leghorn,[59] but the diplomatic agents devoted a good deal of their time
to what would now be regarded as consular business. From 1731
until his death in 1757 Baron Philippe de Stosch resided at Florence
under British protection though he was not accredited to the Tuscan government. He signed his reports John Walton and his real
business was to report on the activities of the Stuart Pretenders
and the Papal Curia as they might affect the security of the
Hanoverians.

To Venice intermittent embassies were sent from 1697 to 1713,
and a regular series of residents, with one or two special embassies,
resided there from 1715 to 1789. Here also there was usually a
British consul. The laws of the Republic imposed such stringent
limitations upon the normal functions of diplomatic representatives accredited to Venice that representation was hardly worth
while. Thus Manchester complained to Shrewsbury: 'The nobles
of my acquaintance avoid me and their law is so rigorous that they
will hardly converse with any that comes to me. The only diversion I can propose to myself is their music, which is now begun,
and will be in perfection this Carnival.'[60]

[59] There was a protracted squabble about the status and privileges of the
chaplain to the Leghorn factory in Anne's reign (H.M.C., *Portland MSS.* iv.
606–7, 649; vi. 6, 29).

[60] H.M.C., *Buccleuch MSS.* ii. 589. Newcastle approved the proposal of a later
ambassador to take leave of the Republic immediately after his public entry to
make it easier to mix with the Venetian nobles (S.P. 99. 64).

No regular appointments were made to Naples before 1753: thereafter two envoys in succession filled the post until 1800. The second of these, Sir William Hamilton, found time to make an exhaustive study of local antiquities and to publish works on volcanic eruptions. He must have believed that the secretaries of state shared his scientific tastes as his dispatches were often devoted to such problems and illustrated by diagrams. According to Gibbon, Hamilton corresponded more with the Royal Society than with the king's ministers. On a visit to Rome he took the risk of being received by the Pope, with whom, of course, no diplomatic relations were maintained in this period. That in the earlier part of our period it was risky for a British diplomatist at a foreign court to invite the papal nuncio to his house may be deduced from Manchester's letter to the secretary of state from Venice in 1700 in which he says: 'I should be glad if with safety I might invite [the nuncio] sometimes to my house. Not that I mean either to visit him in ceremony, or he to return it. The last nuncio did often dine with the Dutch ambassador,' and he adds: 'I believe it may be of some service, if proper.'[61] With the slow decline of religious fanaticism and the disappearance of Jacobitism such caution ceased to be necessary. Proposals to appoint a consul for the Papal states were made in 1735 and again in 1772,[62] and in 1787 there were again rumours of a commercial negotiation with the Papacy. Storer, at least, a former secretary of embassy at Paris, wrote to his friend William Eden: 'What do you think of sending me as Minister Plenipotentiary to his Holiness? The gravity of my character will suit with such a mission perfectly well. I beg you will not consider it as a joke, but think of it seriously as a means of providing for me, and at the same time of procuring me the opportunity of seeing that celebrated capital.'[63] Two years later a merchant at Civita Vecchia applied for the consulship there or at Rome.[64]

Britain was regularly represented at the Scandinavian courts of Denmark and Sweden. The rank of our agents at Copenhagen was normally envoy: sometimes a minister resident was appointed and later promoted envoy. In the earlier part of our period subsidy treaties were concluded and Danish troops hired for use in con-

---

[61] Manchester, *Court and Society*, ii. 147.

[62] See documents and especially L. Dutens's 'Plan for carrying on a trade with the Ecclesiastical States', dated 1 May 1772 in S.P. 85. 13.

[63] *Auckland Journal*, i. 431.

[64] F.O. 83. 11 (letter dated 12 Sept. 1789).

tinental wars, while the British naval squadrons dispatched for various reasons to the Baltic often made use of Danish ports. It was assumed that Britain and Denmark had a common interest in maintaining 'the Protestant cause and the liberties of Europe'. The main importance of Denmark throughout the period was, however, as the guardian of the means of access to the Baltic and collector of the Sound dues. With the marked increase in British ships using this route in the later eighteenth century and the failure of the homeland and the American colonies to produce in adequate quantity and satisfactory quality the timber and naval stores required by our navy and mercantile marine, this became more vital than ever. The British consul at Elsinore spent much of his time counting the ships of various nations which passed the Sound and in settling disputes about the dues. Apart from this, the importance of Denmark in British eyes tended to decline, though there were spasmodic revivals of interest when Sweden and Russia seemed likely to come to grips with each other and the probable military and naval action of Denmark might seriously affect the course of the struggle. The dynastic marriage of George II's daughter, Caroline, to the Danish king, which was intended to consolidate and perpetuate good relations between the two countries, led instead to the Struensee scandal, the imprisonment of Queen Caroline, and the sending of Sir Robert Murray Keith to Copenhagen on a special mission to secure her release. This he successfully accomplished and the incident had no influence on subsequent relations between Britain and Denmark. At the end of our period Copenhagen had the reputation of being 'a dull court and desperately cold'.[65]

With Sweden diplomatic intercourse was less regular and our relations varied from close alliance to actual hostility. From 1717 to 1719 there was a complete rupture of diplomatic relations and a longer and more serious one from 1748 to 1763. An attempt to re-establish relations failed in 1757 and though Sir John Goodricke acted nominally as Minister Resident to Sweden from 1758, he had to discharge his duties as well as he could from Copenhagen. Not until 1764 was he allowed to enter Sweden. That the British government was not vitally interested in Sweden in the closing years of our period is indicated by accidental gaps in our full representation at Stockholm, where mere *chargés d'affaires*

[65] *Auckland Journal*, i. 37.

held the post from July 1773 to March 1774, September 1776 to September 1778, and again from August 1787 to August 1789.

British missions were also regularly maintained in Flanders, Switzerland, and Turkey, and (less regularly) at Warsaw. During the continental wars of William III and Anne the post at Brussels was important and, especially when it was combined with a military commission, afforded opportunities for malversation on a considerable scale—at least such accusations were made against several holders of this post. Brussels was also a vital centre for securing military and political intelligence and at least one holder of the Brussels secretaryship, Marmande, reached it after a career as a spy.[66] After the treaty of Utrecht and the establishment of Austrian rule in the Netherlands the importance of the post declined. From 1715 to 1745 it was held by mere residents or agents, and entirely suppressed from 1745 to 1752. It was again suppressed owing to our rupture of diplomatic relations with Austria from 1757 to 1763. After 1763 it was normally held by a minister plenipotentiary.

British ministers in Switzerland[67] fall into three distinct categories: those accredited to the Swiss cantons who resided mainly at Zürich and Berne, those accredited to the Republic of Geneva, and those accredited to the Grison Leagues. Whereas there was a fairly regular succession of agents to the cantons and to Geneva, missions to the Grisons were occasional, concerned with keeping open in war-time communications between Italy and Austria, combined with negotiations for the hire of mercenary troops. Earlier missions to the cantons were also mainly concerned with negotiations for Swiss troops for use in William III's and Anne's wars and also with securing up-to-date and reliable military and political intelligence.[68]

Early in the Spanish Succession War Godolphin explained to Harley: 'The duke of Marlborough says an active stirring minister in Switzerland would be capable of doing more service than anywhere else, both in supporting and encouraging the Protestant Cantons, and in furnishing the quickest intelligence from all parts.'[69] Mainly for this latter reason there was a revival of British

[66] H.M.C., *Downshire MSS.* i. 674 onwards.
[67] See M. Meier, *Die diplomatische Vertretung Englands in der Schweiz im 18. Jahrhundert, passim.*
[68] Plans for organizing in 1704 a system of espionage based on Geneva will be found in H.M.C., *Portland MSS.* iv. 100–1.   [69] H.M.C., *Bath MSS.* i. 63.

interest in Switzerland during the Austrian Succession and Seven Years Wars. Occasional applications were made by the Protestant cantons for British support[70] and in 1734 the British government tried to hire 6,000 Swiss mercenaries.[71] The regular succession of envoys of the period 1689 to 1714 gave way to intermittent residents between 1716 and 1739 and was followed by a regular succession of 'ministers' from 1743 to 1768. In the closing years of our period Britain was represented at Berne merely by *chargés d'affaires*. By the mid-eighteenth century it was often felt that the *raison d'être* of the Berne legation had disappeared. Keene wrote to his friend Castres in 1757: 'How often have I told you, and you agree to it, that *Swisserland* is the country to be employed in, where there are no admirals, no privateers, no trade nor navigation.'[72]

The Geneva post had a similar history until it was abolished in 1774. One reason why it was so long maintained was the feeling that it was desirable to have some one on the spot to counter the influence of the resident minister maintained by France at Geneva. In 1697 the republic of Geneva protested against this innovation on the ground that the French resident had no other purpose but 'to debauch the citizens by his cabals and intrigues, to alienate them from the fealty and obedience due to their sovereign, and to establish Papacy among them, seeing that otherwise it is sufficient to have an ambassador in Switzerland'.[73] The last holders of the British post at Geneva, the two Pictets, had both been subjects of the republic and had therefore been accepted by the magistrates on condition that they would renounce the outward distinctions and privileges usually allowed to foreign ministers. Matters came to a head in 1774 when the younger Pictet's commission was formally revoked on the ground that 'it is by no means consistent with the King's dignity to keep a minister at Geneva or at any other state, who is not admitted to enjoy every honour and privilege to which he is justly entitled'.[74]

The position of the ambassador at Constantinople was unique in the eighteenth-century diplomatic service. Before the Revolution of 1688 the ambassador had been 'a commercial agent

---

[70] H.M.C., *Polwarth MSS.* iii. 254–6.
[71] S.P. 96. 24, dispatch of 11 Feb. 1734.
[72] *Keene Corresp.*, p. 511.   [73] H.M.C., *Bath MSS.* iii. 163.
[74] S.P. 96. 52, dispatch of 22 Apr. 1774.

masquerading as an ambassador'. The wars against France after 1688 and the consequent alliance with the Hapsburgs, still the chief enemy of the Turks, gradually transformed the ambassador into 'a servant of the Crown sent primarily for political and diplomatic business'.[75] As yet, however, Britain took no direct political interest in the Eastern Question; but she now had, in the first half of the eighteenth century, a strong indirect one in settling disputes between her Austrian ally and the Turks, since these were liable to distract Austria from western Europe and make her a less useful ally to Britain. Carmarthen, writing to Nottingham as early as 1689, remarked that the great defeat given to the Turks might 'be of infinite advantage to us and the rest of Christendom if our allies in Germany and in the House of Commons would agree to improve this advantage the next summer to that degree which will certainly be in their power'.[76] And Carmarthen's view was shared by William III. A special ambassador, Harbord, was dispatched to mediate between the Emperor and the Porte, and the diplomatic agent at Vienna was advised that 'Mr. Harbord is sent on purpose for this service; for he is not to stay as ordinary ambassador [at Constantinople] for the merchants'.[77]

For this reason it was British mediation which contributed to the conclusion of the peace treaties of Carlowitz in 1699 and Passarowitz in 1718. In the second half of the century Britain sought by mediation between them to strengthen her position both at Constantinople and St. Petersburg.[78] While I cannot go so far as Dr. Wood, who holds that Constantinople thus became a nodal point in British eighteenth-century diplomacy, I agree that no eighteenth-century secretary of state could have written what one of Charles II's secretaries wrote about Constantinople: 'that place is soe remote as any intelligence from hence hither (it's conceaved) can be of little use here'.[79]

Whereas the influence of the king and of the Levant Company varied in the choice of ambassadors in the seventeenth century, from 1691 onwards 'the Levant Company was deprived of any real share in the choice of the ambassador, although the nominees of the crown were still submitted to it and a *pro forma* election continued to be held'.[80] Once appointed the ambassador corresponded

---

[75] Wood, *Levant Co.*, p. 130. [76] H.M.C., *Finch MSS.* ii. 247.
[77] Ibid. iii. 293. [78] S.P. 88. 77, dispatch of 2 Jan. 1755.
[79] Wood, op. cit., p. 131. [80] Ibid., p. 133.
6308 D

regularly with the company and received instructions from it. Lord Paget complained bitterly under William III that he had been treated in some of the company's letters 'more like a footman than an ambassador'[81] and on another occasion he spoke of the embassy with its double function as 'that slippery post'.[82] It cannot be said that the ambassadors were successful in protecting and furthering British trade in the Levant, which suffered a protracted and serious recession after 1720, while that of France prospered, although this was due to causes beyond the British ambassadors' control.

In the second half of the century, when British interest in the Eastern Question grew and became direct, British sympathies were with Russia rather than with Turkey. For example, the Turks protested that it was Britain which had made possible the arrival of a Russian Baltic fleet in the Levant during Catherine II's first Turkish war. Nevertheless, Britain for a long time refused to admit a Russo-Turkish war as constituting a *casus foederis* in any alliance between Britain and Russia; and during the Russo-Turkish war of 1768–74 she tried to secure better terms for the Turks than were justified by their military and diplomatic position. By this time the political functions of the ambassador completely overshadowed his commercial duties and from 1768 the government contributed to the upkeep of the embassy and consulates.[83] This system of dual control ended in 1804 with the appointment of an ambassador, paid by the crown, and a commercial agent, chosen by the company but also commissioned by the crown as consul-general.[84] As an indication of the remoteness of Constantinople it may be mentioned that in the early eighteenth century dispatches from the embassy took, on an average, six weeks to reach London[85] and 'the usual time required for an exchange of letters between the factories and home was four to five months, and even this could not be relied upon'.[86] It was a further drawback that plague was endemic at Constantinople and the embassy staff took the most elaborate precautions to avoid contagion, not always with success.[87]

Until the election of Augustus II of Saxony as Augustus I of

[81] Wood, op. cit., p. 132.
[82] Aaron Hill, *Account of the Ottoman Empire,* Preface.
[83] Wood, op. cit., p. 161.   [84] Ibid., pp. 183–4.
[85] *Sutton Desp.,* p. 12.   [86] Wood, op. cit., p. 229.
[87] Ibid., pp. 245–7.

Poland in 1697 William III dispensed with any mission to War-saw. As long as the union of Saxony and Poland lasted the British agent at Dresden attended also to our business with Poland, and was, when necessary, sent to Warsaw, usually to attend the periodical meetings of the Polish Diet. From 1764, when Stanislaus Poniatowski was elected King of Poland, we were regularly repre-sented at Warsaw. The envoys of the middle years of the century gave way to residents and ministers plenipotentiary. In 1778, presumably in consequence of the first partition of Poland, it was decided to reduce the pay of the king's minister at Warsaw,[88] but in practice ministers plenipotentiary continued to be appointed until once again in 1788 a British envoy appeared at Warsaw.

No regular British diplomatic missions were established beyond Europe in this period, though naval officers and consuls combined to maintain 'quasi-diplomatic' relations with the Barbary states.[89] These were the empire of Morocco, with an Atlantic as well as a Mediterranean coastline, and the titular regencies at Algiers, Tunis, and Tripoli on the Mediterranean. Relations with all four were reasonably good in the eighteenth century in marked con-trast to the usual state of affairs in the seventeenth. All had ceased to be important Mediterranean sea powers and all were no longer in any real sense Turkish dependencies. Our main interest in them was to secure supplies of grain, meat, &c., for our garrisons at Gibraltar and Port Mahon and to ensure that French influence did not become dominant on the North African coast.

When it became necessary to conclude peace with the American colonists at the end of the War of American Independence, Richard Oswald as commissioner and David Hartley as minister plenipotentiary were sent to negotiate at Paris with their Ameri-can opposite numbers; but it was not until after 1789 that regular diplomatic representation in the United States began.

Diplomatic contacts were not necessarily limited to the courts at which British missions were regularly or occasionally main-tained. For example, before Britain was represented at Naples, the Sicilian envoy at Dresden handed to his British colleague there a formal letter to His Britannic Majesty notifying the birth of a

[88] S.P. 88. 114, dispatch of 11 Mar. 1778.
[89] Sir G. Fisher, *Barbary Legend, passim*, and especially the lists of consuls on pp. 307–9; M. S. Anderson, 'Great Britain and the Barbary States in the Eigh-teenth Century', in *Bull. Inst. Hist. Research*, xxix (1956), 87–107.

prince at Naples.[90] This was duly sent on to Whitehall and the formal letter of congratulation would normally be forwarded to Naples through the same channel. Such contacts were as a rule used only for ceremonial purposes; they could, however, be used for business, if the courts concerned did not think it necessary or desirable to send a specially accredited minister directly to the other court concerned.

Occasionally diplomatic representatives accredited to one court resided for long or short periods at another. The commonest example of this was when the British government tried to save money by accrediting one agent to two or more courts, as under George I to Genoa and Tuscany. More frequently a diplomatist already accredited to one court might be entrusted with a brief commission to another. These temporary appointments might be business commissions or mere missions of compliment, e.g. to confer the Garter on a German elector or to compliment an Italian prince on his accession to the throne. But on rare occasions a British diplomatist appointed to a court might be refused admission or expelled by the foreign government and, instead of returning home, remained at another court in the hope of being allowed to take up or return to his post at a later date. A good example of this was Lieutenant-Colonel Robert Campbell and his successor Sir John Goodricke, successive residents at Stockholm during and after the Seven Years War. Campbell reached Stockholm but the Swedish Senate refused to accept him as a minister on the ground that as a native of Sweden he was excluded from such office under Swedish law. Though Campbell denied this he had to return home and the British government immediately named Sir John Goodricke as his successor. Goodricke spent the next six years at Copenhagen and then, after the end of the Seven Years War, he was at last allowed to enter Sweden and take up his post. A similar case is that of Captain James Jefferyes, titular minister resident to Russia from 1718 to 1721. Owing to the breach between George I and Peter I he had to retire from St. Petersburg in October 1719 to Danzig where he resided, retaining his character, for another two years until the British government sent him letters of revocation.

Other cases occur in which a diplomatic agent was accredited to one court merely as a cover for his activities elsewhere, the latter

90 Hanbury Williams to secretary of state, 31 May 1752, S.P. 88. 74.

usually falling into the category of secret service or intelligence. Thus Mitford Crowe was sent in 1705 'to reside at Genoa without a character and for colour only has given him a credential to the State [of Genoa] and instructions to make propositions for the mutual advantage of trade',[91] while the real objects of the mission were to watch the Catalan revolt and report naval movements. Similarly Cressener, British minister to Cologne, was expelled by the French in 1759 and resided at Maestricht with a credential to the States General to give him protection in his undercover activities, until the end of the war allowed him to return to Cologne in 1763. Such secret missions were rare, though this may merely mean that they have left little trace in the records. Even allowing for this, I think their frequency in British diplomacy was much less than in contemporary French practice.

Very occasionally a British diplomatist while on a mission was allowed to act also as the accredited representative of another power at the same court. Thus the duke of Manchester, while British ambassador at Paris, was formally accredited to Louis XIV, during the illness of his Dutch colleague, as the Dutch diplomatic representative. This arrangement was formally approved by William III as King of Great Britain.[92]

British missions were staffed by a regular hierarchy of officials ranging from ambassadors and other heads of missions downwards through secretaries of embassy and secretaries with creditive letters to mere *chargés d'affaires*, unpaid *attachés*,[93] and private secretaries. The basic distinction was between those who had been placed on the establishment and could expect to be paid —if they survived long enough—by the Treasury out of the civil list, and those who were still unestablished and drew their salaries or at least received board and lodging from the established diplomatists who employed them. While the line between these two categories was a very definite one, it could be crossed. Many established diplomatists began their careers with a spell as *attaché* in the household of a family friend or were accepted by a stranger on the recommendation of a secretary of state. A competent and industrious *attaché* sometimes discharged the duties of a private

---

[91] S.P. 104. 91, dispatch of 2 Mar. 1705.

[92] Cole, *Memoirs*, pp. 295, 301.

[93] The term *attaché* is not used in the eighteenth century, but it is a convenient anachronism. Professor Bindoff traces it back to 1816 (*Trans. R. Hist. Soc.*, 4th series, xviii. 145).

secretary.[94] Other diplomatists, such as De Visme at Stockholm, had no secretary, 'contenting himself with a boy, who understood no language but his own, merely to copy for him'.[95]

These private secretaries were nearly always men of humble birth. Many of them were foreigners chosen by their employers to remedy their own linguistic incapacity. Lord Lexington had to explain to the secretary of state that at Madrid: 'I treat with all the disadvantage ever man did for I am not master of Spanish and none of the ministers understands anything else except the Marquis of Bedmar, nor will they give me copies of their papers in any other language'.[96] Since foreigners were usually regarded as security risks and, at least after William III's time, could not be given credentials, they had little inducement to remain for long in a badly paid blind-alley occupation with few perquisites.[97] But there were exceptions. One of Robinson's private secretaries, Dunant, resigned after 'having been in the service above twenty years' giving three reasons for his decision: (1) sedentary business was bad for his eyes and made him fatter and heavier day by day, (2) he had to provide for himself and his family, and (3) future prospects, if he remained a secretary, were, he said mildly, uncertain—so uncertain that he preferred to start in trade as a merchant to Turkey.[98] Another, Necker, gave up his job to teach modern European history and public law to the young Englishmen who came to stay at Geneva.[99] On the other hand, some of these private secretaries, foreigners as well as natives, continued to serve one employer at the same court for many years—such were Milliquet, who served at Dresden for thirteen years as a private secretary and was five times left in charge of affairs,[1] and Mattheson, who served successive ministers at Hamburg from 1714 or earlier to 1751.[2]

More interesting are the few private secretaries who failed to become old family retainers but moved rapidly from employer to employer and from court to court. A good example of this

[94] *Keene Corresp.*, p. 161.   [95] *Elliot Memoir*, p. 45.

[96] S.P. 94. 79, letter of 31 Oct. 1712.

[97] Occasionally they seem in the seventeenth century to have received payments for copying newsletters (Clark, *Trumbull*, p. 51).

[98] S.P. 80. 148 (letters of 1 Nov. and 8 Nov. 1741).

[99] S.P. 96. 49.

[1] S.P. 68. 2, letters of 2 Oct. 1782 and 27 May 1784.

[2] S.P. 102. 31 and 73.

category was William Money, who served as secretary to Onslow
Burrish for seven years. On the death of his employer he served
with Robert Keith at Vienna from 1755 to 1757, transferred to
Lord Stormont at Dresden, and was left by Stormont in charge of
affairs at Warsaw 1761–2. Then he went with Buckinghamshire to
St. Petersburg where he claimed to have 'transacted alone all the
business under his lordship' and finally returned to England in
1766.[3] Another secretary in the same category is Tinkler Duckett
whose career began in 1739 as private secretary to Burnaby at
Stockholm. He came home with Burnaby and went abroad again
with Wych to Hamburg, then he transferred to Villiers at Dresden, went to Berlin, and returned with Villiers to England. In
1747 he accompanied Lieutenant-General Wentworth to Turin
and, when his employer died, he took charge of the papers and
handed them over to Wentworth's successor, General St. Clair,
before moving on to Vienna to see about a job as tutor to Sir
Thomas Robinson's eldest son.[4]

A few private secretaries gained a place on the establishment,
but this required both exceptional ability and exceptional luck.
Sir Luke Schaub, who began as private secretary to Lord Cobham
at Vienna and became one of the best-known British diplomatists
of his day, is a good example of how the line could be crossed—
usually as a result of being temporarily left in charge of British
interests at some court or other by a head of mission who was in
too much of a hurry to get home to wait at his post until his successor could arrive. Occasionally a favoured diplomatist, when a
private secretary could not be recruited locally, was allowed to
make use temporarily of one of the clerks in the office of the
secretary of state, as Keene did J. D. Kluft.[5]

If on the whole private secretaries found their employment
frustrating and unremunerative, experienced ambassadors rarely
thought much of their private secretaries. Keene towards the end
of his career wrote: 'I know not a greater plague in this trade than
that of secretaries. Good usage spoils them, and all those I have
met with except Renouard have been mad in one respect or
another.'[6] His last secretary he described as 'a whimsical uneasy
Dutchman',[7] though this characterization was at least partly due

[3] See his 'Case' in Add. MS. 28062, fo. 157.   [4] S.P. 92 53.
[5] Keene Corresp., p. 526.   [6] Ibid., p. 497.
[7] Ibid., p. 499.

to Keene's objection to having women, even his secretary's wife, in his household.

When the head of a mission was a great nobleman he often took with him his chaplain to serve in the double capacity of chaplain and private secretary and occasionally he secured his protégé's appointment as secretary of embassy. In any case, the clergyman-secretary expected to reap the reward of his service abroad in clerical preferment at home either from the crown or from his immediate employer. Lord Raby, for example, wrote to Oxford about his secretary-chaplain, Ayerst:

Your lordship, who takes a pleasure to bring to light and distinguish hidden merit, cannot—I am bold to say—better do it than in procuring him some mark of Her Majesty's favour, since if his merit is not so much known in England, it is his being abroad that is the only cause of it, which he hopes your lordship will not permit to be prejudicial to him, being it would be very hard, if while he is detained on this side the water in some measure on a public account, he should remain—as he has for a great while—unprovided for, while others who have never been abroad in Her Majesty's service run away with double and sometimes treble preferments.[8]

That secretarial appointments were not always highly esteemed is suggested by the attitude of one candidate for preferment who would have liked in 1714 to go as a travelling tutor to Lords Harwich and Holland, but if all else failed 'would reckon himself very happy to go to Vienna as secretary with an English ambassador'.[9]

Intervention in foreign negotiations by unofficial diplomatists with no credentials or instructions from the British government was rare, though not entirely unknown. Unique in my experience is the case of Lady Torrington, wife of the minister plenipotentiary at Brussels, who, in her husband's absence on leave in 1789, superintended his secretary's activities as *chargé d'affaires*. Even when Torrington was actually at Brussels his wife, he told the secretary of state, was 'the soul of my office'.[10] More than once on the death of a consul, his widow put forward a claim to succeed to this office. Now and again it is possible to trace the activities of quite unauthorized agents abroad such as the earl of Lindsay who

[8] H.M.C., *Portland MSS.* ix. 362–3.   [9] Ibid. v. 456.
[10] B.M. Add. MS. 28064, fo. 380.

claimed that, while resident at Geneva as a private person in 1742, he had bribed or otherwise influenced the senators to prohibit the passage of Spanish troops by Domodossola into the Milanese.[11]

The examples, quoted in the preceding paragraph, of unofficial agents attempting to assist the official agents in executing the government's foreign policy are quite exceptional. Still rarer were unofficial missions connected with the parliamentary opposition and deliberately intended to thwart the foreign policy of the government. Perhaps the best known of these in the eighteenth century was the journey of Robert Adair to Vienna and Petersburg at the time of the Ochakov crisis. Burke claimed at the time that Adair's mission was the work of C. J. Fox and that Adair and Fox had conspired against the state 'in setting on foot communications with foreign powers, leading to concert and co-operation with them in measures hostile to the King's Government'.[12] Long afterwards Adair stated his agreement in the abstract with Burke's condemnation of such opposition action, but argued that his conduct had been quite different. 'Taking a warm and open part in public affairs, and anxious for the preservation of our establishments at home and our relations abroad' he had sought 'to impress his hearers not only with a sense of their value, but of the value in which they [were] held by the leading statesmen of his country'. In particular he held it 'to be most important for the interests of peace, that foreigners should know what is national in party disputes, so as to distinguish it from what is merely factious or adventitious'.[13]

In the next chapter the ranks and emoluments of the established diplomatists will be discussed.

---

[11] Rolt, *Life of the Earl of Crawfurd*, p. 354.
[12] *Memorials and Correspondence of C. J. Fox*, ed. Lord John Russell, ii. 385.
[13] Ibid. ii. 386.

CHAPTER III

Rank and Emolument

FROM the institution of resident diplomatic missions in the fifteenth century a basic distinction has been drawn between ambassadors, either ordinary or extraordinary, and ministers of less eminence, often described as residents. By the late seventeenth century, however, various intermediate grades had become established. For example, a decree of the States of Holland, passed on 29 March 1651, mentions 'ambassadors, resident envoys, agents or other ministers'.[1] Much the most important intermediate rank was that of envoy extraordinary, which under Louis XIV became much commoner than before, while the gulf between the envoy and the mere resident grew steadily.[2] The title of resident is said to have been degraded when the lesser German courts gave or even sold the title to persons who had no diplomatic functions at all.[3] The increasing use made of envoys in the seventeenth century was partly due to a desire for economy, but at least as much to the desire of sovereigns to avoid or at least reduce the number of quarrels between ambassadors[4] where there were several ambassadors at the same court and no generally accepted rules of precedence. Thus Frederick William, the great elector of Brandenburg, is said not to have appointed any ambassadors.[5] There was a similar reluctance at Genoa[6] and in Sweden[7] and elsewhere in the late seventeenth and early eighteenth centuries. When Cobden proposed and carried in the Select Committee of 1850 on Public Salaries the abolition of embassies he was much less of a radical

---

[1] Cornelius Van Bynkershoek, *De Foro Legatorum Liber Singularis. A Monograph on the Jurisdiction over Ambassadors* (reprinted Oxford and London, 1946, ed. G. J. Laing), p. 10.
[2] Picavet, *La Diplomatie Française au temps de Louis XIV*, p. 74; O. Krauske, *Entwickelung d. ständigen Diplomatie*, pp. 162–3.
[3] Krauske, op. cit., pp. 165, 174.
[4] These are dealt with *ad nauseam* in Wicquefort and Callières.
[5] Satow, *Guide to Diplomatic Practice*, 4th ed., p. 165.
[6] Vitale, *La Diplomazia Genovese*, pp. 16–17.
[7] *Histoire de l'administration des affaires étrangères de Suède*, ed. S. Tunberg and others, pp. 235 ff.

than his contemporaries thought.[8] Callières, whose famous treatise sums up the experience of Louis XIV's reign, arranges diplomatic agents in a regular hierarchy: (1) ambassadors; (2) envoys extraordinary; (3) residents; (4) secretaries; (5) agents, and explains that the additional title of plenipotentiary is given according to the occasion either to ambassadors or envoys.[9] Writing early in the eighteenth century, Cornelius Van Bynkershoek probably summed up pretty fairly the general practice when he wrote: 'Envoys were formerly less frequently employed than they are to-day; residents were at one time more numerous than they are at present; agents are as common to-day as before, but in earlier times they were held in higher esteem than they are now.'[10]

In England under Charles II there was a clear division into ambassadors, envoys, and residents. William III's practice corresponded very closely with this. As King of England he appointed twelve ambassadors, forty-two envoys extraordinary, one of whom enjoyed also the title of plenipotentiary, six residents, four secretaries (with creditive letters),[11] and three agents. In addition he appointed four secretaries of embassy, a rank ignored by Callières since under Louis XIV they were the private servants of the ambassadors,[12] whereas under the English administration they were appointed and paid by the crown. His other appointments include three 'Ministers', three 'Commissaries', and two diplomatic agents who seem to have received no special rank. Under Anne more ambassadors are appointed and ministers plenipotentiary appear in their own right, without the title of ambassador or envoy, although about a fifth of Anne's envoys also had the title of plenipotentiary.[13] No fewer than thirty-two appointments by Anne

[8] H.C. (1850), xv. xv.

[9] De la Manière de négocier avec les souverains, English translation ed. A. F. Whyte (1919), pp. 71–76. Pecquet, Discours sur l'art de négocier (Paris, 1737), p. 135, recognizes only three clear grades: (1) ambassador; (2) envoy; and (3) resident.

[10] De Foro Legatorum, p. 64.

[11] Excluding mere chargés d'affaires. These and subsequent figures are based, with a few adjustments, on the lists published in B.D.R. They do not include diplomatic representatives sent to international conferences who were not accredited to the sovereign in whose territory the conference was held, nor do they include occasional embassies to non-European countries, especially the Barbary states. For some purposes I have also left out of account agents who received credentials but did not take up the appointment.

[12] Picavet, op. cit., pp. 78–79.

[13] 'The commission of Plenipotentiary', Dartmouth wrote to Prior, 'does not

were made in no special rank, many of them being to temporary naval or military missions necessitated by war conditions. Under George I there was a further marked increase in the number of ministers plenipotentiary and residents, and a parallel decline in the number of envoys extraordinary and ministers with no special

Appointments in the reign of	Ambassadors	Ministers plenipotentiary	Ministers[14]	Envoys extraordinary and ministers plenipotentiary	Envoys extraordinary	Residents	Secretaries of embassy	No special rank	Commissaries[15]	Secretaries or chargés with creditive letters	Agents[15]	Secretaries of legation	Total
William and Mary 1689–1702	12	0	3	1	42	6	4	2	3	4	3	0	80
Anne 1702–14	22	3	2	11	43	10	5	32	1	7	0	0	136
George I 1714–27	15	9	7	17	17	17	5	19	0	4	1	0	111
George II 1727–60	18	29	31	14	19	19	10	16	1	6	0	0	163
George III 1760–89	24	38	16	25	29	10	25	6	1	2	0	5	181
Total	91	79	59	68	150	62	49	75	6	23	4	5	671

rank. Under George II the most obvious changes were a jump in the number of ministers plenipotentiary and ministers[16] and a less marked increase in the number of secretaries of embassy. In the first twenty-nine years of the reign of George III there seems to be a greater readiness to appoint ambassadors: there are certainly

give you a representing character' (*Bolingbroke Corresp.* ii. 324). Cf. the difference in treatment accorded at the French court in the early eighteenth century to envoys who were also plenipotentiaries and to mere ministers plenipotentiary (Coxe, *Lord Walpole Memoirs*, i. 136–7).

[14] Including some who are more accurately described as 'plenipotentiary'.

[15] Only those commissaries and agents who actually undertook diplomatic work are included.

[16] Callières regards the title of plenipotentiary as occasional, given chiefly to ministers accredited to the German Diet at Ratisbon, and Pecquet regards it as 'un titre passager, sans autre décoration que le relief attaché naturellement à un emploi de confiance, qui ne peut rien exiger, mais qui attire de la considération et du respect' (*Discours*, p. 136). Similarly he excludes minister from the hierarchy of ranks as being a vague description 'qui naît de la commission qu'un particulier a d'administrer dans un païs étranger les affaires de son maître. Ce n'est même que depuis peu que l'usage s'en est établi: on l'a jugé plus commode, parce qu'il n'assujettit à aucun cérémonial, et parce qu'il peut être porté par des personnes de différente naissance, sans qu'on puisse en rougir ou s'en trop glorifier' (ibid., pp. 135–6).

more appointments to the rank of envoy, and a rather larger percentage of envoys enjoy the additional rank and pay of plenipotentiary; there is a corresponding decline in the number of residents, but for the first time secretaries of embassy equal the ambassadors in number.

Taking the whole period we have the figures shown in the table on page 44.

The most notable features in this table are the introduction and progressive rise in number of ministers plenipotentiary (0 to 38), envoys with additional rank of plenipotentiary (1 to 25), secretaries of embassy (4 to 24), and 'ministers' (3 to 16). The envoys, who had been the backbone of the British diplomatic service under William III and Anne, form a much smaller percentage of the total appointments under the Hanoverian kings. Residents, after showing a tendency to increase up to the early Hanoverian period, decline under George III; appointments in no special rank declined steadily under the Hanoverians from the peak reached under Anne.

Few British diplomatists reached the dignity of ambassador. If we exclude the anomalous Turkish embassy,[17] there were only sixty-nine ambassadors appointed in a hundred years. Only our diplomatic representatives at the French court were regularly appointed with the rank of ambassador from 1689 to 1789, but owing to the frequent wars they were not numerous. Appointments in the rank of ambassador throughout the period were also frequent (but not regular) to the United Provinces. They were made occasionally to Spain in the first half of the period and regularly after 1746. Occasionally made to Austria and Portugal in the first half of the period, they were frequently made to Russia after 1743. No other country except Venice (with four appointments) received more than two British ambassadors in these hundred years. This tradition of keeping ambassadorial appointments at a minimum continued into the twentieth century. As late as 1910 there were only eight ambassadors in the British diplomatic service compared with the present figure of about fifty.[18]

In the earlier part of the period ambassadors often did not have a secretary of embassy provided by the government: under George III this had become an invariable practice, and it was

[17] On which see A. C. Wood's article, *E.H.R.* xl (1925), 533–61.
[18] Lord Strang, *Home and Abroad*, p. 309.

being extended by the introduction in the late 1780's of an entirely new practice of appointing to the more important legations
a government-appointed and paid secretary of legation.[19] Another
interesting departure which occurs after the early years of
George III's reign is the practice of appointing some of the secretaries of embassy to France and Spain as ministers plenipotentiary, thus enabling them to carry on the embassy business in the
absence of their chief with greater prestige and, it was hoped, increased efficiency and promptitude.[20]

Leaving out of account the heterogeneous class of ministers
plenipotentiary, these diplomatic representatives may be grouped
in six categories, in descending order of rank and emoluments:[21]

1. Ambassador, ordinary or extraordinary, with or without the
   title of plenipotentiary, £100 a week, or less frequently £10
   a day.[22]

2. Envoy extraordinary and plenipotentiary, £8 a day.[23]

3. Envoy extraordinary, £5 a day.

[19] Those secretaries were paid at a uniform rate of £1 a day (46 C.J. 592),
Berlin 1785, St. Petersburg 1787, Vienna 1789, and Copenhagen 1790. According
to Lord Whitworth the experiment was not a success at St. Petersburg since the
secretary was excluded from Petersburg society. He advocated instead appointment of unpaid attachés (H.M.C., Fortescue MSS. ii. 226).

[20] See Satow, Guide to Diplomatic Practice, p. 256, for the continuation of this
practice into the twentieth century. It was anticipated to some extent under
George II (Chesterfield, Letters, i. 433, 465–6).

[21] Particulars of payments to foreign ministers can readily be obtained from
the Treasury records preserved in the P.R.O. (general reference E. 403). Much
information is available in print for the period 1689–1745 in the three series of
official publications, Calendar of Treasury Books (1689–1714), Calendar of
Treasury Papers (1714–30), and Calendar of Treasury Books and Papers (1731–
45). For the middle period (1752–69) statements of civil list payments, &c., to
foreign ministers and consuls are printed in 32 C.J. 466–603. After Burke's Bill
for Economical Reform came into operation 'the salaries of the ministers to
foreign courts being resident at the said Courts' are grouped in one class and the
amounts paid to each are printed annually in the Commons Journals, e.g. 40 C.J.
328–33. Some additional information may be gleaned from the Calendar of
Home Office Papers for the years 1761–75.

[22] Lord Mahon, History of England, i. 30, suggests that in Anne's reign the
higher rate was paid to ambassadors to France, Spain, and the Emperor, the
lower to other ambassadors, but this is because he thinks that the regulation of
1669 remained in force in Anne's reign. In the mid-eighteenth century the lower
rate seems to have been paid only to two ambassadors to Russia and one to
Venice.

[23] The payment of £10 a day in this rank to William Eden as envoy extraordinary and plenipotentiary to France is anomalous (46 C.J. 592). The appointment of a minister in this rank might be a tribute to the sovereign to whom he
was accredited or a reward to the man appointed.

4. Minister, £3–£5 a day.
5. Resident, £3 a day.
6. Secretary of embassy or secretary at a court where no British minister was resident, £2 a day.

Ministers plenipotentiary received anything from £3 to £10 a day, the lower figure being customary when the title of plenipotentiary was added to some other rank in the service, e.g. envoy extraordinary or secretary of embassy.

Special arrangements applied throughout this period to the Constantinople embassy, where the ambassador was paid by the Levant Company at rates which tended to decline after 1689.[24] From 1762 the ambassadors normally received a government subsidy of £3 a day in addition to their pay from the Company:[25] in 1795 the latter was raised from £1,000 to £2,000 a year.[26] After 1804, when the government assumed sole responsibility for the ambassador's salary, he continued to be paid at a lower rate than the other ambassadors; but at least down to 1809 he enjoyed some lucrative perquisites which they did not share.[27]

These ordinary payments commenced on the day of the diplomatist's 'departure out of the presence' and normally continued until 'the day of his return into the presence'.[28] Not infrequently, however, specially favoured ambassadors and envoys were allowed to draw these allowances for months, and even years, after they had ceased to act. In such cases their duties at the foreign courts were discharged by proxy, i.e. by a lowly and poorly paid subordinate. One of the worst examples of this is William Norton, titular minister to the Swiss cantons from 1765 to 1783, who was only resident at his post for about three and a half years. When Catt, the *chargé d'affaires* he had appointed to do his work, died in 1776, Norton went back to Berne for a few days to appoint a successor, Louis Braun, and continued to draw his pay as minister

---

[24] Wood, *Levant Co.*, p. 134.
[25] Pells General Posting Books (E. 403 general reference) in P.R.O.
[26] Wood, *Levant Co.*, pp. 177–8.
[27] *Infra*, p. 59.
[28] Irregular additions or perhaps merely anticipations of ordinary payments (H.M.C., *Bath MSS.* i. 235) were occasionally made, as to the dukes of Shrewsbury and Hamilton in 1712, 'without account', *C.T.B.* xxvi (1712), 427, 530, 532; cf. for a similar proposal affecting Matthew Prior H.M.C., *Bath MSS.* iii. 216. I think George III was wrong when he wrote: 'The giving an audience to foreign ministers when they go abroad is now become customary. It used only to be to ambassadors' (*Correspondence*, ed. Fortescue, iv. 101).

until 1783. On the other hand, Godolphin refused to pay Stanhope as envoy after he had been defeated and taken prisoner at
Brihuega.[29] Occasional pamphleteers tried to make capital out of
the non-residence of the ambassadors at their posts. Thus the
author of *The Present State of the Nation* wrote: 'Foreign affairs
seem to have been almost entirely neglected for these last two
years; the ambassadors appointed for the courts of Madrid, Turin
and St. Petersburg were permitted to enjoy their salaries and their
friends in England.'[30]

In addition to these 'ordinaries', during the time of their missions, most of these ministers received a regular 'extraordinary'
allowance to cover certain expenses, such as postage, intelligence,
and stationery.[31] This varied not only according to rank but to the
court to which they were accredited.

Under Charles II the Committee for Foreign Affairs seem at
first to have advised the king as to the suitable allowance for
equipage, weekly expenses, and extraordinaries in each case. For
extraordinaries the privy seal of appointment had usually authorized the Lord Treasurer to pay such extraordinaries as a secretary
of state should sign: if this was not done the king's express command had been required for any payment under this head.[32]
However, on 4 April 1669 the king approved at Whitehall a regular establishment covering equipage and ordinary allowances.[33]
This scheme on 20 April 1669 was ordered to be entered in the
Treasury books[34] and was intended to apply to all appointments.
Ambassadors in ordinary were divided into two classes according
to the court to which they were accredited. The higher class, to be
sent only to France, Spain, and the court of the Emperor, received
£1,500 equipage and £100 a week, the lower £1,000 equipage and
£10 a day. Ambassadors extraordinary differed from ordinary
ambassadors only in equipage money, which was to be settled
by His Majesty on each occasion. Envoys and residents were

[29] *C.T.P.* xxvii (1713), 62, 450.
[30] 3rd edition, 1768. There was in fact a gap of nearly eighteen months at
Madrid, nearly five years at Turin, and over a year at St. Petersburg.
[31] See, for example, Ruth Clark, *Trumbull*, pp. 173–6. A considerable number
of other accounts of this nature have been printed in *C.T.B.* At a time of crisis
in the Balkans Sir R. M. Keith at Vienna spent £300 on postages alone in the six
months July 1773–January 1774 (B.M. Add. MS. 35506, fos. 240–1).
[32] *C.T.B.* iii, part i (1669–72), 188.
[33] *C.T.P.* i (1557–1696), 6: printed in *Bolingbroke Corresp.* i. 114.
[34] *C.T.B.* iii, part i (1669–72), 324.

similarly divided into two classes, the higher again being those sent to France, Spain, and the court of the Emperor, with differing amounts for equipage and ordinary allowances. Only three months' pay at the beginning of the mission would be paid in advance; thereafter payment would be made at the end of each quarter. No bills of extraordinaries were to be allowed by the secretary of state until the minister had delivered an exact narrative of his negotiation, the state of the court at which he had resided, and the characters of the ministers and other principal persons at that court.[35]

Later in 1669 by a Treasury minute of 10 December an attempt was made to regulate extraordinaries.[36] Certain expenses, such as the cost of hiring a private secretary, were excluded, and the foreign minister was required, if he was a commoner, to swear to the account, or if he was a peer to give it upon his honour and have his steward or secretary swear to it. Nevertheless, on 21 January 1670 the question of 'presents to foreign ministers going hence and the rules about extraordinaries' was still being discussed by the Treasury Lords, the Privy Council, and the secretaries of state.[37] The Order in Council of 1680 by which any expenditure in excess of an establishment must be authorized by the Treasurer before passing the Privy Seal[38] presumably increased Treasury control over extraordinaries.

Similar regulations controlling equipage and ordinary and extraordinary allowances were in force under James II. These elaborated a scale for diplomatic extraordinaries beginning with the envoy extraordinary to France at £200 a quarter and descending to the resident at Ratisbon at £50 a quarter. No other allowance for extraordinaries was to be made except by His Majesty's particular order.[39] Combined and slightly simplified after the Revolution, these regulations provided the financial basis of the British diplomatic service from 1689 to 1789. In other countries, such as Sweden, diplomatic salaries and allowances were raised to meet the increased cost of living,[40] but in Britain such payments were frozen for more than a century.

[35] The influence of French practice may reasonably be inferred here.
[36] *C.T.B.* iii, part i (1669–72), 169–70.
[37] Ibid. 347.
[38] S. B. Baxter, *Development of the Treasury 1660–1702*, p. 55.
[39] Copy in Add. MS. 31150, fos. 23–25 (Strafford Papers).
[40] *Hist. de l'admin. des aff. étrangères de Suède*, pp. 355–6.

From 1690 they were regulated by an Order in Council, dated Whitehall, 9 January 1690, on the basis of a report made jointly on 13 December 1689 by the secretaries of state and the Treasury Lords. Ambassadors to Spain, France, or Holland were to receive £400 each a quarter, other ambassadors £300. Envoys and residents were grouped in three categories with extraordinary allowances varying from £150 to £75 a quarter, according to post, not rank.[41] With a few trifling variations, such as the increase of the allowance at Turin and Berlin from the original £75 to £100 a quarter, these figures remained unaltered until 1789. When new posts were created they were fitted into the scale at an appropriate level, e.g. the British envoy at Naples under George III received £400 and his colleague at St. Petersburg £600 a year.

According to this establishment of the extraordinaries only 'heads of missions' were entitled to draw a fixed allowance, but special arrangements were sometimes made, chiefly for secretaries of embassy.[42] By the middle of the eighteenth century, however, secretaries of embassy had been included in the scheme, but when at the very end of our period secretaries of legation were first appointed they received no extraordinary allowance. Consuls also were excluded and the Lord Treasurer in 1705 ruled that 'a Consul has no title to make bills of extraordinaries. But if he has been at any expenses rel[ating] to prisoners at war he may make a bill of that and it shall be referred to the C[ommissioners] for sick and wounded.'[43] The Treasury's view does not seem to have found acceptance in the secretary of state's office. There is at least one document, apparently dating from Anne's reign, which gives the salaries of consuls at Algiers and Tripoli and adds 'besides which, they both make bills of extraordinary'.[44] They continued to present bills for extraordinaries,[45] and in 1754 regular salaries and extraordinary allowances were fixed for the Barbary coast con-

[41] P.R.O., Warrants not relating to Money XIII, pp. 1–2, summarized in C.T.B. ix, part ii (1689–92), 443, and perhaps more accurately in H.M.C., Downshire MSS. i, part i. 330. No regular extraordinary allowance was paid to the ambassador at Constantinople (cf. Sutton Desp., pp. 49–50).

[42] H.M.C., Bath MSS. iii. 24.

[43] C.T.B. xx (1705–6), 108. In 1691, however, the Cabinet Council had allowed Consul Lodington's extraordinaries (H.M.C., Finch MSS. iii. 404).

[44] P.R.O., S.P. 71. 11. It was easier to make bills for extraordinaries than to get them paid by the Lord Treasurer (C.T.P. (1708–14), p. 557).

[45] e.g. Consul Hudson's from Algiers after his dispatch of 21 Sept. 1720 in S.P. 71. 6.

suls.[46] In accordance with this arrangement the consul at Tripoli, for example, was receiving in the concluding years of our period a regular extraordinary allowance of £250,[47] but the Barbary coast consuls were exceptions. Some, however, were now being allowed to charge extra extraordinaries from time to time, e.g. Consul Merry at Madrid received £193 as the cost of illuminating his house on the accession of Charles IV of Spain in 1788 and Consul Magra obtained £218 in payment of his passage money to take up his post at Tunis.[48]

The Order in Council of 1690 did not merely fix these quarterly extraordinary allowances: it laid down that no other extraordinaries were to be allowed save by the king's particular order or for 'such expenses as shall appear absolutely necessary in case there be not time to receive the King's direction therein'. This enabled a very close check to be kept on any claims for extra extraordinaries, i.e. for expenses not covered by the fixed extraordinary allowance. Thus the whole 'extra extra' payments in 1784 and 1785 were not much in excess of £1,400 per annum.[49] Allowable claims under this head included cost of putting a diplomatist's household into mourning if there was a death in the royal family or travelling in the course of a minister's employment,[50] e.g. with the Saxon court on its biennial pilgrimage to Poland during the

---

[46] S.P. 71. 20 and 22, especially 22, fo. 683.
[47] 40 C.J. 328–33.   [48] 46 C.J. 598.
[49] 41 C.J. 645.
[50] But not, as a rule, journeys to and from the foreign court to which he was accredited. Thus when Lord Rochford put in a claim for his journey to Turin via Paris, the Lords of the Treasury recommended 'that no allowance be made for the future to ambassadors, envoys and ministers employed abroad for their journies to and from the respective courts to which they are commissioned, but in cases where His Majesty gives particular orders for a journey to be made for a particular service' (Minutes T. 29. 31, fo. 236, 7/11/49). Under William III and Anne, however, if the costs of these journeys were exceptionally heavy, claims were often allowed (C.T.B., passim). Daniel Pulteney probably summed up the earlier practice not unfairly when he said, referring to claims for travelling charges and public mournings, that 'these extraordinary demands have, or have not, been allowed as the minister had friends at the Treasury, at least they have remained upon the foot of a pretension which may be obtained on some favourable turn' (H.M.C., MSS. in Various Collections, viii. 361). Under William III the decision whether to pay the bills drawn by a foreign minister was often made by the king himself (e.g. H.M.C., Downshire MSS. i. 739), but this tended to become a matter for decision at the Treasury. In accordance with the Treasury Minute of 7/11/49 R. M. Keith received £500 as expenses of removal from Dresden to Copenhagen and Sir T. Wroughton £400 as equipage money on being posted from Warsaw to Stockholm (S.P. 88. 103 and S.P. 88. 114).

reigns of the Saxon kings in Poland or with the Russian court on its rare migrations from St. Petersburg to Moscow. If a minister were accredited simultaneously to two courts he might receive a special allowance for house rent.[51] Occasionally expenses incurred for secret service were also dealt with under this head;[52] more often it included presents to influential persons at the foreign court.[53] It should be noted that all these payments had normally to be paid out of the diplomatist's own pocket and he was lucky to secure repayment from the Treasury within six months. Not until nearly the middle of the nineteenth century was any arrangement made to allow diplomatists to draw in advance, month by month, sufficient cash to provide for the bulk of their extraordinary expenses.[54] Until then most diplomatic agents must have (like Lord Clarendon) 'borrowed money from my bankers and paid interest for it'.[55] Matthew Prior might ask rhetorically: 'Who would be vexed about extraordinaries, whilst arsenic is but ninepence an ounce and a rope costs but three halfpence?', but to judge by the time and energy his colleagues devoted to securing payment of their extraordinaries few agreed with him.[56]

In addition to these ordinary and extraordinary allowances, ministers received on first appointment, and sometimes on transfer to another court, a sum of money for equipage, corresponding to the allowance for 'outfit' still paid under the 'Regulations for His Majesty's Foreign Service' at present in force. Ambassadors between 1689 and 1789 often received £1,500, but sometimes had to content themselves with £1,000.[57] An envoy extraordinary and

---

[51] *C.T.B.* xxiv (1710), 535.

[52] More often this class of extraordinary payment seems to have been dealt with in the manner described in *C.T.B. and P.* iv (1739–41), pp. viii–ix.

[53] *E.H.R.* xliii. 610–11, prints Hyndford's bill of extraordinaries, which largely consists of such items.

[54] *Report from the Select Committee on the Diplomatic Service*, H.C. (1861) vi, question 540.   [55] Ibid., question 1009.

[56] H.M.C., *Bath MSS.* iii. 39.

[57] Lord Mahon, *History of England*, i. 30, argues that the only difference between an ambassador-extraordinary and an ambassador in ordinary was that the former received a sum for equipage determined by the sovereign on each occasion, whereas the latter received £1,500 or £1,000 according to the court to which he was accredited. This does not square with figures given in two notes about the pay of ambassadors in S.P. 94. 229. If these figures are correct, Charles II was much more generous than his successors. In 1663 Sir Richard Fanshaw is said to have received £4,000 at first setting out, and £4,000 a year for all expenses, while in 1666 the earl of Sandwich was paid for a year and ten months as ambassador at the rate of £8,000 a year. On the next appointment in

plenipotentiary to the Emperor might get £1,200, but the normal equipage allowance for envoys was £500, and £300 for lower ranks, especially secretary of embassy and resident.[58] Equipage money was normally paid, along with an advance of ninety-one days' pay, before the diplomatist left England.[59]

Service was not pensionable, though occasionally lucky diplomatists for special reasons continued to draw pensions from civil list revenues long after they had left the diplomatic service. Manchester claimed that when he was ambassador at Venice he was allowed a pension of £1,500 a year.[60] The civil list accounts of the 1750's and 1760's printed in the *Commons Journals* show regular payments to Frederick Laurence, Charles Holzendorf, and Brinley Skinner. The special case of Laurence was discussed fully by Sir Richard Lodge[61] and in a sense he was still employed actively abroad, but Holzendorf's last appointment had been as private secretary to Chesterfield while ambassador at The Hague in 1728–32 and Skinner's last appointment was as *chargé d'affaires* at Florence in 1733–4. Another anomaly of this kind is the payment of substantial sums to Solomon Dayrolle, the former minister to Flanders, who retired in 1757 from Brussels on the rupture of diplomatic relations with Austria but continued to receive payments of varying amounts until at least 1768–9. There is another slightly earlier case, that of John Burnaby, formerly minister to the Swiss cantons, who received in 1752, two years after retirement, 30s. a day 'till provided for in his Majesty's service'.[62]

Later under George III ministers who had spent the best years of their lives abroad regularly received retiring allowances, usually of £1,000 or £1,200 a year. John Murray, who had been resident at Venice from 1754 to 1766 and then ambassador at Constantinople,

the list after the adoption of a regular establishment (Oct. 1671), that of the earl of Sunderland, the equipage money dropped to £2,500 and the familiar figure of £100 a week apears as his ordinary allowance.

[58] *C.T.B.* xxvi (1712), 297; xxvii (1713), 259.

[59] The preceding paragraphs incorporate, with some modifications, the substance of my note in *E.H.R.* xliii (1928), 606–11. Equipage was paid to officials other than diplomatists, e.g. Lord Chancellor Cowper received £2,000 on his appointment for equipage (*Diary*, ed. Rev. E. C. Hawtrey for the Roxburghe Club [Eton, 1833], p. 15). Speakers of the House of Commons received equipage money (46 *C.J.* 598) and also Lords Lieutenant of Ireland (*C.T.B. and P.* v (1742–5), 800).

[60] Manchester, *Court and Society*, ii. 141–2. Cf. H.M.C., *Portland MSS.* ii. 196: 'Mr. Stanhope will have a pension, being superannuated.'

[61] *Trans. R. Hist. Soc.*, 4th series, ix. 63.

[62] *E.H.R.* xliii. 609.

was in 1770 promised a pension of £1,000 a year till suitable provision could be made for him.[63] Joseph Ewart was compulsorily
retired from his post at Berlin on a pension of £1,000 a year.[64] Sir
James Porter after twenty-three years' service received a pension
of £1,200 per annum.[65] Other examples from this period are
quoted in my Historical Association pamphlet on *Scottish Diplomatists 1689–1789* and justify us in concluding that by the end
of the eighteenth century the grant of a retiring allowance had
become a regular practice in the case of diplomatists who had a
sufficiently long and distinguished period of service abroad.[66] The
Act 22 George III, c. 82, regulating the civil list expressly safe-
guarded by its eighteenth clause the right of the crown to grant
such pensions to persons who had served the crown in foreign
courts, provided the list of such pensions was laid before Parliament. Lord King in 1822 made a furious attack upon the whole
system as it had developed under George III.[67]

In addition to these cash allowances and payments, there were
often perquisites of considerable value. Ambassadors were entitled
to a large quantity of white and gilt plate, estimated in the earlier
part of the period to be worth £2,500. In Anne's reign they also
received a cloth of state of crimson damask with gold and silver
fringe, a chair, two stools, a footstool, and a foot carpet 'as hath
been usual on such like occasions' as well as a large Bible, prayer-
books, altar cloth, &c., for the embassy chapel to an estimate of
not less than £350.[68] By an Order in Council of 31 January 1668 the
secretaries of state 'were to allow no ambassador to take official
plate from the Jewel House unless he promised either to return it
or buy it at the end of his mission',[69] but ambassadors, as a mark
of particular royal favour, were sometimes allowed to retain for

---

[63] Weymouth to Murray, 30 Nov. 1770, in S.P. 97. 46.

[64] Lodge, *Great Britain and Prussia*, p. 212. Cf., however, *Auckland Journal*,
ii. 396, where it is stated at £1,500 gross yielding over £1,000 net.

[65] Larpent, i. 10.

[66] Details in P.R.O., E. 403, 2680/1. Lists of such pensions are printed from
time to time in appendices to *Commons Journals* and *Parliamentary Debates*.

[67] *Parliamentary Debates New Series*, vi. 1284 et seq.

[68] *C.T.B.* xx (1705–6), 376. Cf. for a similar grant, *C.T.B.* xxi (1706–7), 151, to
the earl of Manchester. By the mid-eighteenth century rather more was usually
estimated, e.g. three ambassadors, appointed between 1742 and 1745, all received
plate valued at £3,100 and chapel furniture estimated at £408: *C.T.B. and P.* v
(1742–5), 12, 378, 574, 576.

[69] Baxter, *Development of the Treasury*, p. 13.

their own use the plate issued to them.[70] Even when no such grant had been made royal officials often had difficulty in recovering possession.[71] In 1690 and 1691 the deputy Treasury solicitor was suing certain peers for keeping the official plate loaned to them, though it is suggested that this was effectively a political prosecution, and as soon as Sunderland (one of the peers prosecuted) had made his peace with the king the proceedings against him were dropped.[72] The expense for plate averaged over £8,000 a year under William III[73] and plate (or an allowance in lieu thereof) continued to be issued to individual ambassadors until new arrangements were made after 1815. Ambassadors also received a framed portrait of the reigning sovereign as part of their state.[74]

Diplomatists of all ranks valued highly the privilege of exemption from customs duties which they habitually enjoyed and often abused. The extent of these exemptions varied at different courts.[75] The English practice, as stated by Godolphin to the Commissioners of the Customs in 1707, was to allow foreign ministers to import free of duty household goods, wearing apparel, and equipage along with one tun of wine for ambassadors and two hogsheads for diplomatists of lesser rank; all other customable goods were to pay the usual duties.[76] It was, however, difficult to make certain that such goods were not subsequently sold at a handsome profit and there were continual disputes with the foreign ministers in London.

In 1764 George Grenville wrote to our ambassador in France:

You will have heard of the many difficulties and disputes which we have had with M. de Guerchy [the French ambassador at London]; in some of them, which related to the introduction of prohibited goods,

[70] See, for example, *C.T.B.* xxi (1706–7), 517 (grant of two services of plate to duke of Manchester, one as ambassador to Venice, the other as ambassador to France). Cf. *Stair Annals*, ii. 154.

[71] *C.T.P. 1714–19*, 365, refers to a long list of ambassadors and others who in the thirty-three years up to 1718 had neither returned their plate nor secured a discharge.

[72] Baxter, *Development of the Treasury*, p. 248.

[73] *Parliamentary Papers*, H.C. (1868–9), xxxv. 593.

[74] *C.T.B.* xx (1705–6), 298. Cf. *Bedford Corresp.* iii. 200, and (for the nineteenth century) *Report of the Committee to inquire into the fees and emoluments of Public Offices*, H.C. (1837–8) *Accounts and Papers*, xliv. 118–19; Vera Watson, *A Queen at Home*, pp. 45–47.

[75] There is some information about Russian practice in *Buckinghamshire Desp.* ii. 71, &c.

[76] *C.T.B.* xxi (1706–7), 346–7.

and of an unlimited quantity of wine duty free, I have been particularly concerned.

The notorious abuse which has been practised under colour of this indulgence ... occasioned a great ferment here, and a body of six or seven thousand manufacturers came to the King to complain of it, and to desire that he would order the laws to be put into execution, which his Majesty solemnly directed to be done, and the orders were given accordingly. The rule which has been established with regard to foreign ministers for above a hundred years in this country, and which is confirmed at the beginning of every new reign, was ordered to be followed: by that rule foreign ministers are entitled to have their first entrys duty free, and that première entrée is limited to one tun of wine, their equipages, and the furniture of their house, but not to extend to any merchandize. The time for making this première entrée has been literally construed, and limited only to six months.[77]

At the same time the Bavarian diplomatic agent at London was complaining about the retention by the customs of 'un habit d'été brodé en argent'.[78] There were the same difficulties in the 1770's when, according to Horace Walpole, 'the ministers of smaller foreign courts, whose pay is scanty, taking advantage of their sacred character, were turned notorious smugglers, and, without paying duties, kept warehouses of contraband commodities'. The principal offenders, he adds, were the ministers from Bavaria, Venice, and Naples, and 'the Spanish ambassador was almost the only envoy from a foreign court who disdained to turn his exalted office to trading purposes'. Lady Holdernesse, wife of the former secretary of state, now Governor of the Cinque Ports, made use of her husband's official position to engage in wholesale smuggling.[79] Cornelius van Bynkershoek gives the title 'the Merchant Ambassador' to one of his chapters 'because the profit of ambassadors from trade is now far larger than that of any others, since they do not pay any tariff on the merchandise which they pretend is necessary for their own use but which they afterwards sell at retail'.[80] Comparatively few British diplomatists engaged in business on this scale:[81] they were much more likely to

---

[77] *Grenville Papers*, ii. 393 and elsewhere.   [78] Ibid. ii. 361–2.
[79] Walpole, *Journal of the Reign of George III*, i. 112–13.
[80] *De Foro Legatorum Liber Singularis*, p. 69.
[81] Accusations of smuggling were frequently brought against British diplomatic agents, e.g. by Lady Mary Wortley Montagu against John Murray at Venice (Halsband, *Lady Mary Wortley Montagu*, p. 266), but they are usually unsupported by evidence which would satisfy a court of law.

try to abuse their exemption from customs duties to import goods cheaply for their friends, not to make a personal profit. Lord Hertford was indignant when the customs officials at Dover seized from one of the king's messengers some small presents which Lady Hertford was sending in the diplomatic bag to her friends in England.[82] The *Stair Annals* include references to commissions of this sort discharged by Stair while at Paris including six pairs of silk stockings for the duke of Argyll, a nightgown for the duchess of Marlborough, and plate for her sister.[83]

A diplomatist who successfully negotiated a treaty was entitled to expect a valuable present, not from his own master[84] but from the foreign sovereign. Such presents were rarely refused by the destined recipients.[85] Thus the duke of Bedford on signing the treaty of Paris received from Louis XV a 'snuff-box with the royal portrait set in diamonds in red enamel' costing nearly 34,300 livres[86] while the duchess was given the magnificent service of Sèvres porcelain which is now on exhibition at Woburn.[87] His successor, the duke of Manchester, who negotiated the peace of 1783, received from Louis XVI the king's picture 'ornamented with a crown and circle of diamonds'. Vergennes claimed that the value of this present was 35,000 livres 'but according to the opinion of experienced jewellers, whom the duke of Manchester has consulted, the diamonds are not thought to be worth more than between nine hundred and a thousand pounds. A very costly present of French porcelain has been made to the duchess of Manchester and His Most Christian Majesty's picture set round with diamonds in a snuff box' given to the secretary of embassy.[88] It was estimated that Sir Robert Ainslie, if he had been selected to

---

[82] *Grenville Papers*, ii. 260.

[83] *Stair Annals*, i. 290–4, cf. ii. 136, 445.

[84] Harrington, while secretary of state, ruled that 'it was an absolute unprecedented thing for our court to make (after the custom of the German courts) any pecuniary acknowledgments to our own ministers upon the conclusion of any treaty through their means, how beneficial soever that treaty might be to the public; but threw out at the same time that a riband, or some such mark of distinction, was the usual and proper method taken by our court to distinguish such ministers' (*Bedford Corresp.* i. 126–7).

[85] One example of refusal by the French diplomatists Dubois and Pecquet to accept presents from George I valued at £3,000 and £500 respectively is mentioned in *Stair Annals*, ii. 367, 370.

[86] Joan Evans, 'The Embassy of the Fourth Duke of Bedford to Paris, 1762–1763', in the *Archaeological Journal*, cxiii (1957), 151.

[87] *Bedford Corresp.* iii. 232.   [88] *George III Corresp.* vi. 452.

mediate between Austria and the Ottoman empire at Sistova in
1791, would have received nearly £30,000 in presents.[89] Frederick
the Great offered Hyndford 100,000 rix dollars if he could secure
Maria Theresa's acceptance of the Prussian terms in 1742 and
actually made him a present of 10,000 crowns on the conclusion of
the treaty of Breslau in 1742. When Hyndford proposed to spend
the money on a service of plate to be made at Berlin, Frederick
graciously added a patent authorizing the ambassador and his
heirs to bear the arms of Silesia in memory of the peace of Breslau.[90] Sir Robert Sutton, ambassador at Constantinople, who had
helped to settle Russo-Turkish grievances in 1712, received 6,000
ducats and a sable coat from the Russian negotiator as well as
presents from the Tsar.[91]

Junior officials who brought a treaty, after signature, to the king
could, however, expect a handsome gift in cash from their own
sovereign.[92] When Abraham Stanyan negotiated a loan of £150,000
by the Canton of Berne to the British government he received the
commission of ½ per cent., amounting to £750, 'usual amongst
merchants', while the grateful Lord Treasurer assured him that
his services in this matter would always make the Treasurer justly
distinguish him by forward payments of his allowances.[93] There
are occasional hints that diplomatists who made themselves unpopular with the authorities would suffer delay in receiving their
arrears or might not be paid in full.[94]

Another method which optimistic diplomatists sometimes used
to supplement their income was the one often described in the
eighteenth century as the infamous practice of stockjobbing.
There were obvious reasons why men whose official position gave

[89] B.M. Add. MS. 38229, fo. 161. This is a gross over-statement (*Keith Memoir*,
ii. 481, 492, &c.).

[90] Lodge, *Great Britain and Prussia*, p. 40.

[91] *Sutton Desp.*, p. 8. Cf. the statement that Sir Robert Ainslie, by not being
chosen to mediate at Sistova in 1791, lost nearly £30,000 (M. S. Anderson in
E.H.R. lxix. 52).

[92] The attachés who brought the definitive treaty of Aix-la-Chapelle to
Hanover and to London each received £1,000 while the bearer of the definitive
treaty of Paris at the end of the Seven Years War 'touched his thousand at the
Treasury without any deductions: he is in great spirits' (*Bedford Corresp.* i. 558
and iii. 212).   [93] *C.T.B.* xxiv (1710), 248–9, 349.

[94] Halsband, *Lady Mary Wortley Montagu*, p. 94. Wortley claimed £9,000 on
his return from Constantinople and asserted that his refusal to support the
Peerage Bill cost him £4,000 of this and other advantages which he had been
promised, but his story is quite unsupported.

them access to early and confidential information likely to affect stock-exchange prices should not use this information to make a personal profit. According to Horace Walpole, however, most of the foreign ministers at London 'except the prince of Masserano, the Spanish ambassador, followed that dirty trade'. Amongst others accused by Walpole was the French ambassador, de Guines, whose secretary claimed to have acted as the ambassador's agent in stockjobbing transactions with English bankers which had resulted in heavy losses. Walpole, however, pointed out that 'it did seem an exculpation of the Count that he had lost by the transaction, which was not credible, being master of the secret of pacification on Falkland's Island'.[95] Amongst British diplomatists accused of this malpractice was Stair during his celebrated mission to the Regent Orleans, but he too apparently lost by it.[96] The Russian minister at London, Simolin, was also believed to have engaged in speculation on a large scale.[97]

The ambassadors at Constantinople by extending their protection—at a price—to Jews, Armenians, and other aliens made a considerable profit. According to one of them 'the fees for this protection . . . formed an important item in the emoluments of the ambassador'.[98]

At some courts a valuable present could be expected from the foreign sovereign at the end of each mission.[99] Lord Forbes received 6,000 roubles and a diamond ring valued at £1,100 from the Tsaritsa,[1] Buckinghamshire received a gift of tapestry from Catherine II during his mission to Russia,[2] and Robert Liston was given at the end of his Spanish mission amongst other gifts a copy of the Infant Don Gabriel's Sallust (which could not be bought) and proposed to smuggle it (as a gift to Edinburgh University Library) through the British Customs House in the diplomatic bag.[3] Probably the most expensive gifts were given to the earl of Macclesfield on his mission to Zell and Hanover to present to the Electress Sophia a copy of the Act of Settlement and invest the

[95] Walpole, Journal of the Reign of George III, ii. 9–10.

[96] Stair Annals, ii. 60, &c.

[97] Auckland Journal, i. 279–80.

[98] Larpent, i. 6. Details are to be found in Add. MS. 38229, fos. 156–61.

[99] See the curious references in Auckland Journal, iv. 277–8, 280–1, to a grossly indecent painting given by the King of Sweden as a parting gift to Lord Henry Spencer.   [1] H.M.C., Report II, App., p. 215.

[2] Buckinghamshire Desp. i, p. viii.

[3] National Library of Scotland MS. 3943, fo. 216.

elector with the Garter.[4] These are stated to have exceeded £7,000 in value. When the customary present was not given, acrimonious protests followed.[5]

The custom of paying at least part of the expenses of a resident diplomatist apparently still survived in the early years of our period at one or two continental courts, including Brussels[6] and Constantinople.[7] Davenant after quarrelling with the Tuscan authorities proposed to remove to Genoa, to which state he was also accredited, and, trying to obtain the approval of the secretary of state, used the argument that he would then qualify for a pension from the Genoese republic.[8] Special services highly appreciated by the foreign government might win for a British diplomatist a foreign title such as count of the Holy Roman Empire, a foreign decoration, or an addition to his coat of arms. Thus Malmesbury received, for his services in establishing a British–Prussian–Dutch alliance, a peerage from his own government, from the King of Prussia the addition of the Prussian eagle to his arms, and from the Stadtholder his motto 'Je maintiendrai'.[9] Queen Elizabeth I is said to have remarked: 'I would not have my sheep branded with any other mark than my own, or follow the whistle of a strange shepherd';[10] but it was not until 1834 that a rule was introduced prohibiting (inter alios) diplomatists and consuls from receiving any presents from a foreign government.[11] Such a regulation could, however, be evaded, as it was when, on the conclusion of a convention regulating the Sound dues on ships trading to the Baltic, the King of Sweden gave a porphyry vase to the wife of the British diplomatist who had negotiated the treaty.[12] Palmerston three years earlier had abolished the practice of giving presents of this character to foreign diplomatists at London on conclusion of treaties and at the end of their missions.[13]

It is clear also that British diplomatists were occasionally offered substantial sums as bribes by foreign governments: at other times they had the chance of disbursing considerable sums at foreign

[4] Cole, Memoirs, p. 414.
[5] e.g. H.M.C., Polwarth MSS. iii. 65–66.
[6] H.M.C., Portland MSS. v. 232.   [7] Wood, Levant Co., p. 134.
[8] S.P. 79. 9, dispatch of 17/1/16.
[9] Malmesbury Diaries, i, p. xiii.
[10] Satow, Guide to Diplomatic Practice, p. 269.
[11] Hertslet, Recollections of the Old Foreign Office, p. 175.
[12] Old Days in Diplomacy, by the eldest daughter of the late Sir E. C. Disbrowe, p. 203.   [13] Ibid., p. 175.

courts and possibly retaining a proportion in their own hands.[14] The difference between legitimate perquisites and malversation was not always as clear as it might have been.

A few examples, chosen from the middle years of the eighteenth century, will show the actual sums received in cash by men at the top of the diplomatic tree. Albemarle as ambassador extraordinary and plenipotentiary to France drew well over £7,000 a year and in addition drew another £2,000 a year as Groom of the Stole.[15] Keene's earnings towards the end of his embassy to Spain averaged nearly £7,000 a year. Hanbury-Williams, a mere envoy to Saxony-Poland, until appointed in 1755 to the Russian embassy, averaged over £5,000 a year between 1752 and 1758. Joseph Yorke, son of the Lord Chancellor and minister plenipotentiary to the United Provinces, was drawing between £3,000 and £4,000 in the middle 1750's and in 1761–2 his pay as envoy extraordinary and plenipotentiary to The Hague and as ambassador extraordinary and plenipotentiary to the Congress of Augsburg reached a total in excess of £8,500.[16]

It should be remembered that these sums, large as they seem, were not intended as remuneration for services rendered to the crown but rather as an expense allowance to defray the costs necessarily incurred in representing the crown abroad.[17] The first duty of an ambassador, if he would do honour to his master, was

[14] See, for example, a curious conversation between Lord Rochford and the Russian ambassador at London in which Rochford states that Goodricke, the envoy to Sweden, is trustworthy in every way except with money. Russia was pressing Britain to bribe the anti-French party in Sweden: Martens, Recueil des Traités conclus par la Russie, ix (x), under date 1772. George III on this occasion authorized Goodricke to draw up to £15,000 'provided that sum can defeat the attempts of the K[ing] of Sweden' (Correspondence, ed. Fortescue, ii. 384). Successive agents at St. Petersburg received large sums to be spent at their discretion in winning the favour of the Russian ministers. The earl of Cadogan in 1721 received 50,000 crowns from the King of Prussia to be used as bribes at Vienna (S.P. 80. 43, dispatches of 5 Mar. and 15 Mar.), while John Methuen while ambassador to Spain received over £200,000 from his own government for various purposes connected with the war. Stormont, while ambassador at Paris, was accused by an enemy of embezzling secret-service money (Fife Papers in Aberdeen University Library).

[15] One of his predecessors, Stair, had been given the colonelcy of a regiment of dragoons 'because his Royal Master foresaw that his salary could not defray his expences': The Life of John Earl of Stair by an Impartial Hand (London, 1748), p. 169.

[16] These figures are taken from 32 C.J. 466–603.

[17] For this reason a proposal to arrest an envoy's wages for debt was described as 'not very practicable' (H.M.C., Finch MSS. ii. 301).

to keep an open table.[18] 'The minister's table ought to represent the grandeur of his master by making known the honourable salary he allows him.'[19] Lord Chesterfield also believed that 'to keep a good table, and to do the honours of it gracefully and *sur le ton de la bonne compagnie*, is absolutely necessary for a foreign minister'.[20] Thus the elder Horace Walpole, we are told by his biographer, though by nature and habit strictly economical, acted with a laudable spirit during his embassies. 'Even in his absence a regular table was maintained, and the same establishment (except in his equipages) kept up as when he was present. He was accustomed to say that the best intelligence is obtained by the convivial intercourse of a good table.'[21]

In some continental states appointment to an embassy was almost regarded as indirect taxation of over-wealthy subjects. This was never the case in Britain, but the expenses must often have exceeded the income.[22] The position in Britain was similar to that in France, where Montesquieu commented: 'Les ambassadeurs de France sont tres mal payés; le Roi est un géant qui se fait représenter par un nain',[23] and Pecquet in his *Discours sur l'art de négocier* stated that 'tout homme occupé d'un désir excessif de fortune ou de richesse doit renoncer à l'emploi de Négociateur'.[24] Matthew Prior referred to himself and his diplomatic colleagues under William III as working journeymen 'sent [abroad] to preach politics as the Apostles were on a better errand, without purse or scrip'.[25] Hans Stanley, applying for a diplomatic job in 1761, wrote to Pitt: 'Those who know the nature of these commissions, cannot be ignorant, that they are not to be sought from any hope

[18] Wicquefort (English trans.), *The Ambassador and his Functions*, pp. 207–8.
[19] Ibid., p. 208.   [20] *Letters* i. 421.
[21] Coxe, *Lord Walpole Memoirs*, ii. 455–6. Cf. the story in H.M.C., *Egmont Diary*, iii. 240, of the Member of Parliament who, when Walpole drew a distinction between the dinners he gave in England as plain squire Walpole and those he gave abroad in his ambassador's function, remarked: 'Then I will dine no more with the squire but with the ambassador.'
[22] The most convincing evidence for this relates to the early nineteenth century. The F.O. memorandum as to the Diplomatic Expenditure (11 May 1822) is supported by statements of actual expenditure by some of the leading diplomatists of the day (F.O. 83. 10). But as early as 1713 when Bolingbroke proposes Lord Bingley as ambassador to France he adds: 'His estate will bear it, and his obligations to the Queen will, if she requires it, I suppose, make him willing.'
[23] *Œuvres Complètes*, ed. R. Caillos, i. 1445. Cf. M. Jusserand's remarks, *Recueil des Instructions*, XXIV, xxxiii–xxxvi.
[24] p. 20 of the Paris 1737 edition.
[25] H.M.C., *Bath MSS.* iii. 15.

of emolument.'[26] James Harris claimed to have diminished his private fortune by £20,000 during his fourteen years in the diplomatic service.[27]

Under James II Sir William Trumbull wrote from Paris that unless special arrangements could be made 'it is impossible for me to live here according to my Character without being ruin'd in my little fortune'.[28] And towards the end of our period Sir R. M. Keith, after some years at Vienna, wrote in 1774:

It is a melancholy truth that with more marks of favour conferred upon me than I ever looked for, or merited—with a more grateful and contented disposition than most people are blessed with—I find myself unavoidably verging into beggary; because my place, my principles, my duty towards the King and my countrymen, lay me under *indispensable obligations* of expense which are, from their nature and from inveterate custom, carried to a pitch which exceeds my appointments, and swallows up the last shreds of my private fortune. I live amongst great Austrian lords, whose tables are costly and splendid, and ambassadors from great courts, whose appointments are at least the double of mine. I neither cope with, nor ape any body in magnificence; but the minister of England in the first court of Europe must live not only hospitably, but handsomely, especially if he has frequently a score of young fellows of the first fashion of his country to introduce into the best company of the capital.[29]

At certain other courts the entertainment of British visitors added to the already high expenses.[30] It was on this ground that Sir James Porter solicited his recall from Brussells in 1765 although he had been able to live comfortably and even make a handsome profit at Constantinople on a previous mission.[31] Even at the Constantinople embassy profits were on the decline. There a main source of income was the sale of *barats* or patents of protection, entitling the holders to claim the benefit of the English capitulations to Armenians, Jews, and Greeks, which may well have brought in £2,000 or £3,000 a year and was not ended until 1809.[32] Stair, writing from Paris in 1715, claimed that 'my house

---

[26] *Chatham Corresp.* ii. 118. [27] *Malmesbury Diaries*, i. 457–8.
[28] Clark, *Trumbull*, p. 103. [29] *Keith Memoir*, i. 477–8.
[30] Lord Preston, while ambassador to France, entertained the duke of Northumberland, by the king's order, for nearly six months and expected an extra allowance. H.M.C., *Report VII, App.*, p. 303.
[31] Larpent, i. 10.
[32] Wood, *Levant Co.*, pp. 135, 191.

here and my stables, my servants' wages and board-wages and clothes, will do more than exhaust all my appointments . . . and then there will remain my table and all my own personal expenses and extraordinaries[33] to be taken out of my own funds'.[34] According to his biographer at the end of his mission 'his fortunes and estates were much impaired by the debts he had contracted, which his government allowances as ambassador were never sufficient to liquidate'.[35] He himself admitted, however, that his debts were in part due to gaming and stockjobbing.[36] An earlier ambassador to France, Jersey, calculated that he spent £12,000 in eight months.[37]

The third earl of Marchmont when offered a diplomatic commission remarked that

my father had undone himself in such, and had been kept abroad till all his friends were dead. . . . Upon [Lord Chesterfield's] saying that no gentleman could save himself in such a commission, I told him, that I could not undertake one, if I had not something beside my own estate to trust to, if the Treasury did not pay.[38]

'I would not ruin myself and family', Marchmont told Bolingbroke, 'to come home here forgotten, to walk about soliciting a Scots pension.'[39] Occasionally expenses were reduced by exchange of houses in Paris and London by the French and British ambassadors,[40] but this was rarely practicable. It should be remembered that the figures given are gross payments and liable to substantial deductions. It was estimated in 1821 that 14 per cent. of the equipage, ordinary, and extraordinary allowances was deducted at the Treasury and Exchequer. The Privy Seal office also collected fees from each payment made to a diplomatist, though these are possibly included in the 14 per cent.[41] Moreover, to secure more

---

[33] *Stair Annals*, i. 391, shows that these amounted to nearly £2,000 for the June–Sept. quarter of 1716.   [34] Ibid. i. 266; cf. ibid. ii. 98.
[35] Ibid. ii. 159.   [36] Ibid. ii. 60, 98.
[37] H.M.C., *Bath MSS.* i. 224.   [38] *Marchmont Papers*, i. 90.
[39] Ibid. i. 95.   [40] *Bedford Corresp.* ii. 94.
[41] F.O. 83. 10. Thus fees confirmed by a Treasury minute of 30 Nov. 1782 included a charge of £6. 7s. on all quarterly allowances to ambassadors or to envoys and plenipotentiaries and of £3. 3s. 6d. on each bill of extraordinaries of £100. (Pensions to foreign ministers were charged at the rate of £1. 1s. per cent. up to £500.) On first appointment each ambassador paid £88. 10s. to the Foreign Office fee fund, with an additional £21 for the chief clerk's own use. These and many other details will be found in *First Report of the Committee appointed to inquire into the fees and emoluments of Public Offices*, H.C. (1837–8) *Accounts and Papers*, xliv. Official deductions made from the basic

prompt payment diplomatists got into the habit of appointing Foreign Office clerks and others to act as their agents in collecting the sums due to them,[42] and these agents were entitled to a commission, fixed by Castlereagh in 1816 at 1 per cent. on ordinary allowances.[43] It is also possible, though I am far from certain about this, that diplomatic salaries may have been subjected to land-tax, as they certainly were later on to income-tax.

Other deductions of a less official kind included the cost of supplying friends at home with articles for which the country in which they had their residence was famous. Envoys to Saxony, for example, were continually being dunned for Meissen porcelain, while those in Italy were sometimes expected to pick up cheaply old masters for their friends. Horace Walpole's sister Lady Townshend expected him to bring her back some 'linnen' from The Hague.[44] Apart from a pound of ultramarine for the king, Sir William Trumbull on his return from Paris received orders from various acquaintances for 'a night dress of Point de Paris for the head for my Lady Jeffreys', books on history, geography, and morality, sealing-wax and sand, and 'three pairs of small French scissors'. It was also suggested that he should smuggle into England '3 or 4 suits of hangings and a velvet bed' which Lord Montagu had at Paris.[45]

Some diplomatists, such as Tyrawley, who wrote that the king had appointed him to Lisbon as a good thing in order to retrieve his private fortunes,[46] and Sandwich, who had the same idea about Madrid, expected to make money out of a diplomatic career, but I do not think many succeeded in this, though John Laws, a writing master, was reputed to have made his fortune as resident at Brussels during the Spanish Succession War.[47] According to his

salary of £45 per annum payable to messengers reduced the net amount received to £35. 8s. (V. Wheeler-Holohan, *History of the King's Messengers*, p. 217).

[42] An early example is to be found in H.M.C., *Bath MSS.* iii. 33–34.

[43] *Report of the Committee . . . into the fees and emoluments of Public Offices*, H.C. (1837–8), xliv. 114–23. F.O. 366. 375 contains a mass of papers relating to the question of these agency charges in the nineteenth century, although as early as 1786 the Committee on Fees and Gratuities in Public Offices had reported that such fees are 'improper, liable to abuse and ought to be discontinued'. As late as 1865–7 five Foreign Office clerks showed an average net profit of £422 from such charges. See also a report by the secretaries of state, 23 Feb. 1795, in F.O. 366. 542.   [44] *Honest Diplomat*, p. 349.

[45] Clark, *Trumbull*, p. 165; H.M.C., *Downshire MSS.* i. 219, &c.

[46] S.P. 89. 37, letter dated 22 Sept. 1730; Namier, *Structure of Politics*, p. 288.

[47] *Honest Diplomat*, pp. 47–48.

official biographer, Sir James Porter did well for himself at Constantinople and acquired financial independence, partly by collecting perquisites and partly by 'the judicious economy he established in his household. . . . He soon discovered that the Turks viewed any ostentatious display on the part of an ambassador not only with indifference and habitual apathy, but sometimes with contempt.'[48] Far more typical was Benjamin Keene, who wrote to Bedford from Madrid in 1750: 'My circumstances, after a life of some labour and disagreeable passages, are in every respect much the same as when I made the first step into it. My appointments, and much more, have always been expended in procuring that regard here which was necessary for his majesty's service.'[49]

Some idea of the preparations required at the outset of an important embassy may be obtained from the list of the earl of Stair's suite when he made his public entry as ambassador to congratulate Louis XV on his accession to the throne.[50] One of Stair's predecessors on a similar occasion paid £450 in gratuities alone to the officers and servants of his Most Christian Majesty.[51] One of James II's envoys to Louis XIV, Sir William Trumbull, took with him a household of forty persons.[52] Albemarle, a later ambassador, was accompanied by a suite of forty-one persons.[53] But the record seems to be held by Portland, who took with him to France in 1698 eighty servants and ninety carriage and saddle horses.[54] Sometimes the Treasury made a special payment towards the cost of an ambassador's public entry. Holdernesse, for example, received £200 from the Treasury towards this expense during his embassy to Venice.[55]

Admittedly a suite on the scale adopted by Stair was exceptionally lavish; but as Callières puts it, 'a well-ordered household served by reliable and well-mannered persons is a good advertisement, both of the ambassador and of the country whence he comes'.[56] For this reason the suite of a Genoese diplomatist was

[48] Larpent, i. 6.
[49] Bedford Corresp. ii. 62–63.
[50] The Life of Stair by an Impartial Hand, pp. 199–208. A less pretentious ambassadorial entry is described in H.M.C., Polwarth MSS. iii. 95–96.
[51] C.T.B. xxvii (1713), p. 296.   [52] Clark, Trumbull, p. 18.
[53] Bedford Corresp. iii. 93–94.
[54] C. K. Eves, Matthew Prior, pp. 103–4.
[55] C.T.B. and P. v (1742–5), 672, 803.
[56] De la manière de négocier avec les Souverains (trans. A. F. Whyte), p. 97.

laid down by the law of the Republic and any diminution in state would mean a reduction in his emoluments.[57] When Wortley and his wife went on their celebrated mission to Constantinople Wortley's suite included a secretary, treasurer, resident chaplain, three dragomen, a Turkish scribe, and a guard of Janissaries to protect his family in public against fanatical Moslems. The embassy was staffed by a retinue of servants, most of them Greeks and Armenians hired at Constantinople.[58] Sir William Trumbull's luggage included

a coach, a chaise and twenty horses ... two trunks full of plate, nine boxes full of copper and pewter vessels, fifty boxes filled with pictures, mirrors, beds, tapestries, linen, cloth for liveries, and kitchen utensils, ... seven or eight dozen chairs and arm chairs, twenty boxes containing tea, coffee, chocolate, wine, ale and other provisions; four large and three small cabinets; six trunks and six boxes with Sir William and Lady Trumbull's apparel [and] forty boxes, trunks, bales, valises, portmanteaux containing the belongings of Sir William's suite.[59]

The key appointment was undoubtedly that of secretary. In British practice secretaries of embassy were separately paid by the crown; but envoys and ministers had to provide secretaries out of their own emoluments.[60] A well-qualified private secretary might well cost his employer up to £100 a year in cash, plus of course his board and lodging.[61] A good cook, at least at some courts, we are told, was as important as a good secretary. It was a common practice for an eighteenth-century British diplomatist to take with him one or more young men, friends or connexions of his own, who acted as unpaid attachés and gained experience of diplomatic practice in the hope of being appointed to a diplomatic post. Sometimes the more menial servants were the domestic servants employed in England by the diplomatist in his private capacity and brought out with him from home,[62] but they usually had to be

---

[57] V. Vitale, *La Diplomazia Genovese*, p. 13. Cf. Pecquet, pp. 71–72.
[58] A. C. Wood's article in *E.H.R.* xl (1925), 538–41; Halsband, *Lady Mary Wortley Montagu*, p. 74. This was in accordance with the traditional practice (H.M.C., *Downshire MSS.* i. 224).
[59] Clark, *Trumbull*, p. 19.
[60] For the institution of secretaries of legation see *supra*, p. 46.
[61] Occasionally a great nobleman's chaplain acted also as his secretary, e.g. Ayerst to Lord Strafford in 1713 (*Bolingbroke Corresp.* ii. 376).
[62] Government messengers were often chosen from the menial servants of noblemen with Foreign Office influence, e.g. Arthur Young's *Autobiography*,

recruited from the available labour at the foreign capital. Such recruits were often politically unreliable: others occasionally acted as spies for other governments. Thus our ambassador at Constantinople, John Murray, from 1766 to 1775 had his whole correspondence, ciphers, &c., betrayed to the French by one of his servants, a Pole.[63] Harris claimed that at St. Petersburg no person in his household was too insignificant to escape the temptation of a bribe from his opponents and that 'when he left his secretary writing, he used to lock him up, not from mistrust of his honesty, but of his leaving the door of the room open'.[64] It was a commonplace in diplomatic textbooks that the bad conduct of diplomatists' servants was responsible for many incidents.[65] A surprising number of these can be attributed to *odium theologicum*, though this was often sharpened by more material motives.

'Vivant noblement et dans l'abondance, mais sans profusion ridicule', the good diplomatist 'ne contracte point de dettes'.[66] This, I fear, represents theory rather than practice when we attempt to apply it to British diplomatists. Quite apart from the problematical adequacy of the rates of pay to meet expenditure, payment both of ordinaries and extraordinaries was often much in arrear. As early as 1694 there were difficulties and Sir Paul Rycaut from Hamburg agreed with his correspondent Trumbull that 'the best way to have the foreign ministers paid is to have a vested fund appointed for their maintenance'.[67] Rycaut himself at this time had to accept payment of some of the arrears due to him by tallies on the excise leaving £1,127. 16s. 3d. still outstanding.[68] 'My tallies I cannot sell under 30% loss', wrote Prior in 1696,[69] while arrangements were made to pay off some of the arrears due to Manchester by weekly instalments.[70] By 1697 William III's inadequate civil list was pledged for two years ahead. This was not due to extravagance, but to the deliberate refusal of the House of Commons to vote him money sufficient to carry on

ed. M. B. Edwards, p. 45, and *Old Days in Diplomacy*, by the eldest daughter of Sir E. C. Disbrowe, p. 41.

[63] Information from Dr. M. S. Anderson. See *infra*, Chapter XIV, note 72.

[64] *Malmesbury Diaries*, i. 458.

[65] e.g. Pecquet, *Discours*, p. 130. In extreme cases such incidents produced an actual rupture of diplomatic relations, e.g. H.M.C., *Polwarth MSS.* ii. 558.

[66] Pecquet, op. cit., p. 131.   [67] H.M.C., *Downshire MSS.* i. 449-50.

[68] Ibid. i. 455.

[69] H.M.C., *Bath MSS.* iii. 86. Cf. ibid. iii. 95, for tallies at 45 per cent.

[70] Manchester, *Court and Society*, ii. 66.

the government.[71] The result was that he died owing his foreign ministers £14,502. 2s. 5d. This sum was included in his civil list debts, the great bulk of which was never paid.[72]

The position in the closing years of Anne's reign was for a time even worse. Writing to Lord Strafford in August 1713, Bolingbroke states: 'I neither have received, nor expect to receive anything on account of the journey which I took last year by her Majesty's order [into France]; and, as to my regular appointments, I do assure your Lordship I have heard nothing of them these last two years.'[73] When this was the position of a powerful secretary of state, the plight of lesser men can readily be appreciated. Christian Cole, secretary at Venice, claimed in November 1713 that his pay was four years in arrear.[74] John Molesworth, envoy extraordinary to Tuscany, also in November 1713, claimed that his pay was three years in arrear and pointed out that he would be unable to leave his post until he received payment. The moment he took leave of the grand-ducal court he would lose his diplomatic immunity and his many creditors would descend upon him to the dishonour of the British crown.[75]

In 1708 the Lord Treasurer 'cleared the arrears of all the foreign ministers by "tallies of Pro" upon the tin, bearing no interest',[76] and later in the reign the crown raised £30,409. 15s. 5d. out of loans made by the merchants commissioned to sell Her Majesty's tin abroad and used this to defray some of the arrears due to foreign ministers[77] instead of paying the Cornish tinmen with it. So desperate was the position of some foreign ministers that they begged for payment even in tallies.[78] The Treasury accounts confirm the arrears when they show a jump in the payments made to foreign ministers from £38,798 in 1713 to the staggering figure of £158,874 in 1714. Most of the latter sum represents the liquidation of arrears. This was due to the passing of the Act 12 Anne, c. 11, which authorized the queen to raise a loan of £500,000 serviced

[71] *C.T.B.*, introduction to vols. xi–xvii (1695–1702), pp. xxiii–xxvi.
[72] Ibid., p. xli.
[73] *Bolingbroke Corresp.* ii. 466.   [74] S.P. 99. 60.
[75] S.P. 98. 23, dispatch of 21 Nov. 1713 and authorities cited in *B.D.R.*, p. 79. There are occasional cases of diplomatists leaving unpaid debts behind them, e.g. *Polwarth MSS.* i. 37, 408, 416.
[76] H.M.C., *Portland MSS.* iv. 502.
[77] *C.T.B.* xxiii (1709), 357. Sir Lambert Blackwell received payment of arrears due to him in 1710 by tallies on the [Queen's] tin (*C.T.B.* xxiv (1710), 22).
[78] H.M.C., *Portland MSS.* ix. 300, 321, 330.

by a charge on the civil list for the next thirty-two years towards meeting arrears due to the queen's servants, tradesmen, and others.[79] Since it was most improbable that the queen would live for another thirty-two years, the loan had also to be charged upon her hereditary revenues. A lottery was thus raised and from the proceeds the Lord Treasurer was preparing to make certain payments to our diplomatic representatives abroad in December 1713 which would still leave them with their salaries six months in arrear; but would restore most of them to solvency.[80] Amongst the payments to be made was £1,036 to James Dayrolle, late resident at The Hague, for the period 25 December 1710 to 26 May 1712 when his employment had ended, and £6,385 to the executors of John Wych, late envoy to the Hanse Towns, &c., being arrears from 25 December 1709. There is ample evidence that Wych (as one might expect) was heavily in debt, and when he died in October 1715 £50 was paid by the Treasury to give him decent burial.[81] In spite of this special parliamentary arrangement to meet arrears of pay, Queen Anne died heavily in debt to her servants abroad.[82]

A similar but less acute state of affairs is shown on the death of George I when the corresponding figures are £41,348 (1727) and £113,998 (1728),[83] and similar financial crises occur later in the period. Towards the end of George I's reign it was 'doubted whether any of the [foreign] ministers will receive any pay, until the Parliament meets, when 'tis thought they will raise a new fund'.[84] Robert Trevor, at the end of his mission to The Hague in 1746, warned Pelham:

I must only apprise you betimes that when I have obtained my letters of revocation, I shall not be able to make use of them here, before I am enabled by suitable remittances to provide for the dignity of the King's Commission, and indeed the safety of my own person, the lowness of my private purse putting it morally out of my power

[79] *Statutes of the Realm*, ix. 771–81. The details are best explained by W. R. Ward in *E.H.R.* lxxii (1957), 333.

[80] *C.T.B.* xxvii (1713), 450–1.   [81] Ibid. 62–63, 390, 438.

[82] *C.T.P.*, 1714–19, 60–61, refers to a list of debts due by the crown to foreign ministers on the day of Anne's demise.

[83] *Parliamentary Papers*, H.C. (1868–9), xxxv, part ii. See also Binney, *British Public Finance and Administration 1774–92*, p. 90, note 1, for the Civil List 3 per cents. of 1726.

[84] H.M.C., *MSS. in Various Collections*, viii. 376.

to supply the *vuide* of my arrears; and consequently to comply with the immemorial custom established here . . . of all Public Ministers, even from the most indigent Courts, challenging before they quit this residence all their creditors by public beat of drum for three days running to serve any pretension to their charge.[85]

It is, however, worth while to point out that arrears in pay were no novelty to diplomatists. Danby had calculated in 1673 that 'Embassadors and envoys are behind 34,000[l]'.[86]

> Duns come so boldly,
> King's money so slowly,

as Matthew Prior found in the reign of William III.[87] And as late as 1822 a memorandum relative to the more speedy issue of the salaries due to the king's ministers employed abroad[88] states that these salaries are 'so irregularly issued from the Treasury that no banker will accept their drafts . . . owing to the want of some regulation, although the pensions are paid up to the 10th of October, the ministers' salaries are in arrear since the 5th of April'. On this the author of the memorandum comments: 'The ministers employed abroad are the last whose salaries should be left in arrear —the very nature of their employment requires that their credit should be preserved as sacred as their persons.'

Though the modification of the system so far outlined is really beyond the chronological limit of 1789, it seems worth while to try to indicate the stages in the transition to the nineteenth-century system. The Foreign Office itself does not seem to have retained more than a tiny fraction of the documents which would illustrate this process, and part of what I am now going to say rests on inference, not on firmly established official facts. It is convenient to take as a starting-point in this inquiry the debate in the House of Lords on foreign ministers' salaries in 1822, when Lord Liverpool, speaking for the government, claimed that 'in fact no alteration had been made in the scale of the salaries of ambassadors and envoys from 1721 down to 1804'.[89] In reply Lord Holland doubted 'the noble earl's historical accuracy' and claimed that two committees had sat on the subject, one in 1786 and another in 1790,

[85] H.M.C., *14th Report, App. IX* (Trevor MSS.), p. 154.
[86] A. Browning, *Danby*, iii. 13. [87] H.M.C., *Bath MSS.* iii. 90.
[88] In F.O. 83. 10, dated 8 Nov. 1822.
[89] *Parliamentary Debates New Series*, vi. 1295.

'and the object of those committees was, if possible, to reduce and not to augment the previous scale of diplomatic expenditure. Mr. Pitt was the promoter of these committees.'[90]

Both noble lords seem to me to have fallen into error here.[91] Just at the time when Pitt's two committees were sitting the *maximum* scale for ambassadors was raised from £100 to £160 a week,[92] but when appointments were made on this scale the regular extraordinary allowance was not paid. The net result of this in the case of the first two appointments of which I am aware —both in 1787—was to raise the salary from £6,800 to £8,320. William Eden anticipated criticism in the House of Commons of these increases, but claimed: 'Nobody has ever doubted . . . that the increase was necessary.'[93] Also, at the end of the following decade, the anomalous Constantinople embassy was raised from £3 a day in 1799 to £100 a week, and then in 1804 to £160 a week.

The other change in the scale of payment concerned the highest grade of minister below the rank of ambassador. The first case known to me is that of James Harris who had just returned from his mission to Russia. Harris was summoned to the Foreign Office by Lord Carmarthen and told that

His Majesty's confidential servants were unanimous in their opinion that I was the properest man to be sent to Holland; that they equally agreed that it could not be expected of me to accept that post on the same terms on which I held Russia: at the same time that it was not becoming to send a Minister of a higher rank to the Dutch than they should send here; that, to conciliate this point of etiquette with the personal considerations which were due to me, they [the Cabinet] had come to a resolution to offer me The Hague mission, with the salary and all the emoluments of an Ambassador, but that I should produce in Holland credentials only as Minister Plenipotentiary, till such time

---

[90] *Parliamentary Debates New Series*, vi. 1300.

[91] The remainder of this chapter is based on documents in F.O. 83. 10, supplemented by the Pells General Posting Books E. 403. 2681, and checked by civil-list estimates submitted to Parliament and printed in the *Commons Journals*. The Index to Foreign Ministers' allowances in F.O. 463–5 has also been occasionally used. The nature and uses of the Pells Posting Books are explained in the *Fourth Report of the Deputy Keeper of the Public Records Appendix II* (*P.P. House of Commons*, 1843, vol. 18, pp. 34, 176–8).

[92] This is clearly shown by a comparison of estimated salaries laid before Parliament on 6 July 1786 with the actual amounts paid in the year ending 5 Jan. 1803 (58 *C.J.* appendix 75).

[93] *Auckland Journal*, i. 286.

as either the States General sent an Ambassador, or till some favourable circumstance should make it proper for me to appear in that character.[94]

Two years later William Eden, sent to negotiate a treaty of commerce with France as envoy extraordinary and plenipotentiary, was given the same allowance as Harris, i.e. the lower pre-1787 scale for ambassadors—£10 a day. Pitt explained to Eden that 'it would be my wish, if it were practicable, to place [the appointment] on the highest rank of foreign embassies; but I find [that] there are objections to it, both from former practice and from some peculiar circumstances now'.[95] The increased salary was presumably intended as compensation for the denial of the title of ambassador. A year or two later Lord Sheffield reported that 'Trevor was on the brink of going to Petersburgh. He gave some general hint of wishing to be serviceable. He was offered the red riband, and the appointments of ambassador without the title, and everything'[96] but did not in the end go. As Pitt foresaw, payment at a special rate to one or two favourites led to a mutiny in the diplomatic corps and after 1799 such special appointments were usually at the rate of £100 a week, e.g. Lord Minto at Vienna in 1799, Lord Carysfort to Berlin in 1800, Hookham Frere to Spain and Robert Liston to the Batavian Republic, both in 1802. Even then, the majority of the appointments as envoy extraordinary and minister plenipotentiary continued until 1804 to be made on the old scale of £8 a day and envoys at minor courts had to content themselves with the old scale of £5 a day.[97]

Lord Liverpool was, however, so far right in selecting 1804 as the point when the old eighteenth-century scale was altered in that there was in this year a further increase in the salaries paid to the higher grades of diplomatists. Ambassadors of the highest class

---

[94] *Malmesbury Diaries*, ii. 72–73.

[95] *Auckland Journal*, i. 87. This is confirmed by Eden's privy seal of 1786 which gave him £10 a day (E. 403. 2681). I cannot reconcile this with Professor Cobban's implication that Eden from first appointment received £100 a week unless the difference was paid in some underhand way (Cobban, *Ambassadors and Secret Agents*, p. 174).

[96] Ibid. ii. 223.

[97] A draft circular to foreign ministers dated Sept. 1800 (F.O. 83. 8) states that these regular extraordinary allowances are to continue and to be paid in the old way, whereas authorized extra extraordinaries would be repaid to them if they drew on the Commissioners of the Treasury at three months after sight instead of sending drafts on the secretary of state's office.

went up to £11,056 while envoys extraordinary and ministers plenipotentiary now varied from £7,744 to £3,256, the highest rate being paid at Vienna.

These increases were presumably made possible by the parliamentary vote of an additional £60,000 a year to the civil list in 1804, accompanied by a reduction of £135,000 in the annual payments charged against it. In introducing this proposal the Chancellor of the Exchequer stated that, apart from increased tradesmen's bills, due to the rise in the cost of living, the only other civil list item in which there was any real excess was certain allowances to foreign ministers not exceeding £8,000.[98] Addington interposed to explain that the arrears incurred had been spent on an 'object which was not already sufficiently provided for according to its importance; he meant our diplomatic service, a line in which it was essential to encourage men of talents, rank and fortune to engage. The insufficiency of the present establishment was the cause of this arrear being incurred.'[99] At least two critics of the government's handling of the civil list problem in the preceding years went out of their way to approve of increased salaries to the foreign ministers.[1]

It was an essential part of the new scheme that all *regular* extraordinary allowances were abolished and a consolidated salary was allocated to the various posts in the diplomatic service.[2] In fact extraordinary allowances for specific purposes continued to be paid and trebled between 1805 and 1815. These corresponded closely with the extra extraordinaries of the eighteenth-century system.

Further changes, indeed a general reorganization, took place at the end of the Napoleonic wars. Whereas in 1791 the scale of payment fixed according to rank in 1690 was still almost intact, though beginning to show signs of wear and tear at the upper end, in 1815 payment by rank had been largely superseded by payment according to post held. This change was clearest in the case of the envoys extraordinary and ministers plenipotentiary. In 1791 eight out of nine diplomatists with this rank had been paid at the standard rate of £8 a day, whereas in 1804 eight men with this rank

[98] *Parliamentary Debates*, ii. 903–6.
[99] Ibid. ii. 913.
[1] Mr. Bankes (*Parliamentary Debates*, ii. 906–7) and Mr. Johnstone (ibid. 937–8).
[2] F.O. 83. 10 (cf. 59 *C.J.* appendix 30).

were paid at five different rates according to the presumed importance of the post held. In the reorganization of the diplomatic
service after 1815 three categories of missions to be held by men
with this rank were recognized.

In the eighteenth century diplomatists had been paid according
to rank, with minor adjustments of allowances according to post
held. In the nineteenth century, while payment continued to
depend to some extent on rank, the primary criterion was now the
post held. This might well have happened in any case; but what
actually brought it about was the intervention of Parliament in
the reign of George III into the sacred mysteries of the civil list.
Estimates had now to be submitted to Parliament and it ceased to
be solely in the king's power to send a diplomatic agent of any
rank he pleased to a particular court.

CHAPTER IV

The Cost of the Diplomatic Service

No official estimates have ever been prepared for the purpose of showing the actual cost of the diplomatic service between 1689 and 1789. Such estimates would have to include not only the salaries and allowances payable to foreign ministers abroad, but many other items, some large, some small. If we begin by considering merely the gross total of salaries and allowances in any one year it is still true that there are no regular contemporary estimates submitted to Parliament. Diplomatic salaries were a charge on the king's civil list and it was not until George III's reign that the Commons in a tentative and fumbling way came to take cognizance of the amount of such charges and the way in which they were paid—or rather not paid.

There was in fact, as Dr. W. A. Shaw has pointed out, no regular establishment for the diplomatic service which might have tied the hands of the Treasury or of the king himself to a certain definite expenditure. The king could increase or decrease the number or the status of his foreign missions at his will.[1] Thus William III, pressed by Lord Villiers to secure Matthew Prior's appointment to the post at Ratisbon, replied that though he was satisfied with Prior's service 'he had not so much occasion for a minister at Ratisbon as they told him he had'. Prior added that he was 'afraid the same objections would be against Berlin, though may be Lord Villiers would help me to ask it'.[2] This conversation occurred in 1695 and no appointment was in fact made to Ratisbon until 1702 and none to Berlin until 1698. Similarly, when Lord Falkland, who had been appointed to go as ambassador to The Hague, died in May 1694 before taking up the appointment, William III had no thoughts of sending anyone thither until the winter[3] 'but that there may be somebody at the Hague to do what is necessary in the meantime, his Majesty thinks fit that Mr. Prior, my Lord Dursley's secretary, who has been always very careful in

---

[1] *C.T.B. and P.* v (1742–5), xlii.
[2] H.M.C., *Downshire MSS.* i. 522. [3] H.M.C., *Buccleuch MSS.* ii. 76.

that station, may be continued as the English secretary, with the usual allowance. . .'.[4]

Even late in the eighteenth century, when the Americans, after they had secured recognition of their independence, proposed an exchange of ministers, George III tartly rejected the proposal:

> As to the question whether I wish to have a Minister accredited from America, I certainly can never say that it will be agreeable to me, and I should think it wisest for both parties if only Agents were appointed; but so far I cannot help adding that I shall have a very bad opinion of any Englishman that can accept being sent as a Minister for a revolted state, and which certainly for many years cannot have any stable government.[5]

Even under George II, self-styled prisoner of the Whigs, the duke of Newcastle told Michell, the Prussian agent at London who was trying to get a British minister sent to Berlin, 'that the king would not consent to send a minister to Berlin, though [Newcastle] had proposed it several times'.[6] Chesterfield reported that he too had tried vainly to convince the king that the more the King of Prussia was a 'Fripon', 'the more necessary it was to have a minister who was a spy at his court; that with all this he could not prevail', though the duke of Newcastle finally 'prevailed on the King to send a minister to Berlin'.[7]

The only effective restriction on this royal discretion was that if the king spent more money on diplomatic salaries he would have to economize on some other branch of the royal expenditure or else run into debt. As has been shown in the preceding chapter, sovereign after sovereign preferred the latter alternative. All through the century there were periodical financial crises with salaries in arrear, and appeals to the Commons for help, followed by half-hearted attempts to economize.

In practice foreign-service expenses were likely to be amongst the first targets of economists in government expenditure. Already in 1676 when Danby was seeking economies he proposed to cut 'Embassadors and presents' from £50,000 to £40,000 and he added a note 'Embassadors etc. To reduce to envoyes as soon as may be.'[8] William III is generally supposed to have economized on British

---

[4] Ibid. ii. 77.
[6] *Marchmont Papers*, i. 233
[7] Ibid. i. 238–9.

[5] *George III Corresp.* vi. 429–30.

[8] A. Browning, *Danby*, iii. 22–23.

missions abroad, partly by making use of Dutch agents already accredited to certain sovereigns, though this is hardly supported by the figures printed below, which seem to show that his average annual expenditure on diplomatic salaries was almost exactly the same as that of his predecessor, James II.[9] He did, however, do his best to adhere strictly to the Order in Council of 1689/90. When the envoy to Switzerland tried to get extra extras in 1691, Lord Sydney wrote to his colleague Nottingham that 'the King will give no answer this post to Mr. Cox's extraordinaries; but I believe he will hardly suffer you to allow it, because he hath refused to others that desired the addition of very inconsiderable sums to what is settled by the Treasury'.[10] A few years later according to a Privy Council minute of 1696: 'Mr. Secretary and I [Shrewsbury] are to write to the foreign ministers to restrain their bills of extraordinary, according to Orders in Council in King James' and his Majesty's time, of which copies be sent.'[11] When he received this circular letter Galway protested and was specially excepted from it by the king.[12]

When William III was recognized by the Italian states and began sending expensive embassies to France he tried to economize in other directions. Towards the end of his reign he 'ordered that my Lord Ossulston's house, which was hired for entertaining ambassadors, the lease being now expired, should be put off' and the goods (i.e. furniture) be secured in the Removing Wardrobe.[13] This was part of a general scheme of retrenchment intended to help clear the civil-list debts,[14] but it does not seem to have been followed by any cuts in diplomatic salaries. Certainly, under Anne, Godolphin kept a watchful eye on British diplomatists' claims on the Treasury,[15] but a contemporary critic accused him of negligence and lack of system:

[The reader] will not wonder that a nation full of wise and brave men succeeds generally so ill in foreign negotiations. The foreign ministers are paid out of the civil list, and therefore the consideration of economy made the Minister reduce the number of them; and those he kept were very ill paid, especially when they disbursed money for

[9] Infra, p. 81.
[10] H.M.C., Finch MSS. iii. 88.
[11] H.M.C., Buccleuch MSS. ii. 328.   [12] Ibid. ii. 361, 368.
[13] Ibid. ii. 636.   [14] Ibid. ii. 644.
[15] e.g. C.T.B. xxvii (1713), 62; cf. H.M.C., Portland MSS. v. 346.

expresses and for intelligence, and such often very important and very necessary expenses.[16]

After the dismissal of Godolphin attempts were naturally made to put the blame for excessive expenditure and consequent diplomatic arrears upon the fallen statesman and in 1711 another contemporary critic wrote to Oxford:

When your lordship gives yourself the trouble to look into that expense [of foreign ministers] you will find one third of it might have been saved. When a pretty fellow was to be provided for it had been better doing it with some place at home of two or three hundred pounds a year than throwing away two or three thousand a year abroad in making him an Envoy etc. Public business would have been better done with fewer ministers, well chosen and well paid, which would have made men of the greatest abilities solicit those employments.[17]

Oxford himself three years later wrote that 'he was forced to bear all the reproach of not paying when there was no money' and took credit to himself for raising a half million to pay the queen's debts 'in such a manner as exposed [him] to the hatred of his enemies; and [there] was some little merit in the time and manner of doing it and [it] was what nobody before had thought upon'.[18]

Under the Hanoverian kings the survival of occasional estimates amongst the Treasury and other papers suggests that economists in government expenditure carefully watched the cost of British missions abroad.[19] Sir Robert Walpole more than once objected to missions of compliment. On 29 July/9 August 1725 he wrote to Townshend:

I am sorry to hear you think of sending an ambassador extraordinary to France with a compliment. The expence to the king will be very great and, I think, of very little advantage to the person. The plate for an ambassador, and an allowance for equipage money, the quarter's advance, and the weekly appointments will, in a little time, come to a great many thousand pounds, which I think may as well be

---

[16] Cole, *Memoirs*, p. 474.
[17] H.M.C., *Portland MSS.* ix. 293, Raby to Oxford, 29 June 1711.
[18] Ibid. v. 467.
[19] e.g. the list of foreign ministers [1742] in H.M.C., *Townshend MSS.* 126 and the later figures given in B.M. Add. MS. 32737, fo. 550, printed *E.H.R.* xlii (1928), 607–9. To these should perhaps be added the figures for 1763, 1764, and 1765 in B.M. Add. MS. 38339, fos. 212, 297.

saved, and 'tis better for the king to give Lord Waldegrave 2000*l.* than to make an expence of three times that sum; out of which he cannot with credit save 1000*l.*[20]

While in office George Grenville attempted to reform the system of paying foreign ministers. At least one of them wrote in 1764: 'Mr. Grenville will deserve a statue from all the King's servants, especially those abroad. I see we shall now be paid regularly.'[21] Yet when he was in Opposition only three years later, in 1767, George Grenville, speaking according to himself with greater applause than ever, amongst other articles where saving might be made

instanced that of so many ambassadors extraordinary, viz. the ambassador named for Russia, the ambassador named for Spain, the ministers for Portugal and Turin; ministers in time of peace named to foreign courts, but who received their pay and continued in England. That we were told last year of mighty schemes for strengthening our alliance in the North to balance that of the South; what had it amounted to but to name an ambassador extraordinary to Russia, in the month of July, whose instructions had never yet been made out. That a Minister every way agreeable to the Court of Spain had been recalled from that country at a time when it was most of all necessary to have an able person there, from the ticklish state of that court, and that important negotiation trusted to the care of a clergyman, left there chargé des affaires. A chaplain [to Lord Rochford] of the church of England charged with the great and desirable object of breaking the family compact at the court of the Catholic king, whilst the ambassador appointed to go there was waiting in England 'till time could be found to give him his instructions. That in saying this he did not mean to throw blame on either of the ambassadors so appointed, and who he was persuaded were ready to go; neither did he mean to blame the Right Honourable Gentleman who must sign the order for their pay; nor the Secretary of State in that House, and in whose department one of these ambassadors was . . . but if their [the Ambassadors] presence was not necessary at the several courts, why were they appointed since it was well known that the expense of an ambassador extraordinary for the first year amounted to no less than £13,000.[22]

Extravagant diplomacy had already become a favourite topic with Opposition speakers.

[20] Coxe, *Walpole Memoirs*, ii. 473.
[21] H.M.C., *Report XII, App. 9* (Aitken MSS.), p. 342.
[22] *Grenville Papers*, iv. 216–18.

Later, after diplomatic expenditure came regularly before Parliament in the form of estimates, such protests became almost common form. In 1821 Lord Darnley thought £160,000 a year might be saved on diplomatic salaries and pensions.[23] A year later Lord King argued at length that, in spite of the distressed state of the country and the decline in prices since the end of the war, salaries and allowances were in all cases higher than they had been in 1791 before the Revolutionary war commenced.[24]

In spite of periodic attempts at economy there can be no doubt that the total cost of the diplomatic and consular services rose steadily between 1689 and 1789. Thanks to the initiative of Mr. Gladstone, we have in print a statement year by year of the 'ordinary Entertainments and Extraordinaries' of the foreign ministers.[25] The average charge per annum reign by reign is

(James II	£32,687)[26]
William III and Mary .	£32,063
Anne	£57,390
George I . . .	£67,539
George II . . .	£62,430
George III (up to 1789) .	£79,939[27]

Obviously these statements, even if their accuracy is unimpeachable, do not give the actual cost of the diplomatic service. Until 1782 we should have to include also a large proportion of the cost of running the offices and paying the salaries of the two secretaries of state who were largely occupied with the conduct of foreign policy. After 1782 there would be the whole cost of the foreign office. This, exclusive of emergencies, has been estimated at £14,178. 6s. 8d. for 1782–3.[28] Contingent expenditure was often high and, as it could not be exactly foreseen, was often not included in estimates of expenditure.[29] We must add the expense of

---

[23] *Parliamentary Debates New Series*, vi. 1467.   [24] Ibid. vi. 1284.

[25] *P.P. House of Commons Session 1868–9 Accounts and Papers*, vol. 2 (vol. 35 of Sessional Papers), parts i and ii.

[26] Ibid., part v. 647 (included to suggest that William III's expenditure on diplomacy was not as small as is sometimes thought).

[27] Some evidence of the inflationary effects of the French wars of George III's reign after 1789 is offered by the statement (F.O. 83. 10) that the average of ordinary allowances to ministers abroad from 1814 to 1822 was £140,000. The corresponding figure for 1790 to 1803 was exactly half this sum.

[28] Tilley and Gaselee, *Foreign Office*, p. 30. See *infra*, Appendix B.

[29] See *infra*, Appendix C, for details of the Foreign Office Contingent Account for 1795.

the messenger service, postages, secret service, and intelligence payments, &c.[30] In addition there would be a considerable item for expenses connected with the representatives sent by foreign courts to London. Occasionally ambassadors were entertained at government expense for varying periods. This expense was most likely to arise in an acute form with ambassadors from the Barbary states. In 1706 it cost Queen Anne £500 a week to entertain the Morocco ambassador,[31] while George III in 1762 made an allowance of £696. 14s. 0d. to the Tripoli ambassador.[32] These gentry must also have caused the responsible officials considerable worry, as when the ambassador from the Dey of Algiers brought with him to England 'seven horses, three or four tigers, some ostriches, antelopes and other small matters of the manufactures of the country'.[33] In exchange the Barbary potentates expected costly presents.

More general was the custom of making valuable presents to a foreign diplomatist who had served with acceptance at London. Queen Anne gave the Venetian ambassador her picture set with diamonds at a cost of £800, while two envoys from Italian states received rings worth £300 each and the Venetian ambassador's secretary an inferior ring costing £110.[34] Sometimes these presents were in cash, the fees and charges being added to ensure that the recipient received, for example, £200 or £300 or £1,000 as the case might be clear of tax.[35]

It should also be noted that the figures quoted for most of the period include nothing for the cost of our regular embassy to Constantinople, this being largely paid for by the merchants.[36] In general the expense of our consular service was also met by the merchants through consulage and other fees. Thus in 1699 only the consuls at Algiers and Tripoli were paid out of the civil-list revenues, in all £980 per annum with no extraordinaries.[37] By

[30] Including the salary and allowances of the master of the ceremonies, who received 6s. 8d. a day for attendance on foreign ministers (C.T.B. xx. 731). This office was held by the Cottrell-Dormer dynasty, on which see H.M.C., Downshire MSS. i. 284–5.

[31] C.T.B. xx. 77.

[32] 32 C.J. 466.

[33] S.P. 71. 8 under date 8 Sept. 1749.

[34] C.T.B. xx. 363.

[35] Ibid. xx. 236, 678, 768. See infra, Appendix A, for the cost of these presents for the years 1783–9 inclusive.

[36] £3 a day was, however, being paid to the ambassador out of the civil list from 1768. See 40 C.J. 328–33 for these payments in the 1780's.

[37] P.P. House of Commons Session 1868–9, vol. 35, part ii. 587.

1786 this figure had risen to £7,285 for consuls,[38] and in 1789 to £10,585,[39] but it was still a mere fraction of the actual cost of maintaining our consulates abroad.

It would be very difficult to make reliable calculations of the true cost of carrying on relations with foreign powers in the eighteenth century. Some idea of the additions which would have to be made to the figures quoted earlier may, however, be derived from the civil-list accounts for the years after 1783 which were regularly presented to Parliament and printed in the *Commons Journals*.[40] Thus in 1784 presents to foreign ministers at London cost £1,639 and in 1785 only £767. 17s. 0d. This suggests a drastic reduction when compared with an estimate made at 4 February 1713/14 for 'jewels and plate, including presents of money in lieu of jewels, to ministers of foreign princes' about £15,000 a year.[41] I suspect a superfluous o has been added here in the printed version, since actual cost of these presents was often much less, e.g. £1,317 in 1705–6.[42] Payments to H.M. messengers 'to enable them to perform foreign journies' amounted to £12,256. 17s. 0d. in 1784 and to £10,000 in 1785. Foreign secret service cost £27,006. 1s. 8d. in 1784 and £31,878. 10s. 6d. in 1785. Equipage money and extra extraordinaries together totalled £3,248 in 1784 and £1,601. 15s. 9d. in 1785.[43]

If the figures for diplomatic salaries given to Mr. Gladstone by the Treasury officials in 1868[44] are at least doubled, we might reach a first approximation to the actual cost of the diplomatic service.[45] I have not checked them systematically, but they seem to correspond with the data for Anne's reign in the published *Calendar of Treasury Books*. When checked against the civil-list accounts, printed annually in the *Commons Journals* (40 *C.J.* 328–33 onwards), discrepancies appear. Nor do they correspond exactly with the figures given in the Newcastle Papers for 1747–51 and for 1763–5 in Add. MS. 38339, fo. 212 and fo. 297.[46] Some of the discrepancies are, however, accounted for by differences in the date to which the accounts run, e.g. equipage money for foreign

---

[38] Ibid. 647.
[39] 46 *C.J.* 593.
[40] e.g. 41 *C.J.* 645.
[41] 18 *C.J.* 84.
[42] *C.T.B.* xxi, p. cxxvi.
[43] These payments seem to be included in the figures quoted earlier.
[44] *Supra*, p. 81.
[45] See Appendix A for an attempt to calculate the cost to the public of conducting British foreign policy in the eighties.
[46] *Supra*, p. 79.

ministers cost £5,800 for the year to 5 April 1784 but only £1,800 in a year reckoned to end on 5 January 1785.

If it is desired to include also the cost of maintaining British consulates abroad in the foreign-service expenditure, Mr. Gladstone's figure for diplomatic salaries would have to be multiplied at least by three to reach an approximation to the actual cost of the combined diplomatic and consular services. Compared with the amounts spent on the foreign service in certain continental countries, notably France,[47] the British services were not extravagant and, in spite of unfavourable comments by some contemporaries and many later commentators, seem to have provided reasonable value for the money devoted to them.

[47] Budgets of the cost of the French diplomatic service under Louis XIV will be found in C.-G. Picavet, *La Diplomatie française au temps de Louis XIV*, p. 83, and F. Weiss, *Histoire des fonds secrets sous l'ancien régime*, pp. 151–2; and, for later reigns, in F. Weiss, op. cit., pp. 165–71; F. Masson, *Le Département des affaires étrangères pendant la Révolution*, pp. 48–49, and Luçay, *Les Secrétaires d'État*, pp. 478–83.

CHAPTER V

Recruitment

IN a celebrated chapter in his *England in the Age of the American Revolution* Sir Lewis Namier sought to answer the question why did men go into Parliament? His answer may be summed up that it was fashionable and profitable to be a Member of Parliament. If we ask why men went into the diplomatic service in the eighteenth century we must find a different set of answers, since entry to this service was both unfashionable and on the whole unprofitable.

Few Englishmen were much attracted by the prospect of strutting for a brief hour on the European stage with the title of ambassador. Most of them had done a more or less extended variety of the fashionable Grand Tour in their 'teens or early twenties and returned home firmly convinced of the advantages of permanent residence in England. Hill, envoy to Sardinia, remarked that 'there is neither beef nor veal nor mutton which an Englishman can eat'.[1] John Locke, after a short experience in a subordinate capacity at the court of Brandenburg, repeatedly rejected offers of employment abroad. At Cleves he disliked the food, the religious institutions, and the shops. 'Amidst a great deal of meat and company', he records on one occasion, 'I had little to eat and less to say.' It took him three days to find a pair of gloves and 'the next two days were spent in drawing them on' while a pair of shoes could not be made in less than six months.[2] Later on he refused to return to Brandenburg as envoy from William III partly on the ground that for 'the soberest man' in England the 'warm drinking' of the Germans was beyond him.[3] Eventually Locke accepted instead of 'one of the busiest and most important [posts] in all Europe' as he describes the Berlin legation, the modest home job of Commissioner of Appeals with £200 a year only.[4]

This preference for jobs at home was very general. In 1705 the

[1] Margery Lane, 'Lighter Side of Diplomacy under William III', in *Nineteenth Century*, cii (1927), 562.
[2] Maurice Cranston, *John Locke*, pp. 81–85.
[3] Ibid., pp. 312–13.
[4] Ibid., p. 313.

duke of Newcastle wrote to Harley: 'I return you a thousand thanks for diverting from me a troublesome embassy, in which you have showed your kindness . . . such a sudden journey would always be very troublesome to me.'[5] Matthew Prior, writing to Bolingbroke, said frankly, 'what I hope from my little services, though zealous endeavours, being some small establishment at home, in which I may bless the Queen's goodness and cultivate the honour of Lord Bolingbroke's friendship'.[6] On another occasion, after begging his patron's support for one or other post abroad, Prior added: 'I wish I may part with these chimeras for the solid blessing of being near my patron and protector in England . . . I should like that climate or employment preferably to any other.'[7] And Miss Lane, who made a special study of Prior's diplomatic colleagues under William III, concluded that 'the Mecca of all their hopes and ambitions was a good job in England'.[8]

This generalization is indeed true of the whole of the eighteenth century. Henry Grenville wrote under George III from the embassy at Constantinople: 'We enjoy here a very comfortable share of health but to say the truth a very moderate share of pleasure. Certainly this is no country of delight and joy; fire and plague possess it merely and for ever hang over our heads; and yet, in spite of all, we contrive to make our time pass, if not lightly, yet not heavily, and wait the destined period of our return without repining, which is no small point to accomplish in a situation like ours.'[9] Luckily Grenville's brother was Prime Minister and this enabled him to return home long before the normal time and live happily in England as a commissioner of customs. James Hare, a friend of C. J. Fox, wrote that he would 'rather be a commissioner of the customs in London than King of Poland, if I were obliged to pass my life at Warsaw'.[10]

Experienced politicians were well aware of the much greater competition for places at home. Thus when a candidate for a diplomatic appointment, who was dissatisfied with the rank and pay offered by George II, threatened that he would not go to The Hague, Sir Robert Walpole dryly commented: 'He talks of waiting

[5] H.M.C., *Portland MSS*. iv. 243.   [6] *Bolingbroke Corresp*. ii. 221.
[7] H.M.C., *Bath MSS*. iii. 15.
[8] *Nineteenth Century*, cii (1927), 558.
[9] *Buckinghamshire Desp*. ii. 20. Cf. *Grenville Papers*, iii. 117–18, 191.
[10] Jesse, *Life of Selwyn*, iv. 142.

for some provision at home, not dreaming of the number of competitors for every thing that he will think worthy of him.'[11] When, in a letter, George III made a joking reference to Bristol's embassy to Spain, Bristol replied with complete sincerity how much happier he was 'to be obeying your Majesty's commands as a servant in your royal household instead of executing them in a foreign court'.[12]

Peers, of course, were notoriously 'choosey' about accepting even the best appointments in the diplomatic service. Thus it proved very difficult in 1766 to fill the Madrid embassy. Huntingdon, Buckinghamshire, and others turned it down and in the end a commoner was sent. Horace Walpole's statement that 'Sir James Gray goes to Madrid. The embassy has been sadly hawked about; not a peer that would take it'[13] seems to have been not far from the truth. Later, in 1787, Lord Walsingham gladly relinquished all thought of going as ambassador to Spain and 'kissed hands for the postmastership'.[14] Peers who accepted appointment often regretted it. After a short stay in Spain Lexington wrote to Oxford: 'I protest before God I would not remain here another winter to be king of the country.' Shortly afterwards he repeated his request to be recalled 'from this cursed place as soon as I have done what is proper, and that I may have your word for it, for I do protest that I have had neither pleasure, profit nor health since I have set my foot in Spain, nor shall I have ease of mind till I know my request will be granted'.[15]

Since this was the prevalent attitude to employment abroad, the dispatch of a prominent courtier or politician to a foreign court was often regarded as an honourable kind of banishment. When the Portland–Albemarle rivalry for William III's favour reached its crisis in 1697, a British diplomatist reported to the Secretary of State: 'I did lately tell your grace something about the two favourite lords here, which is still a secret. I now find it is resolved that my Lord Portland shall go over to London very quickly and thence to Paris as Ambassador from the King. This is an honourable kind of banishment.'[16]

A few years later, in Anne's reign, when Lord Dartmouth was

[11] Coxe, *Walpole Memoirs*, iii. 534.   [12] *George III Corresp*. iii. 4.
[13] J. Brooke, *Chatham Administration 1766–68*, pp. 35–37.
[14] *Auckland Journal*, i. 430.
[15] H.M.C., *Portland MSS*. v. 273, 276.
[16] H.M.C., *Buccleuch MSS*. ii. 557

told that Queen Anne designed to send him as ambassador to Venice, he replied that 'if the Queen thought it for her service that I should be out of the way, I need not go so far, having a house in Staffordshire that I could easily and willingly retire to'.[17] And the contemporary historian Cunningham attributes Peterborough's mission to Vienna to a desire 'to prevent his interrupting the measures taken at home'.[18]

The idea that a diplomatic appointment might be a concealed form of exile persisted. When Newcastle was looking for a special envoy to Berlin at the end of the War of the Austrian Succession he selected 'Mr. Harry Legge. There is capacity, integrity, quality, rank and address—all necessary qualifications, and nobody can think that Mr. Legge is sent away at this time only to save appearances.'[19] Again, Lord Chesterfield's first mission to the United Provinces 'was rather an honourable exile than a mark of favour: he would in all probability have been troublesome at home. Walpole did not envy him the honour of shining among the Dutch, and eclipsing a French envoy by his superior adroitness.'[20] Similarly Sir Richard Lodge wrote of Chesterfield's second mission to The Hague: 'George II could offer no stubborn resistance to an employment which kept his enemy at a distance.'[21] The duke of Bedford, in recommending a young man for an attachéship, said that he looked upon a diplomatic career 'as a kind of banishment'.[22]

Many and various were the excuses offered for refusing a foreign commission. Health was perhaps the commonest,[23] but inability to meet the extra expenditure required out of the candidate's own resources ran it close. Others pointed out that residence abroad would harm their political connexions or even cause a breach between themselves and their friends. Now and again one who is approached with the offer of foreign employment replies that once bitten twice shy. Lord Paget wrote bitterly to Oxford in 1711: 'My

[17] Burnet, *History of His Own Time* (Oxford, 1823), v. 140.
[18] *History of Great Britain*, ii. 358.
[19] *Chatham Corresp.* i. 27.
[20] Chesterfield's *Characters . . . reviewed* (London, 1777), pp. 81–82. Cf. *Hervey Memoirs*, p. 72, and the contemporary offer of the Vienna embassy to Stair (*infra*, p. 101).
[21] *Private Correspondence of Newcastle and Chesterfield*, p. xv.
[22] *Infra*, p. 95.
[23] John Locke pleaded his 'weak lungs' as his excuse for rejecting a mission to Brandenburg (M. Cranston, *John Locke*, p. 312).

father is too great an instance of that; for, if serving many years abroad, and that successfully too, could have entitled him to merit, he might reasonably be allowed to have some expectations, and yet after his return to England he was so far from being rewarded that he lived totally neglected and unregarded.'[24]

There are now and again suggestions of a special reason for rejecting foreign employment—the desire not to be too closely associated with the Hanoverian interest which was popularly believed to dominate British foreign policy in the first half of the eighteenth century. According to Andrié, the Prussian agent at London in 1744, Orford's own son-in-law, Lord Cholmondeley, 'would have gone to Berlin in the stead of Lord Hyndford, but that he insisted on full powers, and said he would act as English minister, and not be accountable to Hanoverians, but to the parliament of England'.[25]

It is rare to find all these excuses offered by one man, but the third earl of Marchmont came near to achieving this feat. 'As a gratification to me [a foreign commission] was none' he told Lord Chesterfield

and that by way of serving my country and myself, I could not think of one, under such a secretary as either of the two we had [Newcastle and Carteret], but that if he, Lord Chesterfield, was secretary, who could distinguish one man's merit from another, and with whom I desired to cultivate a connexion, any commission wherein he required a man of confidence, and that was not to keep me abroad a great many years, I would not refuse. Upon his saying that no gentleman could save himself in such a commission, I told him, that I could not undertake one, if I had not something beside my own estate to trust to, if the Treasury did not pay; that this I had seen the effects of, and in that view had thought whereby I could be enabled to support it, and that it naturally must be by some Scots place, where I should have the fewer rivals . . . and that in this view I could find no place that would be so agreeable to me as that of Justice-General, which the Duke of Argyll now held, and which was for life.[26]

The financial returns which a recruit to the foreign service might expect have already been discussed in a previous chapter. They were clearly inadequate and most candidates regarded a diplomatic appointment as a second-best. Few had any intention of remaining abroad any longer than they could help and quite often special inducements had to be offered. At the top of the scale candidates sometimes expected (and occasionally secured) a peerage, or at least the promise of one, as a condition for going to, remaining at, or returning to, a foreign court. A well-known example was the peerage granted to Harrington for returning to Spain to conclude the treaty of Seville in 1729.[27] George Pitt, after serving for some years at the court of Turin, demanded a peerage as the price to be paid for his return to his post only to meet with a decided refusal.[28]

Now and again the reward claimed was a step in the British peerage as when in 1714 Lord Paget was named as envoy to Hanover. He resented the fixing of his allowances at the minimum for an envoy and demanded a step in the peerage. He finally 'refused to go till he was made an earl. The Queen said he should be when he returned; he was angry, did not go, and was made by King George an earl.'[29] Under George III Lord Hertford applied from Paris for a marquessate.[30]

This appears in reverse, however, when Oxford claimed that, in sending Bolingbroke on a special mission abroad, he was at one and the same time doing his rival a favour and compensating him for being created a viscount (and not, as Bolingbroke expected and demanded, an earl). 'The negotiation of peace', Oxford wrote, 'not going on so glibly, and some few things of no great importance remaining, M. Torcy proposed a meeting with the Treasurer [Oxford], but to please Lord B. it was [entrusted?] to him. Upon his return this added new fuel to his vanity': and, like many other noble diplomatists he felt that his services abroad, actual or prospective, had given him an incontestable claim to the Garter.[31] Lord Harcourt, when ambassador at Paris in 1771, begged that 'if another Blue Ruband should become vacant while I have the honour to be employed in this country, I hope my absence might rather plead in my behalf than be a disadvantage to any little claim which I might have to your Majesty's favour'. He then used

---

[27] Coxe, *Walpole Memoirs*, ii. 655.
[28] *George III Corresp.* i. 180–4, 194 (cf. Namier, *Additions and Corrections*, p. 40).
[29] 'Memoranda on the Peerage by the second earl of Oxford' in *Notes and Queries*, 2nd series, i. 326: *Portland MSS.* v *passim*.
[30] *Grenville Papers*, ii. 331.
[31] H.M.C., *Portland MSS.* v. 467.

what was already the stock argument of all diplomatists asking for favours:

It has been the object of my life to deserve well of your Majesty, and to be worthy of some distinguishing mark of your favour. And however desirable such a distinction might have been at other times, it becomes far more valuable to me in my present situation, as it would enable me to serve your Majesty with more weight and credit. Foreign ministers are more or less considered in the courts where they reside in proportion the favour and countenance which their respective princes show them. Of all the courts in Europe, Versailles is the court where the greatest attention is paid to those appearances.[32]

Diplomatists of humbler birth pleaded for the Bath on similar grounds. Keene at Madrid struggled for years to overcome George II's reluctance to give the coveted distinction to a man of humble birth.[33] Andrew Mitchell, renewing a request for the K.B. during the Seven Years War, was able to urge that it would not merely be 'a public mark of the King's approbation of my conduct' but 'a sort of protection to my person; for I have unfortunately, even during this last campaign [1760], been in divers situations where a mark of distinction would have been of the greatest use'.[34] In spite of this plea he did not get the coveted ribbon until 1765.[35] A later British diplomatic agent, who had been transferred from Dresden to Berlin and decorated with the red ribbon, was assured by a rather patronizing elder brother: 'Upon the whole you now clearly and conspicuously stand at the head of the second order. The rest must depend on time and circumstances.'[36]

The Order of the Thistle was occasionally conferred in a similar manner on Scottish diplomatists. It enhanced the value of any of these orders if they could be conferred at the hands of the sovereign to whom the diplomatist was accredited during his residence abroad.[37] Scots, and no doubt Irish, peers sometimes looked forward to a British peerage as a reward for their services.[38]

If some men were attracted to or retained in the service by such marks of distinction, others valued more tangible rewards. Porter, pleading the merits of his friend Robinson with the duke of New-

[32] George III Corresp. ii. 215.
[33] Keene Corresp., pp. xx, 28–29, 37.   [34] Chatham Corresp. ii. 80.
[35] Memoirs and Papers of Sir A. Mitchell, ed. Bisset, ii. 359.
[36] Auckland Journal, ii. 392.
[37] H.M.C., Polwarth MSS. iv. 249–50.   [38] Ibid. iii. 149–50.

castle in 1742, asked first for an extra £1,000 a year in allowances. When the duke in surprise held out instead hopes of the Red Ribbon, Porter replied that though Robinson as a single man might have asked for this, he now 'had a wife and several young children [and] the providing for these made up the essential part of his happiness and for them it was I meant a solid, substantial reward'. Porter therefore pressed that 'his Grace would intercede with the King to give [Robinson] any post or place [at home] or even to secure him one before his arrival, whenever that should happen'.[39] Villiers, after a distinguished career abroad, was told frankly by his friend Bedford: 'What I should most wish, both for your sake and for your friends', would be, when his Majesty's service will permit it, to see you at home, to put in your pretensions for some comfortable place here [in England] in reward for your services abroad.'[40] Villiers himself declined to serve abroad again unless he was promised a place at home,[41] and this was indeed one of the commonest inducements offered to diplomatists whose services the government was anxious to retain. Andrew Mitchell was induced to return to Berlin by the promise of an immediate pension of £500 a year for life.[42]

One 'mark of distinction' requires separate treatment. As early as the reign of Charles II, Sunderland, on his return from a foreign mission, was called to the Privy Council;[43] and as early as 1706 Marlborough held that 'being declared of the Council . . . can hardly be refused to any ambassador that can desire it'[44] before going on a new mission. Sir Joseph Williamson's 'being called to the Council' led Matthew Prior to expect that he would be named as one of the plenipotentiaries to negotiate peace with France in 1696.[45] And according to a minute of the Privy Council in 1715 it was usual for ambassadors to be sworn of the Council on their return from abroad.[46] Sir William Hamilton, while a mere envoy at Naples, incurred the wrath of George III by applying to be made a Privy Councillor. 'It is but lately', the king wrote, 'ambassadors have got that feather which would be improper to be given

[39] Larpent, i. 464–5.
[40] *Bedford Corresp.* i. 127.
[41] Coxe, *Lord Walpole Memoirs*, ii. 304.
[42] *Memoirs and Papers of Sir A. Mitchell*, ed. Bisset, ii. 359.
[43] J. P. Kenyon, *Sunderland*, p. 16.
[44] H.M.C., *Bath MSS.* i. 94.
[45] H.M.C., *Bath MSS.* iii. 96–97.
[46] H.M.C., *Portland MSS.* v. 503. Cf. H.M.C. VII. 262; *Marchmont Papers*, i. xli.

to envoys; the husbanding honours is the only means of keeping up their value.'[47] The reason why the practice extended to lower ranks was not so much the need to pay something on account in advance of the diplomatist's going abroad as to intimate to foreign courts that the diplomatist was high in the confidence of his sovereign.[48] Thus Sir R. M. Keith after his quarrel with the Foreign Secretary, Carmarthen, was sworn of the Privy Council before he returned as envoy to Vienna.[49]

In most cases the inducements offered were less specific, as is indeed suggested by the frequency with which men who had served abroad tried to secure additional rewards after they had returned home. Long after he had left his post, Lord Buckinghamshire pleaded his services in Russia as entitling him to a mark of royal approbation.[50] Edward Wortley, who had been ejected by Walpole from his seat at the Treasury board, later claimed that he had been induced to accept the Constantinople embassy by promises of great rewards at the end of this mission.[51] At the close of his first mission abroad William Eden wrote:

I own that it is not very edifying to me, instead of receiving either solid benefits or external marks of favour at the close of our successful struggles, to be preparing for an exile to that horrid Siberia [Spain]; but do not suspect that I am otherwise than in perfect and cordial good humour. I feel a grateful and friendly sense of the manner in which I have been put into the front rank in the great transactions of the last two years.[52]

Few Englishmen of rank or fortune regarded a diplomatic career as an end in itself: fewer still accepted a first appointment abroad with the intention of making their career in diplomacy. Typical is the conduct of John Wilkes who applied in rapid succession for a seat at the Board of Trade, the Constantinople embassy, and the governorship of Canada.[53] In the opinion of Chesterfield

most of our ministers abroad have taken up that department occasionally, without having ever thought of foreign affairs before; many of them without speaking any one foreign language; and all of them

---

[47] *George III Corresp.* iii. 460 (and cf. iv. 44).
[48] Cf. *Malmesbury Diaries*, ii. 73.
[49] *Keith Memoir*, ii. 242.   [50] *George III Corresp.* vi. 3–4.
[51] Halsband, *Lady Mary Wortley Montagu*, pp. 47, 55.
[52] *Auckland Journal*, i. 264.   [53] *Chatham Corresp.* ii. 94 n.

without the manners which are absolutely necessary towards being
well received, and making a figure at foreign courts. They do the
business accordingly—that is, very ill. They never get into the secret
of those Courts, for want of insinuation and address; they do not
guess at their views, for want of knowing their interests; and at last,
finding themselves very unfit for, soon grow weary of their commissions, and are impatient to return home, where they are but too justly
laid aside and neglected.[54]

This is a severe but only too often a fully justified verdict on many
a promising diplomatic career.

As an example of the protests addressed by dissatisfied politicians who had served a term abroad may be quoted the letter from
Hans Stanley to George Grenville, dated 7 April 1763:

I have served my country in a manner to which every court in
Europe has done justice except my own. I have since, from a sense of
my duty, supported that Administration which had neglected me.
My desire of showing my profound and loyal veneration to the person
of the King solely, joined to my resolution of never taking any part
that should have the least appearance of faction, has alone prevented
my laying the office I actually hold at His Majesty's feet . . . mean-
while I shall trouble no present or future Minister with any solicita-
tion; I may be again slighted; I have not, I will not be refused.[55]

Men of lower position also as a rule drifted into a diplomatic
career rather than chose it deliberately as their life work. Sometimes they had failed through no fault of their own to make a
career in the army. Sir R. M. Keith, 'axed' at the end of the Seven
Years War, was thus forced to try his luck in 'the foreign minister
line'.[56] Some had been travelling tutors who had picked up some
knowledge of foreign courts and languages and had a patron with
sufficient influence to secure for them a temporary appointment in
a low grade. Sir Robert Liston had tried his hand at journalism
as well as tutoring and would have preferred to the diplomatic
appointment he actually received a university chair at Parma.[57]

For young men of good family the army and the law, not to
mention politics, offered much greater prospects than diplomacy.
Horatio Walpole, on leaving the university, would have preferred
the law, for a time considered the army, and returned to law be-

[54] *Letters*, i. 114.   [55] *Grenville Papers*, ii. 43–44.
[56] *Keith Memoir*, i. 112.
[57] *Proceedings of the Royal Society of Edinburgh*, lii. 122–3.

fore he finally accepted an opening in diplomacy.[58] Later in the
century Bedford, in recommending a young man for an unpaid
attachéship, explained that his candidate could have had a commission as captain in Bedford's own regiment but for his father's
'old dislike of an army life'. He had tried and proved 'very averse
to the profession of the law' and 'there is now (considering his age)
no other system of life for him to pursue, but an idle one, or *le
métier d'un ministre aux cours étrangères*, which', Bedford adds,
'though I look upon it as a kind of banishment, is yet much prefer-
able to the former'.[59]

It should be noted that the acceptance of a diplomatic appointment did not automatically end a serving officer's army career.
Many diplomatists, both in war and in peace time, retained their
army commissions, though under George III stricter ideas about
the propriety of this practice came into vogue.[60] Lord Loudoun
during the War of American Independence objected to the appointment of a Guards officer to serve at a foreign court and
George III then refused to make the nomination unless the candidate quitted the military profession.[61] Under William III and
Anne, however, it was quite common for naval and military
officers to hold diplomatic appointments. Marlborough himself
remained accredited to the United Provinces from 1702 to 1712
and it is at least arguable whether his diplomatic skill did not contribute as much to his victorious career as his ability as soldier
and administrator.

One reason for the unpopularity of service abroad was the
absence of any regular ladder of promotion. Service as private
secretary or attaché gave no claim to regular employment abroad
by the crown. Still less did successful discharge of the duties of
secretary of embassy give a claim to headship of a mission. The
higher one rose the fewer were the opportunities for further promotion and the greater the competition from noblemen, court
favourites, and politicians with no diplomatic experience whatever. In fact the eighteenth-century diplomatic service was so
riddled with 'outsiders' in its highest ranges that it is only with
substantial reservations that it can be described as a diplomatic
service at all.

Carteret, himself an example as ambassador to Sweden of the

---

[58] Coxe, *Lord Walpole Memoirs*, i. 5–7.   [59] *Bedford Corresp.* i. 127.
[60] *George III Corresp.* v. 10.   [61] Ibid. v. 25.

'outsider' in diplomacy, gave it as his opinion 'that to do great business in a foreign country a prince should rather choose new men than one that has lived in it a great while: for, by long habitude, one contracts partialities, enmities and friendships, all which, carried too far, are equally destructive of the well-conducting great matters'.[62]

That Carteret's view was widely shared is proved by the fact that out of nineteen appointments as ambassador at Paris between 1689 and 1789, seven ambassadors had had no previous diplomatic experience whatever and some of the remainder had had only the slightest connexion with diplomacy. That the system of using inexperienced men to fill the most important post in the service was not altogether a success is proved by the growth of the practice of sending a working minister plenipotentiary to Paris to assist the ambassador.[63] The last British ambassador at Paris before the outbreak of the French Revolution had with him, for most of his mission, two assistants: the relations between titular ambassador and working minister plenipotentiary are summed up in the contemporary ballad:

> For Dorset at cricket can play
> And leave Billy Eden in France, sir.

Many nineteenth-century observers looked back to this and other eighteenth-century practices as though to a diplomatic golden age. Lord John Russell, for example, explained that he preferred to the existing professionalized diplomatic service the former way 'of appointing persons from time to time from this country, who were men of good information and competent to give an opinion upon foreign politics'.[64] And as late as 1853, Lord Stanley, Malmesbury's under-secretary, publicly expressed a preference for a system 'by which all diplomatic posts above the rank of secretary should normally be filled by men outside the profession'.[65] And eight years later Edmund Hammond, the permanent under-secretary, giving evidence before the Select Committee of

[62] Horn, *Scottish Diplomatists 1689–1789*, 4.
[63] *Supra*, Chapter II, p. 18.
[64] *Report from the Select Committee on Official Salaries H. of C. 1850*, xv, questions 1332–3.
[65] S. T. Bindoff, 'The Unreformed Diplomatic Service 1812–60', in *Trans. R. Hist. Soc.*, 4th series, xviii. 160.

1861 on the diplomatic service, remarked:[66] 'I am not sure that we may not have gone too far in making [diplomacy] a profession, and that the old system of the ambassador, taken generally from political men, and carrying as attachés his friends with him, giving them no eventual claim upon the public, may not have been better for the public service than that which now exists.'[67]

Such appointments were certainly more numerous, in proportion to the total appointments, in the eighteenth than in the nineteenth and twentieth centuries. Some proved costly failures, others were entirely justified by results; but whether they turned out well or ill they were inevitably resented by the men already in the service. 'Outsiders' were particularly resented when sent to a court where there was already in residence a regular career diplomatist. Nettled by the quite unexpected arrival of a special envoy to Vienna, Sir Morton Eden gave it as his opinion that 'these private missions are, in my mind, never of any avail as has been fully proved during the period of the last five years [1790–5]'.[68] A more detached observer, Anthony Storer, who had himself some diplomatic experience, attributed such missions to 'the contradiction which has prevailed of late in our measures, when we must have recourse to personal applications and extraordinary envoys rather than the ordinary method of dispatches to transact business'.[69]

There were, of course, exceptional men who asked nothing better than to serve the crown abroad. Some did this continuously for long periods at the same court. Beginning in 1738 as a mere *chargé d'affaires*, Horace Mann remained at Florence until his death in 1786. In the opinion of the historian Gibbon, Mann's 'most serious business was that of entertaining the English at his hospitable table'.[70] Mann's closest rival in length of service was Walter Titley, who took up his post at Copenhagen as secretary in charge of affairs in 1729 and remained accredited to the Danish king until he died at his country seat in 1768. His diplomatic duties, though at times absorbing, usually left him ample time to

---

[66] *P.P. H. of C. 1861*, vi, question 282.
[67] The preceding paragraphs are based on my pamphlet for the Historical Association, *Scottish Diplomatists 1689–1789*, pp. 4–5.
[68] *Auckland Journal*, iii. 321–2.   [69] Ibid. ii. 388.
[70] *Autobiography*, ed. Hill, p. 162. See too the Yale edition of Horace Walpole's correspondence with Mann: also Doran, *'Mann' and Manners at the Court of Florence*.

cultivate the Muses. He wrote Latin verse, translated Horace, and
his learned works were admired by scholars as eminent as Bentley.[71] Another well-known diplomat of this type is Sir William
Hamilton, who owed his original appointment to Naples to
George Grenville. 'His wife', we are told, 'has a terrible state of
health and he thinks the climate will do her good.'[72] It did; but
long after her death Hamilton clung to his post.

Such men soon acquired a taste for the easy life of a minor continental capital with a modicum of business. Some of them gave as
an additional reason that they lived better abroad than at home.
As Lord Pembroke put it in writing to Hamilton: 'You are certainly right in preferring to live well abroad than starving at
home.'[73] These men could hardly expect to climb to the top of the
diplomatic tree. A modest competence in congenial surroundings
was their utmost hope.

Thus Sir James Porter, who had already served for over
twenty years at Vienna and Constantinople, explained his acceptance of a mission to Brussels: he 'had lost sight of his connexions
in domestic politics: those with whom he had acted [originally he
had been a protégé of Carteret] had vanished from the scene—
partly through death, and partly through the fluctuations caused
by the corrupt system of Parliamentary influence under Lord
Newcastle'. His biographer adds that he possessed 'no borough
or borough friends. Hence he was willing to accept the easy office
of Minister at Brussels, which was rendered the more agreeable
to him by the residence in that city of his old acquaintance,
Prince Charles of Lorraine, who was the Austrian governor of the
Netherlands.'[74]

Although Porter's post was at Brussels, this type of diplomatist
was mainly to be found in southern Europe and especially on the
Mediterranean. Many men coveted Mann's post at Florence, including the swashbuckling Hugh Elliot, who wrote from Copenhagen: 'I have now no other ambition in life than to get a quiet
southern situation. I wish it were possible to procure the reversion
of Florence upon the same terms Sir Horace Mann has it. He is
old, and I think I should have some chance of being also one day

[71] W. Michael, *Englands Aufstieg zur Weltmacht*, p. 598.
[72] *Grenville Papers*, ii. 295–6, iv. 554.
[73] Lord Herbert, *Henry, Elizabeth and George*, p. 45.
[74] Larpent, i. 9, based on a letter from Porter to George Grenville.

grey headed under the influence of so warm a sun. In the rude North my feeble frame will soon be destroyed.'[75]

Other budding diplomatists enjoyed residence abroad but started off, at least, with higher hopes. A good example of this class was William Fullarton, a young man who had already travelled extensively when he wrote:

The truth is, that after I had wracked my invention, planning out a long and wonderfull pilgrimage thro Barbary and Spain, in which I had formed a thousand interesting Adventures and discoveries, some counterpoising projects recurred upon my memory, reminded me of the superior advantages that I might reap from being at London in the busy season when many opportunitys of advancement in one line or another present themselves to the fancy of projectors. These arguments prevailed. I for a time renounced my Chateaux en Espagne, got aboard the packet and arrived in London in the middle of March. Since then I have been in constant pursuit of one object or another, and, to make a long story short, have now brought matters to a bearing, for I am appointed Secretary to the Embassy at Paris, in Room of Colonel St. Paul. This is in many respects a favorable outset as it puts me equally in the way of information and preferment. . . . I had likewise secured a Seat in Parl[t] for which I was about to conclude when I was appointed to this employment and I have not yet determined whether it will be more advantageous for me to accept or decline the Offer.[76]

After experience of the coveted job at Paris he reported that his situation 'gives me innumerable opportunities of seeing all the turnings and windings of mankind and does not by any means take up so much of my time as to prevent me from as much application as will do me good'.[77] It was, however, to be the only post he ever held in the diplomatic service. Many of those who accepted a diplomatic commission lost no time in escaping into more pleasurable and profitable paths.

This raises the fundamental problem of the relation between politics and diplomacy in the eighteenth century; as yet there was no rigid dividing line and men passed fairly easily from one career to the other. There was in fact no legal barrier to stop either a peer or a member of the House of Commons from accepting a foreign mission while continuing, in the intervals of active

[75] *Auckland Journal*, i. 342.   [76] N.L.S., MS. 3943, fo. 31.
[77] Ibid., fo. 102 (letter misdated).

diplomacy, his political career at home. As early as the reign of
William III Ambassador Methuen was making the best of both
worlds. Vernon wrote of him in 1696 that he 'comes over [from
Lisbon] to be at the opening of the Parliament and designs to
leave his son his curate [there] whom he has sent for on purpose
from Italy. I perceive if he then find the Commission of Trade
like to stand and that Portugal may go by entail upon the heirs
male, he will stay here; otherwise he will be slipping back into his
post again.'[78]

Bute's brother, James Stuart Mackenzie, had a mind to go as
ambassador to Paris at the end of the Seven Years War. 'He likes
living abroad, and, as I am told, does not like his present employment, which is that of minister for Scotland.'[79] Hans Stanley, who
had already taken part in peace negotiations with France and
thought himself badly treated on his return, was in 1766 willing
to accept another appointment abroad, partly because his former
patron Pitt had returned to office, but also, according to his own
account, because 'tired and disgusted with all the late scenes of
domestic politics, and anxious about the future, I have accepted
the embassy to Petersburg, as a temporary retreat from the present
confusion'.[80] It was no doubt for this reason that he tried to stipu-
late for a maximum absence of two years from England.[81]

Much the best example of combining politics and diplomacy
was Horatio Walpole, brother of Sir Robert and his trusted adviser
on foreign affairs, who 'constantly spent the summer and autumn
at his post [abroad] and returned to England just before the meeting of Parliament'.[82] Horatio Walpole was, of course, a highly
privileged person; but there are constant examples, on a more
modest scale, of this practice. For example, Andrew Mitchell in
1752 was given leave to come home from his post at Brussels to
attend Parliament[83] and Newcastle wrote to Trevor, Minister
Plenipotentiary at The Hague, that he wished to have Trevor in
Parliament. 'I must own', the duke added, 'I had flattered myself
with the hopes of it, and did not see any incompatibility between
your attendance in Parliament some few months in the winter and

---

[78] H.M.C., *Bath MSS.* iii. 82. Cf. S.P. 89. 17 for fuller details.
[79] Rigby to Bedford in *Bedford Corresp.* iii. 210.
[80] *Grenville Papers*, iii. 284.
[81] *George III Corresp.* i. 381; Namier, *Additions and Corrections*, p. 61.
[82] Coxe, *Lord Walpole Memoirs*, ii. 457.
[83] S.P. 77. 88, dispatch of 19 Jan. 1753.

your business in Holland.'[84] Cope, Resident at Hamburg, advised the Secretary of State that he had been elected M.P. for Downton, Wilts., in 1754 and applied (successfully) for leave to go to England to attend Parliament.[85]

The practice which allowed peers to leave proxies with the government made it rather easier to send them than it was to dispatch members of the Lower House on foreign missions.[86] While members of the Lower House could not do this they could usually count on getting leave to return to England if this was necessary to look after their political interests, e.g. if the constituency which the diplomatist represented was to be contested at a general election. Sir Paul Methuen on one occasion gave as his excuse for not going abroad the fact that his seat was being contested.[87] And when Queen Caroline offered Stair the Vienna embassy she seems to have thought him 'being out of Parliament' more likely to accept.[88] There is also on record at least one case where a secretary of state treats a seat in Parliament and the Russian embassy as being equivalent in patronage value and mutually inconsistent. Sandwich wrote to Buckinghamshire who had pressed for recall and then wanted to stay on at St. Petersburg:

It [the Russian embassy] was fixed for Mr. Macartney before your Lordship showed the least inclination to stay; he gave up his pretensions to a seat in parliament upon the promise of this appointment and expected to be dispatched some months ago. Should his appointment be now postponed ... he would have great reason to complain and to think that he was led on with hopes of this commission because we wished to choose another person into parliament instead of him.[89]

Not many politicians, however, were as scrupulous as Robinson and Keith. The latter, while at Vienna, was elected to the House of Commons, and subsequently decided not to seek re-election, on the ground that 'the indispensable duties of a foreign mission can hardly be made compatible with those of a member of Parliament'. He then proceeds: 'I have, in justice to my constituents, let them know that I shall not expose them at the general election

---

[84] H.M.C., *Report XIV, App. IX* (Trevor MSS.), p. 91.

[85] S.P. 82. 74, dispatch of 2 Aug. 1754. He returned to his post when the session was over, but was back again for the next parliamentary session.

[86] H.M.C., *Portland MSS.* v. 270, 273; *Bolingbroke Corresp.* ii. 301, and *Bedford Corresp.* i. 194.   [87] H.M.C., *Portland MSS.* iv. 616–17.

[88] *Marchmont Papers*, ii. 16.

[89] *Buckinghamshire Desp.* ii. 219–20.

to the continuation of the inconveniences they have felt, for several years past, by the absence of their representative. A better (because a more useful) servant of the public will take my place.'[90] And it is occasionally possible to show that combination of duties was in fact inconvenient. Queen Anne, when the balance of parties in the House of Lords was at stake in the closing years of her reign, proposed for this reason to send to Vienna a Scots peer instead of Lord Jersey.[91] Later Keene in 1745 argued that his departure for Lisbon might have to be indefinitely postponed because 'matters in parliament may so fall out . . . as to make every vote necessary for carrying on the King's affairs'.[92] In spite of such difficulties a diplomatic appointment might well be a mere interlude in a successful career in politics.

Nevertheless, politicians as a class were just as anxious as other Englishmen to escape relegation to foreign posts: those who accepted them often admitted ruefully that their stock of royal and ministerial favour was not as high as they would have liked. A near-contemporary historian remarked of William III after the Revolution that as

the King could not gratify [all those applying for posts] he sent many of those who boasted of their merits out of the way by honorable embassies abroad: Mr. Coxe to the Swiss cantons; Mr. James Johnston, still well-known both on account of his father [Lord Warriston]'s death and his own good services, to the elector of Brandenburg on the recommendation of Dr. Burnet; Mr. Molesworth to the King of Denmark; Duncombe to the King of Sweden; the lord Paget to the Emperor; Mr. William Herbert [Harbord?], a troublesome man, to the Grand Seignor; and lastly . . . the young earl of Pembroke. . . . to the United Provinces.[93]

A similar situation at the Restoration had been met in a similar way. Individual politicians continued to be dealt with in this manner. Cases have already been cited of a foreign appointment as a kind of honourable banishment and others may be added. In Anne's reign Robert Benson, Chancellor of the Exchequer, when the ministry was reorganized, was sent as ambassador to Spain and, to gild the pill, created a peer. According to the *Egmont Diary* in 1734 'Lord Harrington, Secretary of State (who, though

[90] *Keith Memoir*, ii. 96.   [91] H.M.C., *Bath MSS.* i. 216.
[92] *Keene Corresp.*, p. 65.
[93] A. Cunningham, *History of Great Britain*, i. 107.

he has acted in concurrence with Sir Robert Walpole, was never right with him), has been desired to quit, and take on him an embassy to France, but that he refused it and offers, rather than be commanded thither, to lay down'.[94] George Lyttelton, in 1746, although partly influenced by weariness 'of living in a country where I must see my friends quarrel to their own undoing', was also making a conscious sacrifice when he offered to surrender his seat at the Treasury board in favour of Richard Grenville and accept a foreign commission.[95]

Under George III the French and Spanish embassies came regularly to be regarded as bargaining counters when a new ministry was being formed. Bedford wrote to Bute in 1763 urging the need to 'widen the bottom of administration' and added: 'Employments to satisfy these great lords [Newcastle, Devonshire, Grafton, Hardwicke etc.] you have enough—Master of the Horse, President of the Council, Privy Seal, embassy to France.'[96] In 1766 when Pitt was drafting schemes for his ministry he originally proposed Rochford as Lord Lieutenant of Ireland and another peer as a possible ambassador at Paris;[97] but in the end it was Rochford who went as ambassador to France.

Pamphleteers were not slow to protest against the converting of 'foreign ambassages' into 'occasions for bestowing private gratifications on the followers of a ministry',[98] but the practice continued. Augustus Hervey in 1766 proposed Sandwich for the Spanish embassy on the ground that 'as a friend to Administration he thought it might accelerate further arrangements',[99] i.e. strengthen the ministry. Four years later the sending of Stormont to Paris is included in a list of hypothetical changes in the ministry, again by Augustus Hervey.[1] Chatham, when it proved difficult to fill the Spanish embassy in 1766, thought this 'has an unfavourable aspect for the King's service in the hands his Majesty has been pleased to entrust his affairs'.[2] The ministry's inability to fill 'this forlorn embassy'[3] showed up the weakness of administration.

[94] H.M.C., *Egmont Diary*, ii. 35.
[95] *Grenville Papers*, i. 425, and Owen, *Rise of the Pelhams*, pp. 301–2.
[96] *Bedford Corresp.* iii. 229.
[97] C. R. Ritchieson, 'The Elder Pitt and an American Department', in *A.H.R.* lvii (1951–2), 376–83.
[98] e.g. *The Present State of the Nation* (3rd ed., 1768), p. 98.
[99] J. Brooke, *Chatham Administration*, pp. 37, 271–2.
[1] *Grenville Papers*, iv. 526.
[2] *Chatham Corresp.* iii. 98–99.   [3] Ibid. iii. 123.

In 1783 Charles James Fox defended a change at the Paris embassy, contrary to the wishes of George III, as being justified by the convenience which resulted to the ministry 'from the present disposal of that appointment'.[4] And in 1789 the younger Pitt was similarly influenced by 'the facility of these political arrangements, which will depend on the French embassy being open' in sending William Eden to The Hague and not to Paris as Eden would have preferred. Pitt expressed to Eden his appreciation of Eden's sacrifice of his own inclinations to 'the convenience of government'.[5]

Although this tendency to treat top-flight diplomatic appointments as included in the periodical ministerial reshuffles is, I think, a novel feature of George III's reign, occasional anticipations appear earlier. In 1727 Hervey mentions 'Sir Robert Walpole, his brother, Mr. Horace Walpole, ambassador to France, the duke of Newcastle and Lord Townshend, the two secretaries of state' as being 'properly speaking, the whole old administration at the death of the late King'.[6] Even after it became a regular practice, it did not do much to popularize foreign appointments: the politicians continued to prefer places at home. Buckinghamshire turned down the Spanish embassy in 1766 partly because 'his connections in the house of commons required his presence, they having suffered much while he was in Russia [as ambassador]'.[7] This was inevitable as long as places went by royal and ministerial favour. Out of sight was out of mind. *Les absents ont toujours tort.* As old Horace Walpole explained to a would-be placeman:

I am glad to find that you are willing to turn your thoughts to business. . . . I am no less pleased that you have hinted your mind [to Sir R. Walpole], which I would advise you to do by your frequent visits and addresses. Your person and manner cannot, considering your merit and your circumstances, be impertinent or importunate, and, believe me, among the number of candidates that have, or that think they have, merit, being constantly in the way is of great service; and often by surprise and, as it were, against the will of the person in power gets the better of greater merit that is modest and backward.[8]

Jenkinson, after trying for years to secure a paid appointment from Newcastle, wrote: 'I shall stay, however, as little time there

4 *Memorials of C. J. Fox*, ii. 71, 123.   5 *Auckland Journal*, ii. 360.
6 *Memoirs*, p. 29.   7 Brooke, *Chatham Administration*, pp. 35-36.
8 10 Sept. 1737, N.S. (in Newport Public Library).

[in Hampshire] as possibly I can, that I may return again to town to hunt a certain Minister, who never does a favour with a good grace, and must fairly be run down if you mean to have him accomplish any promise he has made to you.'⁹

Once the would-be placeman accepted appointment abroad it was physically impossible for him to be 'constantly in the way', still less to run the minister down. He had then to rely on what was usually the less effective advocacy of his claims by his personal friends and political connexions. This, in turn, raises an interesting point. Politicians who were too successful even to consider accepting for themselves employment abroad, often struck a bargain with the court or with their colleagues that, in exchange for services at home, a friend or relation should be employed abroad. The ill-starred diplomatic career of Sir Charles Hanbury Williams was largely based on his close friendship with Fox. Horace Walpole believed in 1748 that 'Sir Charles Williams is the great obstacle to all arrangement. Mr. Fox makes a point of his going to Turin. The ministry, who do not love him, are not for his going anywhere.'¹⁰ Though Fox ultimately failed to get his friend posted to Turin, he succeeded in having him continued at Dresden; and two years later, by waiving, at the request of the king, his own claims to the Treasurership of the Navy, Fox secured for his friend the Berlin legation.¹¹

While insisting that the diplomatic service was unpopular and rarely lucrative, it would be wrong to imply that only eccentric Englishmen were willing to serve abroad. There was, indeed, often keen competition for certain posts. Horace Walpole's letters provide abundant evidence of this, although they also show how often the candidate to whom a post was first offered turned it down at once or ultimately, on some pretext or other, did not go on the mission. The courts of south-western Europe were relatively popular. Men who recoiled in horror from the thought of exile to Russia or Poland or Constantinople and dreaded the dreary prospect of residence at a German court often went willingly to Italy where the climate was more attractive and they could live largely in the company of their fellow countrymen.

It is often said that one inducement which led politically minded Englishmen to accept employment abroad, even at the less con-

---

⁹ *Grenville Papers*, i. 315. Cf. ibid. i. 333–4.
¹⁰ *Letters*, ii. 354.   ¹¹ Hanbury Williams, *Works*, ii. 208.

genial courts, was the belief that this was a purgatory through which it was possible to reach high office at home. Traces of this idea are to be found at least as early as the Tudor period: they do not finally disappear until well on in the nineteenth century. Between the Restoration and the Revolution this belief, at least so far as the office of Secretary of State was concerned, was not ill founded. The Secretary's most important duty being the care of foreign affairs, it was natural for the king to choose secretaries who had already served the crown abroad with success and in so doing had knowledge which would be of use to them in the Secretary's office.

William III's secretaries, however, were little more than clerks. The king clearly thought diplomatic experience unnecessary. Charles Montague, earl of Halifax, writing in 1694, summed up the position admirably, in writing to his friend the diplomatist, George Stepney: 'Formerly after a man had discharged a commission in foreign parts . . . he was called home and made a secretary of state, but that matter is a good deal altered; and, I believe, we shall not see more instances of that kind. This King is so much a master of all foreign transactions that his choice is directed by some considerations at home more than by their skill in business abroad.'[12] Montague prophesied correctly not only for the reign of William but, although the reasons are different, for Anne's reign. Only one of Anne's secretaries, Sunderland, seems to have had, before his appointment, any diplomatic experience; it is perhaps symptomatic of the discontent amongst those who had served abroad that at the close of Anne's reign Abraham Stanyan proposed the appointment of a committee for foreign affairs to be recruited from diplomatists of seven or more years' standing.

Under the first two Hanoverian sovereigns the professional diplomatists come into their own again. In the case of the northern and now more important department, eight of the nine secretaries had represented their country abroad—the solitary and significant exception being the duke of Newcastle. Townshend had held two diplomatic appointments of the first rank and importance before he was appointed to the secretaryship. Stanhope was the son of a career-diplomatist and had himself served as envoy to Spain for nearly four years. Sunderland had been sent on a special mission to Vienna immediately before his appointment to the southern

[12] Quoted Eves, *Matthew Prior*, p. 53.

department, from which he transferred to the northern department. Harrington was himself a career-diplomatist.[13] Carteret had made his reputation by his embassy to Sweden and had subsequently been named ambassador to France. Chesterfield had twice represented British interests in the United Provinces before his appointment to the northern secretaryship, while Holdernesse had served both at Venice and at The Hague.

A similar state of affairs prevailed in the southern department, except that the line of diplomatically experienced secretaries came to an end rather earlier—in 1755, not in 1761. The secretaries for the south who had no diplomatic experience included not only the duke of Newcastle but also the duke of Bedford, whose diplomatic experience was subsequent to his tenure of the secretaryship. Stanhope has already been considered. His successor, Paul Methuen, was, like Stanhope, the son of a British career-diplomatist. Not only had the younger Methuen been closely associated with his father at the Portuguese court: he had also undertaken three missions to Savoy and Spain. Joseph Addison's diplomatic experience, it is true, was limited to a complimentary mission to the Electress Sophia, headed by Lord Halifax, eleven years before his appointment to the secretaryship; he had, however, been sent abroad as a young man, partly at government expense, to prepare him for a career in the public service and most likely in diplomacy.[14] James Craggs the younger had served in Spain with Stanhope, at first as private secretary and then as secretary of embassy, resident, and finally envoy, before being sent in 1714 to Hanover to inform the Hanoverian court of Queen Anne's desperate condition. Carteret and Holdernesse have already been mentioned. Sir Thomas Robinson had been so long abroad in the diplomatic line that he had almost forgotten how to speak his native language.

Responsibility for these appointments rests with the first two Georges who had no sympathy with English ideas of government by amateurs and also with the duke of Newcastle who preferred peers with diplomatic experience to other candidates for secretaryships. Some of their contemporaries saw clearly what was happening. Chesterfield explained the practice with his usual clarity of view to his son:

[13] See *Hervey Memoirs*, pp. 174, 346, for the contrast between Harrington's reputation as diplomatist and as secretary of state.
[14] P. Smithers, *The Life of Joseph Addison*, pp. 42–45.

We are in general, in England, ignorant of foreign affairs; and of the interests, views, pretensions and policies of other Courts. That part of knowledge never enters into our thoughts, nor makes part of our education; for which reason, we have fewer proper subjects for foreign commissions than any other country in Europe; and, when foreign affairs happen to be debated in Parliament, it is incredible with how much ignorance. The harvest of foreign affairs being then so great, and the labourers so few, if you make yourself master of them, you will make yourself necessary; first as a foreign, and then as a domestic Minister for that department.[15]

Other observers also appreciated what was going on. Daniel Pulteney, towards the end of George I's reign, was inclined to regard Horace Walpole's being named as ambassador extraordinary as calculated for the purpose of preparing for his appointment as Secretary of State.[16] Similarly under George II, after Horace Walpole had filled further diplomatic appointments, Lord Egmont firmly believed Robert Walpole's intention was to get his brother named as Secretary.[17] And when Chesterfield was supposed to be going as ambassador to France in 1727, Horace Walpole wrote:

It is already in the Dutch prints that Lord Chesterfield is to come hither [to Paris] which, together with what his lordship publishes abroad himself, will, I suppose, make the Cardinal [Fleury] ask me a thousand questions . . . which will be difficult to answer, considering he will stand in the eye of the world as the person designed by his Majesty to be hereafter secretary of state.[18]

No wonder that Pelham wrote sarcastically to Hardwicke with reference to the appointment of Holdernesse:[19] 'I find his Grace [of Newcastle] and the King also, thinks there is nothing necessary to make a secretary of state but crossing the water, and having credentials to one of the principal courts as a foreign minister; I heartily wish they may find it so.'[20] Waldegrave, who was in George II's confidence, explained that George II preferred Sir Thomas Robinson as Secretary because he 'was diligent in his office, did as he was directed, understood foreign affairs and pre-

[15] *Letters*, i. 83 (cf. also ibid. i. 114 and 447).
[16] H.M.C., *MSS. in Various Collections*, viii. 361.
[17] H.M.C., *Egmont Diary*, ii. 35, 269.
[18] Coxe, *Walpole Memoirs*, ii. 543.
[19] Cf. Shrewsbury's objection as early as 1711 to Robinson as Privy Seal (H.M.C., *Bath MSS*. i. 207).
[20] Yorke, *Hardwicke*, ii. 101.

tended to nothing further'. When forced to accept Fox, George II was supposed to have made some ungracious hints as to how a man might be a 'talker in the house of commons though in every other respect a very indifferent secretary'.[21]

The experiment of regularly appointing men with diplomatic experience to secretaryships of state had broken down before the opening of the Seven Years War. It proved essential to have at least one secretary in the House of Commons who could put the government case to his fellow members with cogency and acceptance. Although this was not the uniform practice after the war, diplomatic experience was much less highly regarded than it had been under George I and George II. George III indeed repeatedly showed signs of a personal preference for a secretary of state who had served abroad, Joseph Yorke, Stormont, and Grantham. He wrote crossly to North: 'Undoubtedly from every man brought forward into offices of business being either Declamers or owing their situation to such persons instead of being regularly bred as in other countries in the offices in which [they] become secretaries, occasions the endless mistakes in matters of form.'[22] And he recognized Stormont's claim to be Lord Justice General in these words: 'Considering the embassies he has with distinction filled' Stormont 'cannot have a competitor.'[23] North, on the other hand, seeking to strengthen his administration in 1778, proposed three names for the three secretaryships and added that if only two secretaries were appointed Sir Joseph Yorke should be dropped. Yorke 'would be of great use in the Cabinet but, his course of life not having led him to parliamentary studies, he will probably not take an active part in the house of Commons'.[24]

In practice, it was in the opening years of George III's reign that the custom of appointing secretaries without diplomatic experience was resumed. Of the ten secretaries appointed to the northern department between 1761 and 1782 seven had no diplomatic experience. The other three had served abroad, Rochford and Stormont for long periods at several posts, Sandwich only for a year or two at the end of the Austrian Succession War. In the southern department only two of the eight secretaries between 1761 and 1782 had served abroad—Rochford and Richmond, who

21 Waldegrave, *Memoirs*, pp. 52, 81–82.
22 *George III Corresp.* vi. 444.
23 Ibid. iv. 209.   24 Ibid. iv. 55, 58, 76.

had been ambassador to France for the three months preceding his appointment. The division of duties between the secretaries on a functional basis made no difference in this respect—few experienced diplomatists are to be found on the list of Foreign Secretaries.

The surprising thing is that the belief that service abroad was a good route to high office at home survived so long. Stratford Canning's biographer states that every time his hero gave up a diplomatic appointment it was with the vain hope of obtaining public employment at home and as late as 1832 the Austrian diplomatic agent at London saw in the nomination of Lord Durham to undertake a special mission to St. Petersburg the 'grooming' of a rival candidate to supplant Palmerston as Foreign Secretary.[25]

In conclusion, some cases may be briefly mentioned of diplomatic appointments for curious and quite eccentric reasons. Perhaps the most extraordinary was that of Charles Bertie who had been secretary to the Treasury under his brother-in-law Danby. Bertie had been committed by order of the House of Commons to the Tower and Charles II found it desirable to get him out of the country 'with all possible speed'. He was therefore hurriedly appointed envoy to the electors and princes of Germany.[26] Hardly less strange was the giving of credentials from George I to John Law, the financier, after the collapse of Law's schemes in France, as diplomatic agent to Venice, where he died on 21 March 1729.[27] These credentials were intended for protection, not use, and were never presented. Spies and secret agents were occasionally furnished with credentials, sometimes for their protection, more often probably to enable them to carry on under cover their nefarious activities. Thus George Cressener, who ostensibly discharged a series of commissions to the courts of Western Germany during and after the Seven Years War, was really more concerned with collecting useful military and naval information from France.[28] Similarly Colonel Mitford Crowe 'for colour only' had 'given him a credential to the state [of Genoa] and instructions to make propositions for the mutual advantage of trade',[29] whereas

[25] The preceding paragraphs are based on my article 'The Diplomatic Experience of Secretaries of State 1660–1852' in *History*, xli (1956), 88–99.

[26] Baxter, *Development of the Treasury 1660–1702*, pp. 64, 183, 190.

[27] S.P. 104. 210; S.P. 81. 91; and S.P. 99. 63, letter dated 22 April 1729.

[28] *Infra*, Chapter XIV, pp. 273–4.   [29] S.P. 104. 91 (dispatch of 2 Mar. 1705).

his real business was to watch the Catalan revolt and report naval movements.

Occasionally the reasons why an Englishman accepted appointment abroad were sentimental rather than rational. By his own account Hanbury Williams accepted the Dresden legation owing to a fit of melancholy following upon the death of his friend Winnington, 'the man upon earth I loved the best. 'Twas upon his death I begged the King to send me abroad and resigned a very profitable employment to come out of a country where I missed an object that I esteemed and honoured very highly and where every thing daily put me in mind of him.'[30] To this personal explanation of motives it should be added that truth is many-sided. Sir Charles's enemies affected to believe that the real motive for his departure from his native land was to escape a succession of duels forced upon him by indignant and pugnacious Irishmen, who resented his published reflections upon their nationality:

> Nature, indeed, denies them sense
> But gives them legs and impudence
> That beats all understanding.[31]

[30] Add. MS. 23825, fo. 198.   [31] *Works*, i. 93.

CHAPTER VI

Alien Elements

ENGLISH reluctance to accept appointments abroad contributed to the permeation of the diplomatic service by alien elements. This was especially marked under William III. Not only did he prefer to depend upon the Dutch diplomatists already established, before his accession to the English throne, at the key points of European diplomacy. Even when he felt bound to send a diplomatic mission to some court as King of Great Britain, he very often chose for the job a Dutchman, a French Huguenot refugee, or a Swiss Protestant. Thus it was William Bentinck, earl of Portland and William's Dutch favourite, who was sent to make peace with France in 1697. Henri de Massue de Ruvigny, earl of Galway, served from 1693 to 1696 as envoy to Piedmont. Philibert de Herwarth, another Huguenot refugee, served as envoy to Geneva and subsequently to the Swiss cantons.[1] He was succeeded at Geneva by another Huguenot refugee, Gasper Perrinet d'Arsellières.[2] Francis Schonenberg, Dutch minister at Madrid, received also credentials from the King of Great Britain, though the protests of Alexander Stanhope, the native-born envoy to Spain, secured Schonenberg's non-intervention in British business with Spain until after Stanhope's departure in 1699.[3] Since Schonenberg's English was rudimentary, at least one important instruction for him had to be translated into French.[4] Julius Heinrich, Count von Friesen, was twice appointed to undertake diplomatic missions, though in neither case did he actually go. Stepney, probably the most active and successful native English diplomat of William III's reign, went so far as to hope that the King 'may be desired not to suffer strangers any more to concern themselves with our affairs, which is a scandal to our nation, and cannot but embroil us'. On another

---

[1] Adrien Chopard, *Die Mission des englischen Gesandten Philibert Herwarth in der Schweiz.*

[2] See *C.T.B.* xx. 815 for alternative spellings of his title and H.M.C., *Buccleuch MSS.* ii. 199 for a brief account of his career to 1695.

[3] *B.D.R.*, pp. 127–8.

[4] Cole, *Memoirs*, p. 267.

occasion he complained: 'There is no dealing with the King when a Dutchman comes into competition.'[5]

Under George I and, to a less extent, George II, occasional foreigners still managed to obtain diplomatic posts. For a time the two Swiss diplomatists, Schaub and Saint-Saphorin, were prominent.[6] Saint-Saphorin wrote dispatches of such inordinate length that it became an office joke to call any long official letter a St. Saphorin.[7] Even later, minor diplomatic appointments were sometimes filled by Swiss agents such as Jerome de Salis, envoy to the Grison Leagues 1743–50, and the two Pictets at Geneva in the sixties and seventies.[8] Occasionally other foreigners appear on the list of British diplomatists after the accession of the House of Hanover. At least one of them was a Frenchman, Lewis Dutens, but they were, as might be expected, usually Germans, and none of them rose as high in the diplomatic service as the Huguenot refugees and Swiss Protestants had done. Almost the only one to become head of a mission was Lieutenant-Colonel Melchior Guy Dickens, who served abroad successively at Berlin, Stockholm, and St. Petersburg from 1730 to 1755. To secure credentials, at least after the death of William III, it was almost essential for foreigners to become naturalized British subjects. Sir Luke Schaub, however, had credentials as ambassador to France in 1721, although this aroused hostile comment. Ker of Kersland remarked: 'Strange that in an affair of such consequence ... not a subject of Great Britain could be found to understand or capable to treat of such matters so well as a foreigner.'[9]

Occasionally this technical difficulty was circumvented by giving foreigners creditive letters from the Hanoverian chancellary, though in fact it was with British business that their mis-

[5] Margery Lane, 'The Diplomatic Service under William III', in *Trans. R. Hist. Soc.*, 4th series, x. 103.

[6] See A. Lätt, 'Zwei Schweizer Diplomaten im Dienste Grossbritanniens', in *Basler Zeitschrift für Geschichte und Altertumskunde*, xxi (Basel, 1923); Markus Meier, *Die diplomatische Vertretung Englands in der Schweiz im 18. Jahrhundert;* and S. Stelling-Michaud, *St Saphorin et la politique de la Suisse.*

[7] *Private Correspondence of Chesterfield and Newcastle*, ed. Sir R. Lodge, p. 10. Specimens of these dispatches are readily accessible in H.M.C., *Polwarth MSS. passim.* Saint-Saphorin's countryman Schaub ran him close in verbosity.

[8] E. E. Rovillain, 'L'Angleterre et les Troubles de Genève en 1766–7', in *Revue d'Histoire suisse*, vii, fasc. 2 (1927).

[9] *Memoirs*, ii. 112–13. The index to this work has the delightful entry: 'Foreigners, the Dangerous Consequences to be apprehended from their Politics.'

sions were concerned.[10] Alternatively while Saint-Saphorin, though
he had no formal credentials, was the leading British minister at
Vienna, George I tried to conciliate English opinion by maintaining also at Vienna a British subject with an inferior character as
resident or secretary. The native diplomatists had orders to be
guided entirely by Saint-Saphorin, who took the line that these
junior ministers should not be allowed to write dispatches to the
Secretary of State without first submitting them for his approval.
Friction was inevitable and Townshend warned Saint-Saphorin
on 12/23 September 1723 that if he did not keep on terms with
Colman worse might befall him 'as it is necessary to have an
Englishman at Vienna'. If Colman was removed another Englishman would be sent, probably with a higher rank. This in fact
happened. Colman, who was merely the king's secretary at Vienna,
was succeeded in 1723 by Harrison, who was variously described
as minister or resident. There was the further difficulty that Saint-
Saphorin as an alien could not sign formal documents such as
peace preliminaries and Harrison's successor Woodward was accorded full powers for this purpose in 1727.[11] Very occasionally,
when there was a gap in British representation at a court where
there also resided a Hanoverian diplomatist, the latter was authorized to act as *chargé d'affaires*, e.g. Baron von Diescau at Stockholm from 1727 to 1728. About the same time, during a rupture in
Anglo-Spanish relations, the Dutch minister at Madrid, Francis
van der Meer, was entrusted with the care of British interests in
Spain.[12]

It should be added that on rare occasions a British title might
conceal a man who was by birth, education, or sympathy or all
three really a foreigner. Portland and Galway are examples under
William III, Albemarle, less clearly, under George II.[13] The same
effect was sometimes achieved by a change of name. Sir James
Porter was the son of a soldier of fortune named La Rogue or La
Roche, who had settled in Ireland. The son took the name of
Porter at the request of an uncle and married a Dutchwoman.
That the family had not become thoroughly naturalized is sug-
gested by the fact that the grandson of La Rogue in 1819 obtained

---

[10] e.g. Colonel James Pictet, minister to Geneva 1763–7, and the Comte de
Marsay as resident to the Swiss cantons 1734–9 (S.P. 96. 24 and 31).
[11] S.P. 80. 36–61.   [12] S.P. 94. 98.
[13] Cf. *Honest Diplomat*, p. 195.

the Prince Regent's permission to take the surname and bear the arms of de Hochepied.[14]

If, however, the British diplomatic service between 1689 and 1789 became more national in membership and outlook, the native English element was progressively diluted by the infiltration of the Scots and Irish.

Even before the union there was no legal bar (after the decision of James I's judges in the *post-nati* case) to Scotsmen holding office under the English crown, but these cases are comparatively rare, except in the armed forces. Thus J. Macky in his *Secret Memoirs*[15] (1733) gives characters of the leading diplomatists at the beginning of Anne's reign: not one of the twelve was a Scot. On the other hand, when he deals with the army and navy, out of the twenty-two leading generals and admirals, four soldiers and two sailors were Scotsmen. Most of them had previously served in Holland and came over with William at the Revolution: Macky records of Admiral Sir David Mitchell that he 'was born in a little Fisher town in Scotland, and was pressed into the English service, when but a boy. He hath passed through all the degrees of a sailor, and without any recommendation, but his own merits, hath raised himself to the honourable post he now enjoys, and had risen faster had he been an Englishman.'

The Scottish penetration into the diplomatic service may be shown in tabular form. The number of Scots appointed in each reign is shown below:

Sovereign	Length of reign	Total appoint-ments	Genuine diplomatic missions	Other appoint-ments
I. William III and Mary . .	13 years	3	2	1
II. Anne . . .	12 „	6	3	3
III. George I . .	13 „	9	7	2
IV. George II . .	33 „	14	11	3
V. George III (up to 1789) . .	29 „	21	19	2

An even clearer picture is presented when in each of these

[14] Larpent, i. 1–18.
[15] It is now asserted that this scandalous work was written by Bishop Burnet. (*C.T.B., Introduction to Vols. XI–XVII* (1695–1702), p. clxxxii.)

periods we express the number of appointments secured by Scotsmen as a fraction of the total appointments made in the period:

Period I	1 Scot out of every 20 appointments	
Period II	1 „ „ „ 18	„
Period III	1 „ „ „ 9	„
Period IV	1 „ „ „ 8	„
Period V	1 „ „ „ 7	„

Apart from James Johnston, who had been educated in Holland and was known to William III before the Revolution, Scottish
representation in the British diplomatic service of his reign is
limited to the earl of Selkirk, who was sent on a special mission
to Denmark in 1691, and Hugh Greg, resident at Copenhagen
1701–2, and uncle of the William Greg who was executed in
Anne's reign for betraying Foreign Office secrets to France. Greg
is said to be of Scottish origin, but I have been unable to trace his
family—possibly he may belong to a branch of the family settled
earlier in Scandinavia.

Under Anne there is at first a complete absence of Scots, not
unnaturally in view of the strained relations between England and
Scotland and the old tradition of friendship between Scotland and
France, which had become since the Revolution the arch-enemy
of England. The only Scotsman to hold a diplomatic appointment
before the Act of Union was Admiral Sir David Mitchell, whose
'character' by Macky has already been quoted. The Alien Act of
1705 in fact made it illegal from Christmas Day 1705 to appoint
most Scotsmen to office under the English crown, since Scotsmen
who were not serving in the army or navy or established in England were now declared to be aliens, but this was repealed in the
following year. Once the Act of Union was safely passed there was
a marked increase in Scottish diplomatists; and the real beginning
of the Scots as a substantial element in British diplomacy occurred,
curiously enough, under the Tory government which held sway
in the last four years of Anne's reign. At this stage the duke of
Argyll held a semi-diplomatic, semi-military appointment as ambassador to Spain; Admiral Sir James Wishart was authorized to
treat about marine quotas with the United Provinces; and two
obscure civilians, George Mackenzie (alias Mackenzie-Quin) and
James Scott, successively represented British interests in Poland
and Saxony and the former also in Russia. This sudden accession
of the Scottish element is presumably an accidental result in time

of war, due chiefly to the prominence of the Scots in the armed
forces of the crown. Four out of the six Scots employed by Anne
were soldiers or sailors and their missions were at least as much
military or naval as diplomatic. There is no suggestion that the
employment of these Scotsmen was part of any deliberate policy
to conciliate Scottish national feeling after the passing of the Act
of Union.

In the early years of George I, in spite of the end of the Spanish
Succession War, the Scottish element became even more important. The earl of Stair, who had already been employed as envoy
to Poland under Anne, now held the premier post in the service—
ambassador to France—and was assisted by Thomas Craufurd of
Drumsoy, a brother Scot; two Scots peers successively represented
British interests at Copenhagen, a key post during and immediately after the northern war; James Haldane of Gleneagles was
entrusted with a series of missions to the Tsar, the Duke of Hesse
Cassel, and the Elector Palatine; and Alexander Cunningham was
Resident at Venice.

Thus the first great wave of Scots diplomatists covered the years
1709–21. In the twenties the Scots rapidly declined in numbers
and, once Walpole took over control of foreign policy, virtually
disappeared from the service. Contemporary Englishmen no doubt
were just as grateful to him for excluding the Scots, as for his
resolute opposition to Hanoverian influence on English foreign
policy.

The Pelhams were lesser men, and in this as in other respects
carried on the Walpole tradition less strenuously and less successfully. Whereas the only Scottish appointment in the thirties was
that of the eighth earl of Kinnoull at Constantinople (1729–36),
Lord Hyndford's appointment to Berlin in 1741 was the first of a
new series. The steady trickle of Scottish appointments in the
forties, fed partly by semi-military appointments such as that of
the earl of Stair as ambassador to the United Provinces, became,
on the outbreak of the Seven Years War, a broad river. On the
death of George II in 1760, Scotsmen had charge of British relations with the courts of Russia, Prussia, Portugal, Sardinia, and
Saxony-Poland. Owing to the Seven Years War, Russia and Prussia were the only first-rate powers where Britain had then a diplomatic agent; Portugal and Sardinia ranked near the top of the
second-rate courts at this time from the point of view of British

interests; and the Saxon-Polish envoyship usually led to higher appointments.

The high-watermark of 1709–21 was now completely obliterated by the second great wave of Scots diplomatists, which, with temporary slight recessions, crept farther and farther up the beach until the outbreak of the French Revolution. Thus about 1770 Lord Stormont was ambassador at Vienna, Sir Andrew Mitchell envoy to Prussia, and Lord Cathcart ambassador to Russia. Sir R. M. Keith was just starting his brilliant diplomatic career as envoy to Poland, Sir William Hamilton was already well established at Naples, and William Gordon was serving as minister plenipotentiary to Flanders. After the treaty of Paris, which ended the Seven Years War, the European centre of gravity moved eastwards and it is notable that, with the exception of Turkey, British representatives at every court in eastern Europe, Austria, Russia, Prussia, and Poland, were Scotsmen. That Britain played such a sorry part in the Eastern crisis of the seventies, and particularly in the first partition of Poland, was the fault of the government at home, not of its representatives on the spot.

By the late seventies Cathcart, Mitchell, and Gordon had all dropped out, but their places were taken by Hugh Elliot at Berlin and Sir Robert Ainslie at Constantinople. Lord Stormont had been promoted to the Paris embassy and was assisted by William Fullarton of Fullarton as secretary of embassy, while Stormont's old post at Vienna was now occupied by Sir R. M. Keith. When our period ends in 1789, Sir R. M. Keith had served nearly twenty years as envoy at Vienna, and Sir William Hamilton twenty-five years at Naples; Hugh Elliot had spent nearly fifteen years at various foreign courts, and Sir Robert Ainslie nearly as long at Constantinople. Joseph Ewart was at the height of his meteoric career as envoy to Prussia; Robert Liston was envoy to Sweden and Daniel Hailes—if indeed he was a Scotsman—to Poland. Two other Scots, C. H. Fraser and William Lindsay, held minor appointments as secretary of embassy at Madrid and secretary of legation at Petersburg respectively.

This remarkable influx of Scotsmen into what was now becoming an honourable if not lucrative profession did not escape the notice of their English fellow-subjects. Horace Walpole refers to it in his *Journal of the Reign of George III* in December 1773. 'In fact [colonial] governments and embassies were showered on the

Scotch as less ostensible and invidious [than giving them pensions and sinecures], while officers and private men of that nation crowded, or were crowded, into the army and navy.' The hacks who wrote letters to the newspapers in the sixties and seventies found in this theme a congenial subject. 'Whipcord' contributed a remarkable letter to the *Public Advertiser* of 30 March 1773 in which he says:

Let any dispassionate man, not a Scot, now consider the list of the very late appointments to our most lucrative governments and honourable embassies, and then tell me if we are not a ruined and insulted people, if our honour is not lost, if the black whirlpool of the North has not borne down all before it and with unremitting fury *levelled* those venerable, patrician, old English *oaks*, which afforded shelter to our Fathers in every Storm.

Similar citations could be made indefinitely: as late as 1773—ten years after Bute's fall from office—an anti-ministerial writer makes a personal attack on the king:

> Nothing with gentle George's nose will suit
> But Burrs and Thistles from the Isle of Bute.

The contemporary English explanation of this distasteful phenomenon was that it was all the work of the Devil and his servant Lord Bute; but the facts stated in previous paragraphs make this facile generalization quite unacceptable. *Pace* contemporary John Bulls, the Scottish phalanx was well established some years before Bute could have had any direct influence on appointments and there was no marked reduction after his fall from office, nor indeed was there any marked increase during his short tenure of office. But, the Whig journalists argued, Bute, after his fall, continued to influence the king from behind the scenes to secure appointments for his countrymen. If this were true, one would expect a marked diminution in the ranks of Scottish diplomatists after Bute's breach with the king and final disappearance from the political scene in August 1766,[16] especially as Bute himself was compelled to write to at least one close friend and explain his inability to get favours even for his own family. Now a sudden increase after Bute's appointment as secretary of state in 1761 and a rapid decline after his fall in 1763 or 1766 are exactly what did

16 See Romney Segwick's *Letters from George III to Lord Bute*, p. lxviii.

not happen: statistics show a fairly stable number of Scottish diplomatists varying from five to eight in every year from 1760 to 1782 and increasing during the younger Pitt's administration to eight or nine every year up to 1789.

One other Scotsman, Lord Mansfield, was also frequently blamed by newspaper critics for the prevalence of Scotsmen in the public service, but here again there is a complete lack of evidence on which the charge can be reasonably based. No doubt Mansfield's nephew, Lord Stormont, owed his rise to the top of the diplomatic tree partly to Mansfield's influence, but there is a well-known proverb to the effect that one swallow does not make a summer. It is equally clear that these appointments were not made under George III, any more than they had been under Anne immediately after the passing of the Act of Union, with any idea of conciliating Scots nationalism at the expense of English dissatisfaction. Diplomatic appointments were distributed to favourites or suppliants as individuals, irrespective of their English or Scots nationality.

Indeed, as in the case of Admiral Mitchell under Anne, the fact that the applicant was a Scot would in itself be an argument against his appointment, in view of the sensitiveness of English opinion to Scottish appointments. And this latent antagonism was called forth and intensified by Bute's presence for a brief space in the government: Scottish appointments which might hardly have been noticed in the fifties were seized upon by the Whigs and Radicals, who used them to rouse feeling against George III's government in the sixties and seventies. It is recorded of the arch-enemy of the Scots in the sixties on the first-hand authority of the Rev. Dr. Alexander ('Jupiter') Carlyle, that 'the people of that nation [Scotland] were always Wilkes's favourites till 1763 . . . when he became a violent party writer, and wished to raise his fame and fortune on the ruin of Lord Bute'. Carlyle, during a visit to Holland in 1745, met Wilkes frequently and came to know him well, and he tells a quaint story of how Wilkes, then aged eighteen and 'a sprightly entertaining fellow', escaped from his eccentric tutor, whose 'chief object seemed to be to make Wilkes an Arian', and 'Wilkes, for refuge, went frequently to Utrecht where he met with Immateriality Baxter, as he was called, who then attended Lord Blantyre and Mr. Hay of Drummelzier'. Wilkes, with no forethoughts of No. 45 of the *North Briton*, found congenial company in this circle of Scottish students.[17] Bute's sudden rise to power, so far from being the cause of the Scottish appointments, probably hindered Scots penetration of the diplomatic service, since it called forth antagonism to all his fellow countrymen in high places. Thus Lord Hertford on his return to London in 1765 had intended to take David Hume with him as his secretary to Ireland, 'but that, on his arrival at London, he found the cry so loud against the promotion of a Scotsman, that he was obliged to give it up'.[18]

Nothing comparable to this Scottish incursion into the foreign service happened at home until much later—presumably for the reason suggested earlier by Horace Walpole that it was less ostensible and invidious to appoint a Scotsman to a foreign mission or a colonial governorship than to a post of similar rank and emolument at home. Competition was less keen and Scotsmen who secured foreign and colonial jobs came much less into contact with their English fellow-subjects. Walpole's generalization is confirmed by the recent study of the personnel of the English Revenue Commissioners from 1754 to 1798.[19] Scottish names here are few and far between, while of the sixty-two commissioners who had a university education not one came from a Scottish university. A similar state of affairs is revealed by an examination of the semi-official lists of court and civil service appointments which were regularly published in the eighteenth century and no doubt carefully scrutinized by hostile critics of George III's government. On this point it is sufficient to quote a passage from John Wesley's *Journal*:

In my way to Bath [he records] I read a pamphlet which surprized me exceedingly. For many years I had heard the King severely blamed for giving all places of trust and profit to Scotchmen; and this was so positively and continually affirmed that I had no doubt of it. To put the matter beyond all possible dispute, the writer appeals to the Court Calendar of the present year [1778], which contains the names of all those that hold places under the King. And hereby it

---

[17] *Autobiography of the Rev. Dr. Alexander Carlyle* (Edinburgh, 1860), pp. 168–70.

[18] Dr. Hugh Blair in *Caldwell Papers*, pt. ii, vol. ii, p. 45. The preceding paragraphs are quoted from my Historical Association pamphlet, *Scottish Diplomatists 1689–1789*.

[19] W. R. Ward, 'Some Eighteenth Century Civil Servants: the English Revenue Commissioners, 1754–98', in *E.H.R.* lxix (1955), 25–54

appears that of four hundred and fifty odd places, just eight are possessed by Scotchmen; and of the one hundred and fifty-one places in the Royal Household four are possessed by Scots, and no more.[20]

In another place I have drawn attention to the high proportion of these Scottish diplomatists who owed their education to the University of Edinburgh[21] and have attempted to explain the reasons for their success.[22]

It should be noted that there was also an Irish contingent, though it seems to have been smaller in number and less distinguished in achievement. I hope I am not displaying here Scottish chauvinism: no estimate of Irish numbers exists and nothing would please me more than that some Irish nationalist would make such an examination and prove me wrong. One difficulty in giving precise figures here would be that certain diplomatists with Irish connexions would probably have claimed to be English rather than Irish. Not all Irish peers, for example, were Irishmen and officers serving with Irish regiments might turn out to have no other link with Ireland. Genuine Welshmen seem to be even scarcer than Irishmen in the ranks of eighteenth-century diplomatists.

In conclusion, it may be observed that in assimilating the Scots and Irish and eliminating the alien elements which had played such a large part in British diplomacy in the earlier part of our period, the development of our diplomatic service was in line with the general European trend. By the end of the century the diplomatic services of the great European Powers were as overwhelmingly national as their armies. In some countries such as Sweden this had been secured by law: the Swedish constitution of 1720 provided that only Swedes could represent their country abroad.[23] Only in Russia, amongst the great powers, did foreigners continue to play a prominent role in diplomacy in the early part of the nineteenth century.

---

[20] *Journal,* ed. Curnock, vi. 210. J. Hayes reckons that one-fourth of all regimental officers were Scots (*Scot. Hist. Rev.* xxxvii (1958), 23–33).

[21] *University of Edinburgh Journal* (autumn 1944), pp. 27–33.

[22] *Scottish Diplomatists 1689–1789,* pp. 11–15.

[23] *Histoire de l'administration des affaires étrangères de Suède,* ed. Tunberg and others, p. 234.

CHAPTER VII

Education and Training

IT was generally agreed in the eighteenth century that men destined for a diplomatic career should be specially educated and carefully trained. Wicquefort, Callières, and Pecquet all discuss this topic early in their treatises. In Wicquefort's view 'a noble extraction is a singular ornament to embassy; however strength of genius and an excellent nature are incomparably more necessary to the ambassador. But neither birth . . . nor study can form an accomplished ambassador without experience; which consummates what the others only began.'[1] Wicquefort also remarked:

The study of polite literature ought to be a foundation to all the ambassador's knowledge. There true morality is to be learned . . . there is no philosopher that teaches [philosophy] more agreeably than Horace. . . . But the chief study of those that design to be employed in embassies ought to be that of history; I comprehend under that name all that depends thereon and is any way useful to it, as Memoirs, Instructions and Negotiations; and particularly Treaties.[2]

Callières, in the preface to his work, in which he dedicates it to the Regent Orléans, gives as one of his objects 'to exhort those who destine themselves to the foreign service of their country, to render themselves capable of discharging worthily that high, important, and difficult office before entering upon it'.[3] Later in his study Callières explains that the would-be diplomatist should first make himself familiar with European history and politics and with the history, constitutions, and economics of the leading European states as well as with the public law of Europe. Also it is desirable that

before entering the profession of diplomacy the young man should have travelled to the principal courts of Europe . . . at a somewhat riper age when he is more capable of reflection and of appreciating

[1] *The Ambassador and his Functions* (translated by Digby, London, n.d.), p. 53.
[2] Ibid., pp. 51–52.
[3] *On the Manner of Negotiating with Princes*, ed. Whyte (Boston, 1919), p. 3.

the form and spirit of government in each country, and of studying
the merits and faults of princes and ministers. . . . It would be well
that in certain cases they should accompany the King's ambassadors
or envoys as travelling companions. . . . There is nothing better
calculated for instruction upon the manner of events in foreign
countries or for the training of a young man to represent his own
country abroad. It is highly desirable that such novices in diplomacy
should learn foreign languages [so as not to require to depend upon
interpreters]. It is also very useful and fitting for the diplomat . . . to
have such a general knowledge of science as may tend to the development of his understanding, but he must be master of his scientific
knowledge and must not be consumed by it. . . . If one could establish
a rule in France that no one should be employed in negotiation until
he had passed some such apprenticeship as this, and had shown his
capacity to profit by study and travel in rendering a good account of
the countries which he had seen . . . we should be more confident that
the King would be well served in his negotiations, and that by these
means he would be able to raise up around him a large number of
reliable negotiators.[4]

Pecquet is even more emphatic than his predecessors on the
need for special education and training. Callières has failed to
develop the taste for a career in diplomacy in France, but Pecquet
hopes to be more successful. 'C'est au moins dans cette vue que
j'ai entrepris l'ouvrage qui paroît aujourd'hui.'[5] In Pecquet's view
'un négociateur, pour être supérieur, doit être préparé dès l'enfance
à cette profession importante'.[6] He must acquire a knowledge of
foreign languages not merely for ease in negotiation but out of
compliment to the foreigners with whom he is to treat. He must
have a general knowledge of ancient history, particularly of the
causes and consequences of revolutions, and a much more specialized knowledge of modern history. He must study in detail the
classic negotiations of the masters of diplomacy and acquire a
sound knowledge of public and international law. In travelling
abroad the would-be diplomat should study the manners and customs of a country and frequent good society.[7] 'On apprend toute
sa vie à être Négociateur',[8] he concludes, and explains:

Bien que l'état de Négociateur paroisse une chose totalement passa-

---

[4] *On the Manner of Negotiating with Princes*, pp. 48–51.
[5] Pecquet, *Discours sur l'art de négocier* (Paris, 1737), pp. liv–lvi.
[6] Ibid., p. xxxiii.   [7] Ibid., p. li.   [8] Ibid., p. 20.

gère; cependant comme les premiers succès sont un titre pour être emploïé dans de nouvelles Commissions, un Ministre se doit regarder, même dans les momens de repos, comme consacré pour toujours à un service particulier, dont les obligations doivent sans cesse lui être présentes, et faire l'objet de ses études, comme la règle de ses conversations, et de ses démarches. Car, ne nous y trompons pas, ce n'est que la réflexion qui forme les hommes, surtout ceux qui sont destinés à la négociation. Cette méditation devient bien plus utile pour l'avenir, quand une première expérience peut lui servir de guide.[9]

Such extensive quotations from French treatises on diplomacy are justified, since eighteenth-century Britons regarded the French as the supreme masters of the art of diplomacy. When, at the end of the War of the League of Augsburg, Louis XIV filled up his embassies with soldiers, Matthew Prior reported from Paris to Portland:

Count Guiscard is named Ambassador for Sweden for having defended Namur so well; Tallard, d'Harcourt, Guiscard, all *gens d'espée*, are made ministers; the King says they are properer than the *gens de robe* and serve him better. Mons. des Alleurs, another of the same kind of men, has made his court to the elector of Brandenburg in a very new manner....[10]

Wicquefort and Callières were translated into English under the first two Georges and widely used by budding diplomatists. *The Craftsman*[11] commented on Wicquefort's *L'Ambassadeur* and tried to relate it to contemporary diplomacy. In a later number[12] of the same periodical Wicquefort was again quoted on Treaties and Callières's work was mentioned as 'a short and judicious compendium' of Wicquefort's.

Their views were also echoed by native English writers on training for a diplomatic career. Viscount Lonsdale in the reign of William III deplored the absence of such training in England:

He [Lord Lonsdale] had frequent occasions of regretting how very defective this nation was in the education of gentlemen. He remarked that there was sufficient provision for those who devoted themselves to the study of divinity, physic, and the study of the civil law at the Universities; but that the education of gentlemen was a thing so foreign to the notions, birth and studies of those men and the

[9] Ibid., pp. 158–9.
[11] No. lxiii (ii. 188).
[10] H.M.C., *Bath MSS*. iii. 245–6.
[12] No. lxv (ii. 199).

discipline with regard to them so loose, that for a very long time it hath very manifestly been the ruin of all those young persons, who are easily susceptible of bad impressions; while the naturally good and virtuous are instructed in nothing but a little useless sophistry, an awkward garb and habit which requires a long time to unlearn, and which nothing less than two or three years' travel is able to remove. [He adds:] To that negligence are we grown that it is not so much as thought of to educate any in qualifications for foreign ministry or embassy, so that in reality, we are the scorn and contempt of all the Courts of Europe; having scarce anybody that understands anything relating to our own, or the common interest of princes: insomuch that at this time the King is obliged to employ the chaplain of the late envoy in Sweden, and one taken for charity, from a tavern bar, in Germany. In Denmark, I think, he hath none, nor in Italy, nor Switzerland, unless a French refugee.[13]

The author of an anonymous pamphlet, dedicated to Sir Robert Walpole and published in 1730, outlined a comprehensive plan for the education of English diplomatists which owes obvious debts to Callières.[14]

Starting from the assumption that 'the Nobility (caeteris paribus) have an indubitable right to be preferred to the higher offices in the State and to enjoy a greater share of the King's ear',[15] the author turns his attention to fitting them for such employments. 'A graceful deportment . . . and a due proportion of affability and condescension'[16] is a desirable foundation. Truth, virtue, and honour are also essential.[17] After

our young nobleman has made himself acquainted with the nature of government in general, and the constitution of Great Britain in particular, he must then look abroad into the frame of other states; but more especially those which have any intercourse and trade with his own country: and from this enquiry will arise a knowledge of a quite different nature from the former viz the political interest of Nations or Commonwealths with respect to each other.[18]

Later the argument proceeds:

It will, I suppose, be readily owned that a competent knowledge in geography and history is necessary to qualify our young nobleman

[13] *Memoir of the Reign of James II* (York, 1808), pp. viii–ix.
[14] *An Essay on the Education of a young British Nobleman after he leaves the Schools*, &c.   [15] P. 3.
[16] P. 9.   [17] P. 12.   [18] Pp. 15–16.

for rightly understanding the political interest of nations; and as the foundation of that enquiry is commonly first laid by travelling into foreign countries, and conversing with men of letters, the noble youth should be attended by an acceptable companion in his travels. . . . As for history, or the knowledge of past times, what is it else, but making the wisdom of our great forefathers our own? . . . We may, by the advantage of this science, copy all their brave actions, and regulate our lives suitable to the best and most shining parts of their characters. It is the knowledge of the transactions of past ages, that opens our minds and enlarges our views.[19]

Finally:

A general notion of arts and sciences will also be convenient to give him proper ideas of the improvements which are daily making in trade and navigation; with other practical and useful branches of mechanicks. For although these things are not to be considered as proper objects of his study, yet, as his natural genius or ambition for universal knowledge will lead him to dip a little into them, they may be casually laid before him by way of diversion.[20]

After some pages of advice on the choice of a tutor for the Grand Tour, the pamphlet closed on a more original note: 'Before we send this noble youth abroad amongst strangers, it would be of singular use first to let him make a progress through the most remarkable parts of his own country.'[21]

Similar ideas will be found scattered through the works of Lord Chesterfield and especially in the *Letters to his son*. When these letters were first published the blue-stocking Mrs. Montagu pointed out their usefulness for training young men for the diplomatic profession,[22] although Dr. Johnson commented acidly that they 'teach the morals of a whore and the manners of a dancing master'.[23] Chesterfield rightly insisted that merit and knowledge were not enough to command success in a diplomatic career. 'If to your merit and knowledge', he wrote, 'you add the art of pleasing, you may very probably come in time to be Secretary of State; but, take my word for it, twice your merit and knowledge, without the art of pleasing, would at most raise you to the *important post* of Resident at Hamburg or Ratisbon.'[24]

[19] Pp. 21–23.   [20] P. 24.   [21] P. 41.
[22] *Mrs. Montagu*, ed. R. Blunt, i. 285.
[23] Boswell's *Life of Johnson*, ed. Hill, i. 266.
[24] *Letters*, i. 447.

Chesterfield's peculiarity, indeed, is a greater insistence on externals than the classic French authorities accord: in view of the
examples quoted in Chapter VIII probably the need to insist on
these was greater in Britain than in contemporary France. And he
is always careful to link external with mental qualifications:

> Your profession [he wrote to his son] has this agreeable peculiarity
> in it, which is, that it is connected with, and promoted by pleasures;
> and it is the only one in which a thorough knowledge of the world,
> polite manners, and an engaging address, are absolutely necessary.
> If a lawyer knows his law, a parson his divinity, and a *financier* his
> calculations, each may make a figure and a fortune in his profession,
> without great knowledge of the world, and without the manners of
> gentlemen. But your profession throws you into all the intrigues,
> and cabals, as well as pleasures, of Courts; in those windings and laby-
> rinths, a knowledge of the world, a discernment of characters, a
> suppleness and versatility of mind, and an elegancy of manners, must
> be your clue; you must know how to soothe and lull the monsters that
> guard, and how to address and gain the fair that keep, the golden
> fleece. These are the arts and the accomplishments absolutely neces-
> sary for a foreign minister.[25]

When Chesterfield warned his son, an attaché at the Paris embassy, not to let his duties interfere too much with his riding and
insisted that they must not interfere 'with your dancing-master,
who is at this time the most useful and necessary of all the masters
you have or can have',[26] he was not thinking of his son's cutting
a dash at court balls. 'You must dance well', he explained, 'in
order to sit, stand and walk well; and you must do all these well in
order to please.'[27] For much the same reasons eighteenth-century
divines were sometimes persuaded to allow their sons to take
dancing lessons since, as 'Jupiter' Carlyle put it, 'dancing would
make me a more accomplished preacher, if ever I had the honour
to mount the pulpit'.[28]

That Chesterfield failed so totally in his training of his own
son does not prove his ideas unsound: he was dealing with singu-
larly untractable material. Frederick, Prince of Wales, would have
agreed with Chesterfield's insistence upon externals: he 'used
frequently to say that Bute was a fine, showy man, who would
make an excellent ambassador in a court where there was no

---

[25] *Letters*, i. 422.   [26] Ibid., p. 410.
[27] Ibid., p. 387.   [28] *Autobiography*, p. 47.

business'.[29] And, according to Stepney, one of the most regularly employed diplomatists under William III, Callières's 'chief excellency is speaking his own language correctly and politely'.[30] As late as the 1780's the Foreign Secretary, Carmarthen, wrote about a candidate for the Warsaw legation: 'I know some of Sir J[ohn] H[enderson]'s connections and have heard him well-spoken of; he seems a genteel man, and as to outward appearance very fit for the foreign line; probably Venice, or one of the smaller German courts (when vacant) may be agreeable to him',[31] since the Warsaw mission was already promised to another candidate.

Returning to the more general topic of special training and education being required, it should be noted that practical men agreed with the theoreticians of diplomacy that this was desirable, if not essential. Sir R. M. Keith wrote ruefully from Vienna: 'As I hope for mercy, the King should breed his foreign ministers from the cradle to that calling, give them the education of the department they are to belong to, and by denying them the good things which are peculiar to his kingdoms, fit them for the enjoyment of those which belong to others.'[32] And Lord Auckland's views on the education of a diplomat in 1796 did not differ essentially from those held generally at the beginning of the century:

Generally speaking [he wrote] it is to be wished that a foreign minister should, even at his outset, be well grounded in the history and circumstances of his own country and its dependencies; and he should also be well acquainted with the outlines, at least, of the modern states of Europe, their governments and existing alliances; and, in short, with the national transactions and treaties of the last thirty or forty years. It is also useful to have acquired some information respecting the personal history and characters of the several sovereigns now living, and of their respective ministers. Above all it is essential to have studied and practised the French language, so as to be able to converse in it without embarrassment, and to have attained the habit of writing in the English language with accuracy, facility and precision.

The knowledge of the etiquettes of courts, of the unsettled system and principles of the law of nations, of commercial and territorial claims and interests and of past and existing treaties, must be gradually attained to a certain degree; but all this must be a work of time, of steadiness, and of experience. There is nothing discouraging in the

[29] Waldegrave, *Memoirs*, p. 38. [30] H.M.C., *Downshire MSS.* i. 697.
[31] H.M.C., *Leeds MSS.*, p. 53. [32] *Keith Memoir*, i. 442.

prospect, though, at the first view, it seems to be alarming to the mind's eye. It generally happens that a foreign minister passes the first years of his career in stations where there is no call for all the attainments which I have described, and where there is little responsibility.

At any rate, a course of English and French history, from the date of our Revolution, or even from the commencement of the reign of Louis XIV, to the present time would be useful ... and very amusing. [Recommends list of books.] When the foundation is well laid, Mr Stuart [the would-be diplomatist] may have other considerable advantages by an access to Lord Bute's State Papers. I believe that Lord Bute formed a considerable collection, and has added to it. I say nothing of foreign travelling; but it would be very material if Europe were now settled.[33]

It seems unlikely that this *consensus* of opinion on the need for a specialized education and the deficiencies of such training as was available in eighteenth-century Britain produced any practical results. Jenkinson in 1758, while he was undergoing training in the Secretary of State's office, remarked that 'though the English are very great politicians, they have, I believe, fewer books on public law or anything that relates to foreign policy than any other nation in the world'.[34] In 1804 a speaker in the House of Commons remarked, more specifically to the point under discussion, that 'the education of such persons [as are designed for a diplomatic career] should be wholly directed to qualify them for such appointments. Those who were sent to represent his Majesty and the dignity of the country should be men of talent and of character, and not persons who were sent abroad merely because they could not live at home.'[35]

Almost the only official attempt in England to translate these generally held ideas on the education and training of diplomatists into practice was the foundation of the Oxford and Cambridge Regius chairs of modern history in 1724. This scheme was the work of Gibson, bishop of London, who shared the 'illusion of Whig intellectuals that Tory principles could not survive an historical education';[36] and even here, the provision of training for diplomacy was subsidiary to the main aim, which was 'to produce a political change at the Universities'.[37] Twenty young men

---

[33] *Auckland Journal*, iii. 329–31.   [34] *Grenville Papers*, i. 270.
[35] *Parliamentary Debates*, ii. 938.   [36] W. R. Ward, *Georgian Oxford*, p. 132.
[37] C. H. Firth, *Modern Languages at Oxford*, p. 3.

in each university were to be instructed gratuitously in modern history and languages to fit them for the service of the state and, if they proved proficient, given employment at home or abroad. George I appointed two professors of modern history for their instruction. Each professor was to appoint and pay two teachers of modern languages to work under him. All the professors had to do was to give four public lectures at their own university in each academic year. It was clearly stated that the purpose of the scheme was to obviate the necessity of employing persons of foreign nations in the civil and diplomatic services and as tutors to young gentlemen on their travels. The emphasis, therefore, is on language not history teaching. Each scholar was to learn two languages and show progress in periodical examinations.[38] While this is the first scheme of its kind, individual precedents exist in the form of financial assistance occasionally given by the crown to allow promising young men, including Addison,[39] to travel abroad and improve their languages and knowledge of foreign countries.

According to the first report on the Oxford scheme to the Secretary of State only two of the scholars had tackled two modern languages, French and Italian: another six had made progress with French, seven others had made no progress whatever in any modern language.[40] When the second annual report was made to the Secretary of State seven scholars were working at two modern languages, two had made satisfactory progress in French only, six had virtually abandoned the study of modern languages, and three had already secured jobs in Secretary of State Townshend's office or in diplomacy. Two others had left the university, one of them by dying. By the date of the third annual report the scheme itself was clearly moribund. No more appointments had been secured and most of the other scholars had taken Holy orders or left the university.[41] Even if we include scholars who subsequently secured diplomatic appointments the list is short. One scholar was appointed as secretary to Richard Sutton, who was to have gone on a special mission to Berlin, but in the end did not go. This man, William Chetwynd, did, however, go as private secretary to Sutton on a mission to Brunswick-Wolfenbüttel in 1729 and acted there as *chargé d'affaires* for a short time. Another of them, John Burnaby, after a spell in the Secretary of State's office,

[38] Firth, op. cit., pp. 4–7.
[40] Firth, op. cit., pp. 8–9.
[39] Smithers, *Addison*, pp. 42–44.
[41] Ibid., p. 11.

went to Paris as private secretary to Lord Waldegrave and was later secretary at Stockholm from 1739 to 1741 and Minister to the Swiss cantons from 1743 to 1750. Henry Bland, who went to Constantinople with the earl of Kinnoull as his private secretary and was appointed chancellor of the embassy in 1733, was probably another scholar, and Gilbert West may conceivably have been the man Hanbury Williams took with him as private secretary to Dresden in 1747, though this seems unlikely. Whether judged by quality or quantity of the recruits to diplomacy, the Oxford scheme can only be described as a disastrous failure.

The authorities at Oxford had no difficulty in accounting for its collapse. The University was conservative and dominated by the old scholastic learning. Some of the scholars had neither inclination nor aptitude for history and languages. Some people at Oxford did their best to discourage any sort of study which came immediately recommended from the throne.[42] These included notorious Jacobites such as Hearne who referred to the 'pitifull, cringing' address voted to the king on the establishment of the Regius modern history chair.[43] Firth, however, insists that it was the defection of the government which caused the failure of the scheme. When Townshend had provided for three out of twenty scholars he had nothing more to give or else he thought he had given enough.[44] After this the professorship of history and the modern language teacherships became sinecures for the rest of the eighteenth century—indeed well into the nineteenth.[45]

Schemes, different in character and method, but designed to secure a supply of trained men for diplomatic appointments were continually being tried out in continental Europe, though few, if any of them, continued to operate for any length of time. The best known of these was Torcy's scheme at the end of Louis XIV's reign. Six young men were to work in the archives and thereby, by close study of previous negotiations, acquire a grasp of the principles of diplomacy. Another six would also receive special diplomatic training. By 1720 the scheme was dead. Frederick II of Prussia in 1747 set up, on a much smaller scale, a training school for his country, but it was intended merely to produce capable men for subordinate posts and ended in the Seven Years War;

[42] Firth, op. cit., p. 13.
[43] C. E. Mallet, *History of the University of Oxford*, iii. 51.
[44] Op. cit. iii. 13–14.   [45] Ibid. iii. 15–17.

although Frederick made some attempt to revive it in the closing years of his reign. Even the Sultans occasionally experimented in sending young Turks abroad with one of their ambassadors to learn the languages and become familiar with the customs and laws of Western Europe. But the closest resemblance to the Oxford and Cambridge scheme was shown, curiously enough, by the almost contemporary, although slightly earlier, plans of Peter the Great:

Some years ago [before 1721] the Czar began to send at his own expense young men to Königsberg and elsewhere to learn the languages and be otherwise educated. Some of these have now returned to Petersburg and, after being examined, such as are found most capable have been sent to be with the Czar's ministers at foreign courts to give them a polish and fit them for service.[46]

This scheme seems to have been no more permanent than those elsewhere. Catherine II's Establishment of 1779 provided for the attachment of one or two students to be paid by the government to each Russian mission abroad[47] and in 1797 Tsar Paul ordered the admission of thirty young men to the College of Foreign Affairs to be trained.[48]

Although it had no official backing, the University of Edinburgh played the preponderant role in training the Scottish diplomatists of the eighteenth century.[49] The Edinburgh curriculum was broadly based and habits of industry and a taste for study were inculcated. According to Captain Edward Topham, who spent six months at Edinburgh in 1774–5,

there are few places where a polite education can be better acquired than in this city; and where the knowledge requisite to form a gentleman and a man of the world can be sooner obtained. It is one of the greatest faults in our [English] universities that so much attention and importance should be given to studies, which perhaps are of little use to a man in life, when either his fortune or dignity calls on him to exert his knowledge for the happiness of his fellow countrymen: and on the contrary that those qualifications which make a man an

[46] Jefferyes to Polwarth, 15 Feb. 1721, in H.M.C., *Polwarth MSS.* iii. 46.
[47] *Official History of the Ministry of Foreign Affairs* (St. Petersburg, 1902) (in Russian), p. 70.
[48] V. N. Aleksandrenko, *Russian Diplomatic Agents in London in the Eighteenth Century* (in Russian), p. 499.
[49] *University of Edinburgh Journal* (autumn 1944), 'Edinburgh University and the Diplomatic Service 1714–89', pp. 27–33.

amiable friend and an agreeable companion should be held in contempt or perfectly neglected. But here it is quite otherwise. Each
attends that system of lectures which suit either his genius or his
intended pursuits, without restraint or compulsion. No particular
study or science is in higher estimation than another: all are taught;
each has its votaries; and a proper portion of time is allotted to
those inferior qualifications which we every day see assist the greater
accomplishments in the acquisition of reputation and fortune. . . .
Besides the modern languages, music, painting, fencing, riding and
dancing are all taught here in some degree of perfection: and manly
exercises are admired and encouraged. . . . The Scotch are more fond
of fencing than riding and in general excel in it. But their greatest
talent seems to be in acquiring the knowledge of and speaking foreign
languages; which they do with much greater facility than our
countrymen.[50]

When he refers to the facility of the Scots in acquiring foreign
languages, Topham puts his finger upon one of their main advantages as candidates for the diplomatic service.[51]

It should, however, be noted that the classical authors certainly
did not regard a university degree as an essential part of training
for diplomacy. Wicquefort remarked:

I cannot tell whether the men of letters are fitter for embassy than
tradesmen: but I shall not scruple to say, that an ambassador is not
better formed in the college than in the shop. If the one renders us
cowardly and self-interested, the other makes us clownish and
opiniated [sic]; and neither in the one nor in the other is learned what
an ambassador ought to know.

Yet he continues: 'I am so far also from excluding all the learned
from this sort of employment that I could wish that all that enter
upon it were learned, provided that with their learning they had
also all the other necessary qualifications.'[52] In the end he concludes 'neither birth . . . nor study can form an accomplished ambassador without experience; which consummates what the
others only began'.[53]

Callières also deals briefly with this topic:

[50] Edward Topham, *Letters from Edinburgh* (London, 1776), pp. 218–23.
[51] The argument of these two paragraphs is developed and illustrated in
Scottish Diplomatists 1689–1789 (Historical Association Pamphlet, no. 132),
pp. 12–15.
[52] *The Ambassador and his Functions*, pp. 50–51.
[53] Ibid., p. 53.

Other things being equal [he remarked] I prefer a man of letters before one who has not made a habit of study, for his reading will give him a certain equipment which he might otherwise lack. It will adorn his conversation and supply him with the necessary historic setting in which to place his own negotiations; whereas an ignorant man will be able to quote nothing but the will of his master, and will thus present his argument in a naked and unattractive form. It must be obvious that the knowledge gained in a lifetime of reading is an important adjunct in diplomacy, and, above all, the reading of history is to be preferred, for without it the negotiator will be unable to understand the meaning of historical allusions made by other diplomatists, and may thus miss the whole point at some important turn in negotiations. And since it is not enough to think aright, the diplomatist must be able to translate his thoughts into the right language, and conversely he must be able to pierce behind the language of others to their true thoughts. It may often happen that an historical allusion will reveal the purpose of a minister's mind far better than any direct argument. Herein lies the importance of culture in diplomacy.[54]

Many English writers with first-hand experience of English universities and English diplomacy were much less impressed by the advantages of a university education. George Stepney, the leading diplomatist of William III's reign, 'hated all learning'.[55] Malmesbury spoke of one of his colleagues at St. Petersburg as 'merely a man of letters, unacquainted with and unfit for business'.[56] Lady Mary Wortley Montagu believed 'a girl out of a village or a nursery more capable of receiving instruction than a lad just set free from the University. It is not difficult to write on blank paper, but 'tis a tedious, if not an impossible task, to scrape out nonsense already written and put better sense in the place of it.'[57] Chesterfield wrote to his son:

All your Greek will never advance you from Secretary to Envoy, or from Envoy to Ambassador; but your address, your manner, your air, if good, very probably may. . . . I would, upon my word, much rather that you had Lord Bolingbroke's style and eloquence, in speaking and writing, than all the learning of the Academy of Sciences, the Royal Society, and the two Universities united.[58]

[54] *On the Manner of Negotiating with Princes*, ed. Whyte, pp. 62–63.
[55] A. Cunningham, *History of Great Britain*, i. 157.
[56] *Malmesbury Diaries*, i. 260.
[57] *Original Letters from Lady M. W. Montagu to Sir James and Lady Frances Steuart* (Greenock, 1818), pp. 53–54. [58] *Letters*, i. 419.

Malmesbury, undoubtedly the best-known diplomatist of the eighteenth century, looked back at the end of his long career at his education. He recorded his opinion that 'the two years of my life I look back to as most unprofitably spent were those I passed at Merton'. While this may well be true in one sense, he acquired during these two years the lasting friendships, especially with Charles James Fox,[59] which were the essential basis of his later career. After two years at Oxford, Harris spent a year at Leyden,[60] studying the history of Europe, international relations and the Dutch constitution, and frequenting the best society at The Hague and Amsterdam. Next year he made a rather eccentric Grand Tour, visiting Holland, Prussia, Poland, and Paris, which may help to explain his confirmed advocacy in later life of what came to be called the Northern system of alliances. Within a few months of his return to England he secured the post of secretary of embassy to Spain through Lord Shelburne's interest[61] and rapidly climbed the ladder of promotion, being appointed Minister Plenipotentiary in 1770, Envoy Extraordinary and Plenipotentiary in 1777, and Ambassador eleven years later.

If we turn from education to training, the one technical accomplishment demanded of young men who wished to make a career in diplomacy was a knowledge of French. When Gibbon described French as the language of Europe it had already for long been recognized as the language of diplomacy. The anonymous author of *The Ancient and Present State of Germany*, published in 1702, pointed out that 'in truth the French tongue is now grown so common and so familiar in all the courts of Germany that one would think that it was the maternal language of the country'.[62] The last peace conference to record its decisions in Latin was the Congress of Utrecht. At the middle of the eighteenth century Austrian and Prussian diplomatists agreed only on one thing—that French was the language for international discussions and sometimes even for confidential correspondence with their own sovereigns. Even at Madrid, aided no doubt by the accession of a branch of the house of Bourbon, 'the foreign ministers generally make use of the French language to their Catholic Majesties and in writing in

[59] *Malmesbury Diaries*, i. ix. 493.

[60] As did other well-known eighteenth-century English diplomatists, e.g. Benjamin Keene as well as a proportionately larger number of Scots.

[61] *Malmesbury Diaries*, i. ix–xi.

[62] Pp. 218–19.

form to their ministers'.[63] French was almost as much used in Italian and east European courts. British ambassadors sometimes spoke in French in formal audiences at the court of St. Petersburg. Whitworth, sent to apologize to the Tsar for the insult to the Russian ambassador at London, delivered an harangue in English, but his secretary read a translation in French and a Russian secretary then read a translation in Russian for the benefit of the Russian nobles present.[64] When Buckinghamshire declined to make use of French, pleading that his instructions were to make the compliment to the Tsaritsa in English, she replied 'in Russ'; but French was used in Buckinghamshire's formal audience of the Grand Duke Paul.[65] Occasionally, however, the Russian chancellary embarrassed British diplomatists by sending them official papers in German and in Hyndford's opinion the German language was absolutely necessary at St. Petersburg.[66] When a British ambassador was sent to apologize for the violation of Portuguese territorial waters by a British fleet, he intended to offer the formal apology in a French speech.[67]

Inevitably, therefore, candidates for employment were required to possess a knowledge of French. Horatio Walpole 'was frequently heard to say that he never learnt to dance, that he did not pique himself on making a bow, and that he had taught himself French'.[68] None the less, according to his biographer, he 'understood and wrote French with great fluency and propriety and spoke it with equal facility, though with a foreign accent'; while Fleury said of him: 'Il est diablement éloquent avec son mauvais françois.'[69]

Probably this was a higher standard of accomplishment than that reached by most of his contemporaries. It is true that one of our diplomatists, Aglionby under William III, was accused of speaking French too well to be an Englishman,[70] but he was a rare exception. Hans Stanley, putting to Pitt a successful plea to be chosen to negotiate peace with France, explained 'as I have been several times in France and once resided two years at Paris, I not only possess their language with sufficient readiness and

---

[63] *Keene Corresp.*, p. 381.
[64] Dumont and Rousset de Missy, *Supplément*, v. 519.
[65] *Buckinghamshire Corresp.* ii. 77, 80, 196–7.
[66] Add. MS. 11386, fo. 189. [67] *Chatham Corresp.* ii. 18.
[68] Coxe, *Lord Walpole Memoirs*, ii. 453.
[69] Ibid. ii. 460. [70] H.M.C., *Downshire MSS.* i. 215.

accuracy, but I have had opportunities of being introduced to their men of business, of cultivating useful acquaintance, and of acquiring some information with regard to that country'.[71] William Eden, setting out for Paris on a special mission in 1786, confided to his brother: 'I should be very glad to start there in full possession of as good French as you speak; I shall have disadvantages from the want of it, but they are lessening fast, and will lessen every day.'[72] No wonder we hear of a young man who, after a tour on the Continent, 'will be able to speak [French], if not like Mr. Spencer without accent, at any rate sufficiently well for an ambassador, the standard generally aimed at by young Englishmen'.[73]

Naturally enough, Lord Chesterfield fixed his linguistic sights much higher than this:

You cannot conceive [he told his son] what an advantage it will give you in negotiations to possess Italian, German, and French, perfectly, so as to understand all the force and *finesse* of those three languages. If two men of equal talents negotiate together, he who best understands the language in which the negotiation is carried on, will infallibly get the better of the other. The signification and force of one single word is often of great consequence in a treaty, and even in a letter.[74]

Candidates for appointment frequently urged their knowledge of languages other than French. Tyrawley, anxious to succeed Keene at Madrid, claimed to 'speak Spanish, a necessary circumstance at that court'.[75] The second Lord Hardwicke attributed much of Keene's success to his perfect skill in the Spanish language.[76] A knowledge of Italian was useful at Constantinople, and to a certain extent in the Barbary states, where it was also occasionally used as an official language.[77] Sir William Trumbull, while ambassador at Constantinople, wrote approvingly of a candidate for employment: 'He writes so well, and understands Latin tolerably, and French and Italian, and is withal so sober and diligent that whoever employs him will be obliged by the recommendation.'[78] But the duke of Manchester's secretary, Christian Cole, was still better equipped since he could translate into English

[71] *Chatham Corresp.* ii. 117.   [72] *Auckland Journal,* i. 95.
[73] H.M.C., *Palk MSS.,* p. 390.   [74] *Letters,* i. 341.
[75] *Chatham Corresp.* i. 204.   [76] *Keene Corresp.,* p. xxxviii.
[77] *Sutton Desp.,* pp. 113, 183 (but cf. 180 for a Russo-Turkish Treaty of 1713 in French).
[78] H.M.C., *Downshire MSS.* i. 367, of Abraham Stanyan.

from Latin, Italian, French, German, Spanish, and Low-Dutch.[79]
Sir James Porter, a later ambassador at Constantinople, had a 'perfect acquaintance with the French and Italian languages'.[80]

Few English diplomatists had any knowledge of German. Hervey, who was in a position to know, believed in 1737 that 'there were not three natives in England that understood one word of [German] better than in the reign of Queen Anne';[81] and under George III Porter warned his friend, William Gordon, that at Ratisbon 'a secretary who can translate from the German is an essential implement, and if he can, from the Latin better; these two are the languages of the Empire'.[82]

Apart from a knowledge of French as a necessity and other languages as a recommendation, some importance was attached to practical experience. While the formal apprenticeship system of paid and unpaid attachés was the creation of the nineteenth century, the practice by which heads of missions took with them for training young men selected by themselves was firmly established in the eighteenth century. One of these apprentices sometimes did the work of a private secretary: more often secretarial duties were shared. In the larger missions there would normally be a paid private secretary and unpaid attachés all boarded and lodged by the ambassador, while the secrets of the diplomatic profession were gradually revealed to them. They would copy the less confidential papers and dispatches: for this reason Chesterfield regarded 'a genteel, legible, liberal hand, and quick' as necessary equipment for a would-be diplomatist, adding that if he were the ambassador at Paris nothing written in his son's present hand should remain in his bureau.[83]

The attachés also ran errands for their employer and acted in emergency as couriers. They were supposed gradually to learn the distinctions between Confidential, Secret, Most Secret, Private, Apart, and other categories of dispatches and above all never to mix up the embassy business in a general dispatch to the Secretary of State. If he were satisfied with the attaché's progress and reliability, the minister might even employ him to cipher and decipher dispatches. Chesterfield explained all this with his usual accuracy:

[79] Cole, *Memoirs*, p. xi.   [80] Larpent, i. 4.
[81] *Hervey Memoirs*, p. 550.
[82] H.M.C., *Report XII, App. 9* (Aitken MSS.), p. 339.   [83] *Letters*, i. 420.

I am glad [he wrote to his son] that you are employed in Lord Albemarle's bureau; it will teach you at least the mechanical part of that business, such as folding, entering and docketing letters; for you must not imagine that you are into the *fin fin* of the correspondence, nor indeed is it fit that you should at your age. However, use yourself to secrecy as to the letters you either read or write, that in time you may be trusted with *secret, very secret, separate, apart* etc.[84]

While this apprenticeship system came to be regarded with enthusiasm in the nineteenth century, its drawbacks were fully realized by eighteenth-century diplomatists. Sir Paul Rycaut warned one of his successors at Constantinople:

You will have great applications made to you to entertain the sons or relations of gentlemen in order to their preferment or to make their fortunes, and perhaps you will not be able to resist their importunities . . . but you must know that when these gentlemen have been sometime with you, and find that matters there do not correspond with their expectations, they will then desire to return home at your expense and perhaps with various complaints against you.[85]

The wastage rate for attachés was in fact extremely high throughout the period with which we are concerned. As the Earl Marischal explained to James Boswell when the latter was intent on a career in diplomacy: 'Sir, you must begin as secretary, and if you are not with a man to your mind, you are very unhappy. Then, if you should be sent envoy, if you are at a place where there is little to do, you are idle and unhappy. If you have much to do, you are harassed with anxiety.'[86]

Occasionally the practical training was obtained not by going abroad but by serving in the office of one of the secretaries of state or even, still more rarely, in other government offices with no connexion with foreign affairs. George Maddison, after a period of service with the Post Office, became Sir Joseph Yorke's private secretary at The Hague, served as under-secretary to Lord Grantham, when he was secretary of state, and was finally appointed secretary of embassy at Paris, where he died.[87] Nearly a century earlier, Robert Wolseley, envoy at Brussels under William III,

---

[84] *Letters*, i. 410.
[85] H.M.C., *Downshire MSS.* i. 224.
[86] *Boswell on the Grand Tour*, ed. Pottle, pp. 131–2.
[87] Ellis, *Post Office in Eighteenth Century*, p. 94.

had previously been a clerk in the Treasury.[88] But such cases are even rarer than appointments from the offices of the secretaries of state.

As early as 1694 Prior wrote: 'From a seat in the office one may leap abroad after having learnt the routine, and we have precedents of this matter from my lord Arlington to father Vernon.'[89] In 1696 Vernon, at the request of Shrewsbury, asked Prior (who was likely to be secretary to the embassy to negotiate peace with France) 'to reserve a clerk's place for a young gentleman he intends to send over for that occasion, who is now bred in this office ... a youth of great hopes, who writes very prettily, and will copy very well, both in Latin and French; and when he hath had this improvement he is to be returned us again'.[90] Abraham Stanyan had been in the secretary's office before his appointment as secretary to Manchester's first embassy to Venice[91] and seems to have returned to this job until dispatched again abroad with Manchester's embassy to France. Vernon wrote on this occasion to Prior:

[Manchester] has his eye upon [a secretary of embassy] who, I think, is so docile that you may quickly instruct him. I need not tell you it is Mr Stanyan of this office; and as I must part with an useful man for the sake of the embassy, I do not doubt but my Lord Jersey [who was about to take over the duties of secretary of state] will be willing to expect one [i.e. Prior himself who was designed to become Jersey's under-secretary] for a much shorter time.[92]

In a letter to Prior, Jersey's views on the relation between employment abroad and in the secretary's office are clearly stated:

I will first tell you [he wrote] that I cannot disagree with those of your friends who think that the employment you have [secretary of the Paris embassy] gives you a title to something better than a desk to write at in the [secretary's] office; but on the other side I cannot think that it is for your interest to stay abroad, unless you ambition an envoyship to some *petit-prince*, which you may as easily obtain from

[88] S. B. Baxter, *Development of the Treasury*, p. 221. Cf. ibid., p. 182, for a comment on the connexion under William III between the Treasury and diplomatic appointments.
[89] H.M.C., *Bath MSS*. iii. 38.
[90] Ibid., p. 84.
[91] Ibid., p. 109.
[92] Ibid., pp. 335–6.

hence. But if you desire to be settled at home, I know no so sure way as the first getting hither.[93]

These occasional exchanges continued during the Hanoverian period. One or two of George I's Oxford scholars served in the secretary's office before being posted abroad. Sir Stanier Porten, who had served the crown from 1758, was secretary of embassy at Paris from 1766 to 1768, before he became Rochford's under-secretary.[94]

On 19 April 1771 Lord Rochford recommended to the ambassador at Paris a clerk taken from the secretary of state's office to act as the ambassador's private secretary in place of a man who had died at his post 'soon after he transcribed' a dispatch.[95] But on 13 September 1771 Rochford and his brother secretary Suffolk, 'seeing many inconveniences in the practice which has prevailed in some instances of the clerks who have gone with ministers abroad as secretaries continuing to belong to the offices [of the secretaries of state], have determined that they shall, for the future, make their option immediately'.[96] In spite of this ruling, William Henry Higden, who had already served temporarily as secretary to the ambassador at Constantinople in 1777, was in 1783 given leave of absence on health grounds from his clerkship in Lord North's office and sent out to take temporary charge of British interests at Turin.[97] An unsuccessful aspirant to employment who tried this unorthodox route was Charles Jenkinson, later first earl of Liverpool. For two years he acted as a volunteer 'without any profit or emolument' in Holdernesse's office with the design of gaining instruction in foreign affairs.[98] His primary objective was the position of under-secretary but, failing this, he would gladly have accepted appointment abroad;[99] and it was his view, as it was also the opinion of Gibbon's friend, Lord Sheffield, that 'England has for a long time shamefully neglected foreign countries'.[1] Jenkinson therefore wrote pamphlets supporting the government in enforcing against the Dutch 'the rule of 1756' and discussing British interests in furthering peace negotiations with

[93] H.M.C., *Bath MSS.* iii. 354. [94] *George III Corresp.* iii. 12–13.
[95] S.P. 78. 282, dispatches of 23 Jan. and 19 Apr. 1771.
[96] S.P. 94. 187, dispatch of 13 Sept. 1771.
[97] F.O. 67. 3, dispatch of 15 Aug. 1783.
[98] *Grenville Papers*, i. 180.
[99] Ibid., pp. 277, 307.   [1] *Auckland Journal*, i. 443.

France.[2] More successful than Jenkinson was William Eden who secured an under-secretaryship of state and then made it the basis of a prominent and successful career in diplomacy.[3]

More important than a university education, an insinuating manner, a working knowledge of French and other foreign languages, or previous training in diplomacy through experience of the attaché system or employment in the secretary of state's office, in securing an established appointment in the diplomatic service was the possession of the right personal and political connexions. This aspect of the problem will be examined at some length in the next two chapters.

[2] *Jenkinson Papers*, ed. Jucker, pp. viii–ix.
[3] *Auckland Journal*, i. xii.

CHAPTER VIII

Selection—by whom?

In Chapter V the motives which induced Englishmen and Scotsmen to seek appointments in the diplomatic service have been analysed. In this and the following chapter an attempt will be made to deal with the same problem from the opposite end. Who decided upon the claims of candidates to employment abroad and on what grounds were their decisions based? Obviously there can be no single answer to either of these questions. So far as the first is concerned the personal views of the king, although an important factor in decisions affecting most appointments down to 1789, came to have less influence than they had had under William III. For this reason it seems best to begin by considering who had most say in diplomatic appointments between 1689 and 1789.

While it is not strictly true that all foreign appointments were changed at the Revolution,[1] there was almost a clean sweep of James II's men; and it was William III who decided not only who should be sent to a particular court, but whether it was necessary or desirable to send anyone at all. The best indication of the new king's opinion of English politicians' knowledge of foreign affairs is the formal instruction he gave in 1690 to the Committee or Cabinet council, which was to advise the queen in his absence, 'to advise with the Spanish ambassador about foreign affairs'.[2] This being so, he naturally kept foreign appointments in his own hands.

William III decided, at the conclusion of Manchester's special embassy to Venice, that he did not need a resident there.[3] In 1700 he was willing to send a minister but not an ambassador to Venice.[4] It even required a special decision by the king that Manchester, when appointed ambassador to Venice in 1697, should be allowed a secretary of embassy.[5] Similarly, the recall of Herwarth from

---

[1] H.M.C., *Downshire MSS.* i. 335: also Hugo Hughes, who had served James II at Ratisbon, was continued there until at least 1694.

[2] H.M.C., *Finch MSS.* iii. 379.

[3] Cole, *Memoirs*, pp. 11, 28.

[4] Ibid., p. 131.

[5] Ibid., p. 2; H.M.C., *Buccleuch MSS.* ii. 511, 524.

Switzerland was a personal decision of the king who believed that 'there is no occasion for a minister in those parts'.[6] When the Genoese envoy informed the secretary of state that 'the banks and particular persons had' money at Genoa and offered 'if he knew the terms, he would do what he could to serve the King', William resolved instead to send a minister of his own 'on purpose' to the Republic.[7] When he was pressed to send a minister to Ratisbon, he replied, 'I have no occasion for a minister there'.[8] And it was he who recalled, in September 1700, Methuen from Lisbon 'which, I think, His Majesty is the more inclined to out of good husbandry, for he said it was not necessary to have a minister at that place for the present',[9] though he soon changed his mind[10] when circumstances changed. Prior grasped the essential factor in the situation when, writing to his patron Dorset in 1693, he referred wistfully to his friend Stepney who, unlike Prior, could 'almost choose his post, having had the fortune to be placed in such a light that His Majesty has known and approved of him'.[11]

This is not to say that William's advisers, official and unofficial, could not often secure a particular job for a favoured candidate. Portland and Albemarle had certainly more influence upon appointments than any of William's secretaries of state. Even Blathwayt was often accused, by unsuccessful candidates, of responsibility for their ill success and, less often, praised for having forwarded their claims.[12] Jersey, while secretary of state for the southern department, wrote to the secretary of embassy at Paris, who was anxious to return home: 'I suppose Mr Blathwayt will not venture to send you an order to stay [at Paris] without first acquainting me with it.'[13]

Lexington was able to secure nomination for Cressett as secretary of embassy in Spain, although Cressett was unknown both to William III and secretary Nottingham.[14] Yet the idea that the secretaries should have influence over appointments in their own departments already existed. A candidate wrote to one of the secretaries in 1697: 'I am pretty weary of serving and indifferent where I serve, but I would not have the least thought of serving in

---

[6] H.M.C., *Buccleuch MSS.* ii. 104.
[7] Ibid. ii. 275.
[8] H.M.C., *Bath MSS.* iii. 63.
[9] Ibid., p. 414.
[10] Ibid., p. 417.
[11] Ibid., p. 15.
[12] Ibid., p. 62; H.M.C., *Downshire MSS.* i. 520–1, 697–8.
[13] H.M.C., *Bath MSS.* iii. 362.
[14] H.M.C., *Finch MSS.* iii. 48, 128, 133.

your province without your consent.'[15] But the whole tenor of the correspondence between William III and his secretaries suggests that secretarial consent was unlikely to be withheld. Thus Nottingham, after giving advice on a subsidy treaty with Denmark, winds up: 'But I humbly beg your Majesty's pardon if I seem to give any opinion in an affair of this nature, for I intended only to remind your Majesty of such matters of fact as relate to it, that thereupon I might receive your pleasure and obey it.'[16] Shrewsbury wrote in a similar strain in 1696:

When his Majesty shall be informed what we are able to do, I hope he is so well instructed in the interests and inclinations of the Allies that he will take such resolutions as shall be most proper for the circumstances; and we, at least I, who see not far into these foreign mysteries, must submit and endeavour to support whatever is determined in the best manner we can.[17]

On occasion, however, Shrewsbury did recommend appointments to the king, e.g. that of Prior as secretary of embassy.[18] He also urged the king to promote Stepney and Cressett, though he was careful in the case of the latter, who was serving in the other province, to explain that he had the prior approval of the other secretary.[19] Aglionby in 1704[20] and other diplomatists believed that they owed their appointments to Nottingham; and this belief was shared by Godolphin.[21]

Under Anne there was, in the sphere of diplomatic appointments as elsewhere, a significant decline in the personal influence of the monarch. A contemporary diplomatist, who wrote a history of the reign, attributed the continued employment of the Rev. John Robinson abroad to a desire to please the clergy, 'who were proud to have men of their order employed in offices of state'.[22] Anne, as the Church's daughter, may have shared this feeling; but it is indeed difficult to point to cases where the queen was personally responsible for the choice of her diplomatists. According to herself, she 'always thought it very wrong to send people abroad of mean extraction'. Yet on receiving assurances from Oxford that 'Mr Prior will be very useful at this time' she com-

[15] H.M.C., *Downshire MSS.* i. 765.   [16] H.M.C., *Finch MSS.* ii. 420.
[17] H.M.C., *Buccleuch MSS.* ii. 378.   [18] Ibid., p. 397.
[19] Ibid., pp. 479, 484.
[20] H.M.C., *Report I, App.*, p. 15.   [21] *Infra*, p. 147.
[22] A. Cunningham, *History of Great Britain*, i. 320–1.

plied with Oxford's wishes.[23] Although Godolphin in 1704 blamed
upon the senior secretary of state in the first two years of the new
reign the unsatisfactory appointments which had been made in
this short period,[24] the main beneficiaries from the reduced influence of the sovereign were not, in fact, the secretaries of state.

Between 1702 and 1710 Godolphin's influence upon these appointments is easily traceable. He followed up his criticism of
Nottingham's appointments[25] between 1702 and 1704 by proposing Harley's cousin, Tom Harley, for the key appointment. Next
year, when he was unable to grant a favour at home to an applicant's brother, he proposed to Harley, 'if the Queen pleases and it
be not too late, why should not G. Granville [the applicant] have
a mind to go abroad to one of those Northern kings? I think that
it is the readiest way for him to be made easy at home.'[26] And
when Stepney was taken ill in 1707 Marlborough wrote to Harley:
'I have writ to Lord Treasurer to know if he has anybody in his
thoughts to fill Mr Stepney's employment if he should die. I hope
you will agree on such a one as may be able not only to help but
direct me, for in this country all things are in great confusion.'[27]
Godolphin's influence in foreign affairs did not end with the
appointments. He summoned Harley to talk with him at his
house on foreign affairs.[28] Harley sent him private letters from
abroad with the remark that 'the public letters are delivered to
Mr Secretary Hedges, who I doubt not hath attended your lordship with them'.[29] And Marlborough suggested Harley should
'advise with Lord Treasurer' about informing Robinson that
Marlborough is secretly designed to go on a special mission to the
King of Sweden.[30]

Particularly since many missions were as much military as
diplomatic in character, Marlborough was often influential: but
his influence, up to 1712, extended far beyond quasi-military missions. Often he gave unsolicited advice to the queen and her official
advisers about diplomatic appointments. In 1702 he pressed the
claims of Alexander Stanhope in preference to those of Poley and

---

[23] H.M.C., *Bath MSS*. i. 217.   [24] Ibid., p. 63.
[25] 'The truth is, all the ministers sent abroad by my Lord Nottingham have
hitherto done us more hurt than good, and the sooner they are all changed, not
Mr Hill excepted, the better' (H.M.C., *Bath MSS*. i. 63).
[26] Ibid., p. 77.   [27] Ibid., p. 181.
[28] Ibid., pp. 80, 186.   [29] Ibid., p. 109.
[30] Ibid., p. 168.

also advised against giving the count de Frise 'the forms and powers of an envoy'.[31] In 1705 he assured Stepney:

You will see I have endeavoured to justify you from any blame they [the court of Vienna] may pretend to lay at your door, and you may depend upon it that the Queen will have so just a regard to your services as not to remove you until her Majesty has provided otherwise for you, wherein you may be assured at all times of my good offices wherever they may be wanting.[32]

In the following year he advised the sending of Lord Raby to Vienna[33] and urged the Treasurer to secure the transfer of Stepney to Brussels.[34] He felt so sure that this latter recommendation would be acted upon (as it in fact was) that he wrote to warn Stepney to prepare himself to leave Vienna.[35] When Stepney was taken ill, Marlborough wrote to Godolphin: 'If I knew anybody proper for this station, I would take the liberty of naming him',[36] and he arranged for Stepney's ex-secretary, Laws, to receive a 'Character' at Brussels in 1708.[37] When his subordinate, Stair, was sent on a special mission to Poland in 1709, he carried with him something like a private credential letter from Marlborough.[38] And it was Marlborough who authorized Stair to return to his army duties in the spring of 1710:

My Lord Stair being very impatient to be at his command here [Marlborough informed the secretary of state] I have written to the King [of Poland] to desire he will approve of his [Stair's] coming, and assured him [Stair] shall return [to Warsaw] whenever he shall think his presence necessary to him, to which I hope her Majesty will be pleased to give her approbation.[39]

Once these men were formally appointed Marlborough often inspired the instructions they received. Moreover, he did not hesitate to send them private letters which were to all intents and purposes additional instructions. He advised Sir David Mitchell, a naval officer sent to The Hague to treat about naval quotas, to remain there 'a little longer, in hopes the States may at last be induced to come into the measures her Majesty proposes for the

---

[31] *Marlborough Dispatches*, ed. Murray, i. 8.
[32] Ibid. i. 575. [33] H.M.C., *Bath MSS*. i. 94.
[34] *Marlborough Dispatches*, iii. 84. [35] Ibid. iii. 91.
[36] Quoted Eves, *Matthew Prior*, p. 202.
[37] *Marlborough Dispatches*, iv. 161.
[38] Ibid., pp. 663-4. [39] Ibid. v. 14.

public good'.[40] When difficulties arose over the withdrawal of Prussian troops, Marlborough wrote to Lord Raby at Berlin:

The Queen, who has been made acquainted with it, is under no less concern, and would have signified her directions to you in this matter by the secretary of state, but that it is thought what comes from me may be better taken. I am, therefore, commanded to desire your lordship will take the first opportunity to represent to the Court, and even to the King himself, in the most serious manner, the concern her Majesty is under.[41]

When Sir Philip Meadows was sent to Vienna, Marlborough supplied him with letters of introduction and advice. He even ordered Chetwynd, envoy to Savoy, to purchase gunpowder and ball at Leghorn and Genoa without waiting for orders from England.[42] Palmes, who succeeded Meadows at Vienna, was also 'one of the favourites of my lord Marlborough'.[43]

Apart from the men who owed their appointments largely to Marlborough, a list could easily be compiled of men who vainly tried to invoke his support for their claims to a diplomatic post. Thus Sir Rowland Gwynne wrote from Hanover to Harley in 1705:

There are many letters come to this court that Mr Poley is to be recalled. If I had the honour to serve her Majesty in this court, I believe I should be as capable of it as any other. . . . I have writ to my Lord Duke [of Marlborough] upon this point. Therefore I pray at least that you will put a stop to the declaration of anybody till you hear from his Grace.[44]

On the question of responsibility for diplomatic appointments in Anne's reign after the decline and fall of Marlborough and Godolphin, there is much valuable evidence in the *Bolingbroke Correspondence*. While he was secretary of state Bolingbroke looked on certain foreign ministers as standing in a particularly close relationship to himself and sometimes implied that they owed their appointment or promotion to him. When Drummond was appointed to the joint office of consul at Ostend and Resident at Brussels, Bolingbroke implied that this was his doing, though it should be noted that Drummond was also on confidential terms with Lord Treasurer Oxford.[45]

---

[40] Ibid. i. 579.   [41] Ibid. ii. 415.   [42] Ibid. iii. 399–400.
[43] H.M.C., *Portland MSS.* iv. 469.   [44] Ibid. iv. 181.
[45] *Bolingbroke Corresp.* ii. 317; H.M.C., *Portland MSS.* iv. 617.

It would seem that the Lord Treasurer was from 1710 to 1714 more influential than the secretaries of state, although both were concerned with diplomatic appointments. When a minister and commissaries were to be appointed to Madrid in 1713, Bolingbroke wrote to the queen: 'I shall put my Lord Treasurer in mind to be ready to offer such persons to your Majesty as you may depend upon for both these pressing services.'[46] In another letter, addressed to Oxford as Lord Treasurer, Bolingbroke expressly asked 'to have your Lordship's orders what you would have me say to the Queen and write to Prior' about the naming of an envoy to France.[47] He even invited Oxford to correct his drafts and instructions.[48] Strafford, the leading diplomatist of Anne's closing years, depicted himself consistently as the favoured client of the Lord Treasurer.[49] While he was negotiating the treaty of Utrecht Strafford wrote regularly to Oxford, and on occasion informed him of things he did not think it proper to put into a letter to the secretary of state.[50] Earlier than this, in August 1712, he had applied privately to the Treasurer for instructions in what he called 'the most critical juncture' of the negotiation.[51] When St. John proposed to send Henry Watkins, secretary of embassy at The Hague, with a letter to the emperor which Queen Anne had altered unknown to St. John, she inquired of Oxford whether he thought Watkins a proper person.[52] Yet when Bolingbroke and Oxford quarrelled over the recall of Prior and the sending of a minister of higher rank to France in 1713–14, a deadlock was apparently reached[53] and the Treasurer endorsed a letter from Bolingbroke, dated 20 April 1714, in which, as a compromise, the sending of Prior to Baden was proposed: 'He [Bolingbroke] has opposed me about a minister for Baden ever since the peace of Rastadt was known to be concluded and that I proposed one.'[54]

Under the Hanoverian kings appointments continued to be the resultant of a triangle of forces, varying in strength according to personalities and also according to the importance of the appointment. As a rule there would be some discussion between the king, the First Lord of the Treasury, and the secretary of state in whose

[46] *Bolingbroke Corresp.* ii. 533.
[47] H.M.C., *Portland MSS.* v. 339.
[48] Ibid., p. 195.
[49] Ibid. ix. 384–5.
[50] Ibid., p. 392.
[51] Ibid., p. 335.
[52] H.M.C., *Bath MSS.* i. 215.
[53] Eves, *Matthew Prior*, pp. 292–3.
[54] H.M.C., *Portland MSS.* v. 423.

province the post lay. Not infrequently the other secretary would also be consulted, especially if he were regarded, or even regarded himself, as the leading minister for foreign affairs. Important appointments were sometimes approved by the whole Cabinet. When Harris was to be sent to The Hague in May 1784 Carmarthen told him 'that all his Majesty's confidential servants were unanimous in their opinion that I was the properest man to be sent to Holland'.[55] Nevertheless, George III had forecast Harris's appointment six months earlier,[56] before the Pitt ministry had taken office, and the post seems originally to have been offered to Harris by his friend C. J. Fox as early as April 1783.[57] This illustrates the difficulty of assessing precisely responsibility for a particular appointment amongst those concerned.

George I was personally more active in making such appointments than Anne had been, though he must have been hampered at first by lack of personal knowledge of the candidates. While he was First Lord from 1718 to 1721 Sunderland's influence was considerable. Robethon reported that Carteret, who was about to become Secretary of State, had already (in February 1721) influenced Sunderland to employ Polwarth 'in some great embassy, but does not know whether it will be Vienna, Cambrai or Paris'.[58] Diplomatists whose original appointments were not due to the First Lord of the Treasury were well advised to cultivate his good graces. When Polwarth was ambassador at Cambrai a friend wrote to him:

This [correspondence with Sir Robert Walpole] I think you ought to cultivate. . . . His having the direction of money affairs gives you a handle for writing to him and if you shall then continue to give him hints of your proceedings, though it does not properly belong to his post, and that you are not obliged to it in form, I should think it will be well taken and at least make him favour you in your money matters and likewise take off any impressions he may have received of your being C[artere]t's creature; and I do not see how any that wishes you well can take such a correspondence amiss.[59]

[55] *Malmesbury Diaries*, ii. 72.
[56] *George III Corresp.* vi. 455, apparently on the ground that 'he would certainly carry his head high enough, which at the present hour seems absolutely incumbent on whoever goes from hence'.
[57] *Malmesbury Diaries*, ii. 48, 68–69.
[58] H.M.C., *Polwarth MSS.* iii. 48.
[59] Ibid. iii. 287.

Yet the First Lord did not always get his own way. Walpole in 1737 proposed to send Hanbury Williams on a special mission to Don Carlos, but the secretary of state for the southern department objected and finally secured the job for another candidate.[60] Probably more typical was the case of Villiers, who owed his original appointment to Sir Robert Walpole, acting in close concert with Queen Caroline. George II at Hanover had previously been inclined to postpone making an appointment to the Polish legation, but on receiving Walpole's recommendation he 'readily agreed to the nomination of Mr Villiers'.[61] Horatio Walpole, brother of Sir Robert, had a voice in many appointments in the early years of George II's reign and remarked complacently towards the end of his active career: 'However unable I may have been in my foreign negotiations, I have the satisfaction at last to find that those that are now avowedly the most able to serve abroad have either been educated in that business or recommended to it by me.'[62]

But there were occasions when George II resisted the recommendations of the Walpole brothers. He refused 'in a pretty peremptory way'[63] to appoint Trevor, a protégé of Horatio Walpole, as envoy extraordinary and plenipotentiary to The Hague, in spite of the fact that the Walpoles had taken the precaution to secure the support of Harrington, the secretary of state in whose province the post lay. Horatio had to write to Trevor: 'Let not, dear Trevor, your personal desires and disappointment alter your personal friendship and regard for those that have it not in their power to prevent this disappointment.'[64] Trevor's indignation was intense:

His Majesty [he wrote to Horatio] was pleased to value my services, or rather his own character, at The Hague at five pounds a day and *no more*. . . . Had I indeed a fortune of my own, out of which I could make up the difference, I would sacrifice it, sooner than let the world see how cheap our royal master holds my past and future endeavours to serve him. But for want of that I have no resource left, but to conjure your excellency to continue me your friendship and protection.[65]

[60] H. Walpole to Williams, 10 Sept. 1737, N.S. (Newport Public Library): *Hervey Memoirs*, pp. 829–30.
[61] Coxe, *Walpole Memoirs*, iii. 366, 370.
[62] Coxe, *Lord Walpole Memoirs*, i. 298.
[63] Coxe, *Walpole Memoirs*, iii. 533–4.
[64] Coxe, *Lord Walpole Memoirs*, i. 410.
[65] Coxe, *Walpole Memoirs*, iii. 539.

This was in August 1739: not until July 1741 after a battle royal with the king did Trevor finally receive credentials as envoy extra-ordinary and plenipotentiary.[66]

Horatio Walpole records another example of George II's personal intervention when the king absolutely refused to give Robinson either 'an augmentation of salary or an additional place' to induce him to return to Vienna and indeed gave 'positive orders for putting an end to his appointments'. Robinson then capitulated and returned to his post on the same terms as before.[67] Again, when Mitchell was proposed for a special mission to Vienna in 1755, the leading ministers thought he had neither the rank nor the experience required; but, since George II vetoed the sending of anyone with higher rank (and pay), they could suggest no one else.[68] On another occasion George II put an absolute negative on the choice of Chesterfield as ambassador to Holland, adding (to Newcastle) 'a peremptory command not to trouble him with any more of *such nonsense*'.[69] Yet this time also the king ultimately gave way.

One of Newcastle's grievances during Carteret's period of supremacy in foreign affairs was that 'most of the material foreign ministers are as much attached to a certain person [Carteret], and act as much in concert with him as formerly; and, what is worse, I am afraid that it is not only known but approved and done in concert with somebody else [the king]'.[70] After the triumph of the Pelhams in 1746 there was still a similar division—at The Hague, for example, there were two British ministers, one representing Newcastle and the other Chesterfield. Partly owing to these divisions, George II, while receiving suggestions from his ministers, was often able to keep the final decision in his own hands. At the end of the Austrian Succession War he approved of sending some proper person to Paris, but would not absolutely fix upon Joseph Yorke, whose claims were being pressed by Newcastle and others. At the same time George was inclined to send Holdernesse to The Hague 'but that is not quite fixed'.[71] When Newcastle crossed to

---

[66] In the meantime he had been envoy only, without either the rank or pay of plenipotentiary, at The Hague.
[67] H.M.C., *14th Report, App. IX* (Trevor MSS.), p. 14.
[68] Add. MS. 32855, fo. 353b.
[69] Add. MS. 35408, fo. 99, quoted Owen, *Rise of the Pelhams*, p. 244.
[70] Add. MS. 32804, fos. 231–2, quoted ibid., p. 276.
[71] *Bedford Corresp.* i. 397.

Hanover with the king shortly afterwards, he reported to his brother-secretary Bedford: 'The Duke [of Cumberland] wishes that Lord Rochford might go to Portugal in the room of Keene; if you have no objection to it I will speak to the King upon it. . . . I shall not presume to interfere in any of those things.'[72]

George II on at least one occasion took a very unfavourable view of the motives which influenced candidates for employment abroad. Speaking to Carteret of James Porter, the king remarked: 'Did not I tell you he is the only young man who serves [abroad] through zeal and affection?'[73] Hardwicke warned his son Joseph Yorke that his mission 'in Holland may be of very uncertain duration; but as Lord Holdernesse will, I believe, keep in, and the king is extremely well disposed to you, it may not improbably be continued. However that must not be depended upon.'[74] Shortly afterwards George II gave Hardwicke the assurance of his 'strong approbation of [Joe's] services, and of his intention to continue him in Holland', adding 'I won't suffer them to change my foreign ministers at their humour'.[75] In spite of this royal protestation, if the king's ministers were resolute and united, they could by this time ultimately impose their candidate upon a reluctant sovereign.

Walpole's was the dominant influence in sending Harrington to conclude the treaty of Seville in 1729, though Newcastle warmly approved.[76] Pelham, when First Lord, was naturally consulted about Robinson's emoluments as ambassador to the Congress at Aix-la-Chapelle.[77] Soon afterwards George II, on Newcastle's proposal, approved Richmond's appointment to the Paris embassy.[78] On at least one occasion about this time, according to Horace Walpole, there was such competition for an appointment at home 'that at last Mr Pelham said he would carry in two names to the King and he should choose (a great indulgence!). Sir Peter Warren and Villiers were carried in; the King chose the latter.'[79]

George III's attitude to diplomatic patronage did not differ materialy from that of his grandfather. It may even be that his personal influence was in practice greater than that of his immediate predecessor. Certainly when his secretaries of state proposed candidates to the king they were usually tactful enough to imply

[72] *Bedford Corresp.* i. 440.
[74] Yorke, *Hardwicke*, ii. 334.
[76] Coxe, *Walpole Memoirs*, ii. 651.
[77] *Bedford Corresp.* i. 443.
[78] Ibid. i. 463–4.

[73] Larpent, i. 472.
[75] Ibid. ii. 337.

[79] *Letters*, ii. 355.

that the final decision lay with their royal master.[80] At least once when relations between the king and the leading ministers were strained the latter offered to appoint a man whose claims were supported by the king to a foreign embassy in the hope of meriting the continuance of royal favour.[81] If he could not always determine the final decision, George wished to maintain at least an effective royal veto on diplomatic appointments.[82]

Early in the new reign Rigby wrote to Bedford: 'Lord Bute has assured me your Grace may depend upon your release [from the Paris embassy] at the time you desire it, and he will tell you your successor when the King has determined upon him.'[83] By this time, however, if not earlier, the right of the secretary of state to a voice in making appointments in his own province, but not actual nomination to a vacant post, was so clearly established that when Grafton was anxious to drive Shelburne out of the ministry in 1768 without breaking completely with Pitt, he proposed to appoint Lynch to the Sardinian legation, which was in Shelburne's province. He hoped in this way to force Shelburne's resignation on a trivial matter in which he could not expect Chatham's support. Instead of resigning, Shelburne proposed another candidate for the post and, when Grafton opposed his nominee, George III 'previous to . . . coming to any decision' referred the dispute to 'those usually consulted on state affairs'.[84] When Shelburne persisted, 'after the opinions of most of the other confidential ministers were totally adverse', George III expressed his surprise and told Shelburne that 'as he could not recommend a proper person, I [the king] proposed to send Mr Lynch, to which he seemed to acquiesce, but I find sends an express this evening to summon Lieutenant General Conway to the meeting, from some desire of mischief'.[85] Shelburne's indignation was natural: he had already informed the court of Turin that he intended to secure the appointment for his own candidate. The nomination of Lynch

[80] See, e.g., Grantham's letter and the king's reply in *George III Corresp.* v. 225–6.
[81] *Narrative of Changes in the Ministry*, ed. Bateson (Camden Society N.s. 59), p. 76.
[82] Quite eccentric influences occasionally had effects on appointments. Lord Whitworth is said to have owed to Marie Antoinette of France his nomination as minister plenipotentiary to Russia in 1785 (*D.N.B.*, *sub* Whitworth).
[83] *Bedford Corresp.* iii. 211.
[84] *George III Corresp.* ii. 29
[85] Ibid., pp. 46–47.

would therefore convince the Sardinian government of 'the little weight he [Shelburne] can have even in his own department'.[86] The dispute seems to have been still unsettled when Chatham, warned of Shelburne's impending dismissal, resigned office.

Later in the reign George III summarized his views on royal participation in appointments in a letter to Lord North:

The greatest part of your difficulties arise from entering too far with others in plans of business but particularly arrangements of employments, without fairly stating your sentiments unto Me; if on the contrary you sounded my opinion first you would save much trouble and vexation to both of us, and where can you repose your undigested thoughts more safely than in the breast of one who has ever treated you more as his friend than Minister, and who would perhaps frequently put you on your guard against things which if consented to from your being hampered disgrace my service, or if refused distress your mind.[87]

He was not referring specifically to diplomatic appointments, though there seems no reason to think that he would not have applied the same principle to the leading posts abroad.

Though George is usually regarded as a believer in departmental government, he sometimes advocated the right of the First Lord to a voice in diplomatic appointments. When, at the end of the Seven Years War, vacant posts were being filled, he expressed his surprise that the First Lord, George Grenville, had not been consulted by the secretaries of state.[88] Again, when the secretaries pressed Grenville to agree to recall Yorke from The Hague to make way for Hans Stanley, Grenville objected, was supported by the king, and Yorke remained at his post.[89] Yet, in opposition, Grenville argued 'that the secretary of state ought to have the appointment of the ministers in his department, because he was answerable for their dispatches and ought to give them their instructions'.[90] But inevitably, whenever difficulties arose, discussions took place between the leading ministers and the king, as they did over filling the Spanish embassy in 1766 between Chatham, Lord Privy Seal, the two secretaries, and the First Lord of the Treasury.[91]

---

[86] George III Corresp. ii. 49: see, for an interesting comment on this affair, Grenville Papers, iv. 308–9.
[87] George III Corresp. iv. 163.
[88] Grenville Papers, ii. 219.
[89] Ibid., pp. 221–2.
[90] Ibid. iv. 217.
[91] Chatham Corresp. iii. 97, 104–7, &c.

So far we have been concerned with the more important appointments, i.e. heads of missions of varying rank. Secretaries of embassy require separate treatment. In some continental states, including France, they were appointed, lodged, and paid by the ambassador: in others, notably Sweden,[92] they were appointed by the government and seem to have been regarded as a useful check on the activities of their official chiefs. In British practice the right of appointment lay in the crown and they were always regarded as a part of the official diplomatic establishment.

Under William III a personal decision by the king that the ambassador needed a secretary of embassy was required,[93] and under Anne the normal procedure was probably consultation between the queen and her Lord Treasurer. In both reigns, however, the ambassador had a large share in the actual choice of a secretary of embassy. When Manchester was being dispatched to Venice in 1697, he first petitioned to be allowed a secretary. When the king's consent was intimated to him he proposed Stanyan; and finally Blathwayt informed Shrewsbury that

as the King has declared his pleasure that a secretary of the embassy be appointed to attend my Lord Manchester, so Mr Stanyan is the person his Majesty does approve of for that employment; which I would not delay signifying to your Grace, being informed by Mr Chancellor of the Exchequer [Charles Montague] of his being the person proposed by your Grace to his Majesty.[94]

While the royal right of appointment was jealously maintained, it soon became nearly uniform practice to allow the ambassador to choose his secretary of embassy as Keene chose Charles Townshend in 1751.[95] The peers who represented Britain at the French court after 1763 usually proposed a candidate who was then appointed by the crown. One chose his younger brother, others their private secretaries or chaplains. When Bedford was about to leave for Paris to negotiate peace at the end of the Seven Years War, he asked Bute 'who the King intended to send as secretary of embassy?' Bute replied 'that the choice of secretary of embassy would be left' to Bedford, who shortly afterwards 'in pursuance of the liberty His Majesty gave' recommended Aldworth.[96]

[92] *Histoire de l'administration des affaires étrangères de Suède*, ed. Tunberg and others, especially p. 334.   [93] *Supra*, Chapter VIII, p. 144.
[94] H.M.C., *Buccleuch MSS.* ii. 511–12, 524. 529–30.
[95] *Keene Corresp.*, p. 312.   [96] *Bedford Corresp.* iii. 90, 93.

SELECTION—BY WHOM?

Hertford, one of Bedford's successors at the Paris embassy, protested furiously to Grenville when Bunbury was named by the king as his secretary of embassy. Grenville, with difficulty, persuaded George III not to send Bunbury to Paris 'during the present session of Parliament'. Hertford remained dissatisfied, arguing that 'my credit, in this country as well as my own, being so much affected by [Bunbury's appointment] will, I am assured, justify me for pleading against a disgrace which never fell upon any of my predecessors in this place'. But George III refused to cancel the formal appointment already made: Grenville could only hold out to Hertford the hope that if some other arrangement could be found for Bunbury 'the King will avoid any further difficulty upon the subject by not appointing any other secretary to the embassy, in like manner as has been done both at St. Petersburg and The Hague'. Not until 31 May 1765 were Bunbury's allowances determined and on 3 July 1765, on the eve of Hertford's return to England, his own candidate, David Hume, secured at last the coveted appointment.[97] In the absence of the ambassador it was essential to have someone at Paris with an official character.[98] In the meantime Hume, in a letter to a friend, described his position at Paris:

I am not secretary [of embassy] at all, but do the business . . . without any character. Bunbury has the commission and appointment[s] —a young man of three or four and twenty, somewhat vain and ignorant, whom Lord Hertford refused to accept of, as thinking he would be of no use to him. The King gave me a pension of £200 a year for life to engage me to attend his Lordship. My Lord is very impatient to have me secretary to the embassy. . . . The King has promised that my Lord Hertford shall soon be satisfied in this particular; and yet I know not how. I suspect that some obstacle will yet interpose, though nothing can be more scandalous than for a man to enjoy the revenue of an office which is exercised by another. Mr. Bunbury has great interest, being married to a sister of the duke of Richmond and sister-in-law to Lord Holland. The appointments of this office are above £1000 a year, and the expense attending it nothing; and it leads to all the great employments.[99]

Other ambassadors were less persistent than Hertford. When Manchester's secretary of embassy died at Paris, he wrote to Fox,

[97] *Grenville Papers*, ii. 186–7, 247–8, 257–8.   [98] Ibid., pp. 413–14.
[99] Brougham, *Lives of Men of Letters*, i. 248–9.

the Foreign Secretary, that 'the persons mentioned by the duke of Portland and yourself (for successors to Mr Maddison) are, I doubt not, all very proper'.[1] Stormont, on the other hand, chose Fullarton as secretary of embassy in succession to St. Paul;[2] and Rochford as ambassador at Madrid secured the appointment of secretary of embassy for his private secretary, De Visme.[3]

When secretaries of legation appeared in the 1780's they, too, are often the nominees of their immediate superiors. Sir R. M. Keith at Vienna was furious when Hammond, a clerk in the secretary of state's office, was to be specially sent out to fill the newly created post at Vienna. Ultimately Keith secured the appointment of Straton, his own private secretary, and Hammond returned to England.[4]

How awkward things could become with an ambassador and an uncongenial secretary of embassy actually at the embassy is shown by the relations between the earl of Bristol, while ambassador at Madrid, and the secretary of embassy, Ruvigny de Cosne, who had originally been sent to assist the previous ambassador, Benjamin Keene; and, on Keene's death, had been in charge of affairs for nearly a year before Bristol's arrival.

At the beginning of my being in this country Colonel de Cosne always followed me into his closet when I was sent for, and the single time I perceived M. Wall the least moved, when upon the subject of our privateers, was when Colonel de Cosne took the lead in the discourse whilst I was present, and occasioned the Spanish minister's expressing himself to him, but not to me, with the warmth I mentioned in one of my public letters. . . . Since that time I have always gone into the closet alone; and if Colonel de Cosne had persevered in accompanying me, it was settled by M. Wall, through the Conde de Fuentes, that he was to come on extraordinary days, and meet me by myself halfway between Villa Viciosa and Madrid.

I hope sir, you will not disapprove of my determining not to content myself with the name of the King's ambassador, and of my resolution to be so in reality. I have, for that reason, not suffered even one of the office letters I have written to M. Wall, to be penned by any

---

[1] *Memorials of C. J. Fox*, ii. 157. The appointment of the historian Gibbon would have been resented by Louis XVI because Gibbon had written of the French sceptre slumbering in the hands of an Arcadius or Honorius.

[2] S.P. 78, 303, letter of 2 July 1777.

[3] S.P. 94. 170, dispatch of 7 Mar. 1765.

[4] *Keith Memoir*, ii. 233, 235, 247.

other than myself, although Colonel de Cosne had offered me for my signing two he had drawn up; but I think I should be wanting in my duty to the King, and to those whom I am indebted to for my promotion, not to let it be seen what I am capable of doing. If I am not fit for this post, I ought not to be employed in this important kingdom. I am responsible for every part of his Majesty's business which passes through my hands, and I will act to the best of my judgment, without a coadjutor. . . . I can at the same time feel the unpleasantness of Colonel de Cosne's situation. It is disagreeable, after having played even what was known to be only a temporary first part, to move afterwards in a second sphere, especially with one who is determined to act for himself.[5]

By the following summer (1759) Colonel de Cosne had retired to his bed and had 'not, since the month of June, put anything into cipher for me, or transcribed a letter'. Bristol argued that 'being confined to his room at Madrid, and often to his bed, without doing any business, is much the same with his going into another province of this kingdom', which he had apparently done with Bristol's encouragement.[6] Not until 5 April 1760, eighteen months after Bristol's arrival, did the unfortunate colonel leave Madrid; and Bristol then secured the appointment of secretary of embassy for his private secretary, Ralph Woodford.

Even these minor appointments were often the subject of discussion at the highest level. When Sandwich wished to nominate to the post of secretary to his embassy, he wrote to his close friend Bedford, one of the secretaries of state, who replied: 'I will do all that lies in my power to forward [your scheme]; but, as it is not in my province, I can do nothing more than putting the duke of Newcastle frequently in mind of it.' Later, Bedford reported that he thought he had secured the appointment Sandwich wanted, 'the duke of Newcastle having promised to mention it to the King, and I find Mr Pelham is not at all averse to it'.[7] Again, when Lord Cardross was appointed secretary of embassy at Madrid in 1766, the appointment was made as a reward for party services by the Prime Minister, Chatham.[8] When, on another occasion, the two secretaries of state persuaded George III to name a secretary of embassy at Madrid, Grenville, the Prime Minister, objected. 'The King', he records, 'looked confounded and tried to excuse himself

[5] *Chatham Corresp.* i. 372–3.   [6] Ibid. i. 418–19.
[7] *Bedford Corresp.* i. 331, 344, 374.
[8] *Grenville Papers*, iv. 208; *Chatham Corresp.* iii. 106–7, 114, 121.

upon the pressing instances of his two secretaries who, he said, did not do fairly in urging these expenses, without Mr Grenville's participation.'[9]

When it was merely a question of arranging for someone, in the absence of a head of mission, to carry on the official correspondence, the nomination made by the absent diplomatist would usually be accepted at home without argument. The usual procedure was for the departing head of mission to present his private secretary to the Foreign Minister as *chargé d'affaires*. No credential letters were normally given to *chargés d'affaires* and when Harris, employed in this capacity at Madrid during the Falkland Islands crisis, left his post and then returned on receiving fresh orders, the Spanish Minister refused to recognize him as a diplomatic agent until he received credentials from home.[10] If, as at Paris, there was already in residence a junior agent appointed by the crown, he regularly stepped into the shoes of the absent ambassador. If he was not already minister plenipotentiary, this rank might be conferred upon him. Similarly, where there was a British consul and no secretary of embassy, the consul often, though not invariably, became *chargé d'affaires*. Consul Jamineau at Naples objected to the envoy's private secretary being left in charge there in 1763.[11] Similarly when Sir James Wright went on leave in 1769 from his post as Resident at Venice, the secretary of state originally ordered him not to leave anyone in charge. Later, however, Robert Richie, 'an English gentleman settled here in trade', was appointed by Wright and accepted by Weymouth with a warning not to meddle with commercial affairs, which were the preserve of Consul Udny. When Wright again went on leave in 1773, Udny, who had been deeply annoyed by the preference shown in 1769 to Richie, whom he described as one of his clerks, claimed the post of *chargé d'affaires*. Rochford replied that he had nothing to do with this and that the *chargé d'affaires* would not be paid by the Treasury. Wright then appointed Udny, but Wright's successor, Strange, again appointed Richie in preference to Consul Udny in 1775. Richie succeeded Udny as consul at Venice in 1776 and again acted as *chargé d'affaires* from 1786 to 1790.[12] Occasionally a consul was temporarily transferred from his post to the capital

[9] *Grenville Papers*, iii. 119.
[10] *Malmesbury Diaries*, i. 74.   [11] S.P. 93. 20.
[12] S.P. 99. 74–79; F.O. 81. 5–7.

to take charge in the absence of a diplomatic agent. Consul Foulis was thus removed from Ostend to Brussels in 1718. If the secretaries of state had any reason to think that the head of a mission might be absent from his post, duplicate orders were sometimes sent to the consul. This happened frequently at Lisbon,[13] less often at Venice.

Except in such special cases, the absent diplomatist almost invariably named his private secretary to carry on the correspondence and this arrangement would be automatically confirmed by the secretary of state.

When there was no British consul available and the diplomatist had no private secretary, or at least not one regarded as suitable, a difficult situation arose. Sometimes, especially in the first half of our period, the correspondence was allowed to lapse until a new diplomatic representative could be appointed and sent out from London. At other times a volunteer rushed into the breach and found that the secretary of state was prepared to make use of him. This happened at Florence on the death of Sir Horace Mann, when his nephew was allowed to take charge for some months, only to discover that his valuation of his services in hard cash differed widely from that of the secretary of state. When there was a vacancy at Brussels, Edward Wortley Montagu in 1745 offered his services to Bedford.[14]

Thus the secretaries of state, though their influence upon appointments certainly increased in our period, never came to have anything like an absolute right to nominate all the diplomatic agents in their own province. Carmarthen, when Foreign Secretary in 1784, protesting against the appointment of one Johnstone to Lisbon wrote: 'Whatever may be the consequences of his appointment, I beg I may only incur the censure of having submitted to but by no means of having approved the measure.'[15] In regard to minor appointments, especially as *chargés d'affaires* and secretaries of embassy, the head of the mission's views had to be taken into account and were often decisive. Major appointments, on the other hand, required not only the approval of the king to the suggestions offered to him, but also previous consultation with leading Cabinet colleagues. It may be suggested that the secretary

---

[13] e.g. H.M.C., *Bath MSS.* i. 113.
[14] S.P. 77. 92, letter dated 13 Nov. 1745.
[15] H.M.C., *Leeds MSS.*, p. 53. It may be significant that Johnstone did not go.

of state had most control over appointments of intermediate rank. Unless difficult questions of patronage or of personality arose, his colleagues were unlikely to object to his choice; and it would usually be possible to 'square' the king, if necessary by agreeing in advance to find another post for his own candidate.

CHAPTER IX

Selection—Why?

JUST as in the preceding chapter it was found to be impossible to give a single answer to the question 'Who appointed the diplomatists of the eighteenth century?' so it is not possible to give a single answer to the complementary query—'For what reasons were they appointed, retained in the service, and even promoted?' That these reasons varied is clearly indicated by the very different methods used to secure an appointment abroad by a peer or an influential politician in contrast to those necessarily adopted by humbler aspirants. This raises at once what is perhaps the crux of the problem—were diplomatic posts habitually treated as places to be disposed of in accordance with the prevailing system of court and ministerial patronage? Important appointments were normally treated in this way, although rarely with total disregard of another criterion, the good of the service. Appointments even to the minor diplomatic posts, secretary of embassy and *chargé d'affaires*, were often influenced by the same considerations.

Lord King in 1822 claimed that

diplomatic situations were now so much the rewards of parliamentary interest, that persons who had friends with the necessary influence were sent abroad to qualify themselves for receiving pensions. When they were duly qualified they returned and were placed on the pension list, to make way for others who qualified themselves for profitable retirement and returned to enjoy it in the same manner.... Why were these extravagant appointments to be continued? The only answer was that they were the means of patronage.

Our system of diplomacy, Lord King asserted, was not designed to maintain the balance of power in Europe, but the balance in favour of government in the House of Commons.[1] Apart from the development of the separate pension list in George III's reign, there was little novelty in this state of affairs.

The control of a seat in the House of Commons, or better still

---

[1] *Parliamentary Debates New Series*, vi. 1285-7.

in the earlier part of our period of a peerage, gave a would-be diplomatist a great advantage over other competitors and it is no accident that so many diplomatists were peers or members of the House of Commons. Of the members of the House of Commons between 1734 and 1832[2] about seventy-five held diplomatic posts between 1689 and 1789. At least fourteen members of the House of Commons elected in 1741 were also diplomatists. It is true that the peerage or the seat might sometimes be the result and not the cause of diplomatic activity. For example, Keene, after a long period of service abroad, was, on his return home, provided with a seat in the Commons.[3] Sir Robert Sutton, after a diplomatic career including the Constantinople embassy, became on his return home a Member of Parliament.[4] Matthew Prior listed among his qualifications to serve his university in Parliament 'my having acted abroad in several stations'.[5] Similarly, outstandingly successful or sometimes merely extremely lucky diplomatists were rewarded with peerages.

But much oftener it was the peerage or the seat which assisted the candidate to bring pressure upon government to give him a chance in diplomacy. Andrew Mitchell, applying to Lord President Forbes for help in being returned to Parliament, regarded a seat in the House as a step towards employment. 'I desire', he wrote, 'nay I am resolved to act a fair and honourable part, if ever I shall be in Parliament; but I do propose a reward for myself—that of being employed, either at home or abroad, in a station agreeable to me, and in which I may be useful; for my ambition at present is stronger than my avarice.'[6] Tyrawley, an old hand at backstairs intrigue, hearing that Keene at Madrid was 'very much indisposed', proposed himself as Keene's successor:

Now if this embassy does not suit some parliamentary interest, or that it is not to be disposed of so as to influence the election of Newport Pagnel, Melcomb Regis or Haverford-in-the-West, and that poor Keene should be removed, I should not dislike going to Madrid, since I am already so far in my way.[7]

[2] Using the lists in G. P. Judd, *Members of Parliament 1734–1832*.
[3] *Keene Corresp.*, p. xii.   [4] *Sutton Desp.*, p. 6.
[5] H.M.C., *Bath MSS.* iii. 423.
[6] *Memoirs and Papers of Sir Andrew Mitchell*, ed. A. Bisset, i. 52.
[7] He was Governor of Gibraltar and the quotation is from *Chatham Corresp.* i. 203.

Lord Hervey recorded, as though it was the most natural thing in the world, that when a mission of compliment to Don Carlos, on his appointment as King of Naples, became necessary, Walpole 'pitched on one Mr. Williams,[8] a young man with a great estate, who had ever since he was in Parliament voted with the Court, and, contrary to most people who did so, had never received any favour or employment from the Court'.[9] And when Porter, after trying in vain to extract from Newcastle some immediate reward for Robinson's long service at Vienna, asked the duke to secure a place for his friend on his return home, 'the Duke, on this point, stroked his face, settled his wig, hesitated, and asked me, with a slow [low?] voice, stooping towards my ear, has he a borough? can he get into Parliament?'[10]

The earliest case of a diplomatist treating his vote in the Lords or Commons as a bargaining counter with the Ministry appears to be that of Lord Raby, according to his own account in a letter to Oxford, dated 25 September/6 October 1713:

All I can brag on to show yet my gratitude to your lordship is, that when you desired I would forbear giving my vote against the bill for the resumption of grants, though the thing then seemed to turn upon my single vote and I had so great a stake depending and had even the Queen's leave to vote as I would, I then told your lordship if you would take it as a mark of my friendship and respect for you, I would not go to the House; which you was pleased to say you would and afterwards to assure me you took it for such a mark of friendship you would never forget it. I desire now your lordship will show me that friendship you then promised me.[11]

It should be noted that there was no legal bar to prevent practising politicians from accepting employment abroad. As early as 1575 the House of Commons decided that 'any person being a member and in service of ambassade shall not be amoved during such service'.[12] The Regency Acts of 1706 and 1707, with their provisions about old and new offices, caused a brief period of uncertainty, during which Bolingbroke wrote to Oxford: 'Will Bingley go to Spain or will he have a commoner, who may be re-elected,

 [8] Afterwards Sir Charles Hanbury Williams.
 [9] *Hervey Memoirs*, pp. 829–30.
 [10] Larpent, i. 465–6.
 [11] H.M.C., *Portland MSS.* ix. 384–5.
 [12] Hatsell, *Precedents of Proceedings in the House of Commons* (1818 ed.), ii. 22.

joined with him, and a couple of under-workmen, and treat about commerce with the French?'[13] But in 1714 the Commons resolved that 'the office of commissaries to treat with commissaries from France was not a new created office within the meaning of the Act of 6th Queen Anne'.[14] In 1715 they passed a further resolution that a member who had been appointed to go to Vienna as envoy was not thereby disqualified from membership.

Speaker Onslow commented on the resolution of the House in 1715 that since then 'no ministers employed abroad have thereby vacated their seats'.[15] It is interesting to notice the ground upon which Hatsell approved the decisions of 1714 and 1715. He admitted that they might well disfranchise a borough for some years, but thought they were necessary to prevent the king from getting rid of dangerous opponents in the Commons by sending them on foreign missions.[16] More recent experts in parliamentary practice have sought to explain the decision of 1715 in other ways, although they candidly admit that 'the ground for these decisions is not very clear'.[17] Diplomatic appointments may have been regarded as not being offices of profit. Alternatively, the Commons may have felt that it was a good thing for members to hold such appointments from time to time, in accordance with the ancient practice of the House, and therefore decided that foreign ministers should continue to be members in spite of recent statute law which would have excluded them or, at least, compelled them to seek re-election.[18] Appointment as a consul, it should be noted, vacated the seat but the member was eligible for re-election.[19]

Patronage is not of course the only answer to the question: how did men secure diplomatic appointments? Lord Malmesbury, who was to become the leader of the British diplomatic corps in the late eighteenth century, owed his first appointment as secretary of embassy at Madrid to the then secretary of state, Shelburne, in spite of the fact that Malmesbury's father, James Harris,

[13] H.M.C., *Portland MSS.* v. 360.

[14] Hatsell, op. cit. ii. 22–23.

[15] Ibid. ii. 23.   [16] Ibid. ii. 24–25.

[17] Erskine May, *A Practical Treatise on the Law . . . of Parliament* (15th ed., 1950), p. 206.

[18] Ibid., p. 206. I can see no justification for a third conjecture, put forward by the editors, that such offices were regarded as not being held directly from the crown.

[19] Hatsell, op. cit. ii. 54 (cases of Lind and Jefferey); Erskine May, op. cit., p. 552.

M.P., a follower of Grenville, was a political opponent of Shelburne. In this case 'personal friendship . . . cut across party connexion'.[20]

More often probably appointments were made for the good of the service. Contemporary writers, especially when they approve of a particular appointment, usually assume that this was in fact the case. Bishop Burnet, writing of the appointment of Townshend as joint plenipotentiary to the States General in 1709, stated as Townshend's qualifications that he 'had great parts, had improved these by travelling, and was by much the most shining person of all our young nobility, and had, on many occasions, distinguished himself very eminently; so he was a man of great integrity and of good principles in all respects, free from all vice and of an engaging conversation'.[21] While this is obviously highly idealized, the reasons occasionally given for particular appointments indicate that the good of the service had been kept in view or had even been the decisive argument in favour of a successful candidate.

When Mitford Crowe was sent as envoy to the Hapsburg king of Spain in 1706, with instructions to conclude a commercial treaty, the reasons given were that he was 'well-versed in the Spanish trade', had 'knowledge . . . of the people and country', had already shown his zeal for Her Majesty's service, and was well acquainted and in good correspondence with Lord Galway, the commander of the British troops in the peninsula.[22] Sir Charles Hanbury Williams was selected in 1755 for the Russian embassy not so much because of his political connexions as because it was thought he would be personally acceptable to the Tsaritsa. Similarly when Sir James Gray was sent to Madrid in 1767, he was chosen, in default of a peer, because he had already gained the approbation of Charles III during his mission to Naples.[23] To these actual appointments may perhaps be added the proposal to send William Eden to the American colonies after they had secured their independence. The foreign secretary, Carmarthen, approved this because Eden's abilities were 'just of the nature fit for the business of that appointment, consisting chiefly of narrow and illiberal intrigues. I know nothing right or honourable about

[20] J. Brooke, *Chatham Administration*, p. 238.
[21] *History of his own Time* (Oxford, 1823), v. 404.
[22] H.M.C., *Bath MSS.* i. 108–9.   [23] S.P. 94. 175 (dispatch of 25/10/66).

him any further than his being a privy councillor entitles him to claim.'[24]

Whenever ministers can be seen to hesitate between the claims of an 'outsider'—usually a man with political connexions—and those of a career diplomat and finally deciding for the latter, we are probably safe to assume that this time at least they were seeking to secure the best-qualified man for the job. Even in the eighteenth century successful discharge of the duties of a mission to one court gave a certain claim to promotion in rank or to appointment to a vacant and more important post. Yet the motives which produced such promotions of experienced diplomatists were often very mixed. When Horace Walpole was arguing for Titley's promotion from resident to envoy in 1736 he wrote:

Not only Mr. Titley's merit, but even the regard due to his Danish Majesty . . . should engage the King to make Titley envoy. He is a very pretty man and endowed with proper qualities to make an able minister; and nothing less than the making him envoy will put him in a condition to watch the motions of the French and to make an interest with the ladies that govern that court.[25]

Lord Holland, I think, was not far from the truth when he replied in 1822 to Lord Liverpool's boast that fourteen out of the eighteen foreign ministers employed in 1821 had been 'regularly brought up through all the ascending gradations from secretaries of legation', that

he did not know whether it was an improvement upon the ancient practice, from which it was certainly very different . . . in former times such individuals as were selected for ambassadors seldom underwent such a schooling: on the contrary they were selected for their high rank and great fortune; and the persons who were employed under them, though they had the right of rising, rose but very slowly to the rank of envoys extraordinary.[26]

One of Lord Holland's criticisms of Castlereagh's diplomacy was the almost total absence of such minor appointments.

It was true, indeed, that they had converted electors into kings and petty princes into potentates—they had nothing to do with such paltry beings as low margravates [sic] or grovelling republics. They were engaged in pursuing higher things, and therefore it was, they

[24] H.M.C., *Leeds MSS.*, p. 53.   [25] Coxe, *Walpole Memoirs*, iii. 343.
[26] *Parliamentary Debates New Series*, vi. 1297, 1305–6.

had abandoned the old custom of having inferior officers, which was
found to succeed so well in the time of Sir R[obert] Walpole.[27]

Holland was certainly right in believing that in the major appointments during the eighteenth century influence counted for
much more than merit or seniority. Evidence is scanty for part of
the period, but it may be tentatively suggested that all three
Hanoverian sovereigns were more influenced by the idea of professionalism and inclined to value experience (and even training)
more highly than their ministers, who were necessarily intent
on maintaining the strength of government in the House of
Commons.

This close, though not invariable, linking of diplomatic appointments and political patronage raised problems, although the connexion is not so clear and simple as it apparently was in the first
half of the nineteenth century, when Professor Bindoff believes
that the two leading diplomatic posts 'changed occupants with
every change of government'.[28] But there certainly was a tendency
for successive secretaries of state, who remained in office long
enough, to surround themselves with a group of friends, relations,
and political connexions in the diplomatic service. A somewhat
idealized account of the advantages of the practice is given by
Lord Holland in discussing the position of C. J. Fox upon coming
into office in 1783:

He had engaged the affections of the diplomatic agents employed
abroad so entirely during his first short Administration by the pers-
picacity of his views, the frankness of his communications, and the
unaffected interest which he took in the personal concerns of those
employed under him, that his restoration to office was hailed as a
jubilee by nearly all of them. Their zeal was quickened by private
friendship and gratitude, and their efforts were directed by a plain,
prompt and unreserved explanation of the views entertained at home,
uniformly and conjointly to the same public objects.[29]

But Fox was not the only secretary to see the advantages of this
close connexion. As early as 1704 Godolphin proposed to get rid
of the diplomatic agents appointed by secretary Nottingham
between 1702 and 1704.[30] Bolingbroke was deliberately appointing

[27] *Parliamentary Debates New Series*, vi. 1302–3.
[28] *Trans. R. Hist. Soc.*, 4th series, xviii. 169.
[29] *Memorials of C. J. Fox*, ii. 73.   [30] H.M.C., *Bath MSS.* i. 77.

personal friends to posts abroad in the last years of Anne's reign; and the rivalry of Whig factions in the early years of George I's reign left its mark upon diplomatic appointments. Bubb Dodington characteristically explained his resignation of the Madrid envoyship by a desire to follow his friends the Walpoles out of office in 1717.[31] This is perhaps best illustrated by the importance attached by Townshend to getting the king to send Horace Walpole on an informal mission to France, where Britain was officially represented by Schaub, an adherent of the rival ministerial clique. Townshend wrote to Walpole on 25 September 1723:

If he [Horace Walpole] executes his commission with his usual dexterity, the effect will either be that he will make such discoveries as must end in getting Schaub recalled; or at least that Schaub, finding we have credit enough to get so near a relation sent over to superintend him, will so far consider his own situation as to act in a more open and sincere manner towards us, and think it necessary to make a merit to himself of appearing to throw that interest into our hands, which, after such a tacit declaration [by the king] in our favour, it may no longer be in his power to withhold from us. And as that interest has hitherto been the chief, and is at present in a manner the only hold and support of our antagonists, this affair, if managed with discretion, will wound them in the most vital and sensible part; and being therefore of such great consequence to us, I hope you will prevail with my brother Horace to undertake the journey without any difficulty or delay.[32]

In a later letter he added:

This indisputable mark of confidence towards us, and neglect towards Lord Carteret and Schaub, cannot fail to induce the duke of Orleans and the French minister to open themselves towards my brother Horace and to court our friendship.[33]

Similarly, when the Walpole influence began decisively to prevail, Lords Whitworth and Polwarth found themselves in difficulties at the Congress of Cambrai. Whitworth wrote to his friend, under-secretary Tilson:

My heart is full and I know no friend to whom I can open myself saflier than to you. Any great changes at court usually affect the [foreign] ministers who are employed and weaken the mutual

---

[31] J. Carswell, *The Old Cause*, p. 147.
[32] Coxe, *Walpole Memoirs*, ii. 270.   [33] Ibid., p. 281.

confidence there ought to be, at least for a time. You know I have had this disagreeable experience more than once. Since my return hither [to Cambrai] Lord Polwarth and I have considered all the despatches which have been sent from hence or received here from the time of my going to Spa. The orders to follow the French in everything have been so often repeated to us in so short a time that we cannot but apprehend with a good deal of concern that his Majesty's ministers must be very diffident of our conduct and think us capable of transgressing the orders which are sent us, either out of design, the vanity of our own notions and experience or the love of meddling in everything. Perhaps the freedom we have sometimes taken to explain our thoughts to them may have given rise to some such suspicion, but we have been as careful and reserved in every point in opening ourselves to others as we have been free and sincere in laying before the King's ministers an account of things in the lights they appeared to us here, and without this liberty we do not see how his Majesty's service can be carried on usefully. It is our duty to report faithfully what we see, hear or think; and it is the business of the ministers at home to order upon it as they find best.[34]

When Townshend in his turn was being forced out of the secretaryship of state by the Walpole brothers, one of his adherents, Poyntz, wrote to him: 'The thought of remaining engaged in this negotiation [with France] at a time when your lordship may possibly have taken a resolution to retire from public business is insupportable to me, and yet I see no remedy till affairs are concluded one way or another.'[35] But other diplomatists were prepared to make their peace with the dominant ministers at London and Hanover. Horace Walpole wrote a few years later:

I must do Mr. Finch the justice to say that he took several occasions in a handsome manner to let me see he had no other bias than that of serving the king, and with zeal, under the administration he is pleased to employ; and I gave him to understand as civilly that the difference of opinion in some of his relations would have no effect upon my friends with respect to him.[36]

Newcastle accused Carteret, after Walpole's fall, of placing his own friends in the material foreign missions.[37] This is borne out by the conversation with Carteret recorded by one of his protégés, Porter, who had been employed to explain to Maria Theresa

[34] H.M.C., *Polwarth MSS.* iv. 130.
[35] Coxe, *Walpole Memoirs*, ii. 659.
[36] Ibid. iii. 335.   [37] *Supra*, Chapter VIII, p. 153.

Carteret's ideas on foreign policy. Pressed by Newcastle to return to Vienna in 1743, Porter told Carteret:

I was ready to risk life and fortune for the King's national service in an honourable cause, but would rather perish than become a base, low tool in a dishonourable one: and as I had too much seen and felt what had been, I had little hope of seeing matters bettered—or such fortitude and vigour, as became the faith, probity and renown of a great nation;—therefore I thought the post of honour in such times was a private station. 'This, my lord,' I concluded, 'is my political creed, and had rendered my determination not to stir from home, for I most solemnly declare to your lordship, did my passion to serve Mr. Robinson lead me back to Vienna, the same passive dastardly measures continuing, would urge me immediately to beg and require a recall.[38]

Carteret then explained the difficulty of his own position, denounced the policy followed since 1731, and outlined his plans to defeat France, win over Sardinia, and restore Austria to a position of strength. Porter then replied that Carteret's 'personal situation had changed my [Porter's] hesitation into resolution, and he might assure the King that I would cheerfully undertake to execute his Majesty's commands, and return to Vienna with them'.[39] Other cases, such as that of the third earl of Marchmont, could easily be quoted, of refusal to serve under a particular secretary.[40] Buckinghamshire refused the Madrid embassy in 1766 from the government which had succeeded his close friend and associate, George Grenville.[41]

After getting rid of Carteret, Newcastle followed the same line. A few months after the formation of the Pitt–Newcastle ministry, Pitt wrote to Newcastle complaining of the conduct of the British diplomatic agent at Berlin, Andrew Mitchell, who was a dependent of Newcastle:

Andrew Mitchell is not a fool and therefore he must be something not fit to be the instrument of the present system of administration in the vital and essential part of the plan of Europe, your transactions with Prussia. I have long entertained a very indifferent opinion of his

---

[38] Larpent, i. 468.   [39] Ibid., p. 471.
[40] *Marchmont Papers*, i. 90.
[41] *Buckinghamshire Desp.* I. vii. 54. 'Mr. Grenville', Buckinghamshire wrote in 1764, 'is the only friend I can in the least depend upon in the present Administration.' H.M.C., *Lothian MSS.*, p. 185.

correspondence from reasons too obvious to trouble your grace with and I am now entirely convinced that he is mischievous to a degree that perhaps may already have rooted ideas in the King of Prussia's mind which will inevitably overturn the system . . . it is evident to whom he belongs and whose work he is doing. Thus it is my lord in every part of government: the tools of another system are perpetually marring every hopeful measure of the present administration. In a word if your grace is not able to eradicate this lurking diffusive poison a little more out of the mass of government, especially from the vitals, I think it better for us to have done. I do not intend for one that Andrew Mitchell shall carry me where I have resolved not to go.[42]

The *reductio ad absurdum* of the element of personal loyalty between secretaries of state and their subordinates abroad occurred towards the end of the American War of Independence, when Fox and Shelburne, the rival secretaries, sent personal agents to negotiate at Paris.

If [Rockingham and Fox] opened a negotiation, he [Shelburne] commenced another underhand at the same court. Mr. Fox despatched Thomas Grenville to Paris; Lord Shelburne sent one, two or three privately to the same place, and addressed them to different ministers or persons of supposed credit.[43]

George III then thought it desirable to retain another agent in France as a check on Grenville;[44] and when Fox resigned Grenville threw up his mission as a political gesture in favour of his friend. His 'abrupt departure from Paris' was disapproved by Harris and others on the ground that 'every man has a right to have his opinions and leanings, and is to be praised for adhering to them; but in times like these, every thing should give way to the public good'.[45]

It was inevitable therefore that such appointments, natural as they were and perhaps even for the good of the service, often led to trouble when a government was changed or even when a new secretary of state was appointed. Daniel Pulteney, on a change of ministry, wrote to his friend Molesworth, employed as plenipotentiary to the several courts of Italy: 'I do not hear that you are likely to be affected, at least not suddenly, though it will depend

[42] Add. MS. 32877, fo. 256.
[43] Walpole, *Last Journals*, ii. 543; *George III Corresp.* v. 488, vi. 82.
[44] *Geo. III Corresp.* v. 494.   [45] *Malmesbury Diaries*, i. 537.

entirely on the push of some person of interest.'[46] Until harmony
was restored between secretary and agents abroad awkward situations arose as 'when lately Mr. Trevor [envoy at The Hague and
a client of the Pelhams] pressed for a decisive answer from the
Pensionary, or else England must alter her measures, the Pensionary said that the Minister in England [Carteret] did not hold
the same language.[47] These problems became more frequent and
acute with the growing professionalization of the diplomatic service. Career diplomats under George III often found themselves in
a predicament owing to a change of government. Offered by his
friend Fox the mission to The Hague, Harris returned from his
post in Russia just in time to see the fall of the Portland administration. He followed his friends into opposition in December
1783

and voted constantly with them on every question till the middle of
February [1784] when I paired off with Sir Whally Gardiner, my
health obliging me to go to Bath. I had renounced all thoughts, both
of going abroad on a public employment,[48] or of receiving any reward
for my services under the new administration, with none of whom I
had any connexion, and whose manner of coming into office I had so
explicitly and avowedly disapproved.[49]

When, in spite of his behaviour, the Pitt ministry offered to send
him on a mission to The Hague, his chiefs advised acceptance:
'foreign employ', they said, 'was perfectly distinct from home
politics; and that the first consideration ought to be, not how best
to serve *a party*, but how to make oneself the most useful to the
whole community'. Harris then expressed to the foreign secretary,
Carmarthen, his 'willingness to serve on the Continent, providing
no conditions whatsoever were made with me relative to my Parliamentary conduct and providing the employment was such as
I could with propriety accept'. When the new Parliament met in
May 1784 Harris, on the advice of Portland and Fox, refrained
from voting either for or against the government he was now

---

[46] H.M.C., *MSS. in Various Collections*, viii. 361.

[47] *Marchmont Papers*, i. 70.

[48] Cf. *Auckland Journal*, i. 70–71: 'Harris has resigned The Hague; but not on
politics which have nothing to do with the foreign line'—an unorthodox view at
the time. Auckland lived up to it by accepting from Pitt the well-known mission
to France.

[49] *Malmesbury Diaries*, ii. 70–71.

committed to serve abroad.[50] 'I called immediately', Harris explained,

on the Duke of Portland, stated precisely the situation in which I stood, and begged of him to give me his opinion whether, thus situated, I ought or ought not to vote in Parliament. I begged him to set aside all personal considerations, and to determine solely on the grounds of public propriety; that it was not permission to vote one way or the other that I came to ask, nor by an artful apology to conceal an intended desertion of my party, but merely to obtain his advice, which, let it be what it would, I was determined, at all events, to follow. The Duke replied that he was clearly of opinion that I ought not to vote at all. That he so much wished to have me at The Hague, that he should be extremely sorry if I furnished any handle for Ministers to send another person, which my voting against them would certainly do; and that, even supposing them liberal enough not to attend to the way in which I voted, my publicly appearing in Opposition, immediately previous to my accepting so consequential a post, would give bad impressions abroad; it would impede my negotiations by affording to my adversaries a motive to say that I had not the confidence of Ministry, and that I was appointed simply in order to be got rid of. . . . Fox was of the same opinion, although he was too busy in his Westminster election to be so explicit as the Duke. I therefore did not attend Parliament at its meeting.[51]

Similarly Pitt in 1785 appointed another of his political opponents, William Eden, to undertake a commercial negotiation with France. These two missions ran counter to the general trend and it is perhaps significant that Portland was much less forthcoming when appealed to by Eden than he had been two years earlier in the case of Harris. He wrote to Eden:

I own to you that had you consulted me previous to your acceptance, I could not have felt sufficient courage to recommend so arduous and hazardous an employment to you; nor can I now venture any further than to give you the fullest credit for the public spirit which animates you in such a moment. I as readily acknowledge, as I sincerely admire, the liberality of mind and the fortitude which have determined you to subject yourself, for a time, to the jealousy of friends, to the animadversions of the censorious, and what, I think, requires still greater resolution, to the good faith of an Administration, thus avowedly incapable of discharging their duty to the public by their

[50] *Malmesbury Diaries*, ii. 69–73.   [51] Ibid., pp. 71–72.

own instruments or their own adherents, and who, joined to this incapacity, have evidently neither the power nor the spirits to act for themselves.[52]

Before setting off for Paris, Eden, unlike Harris, appeared in the House of Commons and 'sat down with Mr. Dundas and Mr. Pitt on one side of me and Mr. Jenkinson and the Master of the Rolls on the other'. Eden continues:

Upon the whole, I am glad that the matter took the form which it did, and that I was induced to put it so much to the proof: for as two or three of the party papers had been very libellous, though very stupid, it was pleasant to prove to the world that the libels were the language of some two or three private and perhaps low people, and certainly not issuing from gentlemen of the House of Commons.[53]

Eden's acceptance of a diplomatic post abroad was therefore followed almost immediately by a change in his party allegiance which Harris had been able to avoid. In spite of this, he more than once complained later on that the friends of the government in the House of Commons, particularly in the debates on the commercial treaty with France, adopted towards him a 'cold and unfriendly' tone.[54] Eden's friend Lord Sheffield so far agreed that he wrote: 'It is generally allowed that Pitt's speeches on the Treaty [with France] were bad. In general, it has been exceedingly ill defended.'[55] Malmesbury, on the other hand, after returning to England from The Hague and before the juristic termination of his mission, voted against the government on the Regency Bill in 1789. Pitt and Carmarthen naturally took a poor view of his defection, as they undoubtedly regarded it, and his employment was brought to an end.[56]

Hugh Elliot, not a man likely to submit tamely to injustice, when he was removed from his post at Berlin by political opponents of his family, acquiesced 'in the propriety of my removal from a post of confidence by those who must have considered me as by no means coinciding with them in principle or action'.[57] Writing to a friend he remarked of the new government:

The duke of Ormonde says of his son, who fell nobly, 'I would

[52] *Auckland Journal*, i. 89–90.   [53] Ibid., pp. 94–95.
[54] Ibid., p. 285.   [55] Ibid., p. 411.
[56] In addition to the authorities quoted by Holland Rose, *Pitt and the National Revival*, p. 424, see *Auckland Journal*, ii. 317.
[57] *Elliot Memoir*, p. 246.

rather have my dead son than any living son in England;' so, I assure
you, I would rather be considered as attached to the system and views
of the late [i.e. North] administration, dead as it is, than to the wild,
incoherent and, I may add, inconsistent set who have usurped their
place [the Rockingham Whigs].[58]

When these opponents offered him alternative employment, he
described this as 'an offer which, considering the circumstances of
the times and my brother's political line, I think exceedingly
handsome on the part of those who made it'.[59]

The problem survived into the nineteenth century and was
clearly stated by the third Lord Malmesbury to the Select Committee on the Diplomatic Service in 1861:

There are peers who have been ministers abroad, and who have not
only entertained decided political and party views, but who have
publicly stated them in the natural course of their duty, up to the
very moment of their appointment [to diplomatic posts] and for a
long time before. The Committee is aware that peers have a right to
leave their proxies with the government, and do so; and, if those
peers have publicly by their votes declared an incoming minister in
their opinion unfit to govern, it seems to me an anomaly that those
peers should hold under that minister when he comes in, because, for
the benefit of the service, confidence must be reciprocal between the
agent and the secretary of state.[60]

Under eighteenth-century conditions no holder of a diplomatic
appointment would be allowed to oppose the government of the
day, and anyone who attempted such factious opposition would
normally find his diplomatic career abruptly terminated. What
George Grenville said about officers, civil and military, in general,
applied forcibly to diplomatists:

I hoped no officer, either civil or military, would be dismissed from
the King's service for giving his opinion upon this or that particular
measure agreeable to his conscience; but that if any gentleman of
high rank in either capacity should engage in an open, regular and
systematical opposition, it seemed to me very difficult, and unlikely
for him to continue long in that situation.[61]

---

[58] *Auckland Journal*, i. 330.
[59] *Elliot Memoir*, p. 250. Mrs. Schapiro in her unpublished thesis (*supra*,
Chapter II, note 38) takes the view that the manner of Elliot's dismissal was
insulting.   [60] Question 1931.
[61] *Grenville Papers*, ii. 321.

As we have already seen, Harris had found himself in difficulties for this reason in 1783-4. His diplomatic career might well have ended at this point, but his conversion to Toryism in 1793 was followed by further missions abroad.[62] On the other hand, there are occasional suggestions that opponents, potential or actual, of the government were offered employment abroad in order to get them out of the way. This must be the explanation, for example, of Queen Caroline's offering Stair the Vienna embassy in 1734 with the additional offer of Evans's regiment to make it more attractive financially.[63] Other cases of this kind have been mentioned earlier in this book in considering employment abroad as a kind of honourable exile.[64]

If it be asked, did the erratic, casual, and irrelevant methods by which the British diplomatic service was recruited produce satisfactory results, the answer must be at best a qualified one. Adam Smith remarked that 'politicians are not the most remarkable men in the world for probity and punctuality. Ambassadors from different nations are still less so.'[65] Some were admittedly in the foreign-minister line for what they could make out of it. Others were frankly neglectful of their duties, badgered the secretaries of state for leave or additional allowances on quite inadequate pretexts, or even tried to treat their appointments as sinecures.[66] Still more dangerous were the few irresponsible firebrands of the Hugh Elliot type, whose diplomatic career was enlivened by kidnappings, duels, and even a declaration of war against Denmark, without particular orders from his sovereign, though this last escapade was *ex post facto* approved by the government.[67]

But regarded as a body of men who often accepted employment abroad with some reluctance and were usually underpaid and often neglected for long periods by their official superiors at home, they did their best for their king and country. Usually it was not lack of probity or punctuality which was their besetting sin. They were on the whole men of goodwill and more than average industry and intelligence: what they tended to lack was the outward show, which counted for so much at continental courts still living

[62] *Malmesbury Diaries*, I. xiii, II. 434, &c.
[63] *Marchmont Papers*, ii. 16-17.
[64] *Supra*, Chapter V, pp. 87-88.
[65] *Lectures on Justice, Police, Revenue and Arms*, ed Cannan, p. 254.
[66] One of the worst offenders was Tyrawley at Lisbon (S.P. 89. 40).
[67] *Elliot Memoir, passim.*

in the shadow cast across Europe by Louis XIV and, perhaps still
more, the specialized education, insinuating manners, and knowledge of technique possessed by their French rivals.

Thus Horace Walpole, probably the best-known British diplomatist of the first half of the eighteenth century, was described by
Lord Hervey, admittedly a hostile witness, in these terms:

> Horace Walpole, with all his defects, was certainly a very good
> treaty-dictionary, to which his brother often referred for facts neces-
> sary for him to be informed of, and of which he was capable of
> making good use. But to hear Horace himself talk on these subjects
> unrestrained, and without being turned to any particular point, was
> listening to a rhapsody that was never coherent, and often totally
> unintelligible. This made his long and frequent speeches in Parlia-
> ment uneasy to his own party, ridiculous to the other, and tiresome
> to both. He loved business, had great application, and was indefa-
> tigable, but, from having a most unclear head, no genius, no method,
> and a most loose inconclusive manner of reasoning, he was absolutely
> useless to his brother in every capacity but that which I have already
> mentioned of a dictionary. He was a very disagreeable man in com-
> pany, noisy, overbearing, affecting to be always jocose, and thoroughly
> the *mauvais plaisant*; as unbred in his dialect as in his apparel, and
> as ill-bred in his discourse as in his behaviour and gestures; with no
> more of the look than the habits of a gentleman. A free, easy, cheerful
> manner of conversing made some people mistake him enough to
> think him good-natured; but he was far from it, and did many
> ill offices to people and never that I heard of any good ones. Nor did
> he, with all the credit he was known to have with his brother, ever
> make one friend.[68]

Even making full allowance for Hervey's gall, it is difficult to
discern in this portrait any of the lineaments of the *habile négociateur* described by the classical French authorities on diplomacy.

Yet Horace Walpole, with all his limitations, was one of the
better British diplomatists of the century. But what are we to make
of the earl of Manchester, who discharged several important missions under William III and Anne, of whom Matthew Prior's mistress, 'Flanders Jane', complained 'that his Excellence blows his
nose in the napkins, spits in the middle of the room, and laughs so
loud and like an ordinary body that she does not think him fit for
an ambassador'.[69] Philip Stanhope, too, in spite of reams of advice

---

[68] *Hervey Memoirs*, p. 285.   [69] Eves, *Matthew Prior*, p. 138.

from Chesterfield, is said, at a dinner party arranged to show him off to Chesterfield's friends, to have been so delighted with a cherry tart that he cleared his plate by lapping or licking it so that his chin, mouth, and lips were smeared with a rosy hue.[70] The country-house-party method of selecting civil servants may have its weaknesses, but it certainly would have weeded out some undesirable eighteenth-century types.

[70] *Gentleman's Magazine* (July 1774), p. 320.

CHAPTER X

Duties and Difficulties

'The principal business of a foreign minister', Chesterfield wrote,

is to get into the secrets, and to know all *les allures* of the Courts at which he resides; this he can never bring about, but by such a pleasing address, such engaging manners, and such an insinuating behaviour, as may make him sought for, and in some measure domestic, in the best company and the best families of the place. He will then, indeed, be well informed of all that passes, either by the confidences made him, or by the carelessness of people in his company; who are accustomed to look upon him as one of them, and consequently not upon their guard before him. For a minister, who only goes to the Court he resides at in form, to ask an audience of the Prince or the Minister, upon his last instructions, puts them upon their guard and will never know any thing more than what they have a mind that he should know.[1]

In another passage he makes a contrast from this point of view between British and French diplomats. A French minister, other things being equal, will always

get the better of an English one, at any third Court in Europe. The French have something more *liant*, more insinuating and engaging in their manner, than we have. An English minister shall have resided seven years at a Court, without having made any one personal connection there, or without being intimate and domestic in any one house. He is always the English minister, and never naturalised. He receives his orders, demands an audience, writes an account of it to his Court, and his business is done. A French minister, on the contrary, has not been six weeks at a Court, without having, by a thousand little attentions, insinuated himself into some degree of favour with the Prince, his wife, his mistress, his favourite and his minister. He has established himself upon a familiar and domestic footing in a dozen of the best houses of the place, where he has accustomed the people to be not only easy, but unguarded before him; he makes himself at home there, and they think him so. By these means he knows the interior of those Courts, and can almost write prophecies to his

---

[1] Chesterfield, *Letters*, i. 155.

own, from the knowledge he has of the characters, the humours, the abilities, or the weaknesses of the actors.[2]

There is one notable omission from Chesterfield's list of the duties to be discharged by British diplomatists. He clearly did not expect them to exert any influence upon the formulation of British foreign policy. Cases when a foreign minister was summoned home for consultation and to advise the government on the policy to be pursued are rare. This is only partially accounted for by the difficulties of transport and communications. The essential duties of a foreign minister were to give his government the best information he could obtain at his post and to carry out promptly and meticulously any orders he might receive from home. His role was much more that of executant than of consultant and few foreign ministers felt much responsibility for the policy which they were expected to carry out.

What Chesterfield implied was explicitly stated by the author of *Observations on the office of an Ambassador*, who stated that

as a wise and prudent ambassador can never be at a loss to justify his own conduct in any event, so he will never attribute wholly to himself the success of his negotiations; but rather choose to place that honour to the wisdom and judgment of his prince and the conduct of his first minister: for a faithful discharge of trust, by punctually executing their commands, is all that any ambassador ought to claim for his share in the public business; and it is great weakness to aim at or accept of more.[3]

In another passage the author gave his opinion that 'an honest minister cannot prudently act but when his own judgment corresponds with his master's sentiments'.[4]

These views were accepted as axiomatic by nearly all practising diplomatists. In 1684 Lord Preston claimed: 'I have ever avoided to meddle in anything which hath not immediately concerned me as being in this post, or to offer anything which may look like an advice, knowing that I have nothing to do but to obey those orders with which his Majesty is pleased to charge me.'[5] The limited role assigned to British diplomatists is confirmed by

[2] Ibid. i. 422–3. Cf. on the duties of a British diplomatist the advice given by Henry Savile to Sir William Trumbull, printed *infra*, Chapter XI, pp. 209–210.
[3] Pamphlet attached to *An Essay on the Education of a young British Nobleman* (1730) in the Heatley Collection of Edinburgh University Library, p. 56.
[4] Ibid., pp. 51–52. [5] H.M.C., *Report VII, App.*, p. 309.

examination of the written instructions which were drawn up for them when they set out on their missions. Many of these relating to Anne's reign have been printed by Miss Curtis Brown in her *Letters and Diplomatic Instructions of Queen Anne*. Others will be found in the seven volumes of *British Diplomatic Instructions 1689–1789* published by the Royal Historical Society which deal with France, Sweden, and Denmark. Even at the end of the seventeenth century these are largely formal; but the underlying assumption is always that the diplomatic agent will carry out his orders and not attempt to influence the policy of the government.

There were, however, exceptional men who were not content with such a restricted role. Horace Walpole when at The Hague in 1716 disapproved so strongly of the Stanhope policy of signing an alliance with France, without waiting for the United Provinces to come in, that he warned Townshend:

I can never consent to set my hand to that separate act, after having plighted my honour, my faith and my conscience that nothing of this kind should be done. I must therefore repeat my instances to your lordship to get me out of this affair, and for that purpose I have writ you the enclosed letter for desiring his royal highness' leave to return home ... that I may ... get away, in case it is impossible for me by any other way to avoid signing with the abbé [Dubois] alone, without disobeying his majesty's commands, which as I should look upon it to be the greatest misfortune that can befall me, so I depend upon your lordship's kindness to secure me from it by the method I now propose, or any other you shall think fit.

At the same time Walpole wrote directly to Stanhope to desire the king's leave for returning home on account of his health.[6]

Lord Strafford, too, at The Hague, argued in 1713 that as The Hague would remain the centre of the affairs of Europe he ought to receive copies of all dispatches from London to foreign courts. So Oxford's confidential agent, Drummond, reported with the dry comments that he himself 'hoped that Whitehall should have had some share' in the affairs of Europe and that Strafford was returning home partly 'to instruct the Queen's ministers how to serve her Majesty to the best of his [Strafford's] judgment'.[7]

Elsewhere[8] I have argued that Sir Charles Hanbury Williams, after a short experience of diplomacy at Dresden, was able to give

---

[6] Coxe, *Walpole Memoirs*, ii. 105–8.   [7] H.M.C., *Portland MSS.* v. 353.
[8] *E.H.R.* xlii (1927), 361–70, and xlv (1930), 463–6.

a decisive twist to British foreign policy in the 1750's by convincing Newcastle that, if he adopted Williams's plan to elect the Archduke Joseph King of the Romans, he would be able to overcome the opposition of his Cabinet colleagues to the system of subsidy treaties which he believed to be essential to maintain the balance of power against France. The result was a futile competition between Britain and France to give subsidies to German princes which set Germany in uproar and contributed to the final breakdown of the old system of alliances between Austria and the Maritime Powers.

It is also usual to attribute to Joseph Ewart, the young envoy at Berlin, a measure of responsibility for the Triple Alliance of 1788 and still more for the alteration of the British attitude towards Russia which produced the celebrated Ochakov crisis. It is an indication of the role played by Ewart in European politics that his death, in forced retirement, was attributed to poison administered by a Russian agent.

His activities in influencing British foreign policy aroused the indignation of Burke, who wrote of him as

a little, busy, meddling man, little heard of till lately. . . . He is said to avail himself, with each of the courts [of Britain and Prussia] of his influence with the others; and by his mutually playing their games, or rather his own, to obtain ribbons, pensions, titles and other rewards, according to the fashion of this diplomatic season.

With his characteristic genius for using an attack on an individual as the basis for condemning the system which had, he believed, given the individual his opportunity, Burke proceeded:

I have been long persuaded that those in power here, instead of governing their ministers at foreign courts, are entirely swayed by them. That corps has no one point of manly policy in their whole system; they are a corps of intriguers, who, sooner or later, will turn our offices into an academy of cabal and confusion.[9]

By the time Burke wrote Ewart's meteoric career was virtually over and it was left to one of his more successful rivals to claim for diplomatic agents abroad that 'if any good is ever done there, it must be effected through the King's ministers abroad and not by those about his person' since the latter 'were too much occupied

---

[9] Burke, *Correspondence* (1844), iii. 268–9.

in the house of Commons to attend to what passes on the Continent'.[10]

Malmesbury went too far, but certainly one of the worst weaknesses of British diplomacy was the failure of the secretaries of state to keep the agents abroad adequately informed and instructed. Joseph Yorke, for example, wrote in 1750 to Bedford's under-secretary to suggest that he should find out who supplied the Dutch gazettes with their extremely well-informed articles; and then added: 'It is really quite indecent that we should inform all Europe of what we are doing when we don't even let our own ministers in foreign courts into these negotiations.'[11] Lord Polwarth, in the reign of George I, is stated to have 'received more ample information of what was going forward both at home and abroad' from Robethon, a Hanoverian secretary attached to the king, 'than in the strictly official correspondence received by him'.[12] This statement is confirmed by a comparison of his formal instructions on taking up his post at Copenhagen with the much more elaborate and informative memorandum he received from Robethon, who continued to send him information which he did not get from his official superiors until later, if at all.[13] Prior, on the other hand, complained while he was secretary of embassy at Paris that Blathwayt ought to have kept him informed of the king's movements, since the French court 'is inquisitive enough and value those ministers that they see know their business and can give an account of their own department ... a consul in any corner of Italy shall be certainly written to—no matter for the secretary at Paris; for Lacrimae Christi and White Florence are very good wines: but this is too ill-natured a reflection'.[14] Towards the end of the Austrian Succession War, when Britain and Austria were fighting for the liberties of Europe against the house of Bourbon, Robinson at Vienna could write to one of his colleagues: 'I expect nothing from England till the opening of the Parliament when I shall take the King's speech as my clue for the ensuing year.'[15]

Defective liaison was particularly serious when there was a change in policy, as at the Diplomatic Revolution. Keene at Madrid, a key post in view of the importance attached by Newcastle to keeping Spain out of the French orbit, was never informed of the

---

[10] *Supra*, Chapter I, p. 3.
[11] S.P. 78. 237, 18/29 Sept. 1750.
[12] H.M.C., *Polwarth MSS*. i. vii.
[13] Ibid. i. 145–6, &c.
[14] H.M.C., *Bath MSS*. iii. 258.
[15] Add. MS. 23875, fo. 377b.

break with Austria and therefore maintained with the Austrian agent at Madrid relations of cordiality and confidence which were quite unjustified in the new situation of affairs.[16]

Some secretaries of state were worse, in this respect, than others; and their neglect was rarely attributable to preoccupation with the House of Commons. Bedford's long week-ends at Woburn were notorious, but the most neglectful of them all was probably Carmarthen. This partially explains the extent of the younger Pitt's correspondence with leading diplomats abroad in the eighties. Sir R. M. Keith protested so violently from Vienna against Carmarthen's neglect that he was given by his superior the option of withdrawing his protest or resigning his commission. Keith then wrote: 'Not a line of answer was given to fifty successive public dispatches, nor to my earnest yet respectful representation of the situation of my private affairs, and of the well founded claims of my secretary, Mr. Stratton. . . .' Then Keith received one dispatch from the Foreign Office and 'soon after that period the Emperor's declaration of war against the Turks rendered the scene at Vienna extremely interesting. Yet from the date of your lordship's dispatch above-mentioned, I have received but one answer (relative to the business of my mission) to about forty of mine.'[17] What moved Keith to frenzy was the failure of Carmarthen to give him any indication that the British government was about to conclude an alliance with Prussia; Keith goes on to explain that, basing his conduct on the single dispatch which he had received,

I remained in the firm conviction that *if ever* the King in his wisdom should see just grounds for departing from those political principles which he had invariably professed, and had (through his secretaries of state, during my sixteen years' mission) enjoined me to look upon as the strict rules of my conduct; his minister for foreign affairs could not fail to make an immediate change in my instructions, by a *few confidential lines*, and without giving me a larger share in the secrets of my royal master, than the good of his service absolutely demanded. Nothing more could have been required than such an act of common justice, and of state policy, to save me from the possible danger of *committing the King's name* by any ill-timed efforts of my zeal in prosecuting an object, which (though repeatedly recommended to me) could, even if attainable, be no longer embraced. . . . Of all situations, my lord, that of a foreign minister

[16] *Keene Corresp.*, p. 463.   [17] *Keith Memoir*, ii. 228.

wholly deprived of the confidence of his court, and who is allowed, nay, even encouraged to proceed in a political pursuit which, in its complete success, could only lead him to disgrace and disavowal on the part of his master, is the meanest and most shameful.[18]

Another four months passed before Keith received an answer from his principal to this spirited protest.

Milder complaints against Carmarthen came from other quarters. Even William Eden, one of the Prime Minister's trusted advisers, wrote to Pitt: 'I speculate in the dark in my correspondence because I receive so few and such short answers to everything that I write; but I am not quite discouraged by that circumstance.'[19]

This bad tradition continued into the nineteenth century. Sir Charles Webster holds that it was not really until the Palmerston era in diplomacy that foreign secretaries fully appreciated the necessity of supplying ambassadors with information about the whole trend of foreign affairs and circulated dispatches freely so that they could know what was going on at the other courts.[20] This practice was certainly not new, though it was no doubt more systematically carried out by Palmerston. For example, when Stormont was ambassador to France in the seventies, we are told that the government must have 'attached great importance to his opinions, for some of their despatches to other courts are nothing but repetitions of Stormont's observations from Paris'.[21]

It should, however, be remembered that by immemorial custom circular letters were sent to all ministers abroad, or to a particular category of them, on some official occasions. Thus a new secretary of state immediately intimated to all agents in his province that he had received the seals, and that, until further notice, all official letters should be addressed to him or to his under-secretary. Court news was often communicated in the same way, as when Addison, as secretary of state, sent 'a sort of circular letter . . . by the late King's orders, to all the English ministers in foreign courts' to give them the official account of the quarrel between George I and the Prince of Wales.[22] When Parliament was in session accounts of important debates were often transmitted in the same way.

[18] *Keith Memoir*, ii. 229–31.   [19] *Auckland Journal*, i. 295.
[20] C. K. Webster, *Foreign Policy of Palmerston*, i. 71.
[21] *British Diplomatic Instructions: France 1745–89*, ed. Legg, p. 128.
[22] *Hervey Memoirs*, p. 845.

Though these circular letters were not systematically preserved until much later, if at all, many are to be found among the general correspondence at the Public Record Office. Others dating from the reign of George III will be found in special files, such as those about Mediterranean passes, royal marriages, naval victories, exports and imports, &c.[23] Appreciable numbers have been printed, chiefly amongst the publications of the Historical Manuscripts Commission.[24]

The usual answer of the secretaries of state to complaints that they did not keep closely in touch with agents abroad was that these agents had all received instructions, on appointment, to correspond regularly with each other and keep their colleagues informed of anything which it was desirable for the good of the service that they should know. This instruction was, on the whole, punctiliously observed and such correspondence sometimes throws useful light on the more official correspondence between the agents abroad and the secretary of state at home. It must have been invaluable to the diplomatists at the more isolated courts, such as Constantinople and St. Petersburg. At the nearer courts, it was supplemented by the regular practice of sending the dispatches to the secretary of state under flying seal, so that our representatives, for example at The Hague and Paris, were kept up to date on the course of some of the British negotiations abroad without the intervention of the secretary of state's office. Such devices, however, were a mere palliative and broke down badly when there was a sudden change of policy or attitude at home. This discussion concerns primarily the courts at which there was real political business to transact: at many lesser courts our diplomatic agents managed to get along comfortably with only an occasional letter from their official superior.

Neglect by the secretary of state was often mitigated by less formal and therefore usually more valuable letters from an under-secretary or politically active friend. Robinson wrote to Newcastle's confidential secretary, Andrew Stone: 'A single word gives sometimes more light than twenty despatches of state and I hope to have the peculiar happiness . . . not to be abandoned to

[23] F.O. 83. 8.
[24] e.g. *Polwarth MSS.*: here the under-secretary seems to have made a regular practice of writing a personal letter to Polwarth on the flyleaf of the office circular.

the dry necessity of a literal execution of orders.'[25] Partly for this reason, diplomatists resented failure by their friends at home to keep up an active private correspondence. As Buckinghamshire wrote from St. Petersburg:

> I have often complained of the slender information with which my friends in England favour me, but never with the tenth part of the reason which I have now, in that, except deaths and marriages, I know nothing of my own country and am never able to contradict any idle report which the flippancy of a Gazette writer or the real or wilful misinformation of a foreign minister prompts him to propagate.[26]

Keene, on the other hand, told Castres that he had 'no private correspondence upon our interior affairs, partly for indolence, partly for having no private views'.[27]

There was no precise or rigid demarcation of the duties of a diplomatic agent. Not only was the line between the work of a diplomatist and a consul (when both were employed in the same area) somewhat blurred; diplomatists were also expected to make themselves useful in spheres hardly connected with diplomacy. When the institution of the London Foundling Hospital was under consideration in 1739 British diplomatic agents at Paris, Amsterdam, Venice, and Lisbon reported how the existing institutions in these towns were organized.[28] Similarly John Howard, the prison reformer, received invaluable help from some diplomatists. Sir Joseph Yorke provided him with letters of introduction to his colleagues, while Sir R. M. Keith arranged contacts for him at Vienna, including a private audience of the Emperor Joseph II.[29] Whitworth procured for him in Russia a courier's pass 'by which I go smoothly on without stopping for horses, which is often the case when there are ten or twelve in the stable at the post-houses'.[30] And when the younger Pitt was looking around for additional sources of revenue he asked Harris at The Hague to obtain information for him about the Dutch tax on successions 'relative to the detail of collecting this tax, how far it is supposed to be fairly paid, what is its average produce and whether any inconveniency is complained of—especially by persons in *trade* from the necessity of discovering the amount of

[25] S.P. 80. 179, 20 Mar. 1748, N.S.   [26] H.M.C., *Lothian MSS.*, p. 187.
[27] *Keene Corresp.*, p. 293.
[28] J. H. Hutchins, *Jonas Hanway*, p. 19.
[29] *Keith Memoir*, ii. 185–6.   [30] Ibid. ii. 203.

any property they succeed to.'[31] On the basis of Harris's reply Pitt imposed legacy duties in Britain.

Naturally diplomatists were used in connexion with the king's private affairs. Hanbury Williams, while envoy at Dresden, was instructed to try to collect a loan due by the elector of Saxony to George II; and while ambassador to Russia to secure permission, at a time of scarcity, for the export of grain to Hanover. Consul Burnett at Lisbon was told 'to look out for seeds or plants to improve his Majesty's kitchen gardens'. He replied that only the onions of St. Ubes were worth exporting, but subsequently sent Murcian cabbage (a kind of colewort) with long instructions for its cultivation in England. A month later he sent another sort of colewort and seeds of the onions of St. Ubes.[32] George II, shortly after his accession, asked Burnett to send seeds of water-melons and cucumbers[33] and when Queen Caroline was troubled with a cough she obtained from Portugal powders used for this complaint—with what effect, if any, does not appear.[34] Henry Newton, envoy in Italy, was engaged in sending seeds to Queen Anne,[35] and George III made use of Sir Joseph Yorke in the king's private affairs,[36] and also instructed his diplomatic representative to the Hanse Towns 'to convey to her Danish Majesty [George III's sister in exile] authentic information of the health of her royal children [at Copenhagen]'.[37]

Secretaries of state could also count on similar attentions from the *corps diplomatique*. Dormer, while envoy at Lisbon, was busy collecting evergreens for Newcastle's gardens at Claremont.[38]

More often the diplomatists provided a channel of communication for foreigners and British residents abroad who for some reason or another wished to make contact with the British government. Most of these were spies while others were mainly interested in getting permission to reside in Britain. But a considerable volume of entirely unpolitical material found its way through our agents abroad to the secretary of state's office. Much of this was probably filed unread as may well have been the fate of a long and elaborate paper on artificial respiration, published by the Hamburg 'Society for the Promoting of Arts and Useful Trades'. One

---

[31] *Malmesbury Diaries*, ii. 156–7.
[32] S.P. 89. 31.
[33] S.P. 89. 91, dispatch of 8 Dec. 1729.
[34] S.P. 89. 36.
[35] S.P. 79. 3.
[36] *George III Corresp.* i. 207–9, &c.
[37] S.P. 82. 91, dispatch of 7 Aug. 1772.
[38] S.P. 89. 31.

of the remedies suggested was to blow into the corpse air and tobacco smoke, while would-be artificial respirators were urged not to keep the body topsy-turvy nor to roll and move it about imprudently. Impressed by this display of medical erudition, the Hamburg Senate offered a reward of 50 marks or a medal of the same value to any one who had restored to life any such unfortunate persons.[39]

In at least one case we have the secretary of state's reply to a hopeful inventor: 'His lordship is rather diffident of the nostrum of the chymical Jew to extract pitch and tar and vitriol and saltpetre out of our common sea coal and cannot think of encouraging the projector to expect ten thousand pounds for [this] secret.'[40]

Occasionally foreign sovereigns made British diplomatists abroad a channel of communication with the British government. Thus Catherine II employed Alleyne Fitzherbert when she wanted to obtain a telescope of great power, similar to that specially made by Herschel for George III, to secure the royal authorization, without which Herschel refused to construct Catherine's telescope.[41]

A recurring problem which faced many British diplomatists abroad was that of their relations with Opposition factions at the court where they were resident. On this topic they received a great deal of advice from Wicquefort and Callières; but the problem is most clearly stated by Hervey:

In my opinion, there are very few situations in which a foreign minister employed at any Court can act politically by caballing with the enemies to the people in power there. If the nation is ripe for a revolt, or for insurrections and civil wars, and that it is the interest of the court by whom that minister is employed to foment these divisions and weaken the government, he may possibly do his master some little service by promoting such measures, but more probably come to be ruined without doing him any; and as to common cases, though it may be for the honour and often even for the interest of a native to adhere to the under party and oppose the people in power, yet it can seldom or never be so for a foreign negotiator; in the first place, as it excludes that foreigner immediately from any pretence to favour, or any hope of confidence; in the next, as an ambassador to any court is sent to the crown and not to the king, to the minister and not to the man, so whoever wears the one, and is the other, those persons for the time being are the persons to whom an ambassador should

---

[39] S.P. 82. 87.   [40] S.P. 88. 109, dispatch of 14 Mar. 1775.
[41] H.M.C., *Report XI, App. VII* (Leeds MSS.), p. 55.

address himself; and the shifting his applications as fast as the crown changes its master, or the king his servant, is certainly what not only in prudence he ought to do, but what with honour he may do, how ignominious soever the like conduct would be in a native, who must betray the party he last acted with, and the principles he last acted upon, to behave in that manner.[42]

It should be added that as opposition was usually more organized and vocal at London than at continental courts, this was a still more serious question for foreign diplomatists in England. At least from Charles II's time, many of them involved themselves too closely with Opposition groups. Jersey, when secretary of state under William III, described a paper, copies of which had been given by the Spanish secretary at London to all the Lords Justices, as 'complaining to the nation of what his Majesty is doing'.[43] William III expelled the Spanish ambassador from London on the ground that he was stirring up sedition against the government,[44] while the Imperial and Hanoverian ministers who had joined the Whigs in opposing the peace negotiations with France 'were both forbid the Court' by Anne in 1712.[45] Yet Louis XIV is said to have told his ambassador to London in 1712 that English constitutional usage made it inoffensive to the court for foreign ambassadors to have contacts with the Opposition and that he need not therefore avoid social contacts with the Whig leaders.

Under George I the Austrian minister at London, Count Palm, tried to undermine Walpole's position with the king and was known to Walpole, owing to systematic interception of his dispatches, to be in close contact with Pulteney.[46] A few years later Horace Walpole explained to Waldegrave:

I do not know by what fatality, that all the Imperial ministers that come to this court [London], of what condition and quality so ever they are, will think the best way of doing their business, and of being informed, is to seek the acquaintance of those whose views naturally lead them to keep up the misunderstanding between his Majesty and the Emperor. . . . [They] fancy by getting false lights they are able to learn more than others who know the true state of things here [sc. Horace and his brother].[47]

[42] *Hervey Memoirs*, ii. 521.
[43] H.M.C., *Bath MSS*. iii. 376.
[44] *Spain under Charles II*, ed. Lord Mahon (2nd ed., 1844), pp. 192–4.
[45] A. Cunningham, *History of Great Britain*, ii. 386.
[46] Coxe, *Walpole Memoirs*, ii. 507–9.   [47] Ibid., p. 637.

Nor was such conduct limited to the Austrian diplomatists. Horace Walpole bitterly condemned the French ambassador's conduct at the time of the Excise scheme. 'No sooner has any body felt the disgrace of the court', he writes,

but he immediately finds a kind welcome from monsieur Chavigny.... [Chavigny] encourages all persons and practices against the court; ridicules, blames and decries all the English ministers; paints them on all occasions as having lost their parts as well as their credit, as being so odious to the nation, and in so tottering a condition that their fall is inevitable; extols their enemies as able men and good patriots and as having concerted such measures as cannot fail of success.[48]

The confidential relations between the Prussian minister, Andrié, and the Opposition during the War of the Austrian Succession are clearly indicated.[49] Similarly in the sixties George Grenville thought that the Russian ambassador, Vorontzov, was too closely connected with Pitt and consequently sent to his own government unfavourable reports of the ministry.[50] In extreme cases such conduct by foreign diplomatists at London so infuriated the British government that it practically ceased to do business with them, with the incidental result of raising the importance of their own ministers abroad, since these now became the sole channel of communication between the courts.

This brief treatment of the duties of eighteenth-century British diplomatists would seem to support the generalization of an Italian historian that it was during this century that diplomatists' horizons widened from courts to countries.[51]

Another problem which caused much heartburning later to diplomatic agents was almost unknown in the eighteenth century—the danger that their confidential papers might have to be submitted to Parliament and even published. Such publication was rare, though not entirely unknown. The reaction of William Eden to this danger was undoubtedly the normal one when he wrote to the Prime Minister:

Have the goodness to tell me what papers you mean to lay before

[48] Coxe, *Walpole Memoirs*, iii. 139.   [49] *Marchmont Papers*, i. 46–47.
[50] *Grenville Papers*, ii. 240.
[51] *Relazioni di Ambasciatori Sabaudi, Genovese e Veneti (1693–1713)*, ed. Carlo Morandi, pp. xxii–xxiii.

the House. It is with me a general opinion, which every observation has confirmed, that, in foreign politics, the fewer papers you give the better; and that, as to domestic information, it is generally impossible to give too much. [Suggests certain papers may have to be communicated in whole or in part and concludes] Surely it will be right to avoid any further or larger communication of correspondence; perhaps even it is unnecessary to give any papers.[52]

It was already a tradition for the Opposition to ask for the communication of papers relating to foreign negotiations as a preliminary to a full-dress attack upon the government's foreign policy. Some of these motions were drawn in exceedingly wide terms. In 1730 Lord Morpeth moved (unsuccessfully) in the House of Commons 'that his Majesty should be addressed to lay before the House all the papers relating to the negotiations of his Majesty in whatever parts of Europe, or to that effect'.[53] Knowing the use that would be made of them if they were to be communicated, the government naturally used its majority against such demands. Even much more specific requests for papers such as the one made in 1734 to secure communication of the instructions given to British ministers in Poland since 1729 were normally rejected by the court and treasury party.[54] No doubt it was partly from this point of view that Sunderland, an expert in parliamentary management, is reported to have told the French ambassador that 'whenever an English minister has but sixty majority in a house of commons he was undone'.[55] And after Pitt's resignation in 1761 Bute wrote to Grenville: 'I do own I look on this demand for papers in the light of procuring materials in order to try the cause between the King and his late secretary [Pitt].'[56]

In spite of the normal unwillingness of eighteenth-century governments to supply materials for an attack on themselves, dispatches from ambassadors were sometimes produced and led to debates in both Houses.[57] Frequently when such papers were supplied Opposition members immediately asked for more. In 1771 Lord North reported to George III: 'after the papers were read which were presented today to the house, Mr. Seymour made a motion to address his Majesty to inform the house, if there had

[52] *Auckland Journal*, i. 275–6.
[53] H.M.C., *Egmont Diary*, i. 10.
[55] Ibid., p. 150.
[57] e.g. H.M.C., *Egmont Diary*, iii. 287, 291.

[54] Ibid. ii. 12–13.
[56] *Grenville Papers*, i. 417.

been any interference of the court of France in the late negotiation [with Spain] and to acquaint them with all transactions relative to the said interference, if there has been any.'[58] The stock ministerial argument was that to produce the papers called for would be contrary to the public interest and would endanger the success of the delicate negotiations upon which the government was engaged with one or more foreign powers. Pelham perhaps stated this more effectively than his predecessors and successors, but they all used it.

Another difficulty which sometimes caused annoyance to diplomatic agents abroad was the appearance of entirely unofficial agents, sometimes closely connected with leading members of the Opposition. Rochford attributed his failure to deter France from gaining control of Corsica in 1768 to the appearance at Paris of Lord Mansfield and his 'imprudent declaration . . . at one of the minister's tables, "that the English ministry were too weak, and the nation too wise to support them in entering on a war for the sake of Corsica"'. Few such interventions had much influence on the course of events. In the case just cited it is clear that Choiseul had independent information to the same effect from his own agent at London.[59] A few years later, in 1774, Lord Mansfield again visited Paris, ostensibly to stay with his nephew the ambassador, Lord Stormont; but according to Horace Walpole, 'to endeavour a nearer alliance with France in our present situation, the difficulties in the colonies increasing, and the power of the Emperor with his sister the Queen of France threatening us'. In Walpole's view Mansfield was prepared, if the French agreed not to interfere in our differences with America, to 'promise all submission on our part to other views of France'.[60]

But the best known of these unofficial interventions was the Fox–Adair mission to Austria and Russia at the time of the Ochakov incident. Adair long afterwards claimed that he travelled to St. Petersburg via Vienna entirely on his own responsibility, although he admitted Fox said to him: 'Well, if you are determined to go, send us all the news' and for this purpose provided him with a cipher.[61] The Russian ambassador at London, Vorontzov, may also have been privy to the scheme and provided Adair with letters of recommendation to the Russian court. The British

[58] George III Corresp. ii. 214.   [59] Grafton, Autobiography, p. 204.
[60] Last Journals, i. 394–5.   [61] Memorials of C. J. Fox, ii. 383–7.

ambassador at St. Petersburg was at first taken in by the letter of
recommendation Adair brought with him from the duchess of
Devonshire, but soon discovered that Adair showed 'the most
virulent opposition to His Majesty's measures, and takes great
pains to counteract the negotiation'.[62] In Holland Rose's opinion
Adair's 'presence at St. Petersburg and the biassed information
which he supplied greatly harmed the cause of the Allies; and
Pitt, after seeing copies of Adair's letters, was justified in hinting
that his action had prejudiced the success of Britain's efforts at
St. Petersburg'.[63]

For ministers who failed a speedy recall and no further employment were usually regarded as sufficient punishment. George III
thought that 'those who have had unpleasant missions should not
return upon a more favourable aspect'.[64] Charles II, indeed, had
intended to make Ralph Montagu, his ambassador to France, the
scapegoat for his discredited pro-French policy.[65] James II had
actually sent one envoy who had incurred the royal displeasure to
the Tower,[66] but this precedent was never followed. Towards the
end of William III's reign when a dispute arose about the succession to a former ambassador of Charles II's to Spain, who died
leaving all his money to the Jesuits, 'many people were for adding
a clause [to an act declaring such wills void] that whatsoever ambassador should break his trust, his goods should be forfeited to
the king'.[67] Less extreme measures were, however, occasionally
taken with conspicuous offenders. Legge, who had taken some
Hanoverian business out of the hands of his Hanoverian colleague at Berlin and who was said to have attributed to the king's
arrival at Hanover the defeat of this design, 'was summoned to
Hanover and received a severe reprimand'. He had offended Newcastle, one of the secretaries of state, as well as the king by imply-
ing that his Grace was subservient to the Hanoverian ministers.[68]
When Brigadier James Dormer's servants attacked the British
consul at Lisbon in 1727, and led the Portuguese government to
accuse him of trying to murder the consul, Dormer was merely

[62] Quoted in J. Holland Rose, *William Pitt and National Revival*, pp. 623–4.
[63] Ibid., p. 624.
[64] *George III Corresp.* vi. 230.
[65] J. P. Kenyon, *Sunderland*, p. 18.
[66] James Macpherson, *Original Papers*, i. 263.
[67] A. Cunningham, *History of Great Britain*, i. 208.
[68] Coxe, *Pelham Administration*, i. 441.

ordered to dismiss the servants engaged in the unfortunate affair and return to England to justify his conduct to the king.[69]

More serious was the offence of the earl of Peterborough, who had deserted his post in Spain 'to negotiate matters with other Princes [in Italy], without any orders from the Queen for so doing, or any credentials to those Princes'. To make matters worse he had 'taken up great sums of money there at a most extravagant price . . . the same having been drawn without any authority or permission from her Majesty, and at such a price which, if answered, must affect all the remittances that shall be necessary to be made for the public service the whole year'. These bills were dishonoured and he was ordered to 'return forthwith to England to acquaint her Majesty with the reasons and grounds of your proceedings'.[70] After discussion in the Cabinet Council it was agreed Peterborough was to be 'told it is expected he should attend her Majesty and the Cabinet Council with the reasons which induced him to quit the army in Spain and go to the duke of Savoy, without order or leave upon that occasion, though in case any forces had been sent thither he had indeed leave to command those forces'.[71]

The case of Lord Strafford, one of the negotiators of the treaty of Utrecht a few years later, was quite different from this, although he, too, was summoned to appear before the king and Privy Council. According to Lord Wharton's report:

The Council met, Earl of Strafford called in. Lord President told him that, it being the custom that ambassadors at their return, should render an account to the King in Council, of their negotiations, his Majesty had now sent for him for that end (as he had required him before by a Secretary of State) and that, in order to it, it was his Majesty's pleasure that he should deliver to the Secretaries of State all his instructions, orders, letters, copies of letters, etc. relating thereto.

Earl of Strafford said, he owned it was his duty to render such an account, that whilst the King was at The Hague, he had prepared and laid before him such an account as he thought proper thereof, that he hoped he should have since allowed to digest into order what he had to say. That he had but few papers here, a great part of them being in his baggage, not yet come from the ships. Being asked if all there,

[69] S.P. 89. 32–34, especially dispatch of 10 Nov. 1727.
[70] H.M.C., *Bath MSS.* i. 153.   [71] Ibid., p. 178.

said, he had part here. That he executed what he had in charge, as
a faithful servant to the Queen, as a good subject, and as a true
Englishman. That he desired he should be considered, that in the
negotiations of peace he was but second plenipotentiary. That the
Bishop of Bristol, as the first, had all the originals, and he only
copies.

Earl of Strafford withdrawn. Long silence before any motion made.
Lord Wharton at last moved that the Earl of Strafford should be told
that the King would immediately send the Secretaries of State with
him, to receive such papers &c., as he had in town. Lord Sunderland
of the same opinion, and also that other persons should be sent, with
such as the Earl of Sunderland should appoint, to seal up all boxes,
&c., with his baggage.

This pretty warmly opposed by Duke of Shrewsbury as what had
been never done to any ambassador, and assuming those papers being
his evidence.

The King said it had been done to Lord Townshend. Lord Townshend: That he was directed at his return to deliver up all his papers,
and that he, for that reason, never went any whither without them,
but that they were never called for.

Duke of Shrewsbury replied that it was unnecessary, because all
papers, &c., sent or received had duplicates of them in the Secretary's
office; that when that office was searched he never saw papers in so
good order. Lord Wharton replied, that for that very reason it was fit
now to demand his papers, &c., because upon perusing papers in the
office, it was found that there were many papers wanting.

Earl of Strafford called. Lord President declared the King's pleasure.
Earl of Strafford, that he was much surprised to be so treated, like a
criminal, that he was a peer, that this was the first instance of any so
treated, that he had many papers of private concern, not fit to be laid
before the King, and all in confusion. That it would be a great discredit to him; spoke much of his innocence, hoped he should be
trusted, that he would not run away out of his coach, desired he might
go away, as if he were taken in custody by a couple of secretaries. (The
first part of his discourse in a submissive strain very often, but the
latter part disordered.) Withdrew. When he came out, he beckoned
the envoy of Sweden, and whispered him, who went straight away.
Earl of Strafford followed in a very little time. Lord Townshend and
secretary Stanhope went after him to his house, stayed a quarter of an
hour. Earl of Strafford then carried them down to a closet, opened
several cabinets, &c., bid them take what they thought fit. They said
they would take nothing but what he delivered to them. He then took
out several books, and desired them to see if they were what they
wanted. They refused again to look, but said they would only take

what he gave them. After much dispute of this kind, he filled two boxes of papers, and they were tied up; and when they came to be sealed, he refused to put his seal, saying that would be to consent to what was done. To which it was replied that nothing had been, nor should be, done without his consent; and that if he did not seal them they would not meddle with them, but would acquaint the King. He at last sealed the tape where it was tied, and the two secretaries also put their seals, and carried the boxes away to the Council Chamber, where they were also sealed by the Lord President.

The clerks of the Council, and under secretaries who were sent to seal up the baggage, met the waggons coming into St. James's Square, took out, and sealed up the several parcels in them, and put them into a stable, the door of which they also sealed up.[72]

This account[73] makes clear that the object was to gain possession of papers which might compromise Strafford's superiors, Oxford and Bolingbroke, and be used as the basis of a criminal prosecution against them. Unlike the case of Peterborough, so far as there was a personal attack upon Strafford, he was arraigned for carrying out faithfully the policy of the government which had employed him, by the men who had been in opposition at the time, and had violently opposed that policy, and were now in power. This applies equally to the similar proceedings against Matthew Prior, which are detailed in some of the papers included in the first volume of his *Miscellaneous Works*, published in 1740.

Even later than this, occasional threats were made to punish diplomatists whose work was disapproved by a section of the Houses of Parliament. Benjamin Keene, who had negotiated the unpopular Convention of the Pardo with Spain in January 1739, was threatened with impeachment on the fall of Walpole merely because he had carried out successfully the instructions of his superiors.[74] Keene and Castres,[75] and many later diplomatists who concluded unpopular treaties, continued to be roughly handled by the Opposition press.

Cases of deliberate disobedience to instructions seem to be rare: in the first half of the century, when Jacobitism was still strong amongst certain British communities abroad, such disobedience is occasionally attributed to the Jacobite sympathies of the agents employed. These included an ambassador at Constantinople, the

[72] H.M.C., *Portland MSS.* v. 503–5.   [73] Ibid.
[74] *Keene Corresp.*, p. xii.   [75] Ibid., p. 498.

earl of Kinnoull,[76] whose brother had been created earl of Inverness by the Old Pretender, though other explanations of his misconduct seem more plausible.

Attacks on foreign ministers were usually directed against them as agents of the government, rather than as individuals. Horace Walpole often attracted unfavourable notice, largely because he was the Prime Minister's brother and confidential adviser on foreign affairs. The literary value of such attacks is usually low when written in prose and even lower when indignation produced verse:

> To purpose Horace said not much,
> But made a heavy splutter
> Of Treaties when he beat the Dutch
> In the famed point of butter.[77]

One of the few diplomatists to be attacked ostensibly as an individual was Horace Walpole's brother-in-law, Isaac Leheup, who had discharged various minor commissions to the German courts before being appointed as envoy to Sweden in 1727. Travelling to Sweden by way of Hanover he fell foul of the electoral prince, better known in England as Poor Fred, and was accused of insulting words and behaviour towards the ladies of the Herrenhausen court. This produced his peremptory recall after nineteen days at Stockholm; and, according to the *Craftsman*, made him on his return to London 'a constant subject for jest and ridicule for the whole town', including at least one broadside.[78] This ballad described his arrival at Hanover where he was at first mistaken for a post-boy:

> Incens'd at this, he rav'd and storm'd,
> And made a mighty Pother,
> And swore by G—d he'd teach them all
> To know Sir R[ober]t's Brother
>
> . . .
>
> But then at Supper as they sat
> Drinking and gaily sporting
> *Le H[eu]p* with many a smutty joke
> His Neighbour fell a courting.

---

[76] Basil Williams, article in *Blackwood's Magazine* for Jan. 1907, p. 99.

[77] W. W. Wilkins, *Political Ballads*, ii. 195.

[78] M. O. Percival, *Political Ballads illustrating the administration of Sir Robert Walpole*, p. 17.

Leheup's conduct led to a brawl, but Prince Frederick is depicted as keeping his temper:

> And said, This Man my Father sent,
> And shall we use him ill?
>
> No! I to England with this News
> A letter will indite:
> The King and Queen shall know it all,
> And they will do me right.

The real object of this exercise in verse appeared in the concluding stanzas. Leheup was seized upon as a convenient means of attacking the Walpole government.

> My Father will revenge th'Affront,
> And turn out all his Kin,
> From him that does for *Y[armou]th* serve,
> To him that serves for *L[y]n*.
>
> Now God bless both our K[in]g and Q[uee]n,
> And may they quickly do it,
> Or shortly else (full well I ween)
> They will have Cause to rue it.

Another example of personal attack was Sheridan's motion in the Commons for a vote of censure on Lord Auckland in 1793 because he had demanded that any French regicides who fell into the hands of the allies should be 'subjected to the sword of the law'.[79] Although it had Fox's support, Sheridan's motion was rejected by 211 votes to 36. Later in 1793 Auckland was violently attacked in the House of Lords by Lord Stanhope, who compared him to Herod, Nero, and Caligula. Stanhope found no supporters and Grenville, the Foreign Secretary, moved a resolution approving of Auckland's conduct, which was carried without a division.[80]

Such overt and public attacks were rare and nearly always covered by parliamentary privilege; but diplomatists were continually being criticized behind their backs by their contemporaries. The commonest charge was that they did not sufficiently impress upon foreign courts the views and needs of their own government. John Chetwynd, Anne's envoy to Savoy, was described by a visiting soldier as 'rather a creature of the Duke [of

---

[79] *P.H.* xxx, col. 705.   [80] *P.H.* xxx, cols. 1035–43.

Savoy]'s than that of our Ministry'.[81] Lord Halifax wrote of John Methuen, for long envoy at Lisbon:

I have always thought Methuen was the ruin of our affairs in Spain. He was truly the minister of Portugal and not of England. He diverted the war from being made in the West Indies, which would have enriched us and touched Spain most sensibly, to carry it into a place from whence we had no assistance, but they had our money and France the silver of the Indies.[82]

In the same way successive British ministers at Vienna during the vogue of the 'old system' are continually represented at home as being unduly subservient to Austria and neither capable nor willing to stand up to the Emperor or Empress-Queen.

More general criticisms were often made, usually by interested parties, of the whole service. The Deist, John Toland, wrote to Harley: 'I observe you are in many things very ill-served abroad. Do but once order me, and I shall soon convince you what I can draw from The Hague, from Hanover, from Berlin, Dusseldorf and Vienna; and what in all those places I can diffuse.' And all this Harley could have for '£200 a year, quarterly paid', preferably with an immediate loan of £20.[83]

Occasionally, instead of publicly attacking a diplomatic agent, the critic made a private approach to the secretary of state. Grafton, according to his own account, while in Opposition, had a private conversation with Lord Weymouth, in which he censured the behaviour of Stormont as ambassador at Paris. He accused Stormont of negligence or worse, and claimed to give the secretary better information of the intentions of the French court than he would be likely to receive from the ambassador. He can hardly have been surprised when he 'was coldly thanked for my attention and dismissed without being questioned on any one particular'.[84]

---

[81] H.M.C., *Portland MSS.* v. 154.
[82] H.M.C., *Bath MSS.* i. 155, and cf. Consul Milner's criticisms in S.P. 89. 20.
[83] H.M.C., *Portland MSS.* v. 259–60.
[84] Grafton, *Autobiography*, pp. 285–7.

CHAPTER XI

Ceremonial and Privilege

THE importance attached in the eighteenth century to questions of ceremonial and etiquette seems disproportionate to present-day writers. It was certainly no greater than it had been in the previous centuries and most of the celebrated controversies can be traced back at least to the seventeenth century. In diplomacy as in other spheres the twentieth century has certainly become the century of the common man. Not merely has the common man at last found it possible to gain admission to the higher ranks of the diplomatic service. At the same time there has been a cheapening of the rank and privileges accorded by general consent in earlier centuries to ambassadors. Now that insignificant states claim and exercise the right to send ambassadors to Great Powers which would have haughtily declined in the eighteenth century to receive an ambassador except from a state which it recognized as an equal, ambassadorial status has declined.

> Ambassadors cropped up like hay,
> Prime Ministers and such as they
> Grew like asparagus in May,
> And Dukes were three a penny
>
> . . .
>
> When every one is somebodee
> Then no one's anybody!

Moreover, the Great Powers in the nineteenth century reached agreement about diplomatic ranks and gradually evolved techniques in conducting their negotiations which greatly reduced the influence and practical importance of ceremonial. Instead of arguing about the papal list of precedence for temporal sovereigns, or whether Power B was entitled in signing a treaty to claim the *alternat* with Power A, or insisting that, for example, British recognition of the claim of the Tsars to the imperial title should not in any way affect the existing ceremonial between Britain and Russia, the relative precedence of agents of different ranks was fairly clearly established and at great diplomatic congresses the order of signature of international treaties came to be determined by the alphabetical order of the names of the contracting states in the French language or even by mere chance.

No such clearly marked paths existed in the eighteenth-century jungle of diplomatic ceremonial. The only safe rule was to adhere closely to precedents,[1] to scrutinize with meticulous care any alterations in ceremonial and etiquette proposed by other parties and to exploit ruthlessly favourable political circumstances to secure recognition by other powers of your own disputed claims. An ambassador who, in negotiating a treaty, failed to secure the *alternat* was felt to have damaged his country's interests just as much as one who signed away a province unnecessarily at the end of a disastrous war. The consequent loss of 'face' might well have practical political and economic consequences. A state which did not exert itself to secure and increase the respect of other states was clearly on the decline. Other powers would cease to regard it as an eligible ally while enemies might be encouraged to attack it politically, economically, and even on the battlefield.

It was generally agreed that the Holy Roman Emperor, in virtue of his imperial title and ecumenical traditions, took precedence of all other temporal sovereigns. In the seventeenth century Spain and France hotly disputed second place, while England and other rising powers gradually asserted their claims. This dispute between France and Spain cropped up several times and on at least one occasion at London under Charles II led to homicide. After the conflict was resolved by the accession of the Bourbons to the Spanish throne and the manifest decline of Spain from her sixteenth-century pre-eminence, considerable difficulty was experienced in fitting the Russian diplomatists into the West European world of diplomacy. As late as 1768, when the French ambassador at London saw that his Russian colleague had taken the place of honour next to the Austrian ambassador at a court ball, he pushed in between them and later fought a duel with his rival in which the Russian ambassador was wounded.[2]

Cobbett, in his translation of Martens' *Law of Nations*, included a chapter on methods of avoiding ceremonial disputes concerning

[1] *'Le cérémonial se règle ordinairement sur le passé'* said Rousset de Missy in the editorial preface to his massive work (*infra*, p. 213).
[2] H. Nicolson, *Evolution of Diplomatic Method*, p. 45.

precedence. His suggestions were: (1) to observe exact equality or take the lead alternately, (2) to come *incognito* or send a minister of a different rank, (3) to be absent to avoid yielding, or (4) to yield and protest or insist upon written assurances that what is done is not to be a precedent. He believed that 'the politeness of our manners and the respect courts pay to each other' formed a barrier against violences such as had happened at London in 1661 between the French and Spanish ambassadors, though he was compelled to admit that 'modern history ... furnishes some few examples'.[3]

But even if it had proved possible to draw up and secure general acceptance of a table of precedence for states, this would have done little to settle the problems of diplomatic ceremonial. Suppose Britain and France had agreed that at any court to which they were accredited their ambassadors should take place according to the date of their arrival at that court, this left untouched other equally thorny problems. What ceremonial was to be observed when a French ambassador and a British envoy were accredited to the same court? And as new diplomatic ranks were introduced and the hierarchy of diplomatic agents became at the same time more extensive and less clearly defined, such problems multiplied. The vagueness attaching to the common eighteenth-century ranks of Minister and Minister Plenipotentiary has been commented on with regard to their colleagues in the British diplomatic service.[4] But these titles were also used in the diplomatic services of other countries and did not carry precisely the same connotation as in the British service. Perhaps an even better example of this is the case of the secretary of embassy: when he was an official appointed and paid by the crown he might reasonably claim a superior status to that of his opposite numbers in other diplomatic services in which the secretary of embassy was merely the private servant of the ambassador.

One reason for the increase in ceremonial squabbles in the seventeenth century was the new technique of multi-national international congresses, usually at the end of wars which had roused bad feeling and created a situation in which compromise was more difficult than in peaceful times. Also the negotiators themselves tended to suffer from swollen heads, to magnify their own position of eminence and insist upon inessential external marks of distinction. Thus the negotiators at Ryswick in 1697

[3] Op. cit., pp. 143–4.   [4] *Supra*, Chapter III, pp. 44–47.

'agreed with the mediator that the guards . . . should let pass none but those who came in coaches with six horses' with the result that the two-horse-coached minister of Lorraine 'was excluded till some minister with a better equipage come by and took him up'.[5]

Another constant source of dispute concerned the precise extent of the privileges to which a British diplomatic agent, whatever his rank, was entitled at a particular court. When Alexander Cunningham took up his post as resident at Venice in 1715, he discovered that his predecessor had never had a public audience and that no precedents were to be found in living memory for the ceremonial of his reception.[6] Then Cunningham was succeeded by Burges who claimed[7] that in Cunningham's formal audience the doors should not have been shut, as they apparently were, but left open, as was the Venetian practice in receiving envoys from the greater courts. A similar difficulty arose when it was time for Burges to have his formal audience of leave.[8] When Gray was appointed as Resident to Venice in 1746 he decided to avoid taking a formal audience, as Burges had done, and thus escaped the problem of ceremonial. Gray's successor Murray adopted the same course in 1754.[9] The difficulty experienced over this relatively trivial matter is a clear indication that political relations between the two courts were unfriendly or at least regarded as not particularly important. The Venetian Republic had been one of the last powers to recognize William III as king of Great Britain; and as late as 1737–44 there was a complete rupture of diplomatic relations, owing to 'the extraordinary distinctions and honours paid to the Pretender's son at Venice'.[10] There had been as early as 1708 an unfortunate incident in which the British ambassador's servants had been caught smuggling prohibited goods into Venice. When Manchester protested at the affront put upon him, the Republic put its officers into prison, but was very reluctant to restore to Manchester the confiscated goods. Finally these were restored on condition that they were at once given by the ambassador to the Venetian hospitals.[11]

In spite of the long continuance of the old system of alliance

---

[5] H.M.C., *Buccleuch MSS.* ii. 469.
[6] S.P. 99. 61. [7] S.P. 99. 62.
[8] S.P. 99. 63. [9] S.P. 99. 64–66.
[10] *B.D.R.*, p. 84.
[11] Full details in Cole, *Memoirs*, pp. 519–48; Manchester, *Court and Society*, ii. 343–67.

with the Hapsburgs, there were frequent ceremonial difficulties at the court of Vienna. The first envoy after the Revolution of 1688 postponed his audience of the emperor until he could be informed of what the usual ceremonies were at the Imperial court for a diplomatist of his rank; and when the audience did take place he was dissatisfied with the ceremonial observed. In particular the Imperial court would give to the English sovereign merely the title of *Serenitas*, not *Majestas*,[12] on the ground that the Imperial Chancellary never gave the title of Majesty to a mere king. This argument was still going on in the reign of Anne when Stepney suggested that the best solution was to dispense with letters from the Chancellary and insist on having *lettres de cachet* written in French in the hand of the emperor. This was already the French practice, Stepney claimed, and what Austria was willing to do for her enemy, France, she could hardly refuse to her friend and ally, Great Britain.[13] It was partly to avoid ceremonial difficulties that ambassadors were rarely sent to Vienna and when Stormont, at the end of the Seven Years War, was given ambassadorial rank, the secretary of state's office bungled his credentials by describing him as *Ablegatus* (envoy) instead of *Legatus* (the customary word for ambassador). Fresh credentials had to be sent.[14]

Usually when relations between two states were friendly, it was possible to arrange some *modus vivendi*; but when problems of etiquette arose between two hostile states or, as often happened, were deliberately raised in the hope of causing embarrassment to the other state, then it might well tax the abilities of the ablest diplomatists to find a way out of the impasse. This is well illustrated by our relations with France. Louis XIV, with his genius for hieratic organization and precise definition, had prescribed a whole code of rules for the reception and entertainment of foreign ministers of different ranks at his court, while he was nearly always careful to prescribe to his own diplomatic agents abroad a rigid adherence to established ceremonial. These rules often caused embarrassment to British ministers to France. Thus when Stair, in the course of making his 'superb' public entry as ambassador in 1719, proposed to enter the courtyard of the Tuileries 'to

[12] S.P. 80. 17. Cf. H.M.C., *Finch MSS*. iii. 431.

[13] S.P. 80. 26, also 224.

[14] S.P. 80. 199. Stormont's dispatch, dated 31 Dec. 1763, on etiquette has some interesting information.

wait upon the king and the Regent' he was told that only carriages
with two horses would be admitted. Six horses had to be withdrawn before Stair was allowed to enter the courtyard.[15]

Trouble was also caused by the pretensions of the French
princes of the blood. When the prince de Conti arrived at the
British embassy to make a formal visit to the new ambassador,
Stair declined to receive the prince at the foot of the outer stair-
case and remained at the top of the stairs. This so annoyed the
prince that he declined to make his visit. Here Stair was apparently
in the wrong and his superiors ordered him to give way, on the
ground that the Imperial minister at the French court did what
Stair had refused to do.[16] A dispute over the position to be taken
by the coaches of the princes of the blood in the public entry of
an ambassador proved more difficult to settle. It had originated
when England and France were still politically on good terms and
Charles II had tried to solve it by asserting the same privileges for
his own close relations when a French ambassador made his public entry to Charles II's court. In 1677 'Prince Rupert's coach was
expressly ordered to precede the ambassador's because the princes
of the blood in France have possession of the like privilege'.[17] Yet
this particular point of etiquette was still causing trouble to
British diplomatists in France two generations later.

Another long-standing controversy arose between Britain and
France as to whether ambassadors should give the hand to envoys
in their own houses. Here again Charles II tried to settle it on a
reciprocal basis and well into the Hanoverian period the formal
instructions given to British diplomatists before they set out for
their posts usually contained orders to this effect.

What was expected of a British diplomatist on his arrival at the
French court was succinctly stated by Henry Savile in his advice
to one of his successors, Sir William Trumbull:[18]

At your arrival at Paris [the new envoy is informed] the first step is
to send to the Master of the Ceremonies to let him know you are come
upon such an occasion and to learn from him when you may see the
Secretary of State. Having shewed your credentials to the Secretary,

---

[15] *Stair Annals*, i. 101. See for full details of 'The Order of his Entry' *Life of
Stair by an Impartial Hand* (London, 1748), pp. 199–208.
[16] Ibid. i. 101–3.
[17] H.M.C., *Finch MSS*. ii. 36.
[18] Printed in H.M.C., *Downshire MSS*. i. 88–89.

you ask him when the King will receive you; the day being appointed you are carried in the King's coaches, every coachman's fee upon that occasion being two pistoles. You are to send to all foreign Ministers notice of your arrival; those of your character and below it, will thereupon come to see you; the Ambassadors will send, but I suppose with them you will meet only in third places, except such as will give you the hand in their own houses if there be any such.

As most of them are altered since my time I can only recommend you to him of Mantua,[19] who having been there these 20 years knows more than his neighbours, and upon living civilly with him, will impart to you what he knows which will perhaps be the best part of your intelligence, till acquaintances of your contracting provide better for you, and in order to this, your own seeming to distinguish him from the rest as the choice of your judgment will go further than any recommendation can be given you, though for an introduction you may name me to him as one I thought worthy your first friendship.

Considering the difference of our circumstances probably my rules of economy will not fit you, but I thought it turned extremely to account to keep all my servants in livery at board wages of 20 sols per diem and no wages, so that without further counting they were easily dismissed in case of misdemeanour.

Your countrymen that pray with you on Sunday will expect to dine with you, I mean the better sort; one dinner more a week to such as are most deserving on one of the days you expect news from England (especially in Parliament time) will do your business as to the creditable part of your living; less hardly will. I had many spies upon me of Scotch and Irish; you will have more, especially priests; I despised and evaded them; whether that will be the best method in this conjuncture your own judgment will best tell you. Your predecessor drank with them, and perhaps it did him good, however that good was dear bought by keeping so ill company.

At Court you will meet many open faces; let yours be so too, but your mouth shut, for except very few they are given to repeat with additions, and those are the most dangerous who will by commending your own country lead you into the discourse of it.

I see not how you will get amongst the Court ladies whose tittle-tattle is sometimes informing unless you will either play or love, or give presents worth more than their acquaintance, though I must repeat some of them are informed betimes of things worth knowing.

In essentials, this advice relative to the court of France would

---

[19] See on this diplomatist, Count Camillo Balliani, *Recueil des Instructions*, xv. 397–8.

have been as sound in 1789 as in 1689. Moreover, its usefulness would not have been limited to diplomatists accredited to France. With a few trifling changes it was applicable to nearly all the courts to which British diplomatic agents were regularly sent between 1689 and 1789.

Occasionally ceremonial quarrels arose not between diplomatists and exalted subjects of the state to which they were accredited, but with British nationals. In 1711 Lord Cornbury quarrelled with the queen's minister at Florence 'about the first visit'. Alexander Cunningham refused to meddle 'between the Queen's cousin and the Queen's minister' but thought that 'Lord Cornbury should have notified his arrival to the envoy, and that the envoy should have prevented his visit, upon my lord's being a peer'. He attributed the quarrel to Cornbury's being 'in company with some gentlemen that have no regard to the Q—'s character, nor own her Majesty's right to give one'.[20] Such examples of punctilio were of no practical importance since the contestants had ultimately to accept as final the decision of their sovereign.

Another category of diplomatic quarrels arose over the precise definition of diplomatic privileges and immunities of the diplomatic agents in general wherever resident. The practical basis of these claims was that, without them, diplomatists could not efficiently carry out their duties, although international jurists tended to base them on the Law of Nations. Vattel argued that since embassies are of such great importance in the universal society of Nations, and are so necessary to their common welfare, the person of the ministers appointed to them should be *sacred* and *inviolable* among all Nations (Book II, s. 218). Whoever does violence to an ambassador or to any other public minister not only does an injury to the sovereign whom the minister represents, but attacks the common safety and welfare of all Nations.[21]

This basic privilege had, however, been greatly extended by custom before the end of the seventeenth century, as may be seen from Professor Adair's *The Exterritoriality of Ambassadors in the 16th and 17th Centuries*. One of the most important of these extensions was the right to the free exercise of the ambassador's religion, which Vattel regarded as not 'absolutely necessary to the due success of his mission' but 'very suitable'. At the present day, he added, 'ambassadors are not denied [it] in any civilised

[20] H.M.C., *Portland MSS.* v. 70.   [21] Op. cit. iii. 371.

country, for a privilege which is founded on reason can not be refused when it is attended with no ill-effects'.[22]

The precise ceremonial and extent of these privileges had been laid down at most courts by the slow accumulation of precedents. Each court had its master of ceremonies or marshal of the *corps diplomatique* whose business it was to know all the answers. In England, in the early seventeenth century, this post was held by Sir John Finett from 1626 to his death in 1641. His work, *Finetti Philoxensis: Som choice Observations ... Touching the Reception, and Precedence, the Treatment and Audience, the Puntillios and Contests of Forren Ambassadors in England*, was published at London in 1656. He was succeeded as master of the ceremonies by members of the Cotterell–Dormer family and it was their duty, for example, to know whether, when the duke of Savoy's ambassador had his formal audience of William III, he should be introduced by earls and attended by three Trumpets. Early in the century only ambassadors from crowned heads had been entitled to be introduced by earls, but the privilege had been gradually extended. 'Venice', according to Sir Charles Cotterell, 'has been allowed that privilege time out of mind. Savoy had it from King Charles the Second at the request of the Queen Mother, to make a compliment to the then Duchess of Savoy, her near relation. Holland was never allowed it till since this Revolution; but now they all three enjoy the privileges of crowned heads.'[23]

Most of the writers on international law and diplomatic practice, quoted elsewhere in this book, included in their works a section on diplomatic ceremonial and privilege in which they either reproduced the current practice of their own court or else attempted to give a generalized account, based on the practices most generally followed at the time by the leading courts of Europe, and particularly of western Europe. Bynkershoek devoted a whole book to a discussion of jurisdiction over ambassadors in both civil and criminal cases;[24] but the best brief account of ceremonial and privilege available in English is probably that of G. F. von Martens in Cobbett's translation.[25] The fullest account is certainly that by Jean Dumont, *Corps universel diplomatique*

[22] Op. cit. iii. 384–5.
[23] H.M.C., *Buccleuch MSS.* ii. 633.
[24] *De Foro Legatorum*, ed. G. J. Laing for the Carnegie Endowment for International Peace (Oxford, 1946).
[25] *The Law of Nations* (1st ed., 1802), book v.

du droit des gens with the supplement by Rousset de Missy, published at Amsterdam in 1739. Volumes IV and V of the *Supplement* contain *Le Cérémonial Diplomatique des Cours de l'Europe ou Collection des Actes, Mémoires, et Relations qui concernent les Dignitez, Titulatures, Honneurs et Prééminences; les Fonctions publiques des Souveraines, leurs Sacres, Couronnemens, Mariages, Batêmes, et Enterremens; les Investitures des grands Fiefs; les Entrées publiques, Audiences, Fonctions, Immunitez et Franchises des Ambassadeurs et autres Ministres publics; leur Disputes et Démêlez de Préséance; Et en général tout ce qui a rapport au Cérémonial et à l'Etiquette.*[26]

Most of the material in these volumes was taken from previous writers who had dealt with the subject in published works, but a good deal was derived from manuscript sources contributed directly or indirectly by the Introducers of Ambassadors and Masters of Ceremonies at the various courts. Rousset insisted in the editorial preface that he had approached diplomatic ceremonial not, as most of his predecessors had done, from the standpoint of international law, but from the purely practical side of conducting diplomatic relations between states.[27] He also found it necessary to insist that the arrangement of his work, by which French ceremonial, followed by the ceremonial of the Imperial court, occupied Volume I while the remaining courts were relegated to Volume II, was not in any way intended to imply an order of precedence between the leading courts of Europe. It had, he added, been adopted merely by the accidental order in which his materials happened to reach a state of readiness for the printer. Volume V of the *Supplement* opened with Papal ceremonial and the ceremonial of the court of Great Britain occupied pages 447 to 534. In one respect, however, Rousset certainly followed the established rules of precedence among sovereigns. He brought together at the end the ceremonial observed by the leading republican states, the United Provinces, Venice, and Switzerland. It was generally agreed that republics were lower in rank than monarchies and that amongst crowned heads hereditary monarchs rightly took precedence over such elected monarchs as the King of Poland.

[26] The copy of this magnificent folio set purchased by Lord Hyndford before 1743 is now in Edinburgh University Library.
[27] Op. cit. Supplement, iv (at beginning but not paged).

So far as foreign diplomatists in England were concerned, most of the trouble arose over what were clearly abuses of diplomatic privilege, such as stockjobbing transactions, evasion of customs duties, &c. In spite of Lord Mansfield's assertion in 1767 'that the law of nations, in its full extent, was part of the law of England', it appears that the common law of England allowed less extensive privileges to foreign diplomatists than were usually allowed them in certain other states by the current interpretations of the law of nations. The Statute 7 Anne, cap. 12, had been 'specifically passed because international law was not part of the common law of England' to secure freedom of ambassadors and their recognized servants from arrest or imprisonment and to prevent seizure of their goods.[28] Apart from the actual case of the Russian ambassador, Matveev, which led to the passing of the Act, there had been similar infractions of diplomatic immunity between 1689 and 1708, especially the arrest in 1691 of one of the Spanish ambassador's servants for a debt of the ambassador's.[29] When the ambassador himself died a few months later, the queen had to arrange a refuge for his thirty servants 'to prevent the affront of arrests, till they can settle their affairs' and to allow them each so much a day for six weeks while they were lodged 'somewhere within the limits of the court'.[30] The Act of 1709 did not in practice prevent the repetition of such incidents, and, although it made provision for the punishment of any person bringing suit or executing a process in connexion with it against an ambassador, no recorded case of prosecution for breach of the Act appears to be known.[31] In 1764, however, when the French ambassador Guerchy's servant was arrested, the ambassador procured the imprisonment of the constables who had made the arrest.[32] And in 1765 the Grand Jury of Middlesex found an indictment against the same French ambassador; but, after a meeting of the Cabinet, legal proceedings were effectually stopped.[33]

When, at the height of the Jacobite rebellion in 1745, a royal proclamation ordered the arrest of Jesuits and Popish priests in

---

[28] See Adair, *Exterritoriality of Ambassadors*, pp. 237–43, and 'The Law of Nations and the Common Law of England' in *Camb. Hist. Journal*, ii (1927–8), 290–7.   [29] H.M.C., *Finch MSS.* iii. 65, 391.

[30] Ibid. iii. 181, 193, 403.

[31] Adair, *Exterritoriality of Ambassadors*, 238.

[32] *Grenville Papers*, ii. 360–1.

[33] *George III Corresp.* i. 70–72; Namier, *Additions and Corrections*, p. 22.

the London area, it excepted only 'such *Popish* priests, not being his Majesty's natural-born subjects, as by the law of this realm are permitted to attend foreign ministers'. The Roman Catholic *corps diplomatique* at London at once protested that this was an infringement of their diplomatic privileges. They alleged that owing to the scarcity of foreign priests in London they had, according to immemorial custom, made use of British subjects as chaplains, and that the proclamation would result in depriving them of the free exercise of religion as required by the law of nations and the Act of 1709. While declaring their readiness to hand over any of their domestics guilty of any crime against the British government, they demanded the immediate release of those domestics who had been arrested as a consequence of the royal proclamation and the punishment of the constables who had carried out the arrests. In reply, the secretary of state maintained that any privilege derived from the law of nations must be consistent with the internal security of the state; but the number and secret plottings of national British priests, 'especially at a time of open rebellion in favour of a pretender of the same religion' threatened the security of the government. The 'open chapels' maintained by some foreign ministers in London with an enormous number of priests wherein mass was 'celebrated from morning to night' were not really for the use of the foreign ministers' families, but 'rather for the sake of furnishing his Majesty's converted subjects with opportunities of being present at it against Law'. As for the Act of 1709, this was never intended 'to authorize foreign ministers to protect state criminals, disturbers of the peace or persons dangerous to society or suspected by the government upon any account whatsoever'. While 'the King does not pretend to subject foreign ministers to his ordonnances . . . he has a right to require the obedience of his own subjects to the laws of their country'. The secretary of state therefore appealed to the Roman Catholic foreign ministers 'to discharge from their service every Popish priest who is a subject of the King's; and that they will for the future make use of foreign ones only'.[34]

Although the '45 made this problem acute, it was one that kept recurring in the seventeenth and eighteenth centuries. At the time of the Popish Plot messengers had been sent to seize English

[34] William Maitland, *The History and Survey of London* (3rd ed., 1760), i. 649–52.

Roman Catholics who were seen coming out of the embassy chapels and the foreign ministers had been warned to dismiss any British subjects whom they had with them as chaplains. Similar measures were taken in William III's reign at the time of the assassination plot; but the foreign ministers took so little notice that their chaplains in 1698 were nearly all English or Irish 'and the number in some of these houses is very extraordinary. The Portugal envoy alone hath ten chaplains, and nine of them are his Majesty's subjects' while the French and Spanish ambassadors had six each 'and but three foreigners between them'.[35] When the French ambassador protested, secretary of state Vernon remarked that 'unless they intend my Lord Jersey [British ambassador to France] shall bring as many Huguenot ministers with him to Paris', the French court 'will hardly direct him to keep English or Irish priests'.[36] Matthew Prior at Paris tried to persuade his Roman Catholic colleagues of 'the reasonableness of our acting in this manner' and 'that these priests were pointed at not as being chaplains but traitors and rebels'.[37]

A memorial to the House of Commons in 1700 after referring to a remarkable growth of Popery and pointing out that

our envoy at Florence is not allowed a minister . . . yet we see here two ministers of the Emperor . . . who have each Popish service in their house. . . . It has been signified to the ministers of the Popish princes not to admit in their chapel service any of his Majesty's subjects. This suffices not: they are to receive orders but from their masters. Guards must be set to the entrance of their chapels. The little commonwealth of Geneva has at this day the courage to do it.[38]

Again in 1733 Lord Egmont was informed by one Dr. Bundy 'that the Spanish ambassador alone has eighty English priests for his chaplains';[39] and at the time of the Gordon Riots in London attacks were for this reason made upon the houses occupied by some Roman Catholic members of the *corps diplomatique* and the Bavarian minister's house was burned down. It will be clear from the preceding paragraphs that difference in religion was one of the commonest causes of diplomatic incidents in the seventeenth and eighteenth centuries.

---

[35] H.M.C., *Bath MSS*. iii. 227–9.   [36] Ibid., p. 233.
[37] Ibid., p. 242.   [38] H.M.C., *Portland MSS*. viii. 67–68.
[39] H.M.C., *Egmont Diary*, i. 405.

CHAPTER XII

Communications

WRITERS on diplomacy with a flair for journalism often contrast the position of a twentieth-century British diplomatist, in hourly telephonic communication with his own foreign office and receiving a continuous stream of letters and telegrams for his information and guidance, with that of his predecessor in the early modern centuries. While the contrast and resulting freedom of manœuvre for the diplomatist on the spot can be exaggerated, there is no doubt that changing methods of communication have exercised a decisive influence upon the development of diplomatic techniques and the position of the resident diplomatists at the leading capitals in the last 150 years. These changes, however, did not exert an appreciable influence until after the close of the eighteenth century. The methods by which the diplomatists abroad kept in touch with their superiors at home in 1689 remained essentially unaltered in 1789. All that one can say is that there had been some increase in the frequency and regularity of the services which already existed in 1689. It is possible, though I should not care to be dogmatic about this, that there had also been some reduction in the time required to send a message to, and receive an answer from, the more distant courts. With the geographical extension of the British diplomatic network which occurred during the eighteenth century, the problem of communications became more important and also more difficult to solve satisfactorily, until technical developments made available new methods.

Mr. Peter Fraser has recently described the postal routes used by the secretaries of state in the Restoration period. From Ostend or Nieuport letters were regularly forwarded by post to the Baltic, Italy, and Spain. Letters for Spain travelled also via Paris and Bordeaux. The route to Lisbon was by the Flanders post to Madrid and from Madrid to Lisbon the service was fortnightly. Letters for Italy could be sent via Paris and Lyons to Turin or via Brussels to Innsbruck and Mantua, which was linked weekly with the leading cities of Italy. Thus from Venice in each week there was one post for England via France and another via Germany.

Occasionally letters from and to Leghorn went by sea to Marseilles and thence overland to Calais. Italian posts and couriers were largely under French control[1] and the secretaries of state had thus reason to use the alternative route. Letters for the Baltic usually went by Helvoetsluys to Hamburg, from which town there was a weekly service by Elsinore to Stockholm and a twice-a-week service to Königsberg, Danzig, and Riga. From Riga a fortnightly extension ran on to Moscow, and from Danzig weekly to Poland. Vienna was usually reached via Flanders, Constantinople by the long sea route or overland via Venice.

Times taken, under favourable conditions, varied from 3 days to Paris or The Hague, up to 18 days to Madrid, 21 to Rome or Stockholm, and 46 to Constantinople. These times could, of course, be improved upon if special messengers were employed; but this was a costly business and often saved less time than had been hoped. In negotiating with foreign post offices England was not geographically in an advantageous situation and her usual technique was to try to play off alternative routes, e.g. via France or via the Netherlands, against each other.[2] As we shall see, the most important developments after 1689 were the institution of the Falmouth packet service, the increased place of the Harwich–Helvoetsluys packets and some improvements and extensions of postal services in eastern Europe. Minor changes in routes and regulations took place also in continental western Europe, but the system established there in the seventeenth century was not fundamentally changed before 1789.[3]

Broadly speaking, once the diplomatic agent had set out for his post, communication had to be in writing; and this is fortunate for the historian of eighteenth-century diplomacy. The practice of summoning a diplomatist home for consultations hardly existed, although there are traces of it when the king was resident at Hanover. Occasionally, too, a trusted subordinate with an oral message might be sent home, as Benjamin Keene was sent from Madrid to London when the ex-minister Ripperda took refuge in the British embassy and offered to disclose the secrets of the Spanish court. Such cases, however, remained exceptional. Written communication was the almost invariable rule.

---

[1] Vaillé, *Histoire Générale des postes françaises*, iv. 262 ff.
[2] Fraser, *Intelligence*, pp. 60–64 and map.
[3] Some details in Vaillé, op. cit. iv–vi *passim*.

Once the message had been written it could be dispatched by various methods and often by different routes. It might be entrusted to the post office and sent as ordinary mail, or it might be sent 'express' or 'by estafette', i.e. by relays of post-office messengers[4] in the hope of reducing the delays to which ordinary mail was subject. These methods, usually the former, had to serve for the great bulk of the written communications which passed between London and the embassies and legations abroad. It was generally felt that cipher should be used sparingly, if at all, in letters sent by this method, since the more ciphered material that was available to the decipherers abroad the more likely they were to break the cipher. The second method was to make use of the official British messenger service after securing from the foreign government a courier's pass for the messenger. Occasionally the Hanoverian couriers who travelled regularly between London and Hanover could be used. As a rule British messengers, each of whom carried a silver greyhound badge,[5] were allowed to pass freely. Martens wrote towards the end of the eighteenth century that 'to commit an act of violence against a messenger is now looked upon as an enormous offence', although he had to admit that 'in time of war this inviolability is not so much respected'.[6] Moreover, in peace-time at least, they often enjoyed priority in securing post-horses over the regular mails.[7]

If no official messenger was available, then it was a common practice to send some member of the ambassador's family, a young attaché, or a trusted servant. If the letter involved matters of confidence rather than of urgency, the diplomatist might entrust it to the captain of a British ship[8] or even to a British tourist who happened to pass through the foreign capital at a suitable time.

Accidents inevitably occurred from time to time both to the professional and amateur messengers. The vessel might be delayed for weeks by contrary winds or shipwrecked on a hostile shore. The messenger might be drowned crossing a river, as was Manchester's gentleman of the horse in 1701, with the result that the

---

[4] Martens distinguishes between 'state messengers' and 'simple couriers' who went 'but from one post to another' (*Law of Nations*, p. 267).
[5] V. Wheeler-Holohan, *History of the King's Messengers*, p. 135.
[6] Martens, *Law of Nations*, pp. 267–8.
[7] *Keith Memoir*, ii. 203.
[8] For 'ship letters' see Robinson, *The British Post Office*, pp. 163–4.

packets he was carrying fell into the hands of the governor of
Navarre and were sent back to Madrid.[9] There was also the risk
that some petty functionary, acting either through excess of zeal
or under instructions from the foreign sovereign, might arrest the
messenger on the ground of some technical infringement of the
regulations and thus delay the arrival of the news in England, if
he did not actually seize the packets themselves. When this happened protests were at once made to the government concerned,
usually with the warning that if it happened again in, e.g. France,
similar incidents would befall French couriers in England.[10]

Down to 1772 the official messengers were controlled by the
Lord Chamberlain, although the secretaries of state could requisi-
tion messengers for the carrying of important dispatches. In 1772
sixteen of the official messengers were placed entirely at the disposal of the secretaries of state and the right to nominate to these
sixteen messengerships, if vacant by death or dismissal, was transferred to the secretaries.[11] The duty of supervising and paying
these sixteen messengers was transferred from the clerks of the
cheque to the under-secretaries of state.[12] Earlier secretaries,
notably the duke of Newcastle, had complained about their lack
of control over the messenger service and the method by which
messengers were paid. In 1743 Newcastle wrote to the Lords of the
Treasury suggesting that £1,000 be issued to the Treasurer of the
Chambers to be advanced to messengers on their being sent
abroad.[13] Long before this the secretaries or their clerks had
drawn up lists of sums requisite to be advanced to messengers
journeying to various countries.[14] When diplomatists abroad sent
back these messengers to England they usually had to advance
similar sums to them and hope to recover the advances, in time,
from the Treasury. I am sceptical of the statement that a considerable number of messengers were stationed at Hanover, unless this
is intended to apply only to the periods of royal residence there.[15]

The messengers were recruited in the most haphazard way.
Some of them had been the private servants of the secretaries or of

[9] Cole, *Memoirs*, p. 300.   [10] Ibid., pp. 201–3.
[11] M. A. Thomson, *Secretaries of State*, p. 142.
[12] V. Wheeler-Holohan, op. cit., p. 28.
[13] T. 29. 29, minutes of 26/10/42 and 8/6/43; T. 29. 31, minute of 26/4/48
refusing to alter the establishment of the messengers of the Chambers.
[14] One in S.P. 80. 42 *ad fin.*, c. 1720.
[15] V. Wheeler-Holohan, op. cit., p. 20.

influential noblemen.[16] No provision was made for retirement and, in Mitchell's opinion, many of them were more fit for a hospital than for travelling.[17] More often, complaints were made not about their physical fitness but about their zeal and reliability. Matthew Prior wrote from Paris to James Vernon in 1698:

I am mighty glad you have found the secret of making the messengers useful to us. I confess they are very far from being so, whilst not a man of them would stir (or could) from hence for our letters at Calais till he was equipped with 12 or 14 *louis*. ... If the business is no better done for the future than hitherto it has been, I protest I will send them home again.[18]

That Prior's forebodings were justified is suggested by Vernon's letter to him, dated 5 January 1699 N.S.: 'We must have some establishment for couriers. ... I wish you would draw up a scheme what the charge will amount to, that I may lay it before his Majesty, and get something resolved that we may depend on; and if it can be done in a cheaper way than by messengers, there would be less difficulty to obtain it.'[19] Harley, when secretary of state, annotated the list of available messengers with such comments as 'capable', 'superannuated', 'seems honest', 'drunken, good rider', 'Irish', &c.[20]

Sir Edward Hertslet in *Recollections of the Old Foreign Office* painted a gloomy picture of conditions in the messenger service in the period immediately following 1789. He referred to

the arduous and dangerous duties which they were frequently called upon to perform, especially before the introduction of railways or steamboats; the great confidence which had invariably been placed in them by H.M.'s Government; the many instances in which they lost their lives by shipwreck, or were murdered; the innumerable cases in which they suffered bodily injury by being thrown from their

[16] A. Young, *Autobiography*, p. 45; *Keene Corresp.*, p. 42. I know of no evidence for Mr. Wheeler-Holohan's theory that there was a lowering of social status of king's messengers due to recruitment of 'temporary diplomatic couriers' during the French Revolutionary Wars (op. cit., pp. 30–32). He himself refers in another connexion to the illiterate handwriting of most of the eighteenth-century messengers and to their employment of agents to draw up and present their accounts (op. cit., pp. 220–2).

[17] B.M. Add. MS. 6806, fo. 53. One or two of them became military knights of Windsor (E. H. Fellowes, *The Military Knights of Windsor*).

[18] H.M.C., *Bath MSS.* iii. 194.   [19] Ibid., p. 307.

[20] H.M.C., *Portland MSS.* iv. 280.

horses or carriages; their sufferings from frost-bite, exposure and so forth.[21]

Even when they escaped such disasters, hardship might well be their lot. Sir Edward Hertslet's grandfather, Louis Hertslet, 'was travelling for over four consecutive months and was in his saddle for fifty-two days, off and on'.[22] Such periods of excessive activity were probably to be set against longish spells when messengers were detained at Madrid or St. Petersburg until the dilatory foreign government thought fit to send a reply which our diplomatic agent on the spot considered important and specific enough to justify him in dispatching a messenger to London. Sometimes, when two or three messengers were known to be at a particular court, the secretary of state instructed the diplomatist there to send one of them back to London, even if there was no message worth sending by special messenger; but it seems to have been true that the foreign messenger service was under- rather than over-staffed.

This at least was the view expressed jointly by the three secretaries of state in 1795. The sixteen messengers allocated in 1772 for the purpose of performing foreign journeys were insufficient and recourse was constantly had to the remaining eighteen. There ought to be at least thirty effective messengers for the three secretaries' offices, 'each messenger taking his regular routine of attendance nearly on the same footing as at present', while old and infirm messengers should be pensioned. These proposals were, with unimportant exceptions, approved by the King-in-Council on 27 February 1795. Under this scheme the basic salary of each messenger was to be £60 per annum plus board wages of £2. 12s. 6d. a week while in waiting.[23] When messengers were actually employed the scheme differentiated between 'rides' up to thirty miles, 'posting-journeys' to The Hague, Paris, Brussels, Ireland, and the army, and 'foreign journeys' to all other places abroad.[24] That the staff of messengers at this time was not adequate for the needs of the Foreign Office is also suggested by the fact that in this year (1795) £819. 15s. 10d. was spent on 'extra messengers attending the office, when the established messengers were employed on foreign service'.[25]

[21] Op. cit., p. 157.   [22] Ibid., p. 160.
[23] F.O. 366. 542.   [24] V. Wheeler-Holohan, op. cit., p. 46.
[25] F.O. 95. 591.

If the work was arduous and sometimes dangerous, as when messengers crossed the Channel in small boats at times when the captains of the mail-packets thought conditions too dangerous to put to sea, or carried cash into a besieged town by creeping 'through an aperture in a wall within range of point-blank shot' while the enemy was firing,[26] the financial rewards were not inconsiderable. In the Restoration period the mileage allowance abroad varied according to the country through which the messenger had to travel and he received in addition two shillings a stage and ten shillings a day for riding or being at sea.[27] In Queen Anne's reign a messenger when abroad on journeys was allowed 10s. a day and 5s. 'for an assistant when an extraordinary case requires one'. When abroad but not travelling he was allowed 5s. a day. Instead of these mileage rates some journeys were 'to be ascertained at the old allowances'; but the only foreign journey included in this list was to The Hague, for which the messenger was to receive £25, actually £5 less than was allowed for the journey to Dublin.[28]

Messenger Lamb, later to be Arthur Young's landlord at Samford Hall in Essex, is reported as saying that 'a journey to Petersburg or Constantinople paid him a neat profit of a hundred guineas'. The scale of payment was deliberately arranged to encourage messengers to travel economically and make a profit on each journey.[29] Each messenger who was sent abroad received a small basic salary *plus* board wages at so much a day while he was in England and at a much higher rate when abroad. In addition his expenses while travelling abroad were met by government and he also received an allowance of so much a mile. This allowance varied according to the mode of travel used by the messenger. Two messengers' bills, one for a journey to Paris in 1772 and the other to St. Petersburg in 1780, show that the system of payment and even the amounts paid were much the same as in the Restoration period. The basic payment for a journey, e.g. to The Hague, was still £25, but various extras, including allowances per stage, for riding, for extra guides, for a third horse and for ports, barriers, and crossing rivers, &c., were added. The total claimed by the messenger to Paris was £48. 10s. 8d. and to St. Petersburg

[26] Laetitia-Matilda Hawkins, *Memoirs*, i. 7.
[27] V. Wheeler-Holohan, op. cit., p. 13.   [28] H.M.C., *Portland MSS.* iv. 178–9.
[29] A. Young, *Autobiography*, p. 45.

£459. 3s. 4d. In each case the figures are for the return journey.[30]

In the early nineteenth century, while this system was still in force, an active and zealous messenger could make a clear profit of more than £1,000 a year;[31] but in the period with which we are concerned the direct profits must have been appreciably less. In the 1780's it was usual to include in the civil-list accounts an item 'H.M. messengers to enable them to perform Foreign Journies'. This varied from £7,000 in the year 1787 to £19,000 in 1788 and averaged from 1784 to 1790 about £14,000 a year, divisible amongst sixteen messengers. It presumably included the actual cost of journeys, the increased board wages while the messengers were abroad, and the mileage profit. When basic salaries of the sixteen messengers are added, the cost of the messenger service in the eighties would exceed £15,000 a year at a time when the total cost to the public of conducting British foreign policy may be estimated at £130,000 a year.[32]

It may well be that in the eighteenth century the indirect profits of the messengers were more important than the salary and allowances. Messengers certainly carried letters and messages for private persons in exchange for rewards: sometimes they conveyed in their coaches travellers who were in a hurry.[33] Since their belongings were not liable to inspection, they had opportunities for large-scale smuggling, of which some of them took advantage. One customs house official in 1746 attributed it to smuggling by the king's messengers that 'the millinery shops in London come to be filled with prohibited Dresden needle-work and other goods of Germany'. The secretaries of state, on the other hand, protested that over-zealous customs officials delayed the messengers and even detained their baggage. Under-secretary Delafaye in 1728 wrote: 'Supposing the Messengers themselves should bring over any small matter of goods, it can be but a trifle but as to that let them a' Gods name be searched to their skin, but pray let it be done with dispatch, and let the King's packets and letters meet with as much regard at least from his own officers as they do from those in France.'[34] As one would expect, control over the activities

[30] V. Wheeler-Holohan, op. cit., pp. 29–31, 216–18.
[31] *P.P.H.C. 1861 Select Committee on the Diplomatic Service*, question 3058.
[32] See Appendix A.   [33] Ibid., question 3088.
[34] E. E. Hoon, *Organization of the English Customs System 1696–1786*, pp. 83–84.

of the messengers was lax and spasmodic. Not until 1799 did the Foreign Secretary draw up a form of certificate to be completed by the minister abroad on each occasion on which he dispatched a messenger to the Foreign Office.[35]

Only a tiny part of the Foreign Office mail could ever be carried by the king's messengers, and volunteer messengers were only employed in emergency. To send a courier was often to attract undesirable attention, while if two or three couriers arrived in rapid succession at a particular court the diplomatic corps spent most of their time trying to find out, or at least to guess, what was in the wind. The normal method of communication in 1789 as in 1689 was through the post office, which had organized in earlier centuries a packet-boat service across the Channel from Dover to Calais, where the letters had to be entrusted to the tender mercies of the French post office. With increasing interest in foreign affairs and (to a less extent) the growing importance of overseas markets for English commerce, there would in any case have been a development of the packet-boat service after 1689. But the precise form which this took was determined mainly by political considerations. Continuous hostility to France, and the frequent periods of actual warfare between Britain and France, not only led to interruption of the Dover–Calais service,[36] but determined the British government, as far as possible or convenient, to by-pass France even when there was a truce between the two countries.

Relations between the French and British post offices were usually bad.[37] The postal treaty of 1698 provided that French letters delivered at Dover were to be sent on immediately by a special post and that English letters delivered at Calais were similarly to be dispatched at once by express to Paris. In practice it was found that if the packet-boat landed the English letters even a few minutes after the normal post had left Calais for Paris, they remained in the Calais post office until the next ordinary post left for Paris twenty-four hours later.[38] Similar or even longer delays occurred at Lyons with English letters sent through France for

[35] F.O. 83. 8, circular dispatch dated 25/6/99.
[36] This did not automatically follow upon a declaration of war, but usually resulted six months or more later on. (Cf. *George III Corresp.* iv. 379; Picavet, *La Diplomatie française*, p. 228.)
[37] See Vaillé, op. cit. iv. 305–22, v. 401–16.
[38] H.M.C., *Bath MSS*. iii. 363.

delivery in Italy.[39] While these delays were irritating, probably the main factor in the organization of British postal services to avoid crossing France was the desire to escape the 'impertinent curiosity of the French postmasters'.[40]

In the Commonwealth and Restoration periods a new route from Dover to Ostend and occasionally direct to Holland had been developed.[41] With the accession of William III and the increasing preoccupation of the British government with the politics of central and northern Europe, this route became vitally important. When Britain and France were at war, the Dover–Ostend service could hardly operate with regularity.[42] The English packet-boats on this service were transferred to Harwich and soon operated regularly between their new base and Helvoetsluys (The Brill). This became, alike in war and peace, the normal route for letters to Holland, Germany, Scandinavia, Poland, and Russia. Although one of the Brill packets was taken by a French privateer in 1691,[43] this route proved much freer from hostile interruption than the Dover–Ostend line of communication had been.

The outbreak of war with France in 1689 led the Post Office to begin another packet-boat service from Falmouth to Corunna (the Groyne), from which port letters were regularly forwarded to Spain, Portugal, and the Barbary states and occasionally to other Mediterranean ports. Falmouth was chosen for this purpose because of its good harbour and geographical position. 'From no other harbour in this country can an outward-bound vessel clear the land so soon. No other is so quickly reached by one homeward-bound running for shelter . . . sailing vessels can leave it in any wind, save one blowing strongly from the east or south-east. The prevalent gales in the English Channel are from the west.'[44]

Oliver Hill, sent over to Spain in 1690 to make the necessary arrangements for the transport of letters from Corunna, was soon regarded as a madman and clapped into prison by the Spanish authorities. As Hill had a 'character' from King William, Alexander Stanhope tried at first to secure his release; but soon Hill's commission was terminated and he was threatened with prosecu-

---

[39] Joyce, *History of the Post Office*, p. 77.
[40] H.M.C., *MSS. in Various Collections* (Clements MSS.), viii. 302.
[41] Fraser, *Intelligence*, p. 23.
[42] H.M.C., *Finch MSS.* iii. 13.   [43] Ibid., p. 37.
[44] A. H. Norway, *History of the Post Office Packet Service between the years 1793–1815*, p. 16.

tion for uttering scandalous words against William III.[45] Hill was succeeded by William Aglionby, who soon concluded a bargain satisfactory to his employers.[46] Just as Louvois had argued in 1685 that the growing English practice of sending letters for Italy through the Netherlands was a breach of an earlier agreement with France,[47] so at the end of William III's war with France the French postal authorities insisted that the Falmouth–Corunna service was an infringement of their rights and demanded its abolition. The English postmasters general replied that in their opinion France would not lose by the new service, 'for the merchants will generally write through France as being a more certain conveyance, and, if any of them shall write by Corunna, we believe even then they will send duplicates overland'.[48]

It was partly because the English postmasters declined to give up the Corunna service that the French postal authorities refused to grant special rates for the conveyance of English letters through France to other destinations.[49] In time of war, as British interests in the western Mediterranean grew, the Falmouth service was increased in frequency from a fortnightly to a weekly one and then reduced again at the end of the war. Early in the Spanish Succession War it was extended from Corunna to Lisbon[50] and during the middle years of the eighteenth century it connected with packet-boat services to Gibraltar and Port Mahon.[51] While Benjamin Keene was at Madrid each packet-boat carried a king's messenger, who landed at Corunna and went direct to Madrid with his dispatches.[52] These developments were due primarily to politico-military considerations, not to commercial needs, although, once established, the services were used and valued by British merchants.

At the close of the Spanish Succession War, on 2 November 1713, a new Franco-British postal treaty was signed after much haggling. It did little more than bring up to date the arrangements made by the previous treaty of 1698. The operation of this

[45] S.P. 94. 73 and 229.
[46] S.P. 94. 75; see also for the views of the English postmasters-general on Aglionby's instructions H.M.C., *Finch MSS.* iii. 121, 151.
[47] Vaillé, op. cit. iv. 317–19. [48] H.M.C., *Bath MSS.* iii. 207.
[49] Ibid. iii. 207; Hemmeon, op. cit., p. 115.
[50] Joyce, *History of the Post Office*, pp. 77–78.
[51] H. Robinson, *The British Post Office*, p. 163.
[52] *Keene Corresp.*, p. 470.

agreement was suspended during the subsequent periods of warfare between Britain and France; but when peace was restored the postal arrangements of 1713 were also restored unchanged so that the postal treaty of 1713 remained in force until a new treaty was made at the end of the War of American Independence.[53]

Although the packet-boats on all routes carried passengers and merchandize, except when this was prohibited in time of war, the government always insisted that their essential duty was the speedy carriage of letters, and especially of the state letters. On the Harwich route, the state letters were carried in a special bag and sent away on arrival at Helvoetsluys ahead of the ordinary mails.[54]

The question of security, especially in time of war, was a constant source of preoccupation. The merchants usually argued that the packet-boats should be large, better armed, and more heavily manned vessels to give them a better chance of resisting capture.[55] William III held that small boats 'of no force' but remarkable for their speed would be more likely to escape capture, whereas, if heavily manned and armed, they might be tempted to attack enemy ships and thus endanger the mails. That William III was right is suggested by the fact that the adoption of his views was followed by nineteen years of war out of the next twenty-four, and yet only two of the boats built to his specifications were captured.[56] When this problem recurred in the Austrian Succession War, Newcastle was convinced by the merchants' arguments, but Pelham successfully maintained the attitude of William III.[57]

Throughout the eighteenth century the prevalence of piracy by the packet-boats was the standard argument against arming them heavily; and in 1793, on the reopening of the French wars, their armaments instead of being increased were cut down. At the same time new instructions were issued to the commanders: 'You must run where you can. You must fight when you can no longer run and when you can fight no more you must sink the mails before you strike.'[58] Even if the packet-boats obeyed these instructions, war-time service on board was clearly dangerous. The sailors were exempted from impressment and a scheme of compensation for

[53] Vaillé, op. cit. v. 407–13.
[54] Joyce, *History of the Post Office*, p. 83.
[55] Ibid., pp. 173, 320.   [56] Ibid., pp. 75–76.
[57] Ibid., pp. 172–3.
[58] Norway, op. cit., pp. 21–24, 37–38.

death or injury arising in the course of service existed, financed by
deductions from pay.[59]

In spite of government refusal to arm the packet-boats heavily,
many of them undoubtedly engaged in piracy in war-time and all
of them devoted much of their energies to smuggling at all times.
'Their frequent disappearance for long periods together when the
wind was blowing from the quarter most favourable to their
return, and their occasional punctuality when the wind was contrary and they were least expected, involved a contradiction which
the postmasters-general found it hard to reconcile.'[60] On the
ground that (theoretically) passes from the secretaries of state were
required for all goods and passengers[61] carried by the packet-
boats, their captains claimed exemption from customs examination. Parcels of lace were concealed in the flap of the mails and
during the Spanish Succession War Paul Methuen complained
that at Lisbon 'there is a public market for English goods as often
as the boats come in'.

While the ministers and officials steadily set their faces against
packet-boats engaging in piracy, some of them connived at smuggling. In 1744 the postmasters-general protested to the Board of
Customs that if violent measures were resorted to, no captain 'of
real worth and character' would be found to command, and 'no fit
and able' seamen to serve on a packet-boat. In the second half of
the eighteenth century the practice of collusive seizure of cargo
carried by the packet-boats developed, by which the customs
officers seized small quantities of goods and allowed the rest of the
contraband cargo to pass on condition of receiving a share in
the profits. In the opinion of the eminent Victorian historian of
the Post Office, Joyce, the practice of smuggling was partly justified by the excessive arrears in payment of wages to the sailors
who manned the packet-boats.[62]

The agents in charge of the packet-boats at each station had
orders that outward mails were to be sent off immediately for
Holland or Portugal. Orders, however, were often sent to delay
them until a king's messenger could arrive: at other times they
were hurried off before their regular time for departure.[63] Diplo-

[59] Hemmeon, *History of the British Post Office*, p. 116; Joyce, op. cit., p. 84.
[60] Joyce, op. cit., p. 91.   [61] e.g. H.M.C., *Finch MSS.* iii. 246, 411.
[62] This paragraph is based on Joyce, op. cit., pp. 91–238.
[63] Hemmeon, op. cit., p. 114.

matists regularly made use of them on their journeys, and John
Macky, who combined the functions of Post Office contractor and
agent with those of a spy, included in his *Memoirs of Secret
Services* 'characters' of the leading diplomatists of Anne's reign.
Each 'character' begins with a reference to the diplomatist's personal appearance, suggesting that Macky had met them all as
passengers on the packet-boats. Recruits for British forces abroad,
the officers in charge of them, and shipwrecked mariners returning home were carried free of charge by the boats.[64] Not more
than two mails were supposed to be entrusted to the same packet-
boat, though this rule was often broken. Weights were to be
attached to the mails so that they could be sunk at once if the
boat was in danger of being taken by the enemy.[65]

The Falmouth packets were considerably larger than those used
on the other routes, nearly 200 tons, whereas Harwich was served
by 'hoys' of 40 to 60 tons.[66] In 1744 there were four boats on the
Falmouth–Lisbon run, four on the Harwich station, six running
from Dover to Calais or Ostend, two between Gibraltar and Lisbon, and two on the Minorca station, eighteen in all. When war
was declared against France in the same year, three boats which
served between Dover and Calais were transferred to Harwich to
augment the services to Ostend and Helvoetsluys.[67] While the
Harwich–Helvoetsluys route was less liable to danger from French
and Spanish privateers, the size of ships used and the conditions
of navigation in the North Sea made it frequently impossible to
maintain the service. George II himself on at least one occasion
narrowly escaped with his life and many stories were current of
miraculous escapes by less highly placed persons. Alexander Cunningham told a really 'fishy' story of how a packet-boat, about to
sink in a tempest, when the pumps were unable to cope with the
water pouring in from a leak, suddenly found the leak had been
stopped by a large fish which had been driven into the hole by the
force of the tempest. 'Without this wonderful providence', he
added, 'they must all have perished in a moment.'[68]

[64] Joyce, op. cit., p. 85.
[65] Ibid., p. 82; Norway, op. cit., pp. 17–18. On the rare occasions when packets
were captured by the enemy this instruction was usually carried out, e.g. H.M.C.,
Finch MSS. iii. 37.
[66] Joyce, op. cit., pp. 73, 75; Norway, op. cit., p. 15.
[67] Hemmeon, op. cit., p. 121.
[68] Cunningham, *History of Great Britain*, ii. 270.

The number of boats employed continued to rise, but, mainly owing to gross official corruption, the annual deficit rose much more rapidly. The official commission of inquiry into the Post Office calculated in 1788 that in seventeen years down to 1787 the total cost of the packet-boat service had been over a million pounds. Of this sum £800,000 had been lavished on the Falmouth station.[69] The packet-boat services had never been self-supporting, but the extent of the loss led to a radical reorganization and a much more effective control over the service.

Using the packet-boats, from 1689 letters left London on Mondays and Thursdays for France, Italy, and Spain and on Mondays and Fridays for the Low Countries, Germany, Sweden, and Denmark. Later in the period a direct service operated to the United Provinces on Tuesdays and Fridays.[70] This meant that, instead of a steady flow of activity in the office of the secretaries of state, there was a slack period in the middle of the week and frantic activity in writing, copying, ciphering, and dispatching letters and papers on Mondays and Fridays. The penchant of the superior officials for the long English week-end further complicated matters. The clerks were kept hard at it and frequently found it physically impossible to get everything ready by the time the mail had to go out. In this case a special messenger would be sent in the hope of catching up with the mail before the packet-boat sailed. If he failed to do so it was a standing order that instant passage must be provided for him, as indeed for any messenger.[71] Similar pressure on post days was naturally felt in the secret office, where the copyists and decipherers and technicians worked, if necessary, all through the night. Reformers began to advocate a daily postal service to the Continent and this was included in the recommendations of the commissioners who inquired into the administration of the Post Office in 1788.[72] In the early years of the French revolutionary war the government felt that such a service would produce revenue as well as intelligence, but it was not adopted until later.[73]

In time of war it was common to send duplicates of important dispatches and documents by successive posts; or, when alternative routes existed, duplicates would be sent by both routes at the

[69] Joyce, op. cit., p. 239.
[71] Ellis, *Post Office*, p. 34.
[73] Ibid., p. 99.

[70] Hemmeon, op. cit., pp. 31, 38.
[72] Ibid., p. 113.

same time. Thus an important dispatch from Madrid might be sent overland by messenger and also by the packet-boat service to Falmouth. Probably the extreme example of this practice occurred in 1778 when it was proposed to send 'orders for an attack on Chandenager and Pondicherry . . . by Leghorn, Alexandria and Suez, duplicates by Constantinople and Aleppo, and triplicates by [the East India Company's] own packet-boat to Alexandria'.[74]

My impression is that, owing to the precautions taken, only a tiny percentage of the official and private letters passing between London and the embassies and legations abroad did not arrive at its destination. On the other hand, during the American Revolutionary wars, one-third of the diplomatic correspondence of the colonies failed to reach its destination in spite of the general adoption of the practice of sending dispatches in duplicate and even in triplicate by successive mails.[75] In the case of the British government, at no period between 1689 and 1789 was anything like this percentage of diplomatic correspondence intercepted or lost. Delays were common; but the complete disappearance of a letter entrusted either to a messenger or to the Post Office extremely rare. On the few occasions when a packet-boat was taken by the enemy, after the mail had been flung overboard, the secretary of state wrote at once to the diplomatic agents asking for a duplicate of any letter which might have been on board to be sent to him.[76] This, in itself, is an indication of the efficiency both of the messenger service and of the foreign post office, which remained throughout our period distinct from the General Post Office.[77] It is likewise a tribute to the packet-boat service upon which both messengers and mails depended.

The secretaries of state consistently put security, and even official convenience, before considerations either of revenue or of public convenience. The obvious weakness was that neither they nor the postmasters-general had any really effective means of control over the foreign postmasters who were in charge of the mails once they had been landed from the packet-boats. Postal treaties were concluded from time to time with various states, but it was often easier to arrange the terms of such treaties than to get

[74] H.M.C., *Report X, App.* 6, pp. 20–21.
[75] G. H. Stuart, *The Department of State*, p. 4.
[76] S.P. 91. 65, dispatch of 26 Apr./7 May 1757.
[77] e.g. letters arriving from abroad were delivered by a separate staff of letter carriers and not mixed up in delivery with the inland mails.

them carried out with regularity and punctuality. Close contact was maintained with the hereditary postmasters of the empire, the Counts of Taxis.[78] Attempts were also made from time to time to secure preferential treatment for English letters by private bargains with individual postmasters and other officials. This was easier because official letters still formed a very large proportion of the total mail, at least with the more distant areas of central and eastern Europe.

The frequent wars on the Continent between 1689 and 1789 caused disturbance in normal postal communications; and, even in peace-time, continental sovereigns often preferred to arrange routes for mail and dispatches which would avoid the territory of a power that they regarded as unfriendly. In 1755 Bestuzhev insisted upon a courier dispatched with letters from Hanbury Williams to the secretary of state going to Hanover via Vienna without touching Prussian territory, with the result that the courier would take many days longer on the journey.[79] Williams himself at this time paid a pension to keep open a postage route for his letters which kept clear of the Prussian territories.[80] The messenger returning by the usual route from London a few months later to Petersburg took twenty-three days on the journey, as he was detained in the Prussian dominions by the post and customs-house officers.[81] After the actual outbreak of war between Russia and Prussia, the foreign ministers at Petersburg were warned by the Russian government that couriers would not be allowed to pass to and from Russia and Prussia and advised to employ other routes in dispatching couriers.[82] A few months later Hanbury Williams reported that although he had received twenty-eight days later a dispatch sent to him from London via Sweden, 'the posts and everything else have been here most irregular and violent in this country. Five mails at a time have been sent back from Memel and I have not received a letter from your lordship this nine months with the impression of the seals upon it.'[83] At such critical times the special postal arrangements required

[78] Their co-operation was particularly valued as offering an alternative route to Italy by the Low Countries and Innsbruck, clear of French influence (Vaillé, op. cit. iv. 317–18).   [79] S.P. 91. 60, dispatch of 17/28 June 1755.
[80] A.E. Russie Supplément 1755–6, fo. 50.
[81] S.P. 91. 61, dispatch of 12/23 Dec. 1755.
[82] S.P. 91. 65, dispatch of 30 Apr./11 May 1757.
[83] S.P. 91. 65, dispatch of 30 Aug. N.S. 1757.

to keep open communications between London and the British diplomatists abroad were sometimes explained to them in circular letters from the secretary of state.[84]

In times like these cipher was used more freely than usual in letters entrusted to the continental post offices. This was less dangerous than it seemed, because the men in charge of the important missions usually had a choice of ciphers, some of which had been in general use for considerable periods. It was often assumed that these common ciphers could be read without much difficulty by interested parties. As early as 1682 Lord Preston was entrusted with five different ciphers when sent on a diplomatic mission to Paris.[85] When Hanbury Williams was sent as ambassador to Russia he was given 'a new double cipher and decipher which none of the King's ministers abroad yet has, but Mr. Keith'.[86] These new ciphers were sometimes kept for use in dispatches sent by messenger and there was the less objection therefore to the occasional use of less precious ciphers in letters entrusted to the ordinary post. Occasionally the secretaries of state sent dispatches out of cipher by ordinary post in the expectation that these dispatches would be read by interested parties.[87]

New ciphers in the late eighteenth century are stated to have cost £150 and the secretaries were therefore reluctant to change them.[88] Prepared in the reign of George I by the senior clerks and then 'vetted' by the deciphering experts, they were from 1745 at the latest constructed by the Deciphering Branch, which not unnaturally had a very high opinion of its own handiwork. Since they had been able to suppress frequencies, their opinion may well have been well founded when these ciphers were originally adopted. But as they passed into general use 'a breach of security at one court imperilled communication at others'. Even an experienced secretary of state like Rochford once sent in cipher to a British diplomatist abroad copies of intercepted correspondence, while many British diplomatic agents on the Continent disregarded their instructions and sent to the secretary of state in cipher documents they had received from the government to

---

[84] e.g. S.P. 91. 65, dispatch of 6 May 1757.
[85] H.M.C., *Report VII, App.*, p. 261.
[86] S.P. 91. 60, dispatch of 11 Apr. 1755.
[87] S.P. 88. 71, dispatch of 8 Feb. 1751.
[88] Tilley and Gaselee, *The Foreign Office*, pp. 31, 148. This sum seems, however, to have been paid for 'New Ciphers' not *a* new cipher (F.O. 95. 591).

which they were accredited. Hyndford did this from Berlin with the result that the secretary of state had to send him a new cipher,[89] while John Strange from Venice 'repeated *en clair* the contents of a dispatch sent in cipher'. As the secretaries of state had to point out again and again, any clue to the subject of a ciphered dispatch, let alone a knowledge of its contents, made it much easier to break the cipher.[90]

Diplomatists had to take care to make use of the right cipher for correspondence not only with the secretary of state but also with their colleagues in the diplomatic service. If a new cipher was used in writing to a colleague at a minor post, the recipient would be quite unable to read the letter. At other times, muddle-headed secretaries forgot which cipher would be used by a correspondent and appealed for help to the secretary of state, only to be told that a copy of the cipher which had been used had been sent to them some years earlier.[91]

This applied also when, either in accordance with standing instructions or upon an emergency, dispatches from a British diplomatist at a distant court were sent to London 'under flying seal' so that they could be read by one or more British diplomatic agents posted along the route to be followed by the courier. Thus dispatches sent overland from Madrid through France were customarily read *en route* at the British embassy at Paris. Similarly, British diplomatic correspondence from eastern and northern Europe was often made available in this way to the ambassador or envoy at The Hague. In times of crisis special temporary arrangements of this kind were often made. Thus Hanbury Williams at St. Petersburg on the eve of the Seven Years War was instructed by the secretary of state to dispatch all messengers by way of Berlin and leave open all his letters upon general business for Mitchell's perusal in order that Frederick the Great, who had no diplomatic agent of his own in Russia, might receive the latest news of what was happening at St. Petersburg.[92]

Private ciphers were occasionally used by diplomatists for official purposes as when Mitchell at Berlin, anxious to get news of the battle of Leuthen to The Hague, had his dispatch translated

[89] Lodge, *Great Britain and Prussia*, p. 67.
[90] This paragraph is based on K. L. Ellis, 'British Communications and Diplomacy in the Eighteenth Century', in *Bull. Inst. Hist. Research*, xxxi (Nov. 1958), 159–67.   [91] S.P. 91. 59, dispatch of 20 Dec. 1754.
[92] S.P. 91. 62, dispatch of 13 Apr. 1756.

into Hebrew by Frederick the Great's confidant, Ephraim the Jew. It was then sent to Ephraim's correspondent at The Hague with directions to turn it into French or English and carry it directly to Colonel Yorke.[93] No one has tried to study the ciphers used in the eighteenth century by the secretaries of state, although there is an interesting discussion of earlier ciphers (with a list of authorities) in Thompson and Padover, *L'Espionnage politique*.[94] The contemporary eighteenth-century theories are explained in Philip Thicknesse's *Treatise on Deciphering and of Writing in Cipher* (London, 1772). Some information about actual practice may be gleaned from documents preserved amongst the State Papers at the Public Record Office and British Museum or printed by the Historical Manuscripts Commission.

[93] A. Bisset, *Memoir of Sir Andrew Mitchell*, i. 297, 385–6.
[94] Op. cit., appendix, pp. 244–55, 265.

CHAPTER XIII

Diplomatists and Consuls

THE history of the British consular service in the seventeenth and eighteenth centuries has still to be written. It is clear that if such a service existed it was even more inchoate and less organized than the contemporary diplomatic service.[1] Professor Barbour believed that under the Restoration kings the increase in the number of consuls was largely due to Charles II's desire to reward his friends at someone else's expense and that the merchants at the ports selected for this purpose usually objected with vigour to the institution of a consulate as costly and unnecessary.[2] Indeed in 1663 the House of Commons passed a resolution that no consuls unacceptable to the merchants should be appointed, and that, if so appointed, they should receive such salaries and allowances as the merchants should consent to give them. Charles II refused to accept such an encroachment on the royal prerogative.[3] On the other hand, there were a few occasions when the merchants interested in trade at a particular port actually petitioned in favour of the establishment of a consulate and even professed willingness to pay the recognized consular dues or consulage.

More recently it has been suggested that Charles II's consuls were appointed 'largely in consideration of their value as intelligencers. . . . The consuls in important locations received a weekly newsletter from Whitehall, as did all ambassadors and envoys abroad, and certain other correspondents.'[4] Out of fifty-four persons on Secretary Arlington's lists of official correspondents from 1667 to 1669, thirty were either diplomatists or consuls.[5] In exchange, consuls were expected to write directly to the secretary of state for the province in which they resided, although in Spain

---

[1] This would apply also to the early history of the American Consular Service, on which see W. J. Carr, 'The American Consular Service' in *The American Journal of International Law*, vol. i, pt. 2 (1907), 891–913.

[2] 'Consular Service in the Reign of Charles II' in *A.H.R.* xxxiii (1927–8), 553–78.

[3] 8 *C.J.* 467–8, 485.

[4] Fraser, *Intelligence*, p. 5.

[5] Ibid., p. 64.

and France they had also to correspond with and supply intelligence to the resident British diplomatist at the national capital.[6]

International jurists drew a clear distinction between diplomatic agents and consuls. Wicquefort declared that consuls, unlike diplomatists, 'do not enjoy the protection of the Law of Nations, and that they are subject, in both civil and criminal matters, to the jurisdiction of their place of residence';[7] but Vattel pointed out[8] that one or two instances to the contrary were to be found in Wicquefort's own treatise. Nevertheless, Vattel concluded that 'consuls are not diplomatic agents . . . and cannot claim their privileges. However, as they bear a commission from their sovereign and are received in this quality by the sovereign in whose state they reside, they must be accorded, to a certain extent, the protection of the Law of Nations.'[9] He attempts to define consuls as 'persons sent by a Nation to the chief commercial towns, and especially to the ports of foreign countries, with a commission to watch over the rights and privileges of their Nation, and to settle differences that may arise between its merchants'.[10]

In view of the tendency which manifested itself in the course of the eighteenth century to describe the highest rank in the British consular service as 'Agent and Consul General', it is worth while to point out that Vattel distinguished carefully between agents with and without credentials. Those with credentials and appointed to transact public business are *ipso facto* public ministers, whatever their title. Those without credentials, or who are sent merely to transact the private affairs of their sovereigns, are not public ministers, 'but out of deference to the prince whom they serve a more special protection is due them than is given to other foreigners or citizens, and a certain respect is shown them'.[11]

The eighteenth-century Dutch jurist, Cornelius van Bynkers-

[6] Fraser, *Intelligence*, pp. 67–70.
[7] Book i, section 5. This would seem to be the view of the leading modern authority on diplomatic immunity in the seventeenth century—E. R. Adair, *The Exterritoriality of Ambassadors in the Sixteenth and Seventeenth Centuries*, pp. 62–63, 244–5.
[8] Edition (text and translation) of the Carnegie Institution (Washington, 1916), iii. 125.   [9] Ibid., p. 124.
[10] Ibid.
[11] Ibid., pp. 368–9.

hoek, in his work *De Foro Legatorum*, was less impressed than Vattel by the claims of consuls to diplomatic immunity.

If we want the truth [he concluded] these consuls are nothing but the defenders of the merchants of their country and at times also their judges; furthermore they are generally merchants themselves, not sent to represent their prince in the country of another prince, but to protect the subjects of their prince in those matters which pertain to commerce and often to administer justice among them in commercial disputes.[12]

Almost the only discussion of this topic by a British author, relevant to our period, is that of Wyndham Beawes, Merchant, in his *Lex Mercatoria Rediviva: or the Merchant's Directory. Being a Compleat Guide to all Men in Business . . . containing An Account of our Trading Companies and Colonies . . . the Duty of Consuls* [&c.].[13] Beawes pointed out that there were differences between consuls of different nations, especially British, French, and Dutch;[14] but in the main his treatment followed closely that of the international jurists.

A *Consul*, to be properly qualified for his post, ought to be master of the language where he resides, and to have a thorough knowledge of the genius and trade of the natives, as well as a capacity to judge of and decide the differences arising among those of his own nation referred to him; and he ought likewise to support the dignity of his office, and not suffer it to be sullied by a practice of any meanness, or a derogating from such a behaviour, as may justly be expected from one who has the honour to serve his Majesty; it is also his duty to secure the esteem of the governing people where he lives, if possible, as by this means he may often influence and obtain favours for his fellow-subjects in their commercial concerns.[15]

Yet in spite of this idealized portrait, Beawes decided that

a consul is no public minister, as he has no affairs of state to manage, and consequently has no pretence to a protection from the *Law of Nations*, but from *that* which the subsisting treaties of peace and commerce give him; however, as a servant of the state that employs him, he may expect that countenance and support, as a good

---

[12] Edition (text and translation) of the Carnegie Institution (Washington, 1946), p. 53. Cf. *infra*, Appendix D.

[13] London, 1752, dedicated to Arthur Onslow, Speaker of the House of Commons.

[14] Ibid., p. 261.   [15] Ibid., p. 258.

master would (for his own sake) afford his domestic or dependent, and this has been demonstrated on many occasions. . . . The generality of consuls are only merchants, who, notwithstanding their office of *Judge in the controversies* that may arise among those of their own nation, carry on at the same time a traffic, and are liable to the laws of the place where they reside, as well in civil as in criminal matters, which is altogether inconsistent with the quality of a public minister; though, where it is otherwise, and a consul does not trade, I think a proportionable regard and respect ought to be paid, as due to his character.[16]

Lastly, as indicative of the views held at the very end of the eighteenth century, may be quoted the work on *The Law of Nations* by G. F. von Martens, as translated and published in English by William Cobbett. Although consuls

are under the particular protection of the law of nations, they are far from enjoying the advantages that custom allows to ministers, either as to jurisdiction, imposts, religion or honours. So that it is only in a very extensive sense of the words that they can be called public ministers. The greatest part of the consuls out of Europe approach much nearer to the rank of ministers; some of them are, indeed, ministers and consuls at the same time.

In a footnote it is added that 'the consuls may dispute about rank among themselves, but no consul takes the lead of a minister, even of the third order'.[17]

We may conclude that from the juridical point of view the humblest diplomatist was incontestably a public minister and a consul, within Europe at least, could only be described with many qualifications and reservations as a public minister, if indeed he could be so described at all. Another legal distinction, so far as British consuls were concerned, related to the manner of appointment. All diplomatists, except the most transitory of *chargés d'affaires*, received credential letters from their own sovereign addressed to the sovereign at whose court they were to reside. Consuls received no such letters; but a royal patent addressed 'to all and singular to whom these presents shall come'.[18] It was, of course, impossible to establish a consulate by

---

[16] Beawes, op. cit., p. 260.
[17] Op. cit. (London, 1829), pp. 155–6.
[18] e.g. Beawes, op. cit., p. 259. Copies of consular commissions abound amongst the S.P., especially S.P. 102 and F.O. 90.

unilateral action—the concurrence of the sovereign in whose territory the consulate was situated had to be secured. Most of our eighteenth-century consulates were the direct outcome of commercial treaties with foreign potentates, e.g. the Danish treaty of 1661 provided for mutual exchange of ministers in each other's courts and of consuls in certain ports 'for the better and more easy communicating and proposing such things as they [the kings of Britain and Denmark] shall think advantageous to the public interest, or private concerns of any particular person'.[19] Since diplomatists were sent to political capitals and consuls to commercial ports, there were very few towns in which both a British diplomatist and a British consul regularly resided. Amongst the duties of the consul as set forth in his commission would be included as a rule, if not invariably, 'to take care of the commerce of our subjects who reside or commonly go there [the place of the consul's residence] to trade'.

The classic authorities on diplomacy tacitly assumed that consuls, being primarily concerned with trade and navigation, could be excluded from consideration; although Callières drew a distinction between consuls and commissaries in European posts, who were not recognized as public ministers, and those appointed to the principal towns of Asia and Africa, who ought to be treated as public ministers. They were, however, usually careful to include commercial negotiations and the advancement of their country's trade amongst the duties of a good diplomatist,[20] so that one cannot argue that there was, in their view, necessarily a functional distinction between diplomatists and consuls.

If, however, we descend from the realms of law and theory to the realities of life, attempts to distinguish with absolute precision between diplomatic and consular agents at once break down. At St. Petersburg in the first half of the century the British resident agent was almost as much consular as diplomatic. The first agent appointed after 1689 was both Minister and Consul-General and

[19] *British and Foreign State Papers*, i. pt. i. 392. Similar provisions will be found in treaties with Portugal (1642 and later), Spain (1667), Morocco (1751), and Turkey (1675 and later modifications) printed elsewhere in the same volume. The Eden commercial treaty with France of 1786 provided by its 43rd Article for the re-establishment of British consulates in France and was followed by the consular convention of 1787.

[20] Charles Wilson in the *New Cambridge Modern History*, vii. 47, believes that the spread of diplomatic offices diminished the risks of foreign trade.

several of his successors were appointed as Consul-General and later promoted Minister Resident. But when Wolff, who had been Consul-General from 1744, was, to please the Chancellor Bestuzhev, promoted Minister Resident, he was debarred from 'any pretence to interfere in [diplomatic] business' and his successors as consuls-general, Samuel Swallow and Walter Shairp, were not promoted at all.[21]

Apart from these Russian examples, a small but significant percentage of diplomatic agents had served as consuls in Spain or Portugal immediately before being appointed to diplomatic posts at Madrid or Lisbon. It was a common occurrence for the consul-general at those two capitals to become secretary of embassy or minister when a vacancy occurred at the same court. There were also extremely rare cases when he was appointed in a diplomatic capacity to another court, e.g. as secretary of embassy at Paris.[22] It is hard to say whether this local practice developed because the consuls-general at Madrid and Lisbon were often of a higher social class than most of their colleagues elsewhere or whether salaried appointments with the prospect of promotion to diplomatic rank attracted more upper-class candidates. Beawes certainly thought a consul who received a salary superior to a merchant consul who traded himself while collecting consulage from his fellow merchants. Further promotion was virtually unknown in the eighteenth century. Interchange between the consular and diplomatic services became commoner in the nineteenth century, but even then few men who started in the consular service reached the top of the diplomatic profession.[23]

There are also in the seventeenth and eighteenth centuries, in addition to the cases already mentioned at St. Petersburg, a few examples of men who held simultaneously a diplomatic and consular appointment. Secretary Blathwayt informed Shrewsbury in 1694 that 'His Majesty has been pleased to appoint one Mr. Kerby, an inhabitant of Amsterdam, to be their Majesties' Consul and Agent there'.[24] Rather earlier, Sir Thomas Dereham had been employed both as consul and resident to the Grand Duke of Tus-

---

[21] B.D.R., pp. 115 et seq.

[22] Sir Stanier Porten in 1766, F.O. 27. 18, memorial dated 23 May 1786. Consuls often, though not invariably, acted as *chargés d'affaires* in the absence from his post of a diplomatic agent (*supra*, Chapter VIII, pp. 161–2).

[23] Bindoff, 'The Unreformed Diplomatic Service', in *Trans. R. Hist. Soc.*, 4th series, xviii. 157–8.   [24] H.M.C., *Buccleuch MSS.* ii. 113.

cany;[25] and his successor Sir Lambert Blackwell had credentials
as envoy, although the Grand Duke received him as consul only
from 1690 to 1696. Bolingbroke in 1713 secured for Drummond
the posts of consul at Ostend and 'secretary and resident at Brussels', adding that 'these two employments, which are very compatible and perhaps better placed in one than in two, will, I believe,
render your post very agreeable to you'.[26] Benjamin Keene at
Madrid was for a time paid both as consul and minister plenipotentiary.[27] Such cases are very rare and were certainly regarded
as anomalous by contemporaries.

A clear practical distinction between consuls and diplomatists
was that they were remunerated on a different scale and from distinct sources. Diplomatists were paid by the crown out of the civil
list on a predetermined scale, depending mainly on rank but
taking also into account the post held. After Charles II had virtually renounced 'the right to determine either the amount of
consulage or the manner in which it was to be raised', each consul
had 'to make the best bargain he could with the merchants,
masters and factors on the spot'.[28] Henceforth consuls usually
depended for their remuneration chiefly upon the amount of trade
between the home country and the port at which they resided and
upon other fees and perquisites. 'A consul's income', Beawes said,
'varies according to the place of his residence.'[29] And the profits
varied not only from post to post but fluctuated violently from
year to year at the same post.

The outbreak of war, for example, might bring British trade
almost to a standstill in the Mediterranean, where most of our
consulates were situated. On the other hand, a consul might be
appointed as agent for prizes and reap a rich harvest from naval
warfare.[30] Lord Grantham, at the end of the War of American
Independence, thought that appointments as consuls in Spain
'now reduced by the loss of American trade are scarcely beneficial
to any persons, but such as have houses or connections in Spain'.[31]
As a rule there was nothing to prevent consuls from engaging in
trade on their own account and often the official information
which they received and the prestige attaching to the office in a

[25] Ibid. ii. 374. [26] *Bolingbroke Corresp.* ii. 317.
[27] *C.T.B. and P.* ii (1731–4), 334.
[28] V. Barbour in *A.H.R.* xxxiii (1927–8), 563.
[29] Op. cit., p. 258. [30] *C.T.B.* xx. 366.
[31] *George III Corresp.* vi. 250.

mercantile community must have been valuable assets. Not until
well on in the nineteenth century did the generality of consuls
become whole-time salaried officials.

Consulage was normally in the eighteenth century the main
source of the consuls' incomes: it was differently calculated at
various consular posts. At Elsinore in 1715 the consul was 'to receive the usual consulage his antecessors have enjoyed, namely
two rix dollars of every leadned ship, and one rix dollar of every
ship in ballast'.[32] At Madeira in 1719 the British consul was
entitled to levy 12 milreis per ship 'let her bulk or loading be more
or less' and it was estimated in 1719 that the consulship at Oporto
was worth £600 and that at Madeira £400 per annum.[33] The
consul-general at Lisbon, however, was forbidden to engage in
trade and had 'to bear all the charges of disputes with the crown
of Portugal' as well as entertain the masters of ships arriving at
the port. His profit, none the less, was estimated at £1,200 a year
in time of war 'when Portugal was in great want of corn and many
ships arrived there from North America as well as Ireland, besides
the transports with soldiers, which likewise paid consulage if they
loaded back'. In peace the profits were less, but the average was
reckoned at £1,000 a year.[34] In 1786 an applicant for the consulship at Genoa reckoned fees at about £200, *plus* a salary of £200.[35]
The rate of consulage at ports controlled by the Levant Company
varied in our period from 1 per cent. to 10 per cent. of the value of
all goods exported or imported, although this was payable to the
company and not to the consuls,[36] who were remunerated by
salaries and expense allowances.[37] When, as part of the reorganization of the consular service in 1825, consuls were forbidden to
engage in trade, this restriction had to be relaxed a few years later;
and the Select Committee of 1835 expressly approved of consuls,
at many consular posts, engaging in trade if this would secure a
'better class of persons' as consuls 'at a more moderate charge to
the public'.[38]

Special arrangements had had to be made in the Restoration
period for the Barbary states, where the amount of trade was

---

[32] H.M.C., *Polwarth MSS.* i. 23.
[33] *Journals of the Commissioners for Trade and Plantations*, 21 Jan. 1719.
[34] Ibid., 23 Jan. 1719.
[35] F.O. 83. 11, letter of ? June 1786.
[36] Wood, *Levant Co.*, pp. 209-10.   [37] Ibid., pp. 217-18.
[38] *P.P. H. of C. 1835 Reports from Committees*, VI. iii (paper no. 449).

often small and the duties were at least as much political as economic. Captives had to be ransomed, supplies obtained for British men-of-war and for the garrisons at Gibraltar and Port Mahon; naval intelligence procured and sent to the Admiralty and the Mediterranean trade route kept open, largely by an elaborate system of passes (Privy Council Register 2. 88, fo. 13 and 120, fo. 88). Since these passes were often abused it was an important part of the Barbary consuls' duties to try to control such abuses and soothe the ruffled feelings of the North African potentates. Most of these duties, it is true, were also performed by British consuls elsewhere in the Mediterranean, but it was felt that they were sufficiently rewarded for such public service as they rendered by the ordinary fees and perquisites.

Charles II ordered the Treasury in 1681 to consider whether 'any allowances be made to any of his Majesty's consuls at any place upon the coast of Barbary or elsewhere'.[39] Immediately after the Revolution special arrangements were made to maintain the Restoration consulates at Algiers and Tripoli. Thomas Baker was appointed by the queen and the lords justices as consul at Algiers.[40] He was to be paid £600 a year with £300 for equipage and allowed to make bills for extraordinaries.[41] Similar arrangements were made at Tripoli, where the consul received £380 a year. At the end of William III's reign they were the only consuls who received payment out of the civil list.[42]

Godolphin and his successors at the Treasury tried to prevent salaried consuls from making bills of extraordinaries, but the efficient discharge of their varied and important duties required special payments[43] and the secretaries of state gradually wore down Treasury opposition. While this departmental battle was being fought, consuls were often placed in the same awkward predicaments as their colleagues in the diplomatic service. The Dey of Algiers wrote to Queen Anne, 'the most select of potentates amongst the followers of Jesus', that 'Mr. Cole, your servant and celebrated consul being indebted to us a sum of money, the

[39] P.C. 2. 69, referred to and partly quoted in Fisher, *Barbary Legend*, p. 270.
[40] H.M.C., *Finch MSS.* ii. 336, iii. 380.
[41] Ibid. iii. 385, 388, 403.
[42] *P.P. H. of C. 1868–9*, xxxv, part ii, 587.
[43] It was quite unreasonable to expect consuls to pay out of their own pockets such 'national and charitable' outlays as are listed by Consul Skinner (Leghorn) in S.P. 98. 26.

friendship between us and him was changed into coldness and indifferency'.[44] By 1754 regular salaries and extraordinary allowances had been fixed for all the Barbary consuls.[45]

Once the precedent of paying salaries to consuls out of the civil list, in addition to their fees and perquisites, had been established for the Barbary states, it was bound to be extended to other consular posts, although the process was a slow one. Under Queen Anne when John Butts, who had received a commission as consul for Denmark and had exhausted his substance in the service, applied for payment, he was told 'that the Queen would not make a precedent to allow him anything as a consul; but if he did anything of service there he should be rewarded accordingly'.[46] Special arrangements were made at Lisbon and Madrid and a list amongst the Townshend Papers[47] for 1742 showed civil list salaries to consuls at Algiers £600, Tripoli £380, Tetuan £250, Flanders £200, Oporto £500, and Faro £200. In addition the consuls at Algiers and Tripoli received extraordinary allowances of £500 and £250 per annum respectively.

This list is, however, incomplete and another, c. 1752,[48] showed £200 for the consul in Flanders, £400 plus £250 extraordinaries for the consul at Tetuan 'in lieu of all demands', and £300 plus £200 extraordinaries 'in lieu of all demands' for the consul at Tunis. The consuls at Algiers and Tripoli were still receiving the traditional £600 and £380, but this time there is no mention of extraordinary allowances to them. In addition, consuls at Madrid, Cadiz, and Naples received £500, £200, and £200 respectively. For the year to 5 January 1786 consular salaries and allowances had risen substantially and may be shown in tabular form:[49]

	£		£
Madrid	1,000	Corunna	250
Cadiz	200	Naples	400
Carthagena	300	Genoa	250

[44] S.P. 71. 11.

[45] S.P. 71 passim (and especially S.P. 71. 22, fo. 683). On the later organization of the Barbary consulates see Hilda I. Lee, 'The Supervising of the Barbary Consulates 1756–1836', in Bull. Inst. Hist. Research, xxiii (1950), 191–9.

[46] H.M.C., Portland MSS. viii. 370.

[47] H.M.C., Townshend MSS., p. 126.

[48] B.M. Add. MS. 32737, fo. 550.

[49] Sinclair, History of the Public Revenue, part iii, appendix 1, based on the annual returns in Commons Journals. The return for 1792 shows only twenty consuls, but excludes both the Barbary and Levant consuls (72 C.J. 816).

£		£	
Morocco	800	Grand Cairo	112. 5s. 1¾d.
Tunis	300	(from 12/9/85 to 1/1/86)	
Tripoli	380 + £250 extras	Nice	
Flanders	200	(Vice-Consul)	340
Trieste	120	Campvere	
Majorca, &c.	200	(Deputy	
America	1,000	Conservator)	120

While payments from the civil list to consuls had risen in a century from under £1,000 to over £7,000 a year,[50] these figures show that consuls in the main were as dependent on fees and perquisites at the end of the eighteenth century as they had been at the beginning. They did, however, occasionally receive gratuities on retirement.[51] Diplomatists, on the other hand, although they found perquisites a useful supplementary source of income, depended primarily on salaries and fixed allowances from the civil list.

Another distinction between diplomatists and consuls was that members of the House of Commons could accept diplomatic appointments without vacating their seats, whereas if they accepted a consular post their seats were vacated and they had to stand for re-election if they wished to continue as members of the House. Partly for this reason, and partly because most members of the House regarded a consular appointment as beneath them, comparatively few members, past or present, of the House, appear on the list of consuls.

In one respect consuls were usually superior to all but the highest ambassadorial grade of diplomatist. Ambassadors and consuls habitually enjoyed the ministrations of a chaplain who conducted in the official chapel services according to the rites of the established church. This privilege was presumably accorded to consuls on the assumption that where there was a consul there would normally be a colony of resident British subjects, probably organized in a Factory.[52] Thus Consul Broughton applied from Venice in 1696 'for the privilege of having a chaplain, which is very necessary for the edification of many English merchants, and even of

---

[50] *P.P. H. of C. 1868–9*, xxxv. 647.
[51] S.P. 93. 26 under date 25 Jan. 1771.
[52] See on consular chaplains in the eastern Mediterranean Wood, *Levant Co.*, pp. 222–4.

foreign merchants who are Protestants, at Venice' and his request was favourably regarded by the secretary of state.[53] Attempts were often made by the more bigoted Roman Catholic princes of Italy to end or circumscribe more narrowly the activity of consular chaplains within their dominions, while there were continual complaints from English merchants that their children or apprentices were being seduced or kidnapped by Papists.[54]

In practice, in the first half of our period at least, some of the Factories had a strong admixture of Roman Catholic Irish and Scottish Jacobites. As late as the 1750's Keene refused to recommend Kinloch, whom he had picked up while consul at Lisbon and employed at Madrid as his private secretary, as secretary of embassy at Madrid, on the ground that members of his family were notorious Jacobites.[55] At Riga in the 1720's we hear from an English merchant that 'the minister [of religion] when I was there was ... an open, bigotted Jacobite, with whom were joined about half-a-dozen more'.[56] While the Scots were numerous in the Baltic area, with which they had long had close trading connexions, the Irish were strongest in the Roman Catholic countries of south-western Europe, and above all Spain. In 1767 the entire Factory at Malaga was composed of such people, all but two of whom appear to have become Spanish subjects, while in 1769 there were many Irish Catholics also at Cadiz.[57] Legally Roman Catholics were debarred from attending meetings of the Factory, but this rule seems rarely to have operated in practice.

Whereas consuls were nearly always English subjects by birth or naturalization, vice-consuls were often foreigners, usually natives of the country in which they performed their duties. This was a constant source of complaint from contemporaries, though many of those who complained wanted such jobs for themselves and their evidence cannot be accepted without substantial reservations. John Jackson, in his *Reflections on the Commerce of the Mediterranean*,[58] argued that 'from these gentlemen [foreign vice-consuls] we cannot expect that they will attend so much to the interest of this country as the natural born subjects. ... The

---

[53] H.M.C., *Buccleuch MSS.* ii. 371, 387.
[54] See various documents in S.P. 98. 22, especially one dated 19 Sept. 1705, and S.P. 98. 86.   [55] *Keene Corresp.*, p. xxiv.
[56] *A particular description of the city of Dantzick* (London, 1734), pp. 40–41.
[57] P.R.O. Adm. 1/3837.
[58] London, 1804, pp. 41–42.

vice-consuls are usually Greeks or Italians, and therefore will always practice their impositions upon all strangers that employ them', such as charging British men-of-war and merchant ships as much as 35 per cent. on necessary supplies, 'exclusive of the usual commission, which only serves as a cloak for their more exorbitant charges'.

The presence of foreign elements in the consular service affords an interesting parallel to the diplomatic service which had, more particularly in the first half of our period, a strong admixture of aliens in the lower ranges. While it is impossible to be dogmatic, my impression is that the foreign element was stronger in the consular than in the diplomatic service and persisted longer.[59] There was also, although to a less extent than in the diplomatic, some penetration of the consular service by Scotsmen in the eighteenth century. Several of Charles II's consuls were Scots and this probably aggravated the objections taken by English merchants to the establishment of consulates.[60] In the eighteenth century Scottish consuls included Nathaniel Davidson at Nice and Algiers, Charles Gordon at Tunis, Sir John Dick at Leghorn, Charles Logie at Trieste, Edward Hay at Cadiz and Lisbon, Sir James Duff at Cadiz, Archibald Campbell Fraser at Tripoli and Algiers and James Bruce at Algiers, as well as successive holders of the conservatorship at Campvere.

Although the remuneration of diplomatists and consuls was based on different principles and, in general, paid from different sources, both classes of officials in the eighteenth century suffered heavy deductions in the form of various fees payable to government officials on stated occasions, e.g. on appointment the lowest grade of diplomatist paid £33. 12s. and a consul £12. 15s. to the Foreign Office fee fund. In addition the chief clerk of the Foreign Office collected for his own use on the first appointment of an ambassador £21 and of a consul £5. 5s. Similar but smaller fees were charged on letters written to the Treasury for the issue of salary instalments, special allowances, &c. When Castlereagh drew up new regulations for the foreign service after the peace of 1815, such fees became payable by the government and not by the individual diplomatist, in accordance with the recommendation

---

[59] An appreciable number of applications for consulships in the 1780's were received from persons who appear to have been foreigners (F.O. 83. 11).

[60] V. Barbour in *A.H.R.* xxxiii (1927–8), 557–8; Fraser, *Intelligence*, p. 71.

that diplomatic servants of the crown should receive their salaries free of fee or deduction of any sort. Consuls, on the other hand, had still to pay such fees out of their own pockets and this introduced a new technical distinction between diplomatists and consuls until such fees were abolished in the 1830's and consuls gradually became whole-time salaried officers. The consular regulations of 1826 marked an important stage in this process. Consular fees on British trade and shipping were abolished and salaries 'proportioned to the nature and importance of the respective duties of each consul' were substituted.[61] Both consuls and diplomatists continued to be liable to agency deductions on salaries and allowances,[62] payable mostly to the Foreign Office clerks who undertook their collection, until such charges were in turn abolished a generation later.

In some ways the clearest distinction between diplomatists and consuls was the social one. The select group of peers and influential politicians who tended to monopolize the highest appointments in diplomacy had no counterpart amongst the consuls. Even middle-class men, who would have been honoured to serve the crown as diplomatists, hesitated to accept consular appointments. Commercial connexions which were regarded as a hindrance or even a bar to candidates who aimed at diplomatic careers were a positive advantage in the consular service. When British consulates were to be re-established in France in 1786, Eden considered that it was very important to have 'the most respectable and most experienced merchants' as consuls.[63] When Newcastle proposed Sir Everard Fawkener as envoy to Berlin, Chesterfield objected that 'Sir Everard had been a merchant, which would not procure him esteem in Germany'.[64] In April 1702 Aldersey, the king's agent at Hamburg, was refused credentials as resident because of his employment among the Hamburg Company. He then offered to give up this employment, but by this time another candidate had been appointed.[65] On the other hand, when applications for a consulship were being considered, supporters of a candidate often included amongst their candidate's qualifications

---

[61] For all this see *P.P. H. of C. 1837*, xliv, Paper no. 162 (Report of the Committee to inquire into fees of public offices).

[62] F.O. 366. 375.

[63] F.O. 83. 11, letter of 12 Oct. 1786. Cf. John Jackson, *Reflections on the Commerce of the Mediterranean*, p. 40.

[64] *Marchmont Papers*, i. 239–40.

[65] S.P. 82. 20, 14 Apr. 1702.

that he had been a merchant[66] and was well acquainted with local conditions.[67]

As the eighteenth century proceeded there may have been a rise in the social status of Mediterranean consuls.[68] One or two of them were closely connected with the peerage, at least one baronet held a consular appointment at Lisbon[69] and there were occasional cases of knights acting as consuls. Yet Horace Mann wrote with reference to Sir John Dick, consul at Leghorn, who had received a Russian decoration for services to the Russian fleet in the Mediterranean: 'Sir John will next appear in England with his new decoration of the Order of Saint Anne of Holstein, which he has deferred putting on till he can quit the abject name of consul.'[70] The diplomatist Keene in 1745 even expressed doubt whether it would be proper for a minister plenipotentiary and a mere consul to live under the same roof, owing to the social gap between them.[71] And when his friend Castres was promoted from Consul at Lisbon to Envoy to the Portuguese court, he made it quite clear that this was an honour although 'honour buys no beef nor shoes or stockings for the little ones'[72]—in other words the post of consul might well be more profitable, but was certainly of lower status. On the other hand, John Murray was resident at Venice at the same time as Joseph Smith, who had married Murray's sister, was consul. And there are other cases where a diplomatist tried to use such influence as he possessed with the secretary of state to procure a consular appointment for a close relative. Perhaps the position may be summed up by saying that a diplomatic appointment, even as *chargé d'affaires*, conferred social distinction for life while the holding of a consular appointment, even if it did not attach a stigma to the holder, certainly did nothing to raise his social status.

In spite of this it must not be thought that in the eighteenth century there was a clear line drawn by contemporaries between

[66] e.g. many of the applications and recommendations in F.O. 83. 11.
[67] e.g. *George III Corresp.* i. 384.
[68] One applicant stated (19/10/86) that he had a moderate private fortune; another was willing to serve without a salary (F.O. 83. 11). Cf. the application of Joseph Denham for the consulship at Naples, which suggests either that there were valuable perquisites or that it was coveted for non-financial reasons (Add. MS. 28064, fo. 38).
[69] Sir Harry Frankland, Bt. (S.P. 89. 54).
[70] Doran, *Mann and 'Manners' at the Court of Florence*, ii. 293.
[71] *Keene Corresp.*, p. 69.   [72] Ibid., pp. 142–3.

diplomatic and consular duties and functions.[73] Thus British
agents to the Hanse Towns were given diplomatic rank although
their duties were primarily consular and commercial. One of
them suggested he should be given an additional appointment to
Cologne and Brunswick 'to promote the commercial interests of
his Majesty's subjects'. His request was granted and he was given
the rank not of consul but of envoy.[74] When the duke of Manchester, ambassador to Venice, heard that a Venetian resident
was to be appointed to London, his reaction was that 'it may be
serviceable and convenient for our commerce' to have a *resident*
at Venice.[75] When an appointment was made, expressly or inci-
dentally, to negotiate a commercial treaty with a foreign state, the
person appointed normally received diplomatic rank. The best-
known example of this practice was presumably Pitt's appointment of William Eden to negotiate the celebrated commercial
treaty with France, but many other cases could be quoted. Similarly, when an ambassador and a consul are both in residence at
Lisbon, instructions to lodge a protest against the institution of
the Wine Company of the Douro, contrary to treaties between
Portugal and Britain, were sent to the ambassador and not to the
consul.[76] The envoy at Dresden was instructed to discuss with the
Saxon court the duties on foreign earthenware in 1778.[77] Often
the formal instructions given to diplomatists at the beginning of
a mission order them 'to protect and countenance' the trade of our
subjects,

to apply yourself by all proper means to render their commerce as
free and as beneficial to them as possible . . . and in case any complaints of grievances which are well grounded shall be brought to you
by our subjects you are in our name to make the proper instances for
procuring redress . . . but . . . you will avoid interposing in matters
which are too frivolous and ill-founded to deserve your favour and
assistance.[78]

If any general principle can be deduced from these multifarious

[73] The duties of a consul are best explained by Miss Barbour in *A.H.R.* xxxiii
(1927–8), 567–9.   [74] S.P. 82. 75.
[75] H.M.C., *Buccleuch MSS.* ii. 591.
[76] S.P. 89. 52, 18 Jan. 1760.
[77] S.P. 88. 115, 20 Jan. 1778. See also S.P. 88. 109 (letter from Josiah Wedgwood,
20 July 1776, favouring lower duties on imports from Saxony if the Saxon
government will reciprocate).
[78] S.P. Royal Letters Poland 42, 28 Feb. 1747.

cases, it must be that contemporaries regarded the making of representations to foreign governments on commercial matters as being a diplomatic rather than a consular function. Yet when there was no diplomatist on the spot, the secretaries of state had no hesitation about employing the consuls for exactly the same kind of work. This is perhaps most apparent in our dealings with the Barbary states, but is by no means limited to this area.

Even when the home government had no representations to make to a foreign power, but merely wanted commercial information for its own guidance, the secretaries of state applied indifferently to diplomatists and consuls. The Board of Trade on 1 March 1711 proposed that

all the British consuls in foreign parts, and, where there are no consuls, her Majesty's ministers there, may receive her Majesty's directions every six months, to assemble the British merchants, trading in the place of such consul or minister's residence, and consult with them upon the then present state of British trade to that place, and to propose what they think proper for the improvement or advancement thereof; and that such their deliberations be writ down, and signed by the said merchants, and by the said consul or minister transmitted to her Majesty, by one of her principal secretary's of state, and to her commissioners for trade and plantations.[79]

A few years later all consuls and ministers abroad were desired to inform the Board of Trade whether 'any new duties or hardships, and what, have been laid on the British trade in the several places where they reside'.[80] And when, under George III, the attempt to secure reliable commercial statistics about our foreign trade was resumed, the necessary instructions were sent to the consuls and, where there were no consuls, to the diplomatic agents.[81] Some of the consuls and ministers continued to send in regularly commercial reports and statistics for many years after 1765.[82]

Similarly both consuls and diplomatists were required, not only to correspond regularly with the secretary of state, but to send home for publication in the London Gazette 'all such articles of foreign intelligence or news as may appear proper for that paper,

[79] Journal of the Commissioners for Trade and Plantations, 1 Mar. 1711.
[80] Ibid., 16 July 1729.
[81] Ibid., 8 Jan. 1765 and 10 Jan. 1766.
[82] Fuller details in E.H.R. liv (1939), 476–80. Copies of the 1765 reports were collected in C.O. 388. 95, and letters from the Board of Trade in S.P. 37. 16.

taking particular care, as the *Gazette* is the only paper of authority printed in this country, never to send anything concerning the authenticity of which there is the smallest doubt'.[83] Again, both diplomatists and consuls were expected to supply information about smuggling or breaches of the Navigation acts,[84] and, especially in time of war, intelligence of enemy plans and manoeuvres.

One reason for the lack of differentiation between the two services was the limited areas in which they overlapped. Only in a few cases was a British diplomatist resident in the same town as a British consul. Under Charles II consuls resided at Elsinore and Hamburg in northern Europe; at Ostend, Dunkirk, Bordeaux, Bayonne, and Marseilles in the Channel ports and France; at San Sebastian, Bilbao, Corunna, Lisbon, Seville, Cadiz, Malaga, Cartagena, Alicante, Barcelona, and Majorca in the Iberian area; at Villafranca, Turin, Genoa, Pisa, Leghorn, Naples, Trapani, Messina, Gallipoli, and Venice in Italy and Sicily; at Zante, Smyrna, Aleppo, Tripoli, and Cyprus in the eastern Mediterranean; at Alexandria, Santa Cruz (south Barbary), Tripoli, Tunis, Algiers, and Tetuan in North Africa; and at Santa Cruz de Tenerife in the Canary Islands.[85] These places are sea ports and, although one or two might also be described as political capitals, only at two or three of them were English diplomatists resident for any part of the Restoration period.

No appreciable extension of this network of consulates took place until well on in the eighteenth century. Indeed some of the Restoration consulates ceased to function. This is especially true of the consulates in France which had been maintained with increasing difficulty during the period of Anglo-French *entente*,[86] disappeared completely after the Revolution of 1688, and were not restored until provision was again made for them by the Eden commercial treaty of 1786.[87] Beawes gave a list, admittedly incomplete, of British consulates *c.* 1752:

[83] *Cal. H.O. Papers 1766–9*, no. 1245.
[84] E. E. Hoon, *Organization of the English Customs System 1696–1786*, p. 91, note 5.
[85] Fraser, *Intelligence*, appendix 7 and map facing p. 64. Cf. the list in *A.H.R.* xxxiii (1927–8), 578.   [86] Clark, *Trumbull*, p. 170.
[87] F.O. 27. 27; *Auckland Journal*, i. 265. Choiseul had been strongly opposed to a resumption of consular relations with Britain (A.E. *Correspondance politique Angleterre*, vol. 477, dispatch of 26 Mar. 1768. I am indebted for this reference to Dr. M. S. Anderson).

Besides the consuls aforementioned in Barbary, there are others at Tetuan, Salle, and St Maura on that coast; in Spain at Madrid, Cadiz, Malaga, Carthagena, Alicant, Barcelona, Sevil and St Lucar, Port St. Mary's, Corunna (or the Groyne), St Andero and St. Sebastian; in Italy at Leghorn, Venice, Naples, Genoa, Messina and at Zant; and in Portugal at Lisbon and Oporto, many of which nominate Vice-Consuls at different places in their respective districts.[88]

In addition in 1755 there were consuls at Nice, Cagliari, the Canaries, Ostend, Elsinore, St. Petersburg, and Campvere.[88a] For the 1780's onwards there are annual lists of consuls in the *Commons Journals*, usually limited to consuls who received some part of their emoluments from the civil list. Sir Godfrey Fisher argues that the consular organization, which had prospered and proved its national utility under the Stuarts, was unsuited to or at least unappreciated by the Hanoverians. Its strength had been due to co-operation, first in the Factories themselves, then with the local authorities, merchant shipping, other Factories, naval commanders and finally, through the London merchants, with the secretaries of state who were friendly and sympathetic.[89]

Certain developments did, however, take place before 1789. The most important additions were the establishment of a consul-general at Madrid, subordinate to and in close contact with the diplomatic staff at the Spanish capital; and the institution of new consulates in the Baltic, at Riga and St. Petersburg. Hamburg, with its associated Hanse Towns, was raised from a consulate to a diplomatic post. Thus in the eighteenth century British diplomatic and consular officials rarely resided in the same town, except at Madrid, Lisbon, St. Petersburg, and some Italian towns, especially Genoa, Venice, and Naples.

So far as I know, there was no eighteenth-century precedent for Lord John Russell's circular dispatch to all consuls, dated 2 May 1861, in which he informed them that 'the consular service is in all matters strictly subordinate to the diplomatic service, and that the diplomatic representative of her Majesty is, subject to the authority of the secretary of state, invested with full authority and control over all her Majesty's consular servants, in the country

---

[88] Beawes, op. cit., p. 260. He omits the Levant Company consulates and the few consulates which existed in northern Europe.   [88a] Adm. I. 4120.

[89] Fisher, *Barbary Legend*, pp. 294–5.

in which he and they reside'.[90] Nevertheless, the basic principle would seem to have been generally accepted. When the resident at Venice gave the consul there leave to go to Holland in 1763 this was not disapproved by the king.[91] It was in fact natural and inevitable that, whenever a consul found himself in difficulty with the foreign government in whose territories his post was situated, he should apply for help to the diplomatist accredited to that government by his own. Diplomatists were sometimes expressly instructed to give help to the consuls within their sphere of activity.[92] Ambassador Keene at Madrid was able to secure the transfer of Consul Parker from Oporto to Madrid and then made use of him to discharge the duties of a private secretary. In exchange Keene persuaded 'our great folk' to double Parker's salary.[93]

Such harmonious co-operation was the exception and not the rule. Keene's friend, Castres, had trouble with Consul Crowle at Lisbon, and found Crowle's successor, Hay, little more congenial.[94] Part of the trouble here was probably due to the idea that the consul at Lisbon had a quasi-right of reversion to the diplomatic post; but, long before this practice developed, there had been bad feeling. Consul Earle accused Ambassador Methuen of seducing Earle's wife and dismissing his own, and also of getting hold of the title deeds of Earle's lands. Now to crown all, Earle wrote in 1704, the ambassador was trying to get him sacked from his position as consul.[95]

Perhaps the most notorious case of diplomatic-consular hostility at Lisbon occurred in 1727. The envoy, Brigadier James Dormer, was so enraged by the behaviour of Consul Burnett, who had publicly celebrated the king's coronation day and the name day of the king of Portugal, that he encouraged his servants to stop Burnett's coach and have Burnett beaten in order 'to put a public disgrace upon him'. The court of Portugal then accused Dormer of trying to murder Burnett and forbade him to approach the court. Dormer was then reprimanded and recalled by his own

---

[90] Detailed instructions for their conduct follow (*P.P. H. of C. Select Committee on the Diplomatic Service 1861*, p. 492). In Sweden a statute of 1793 achieved the same result (*Histoire de l'administration des affaires étrangères de Suède*, ed. Tunberg and others, p. 350).

[91] H.M.C., *Report X 'Eglinton MSS.'* (Weston-Underwood MSS.), p. 451.

[92] Clark, *Trumbull*, p. 170.

[93] *Keene Corresp.*, pp. xxiv, 89, 496–7.

[94] Ibid., pp. 344, 353, 423.

[95] S.P. 89. 88, 13 Dec. 1704.

government.[96] One of Dormer's successors, another fire-eating soldier, Tyrawley, received a present of a cap from Consul Compton's wife and at once wrote a rhymed letter of thanks. This begins:

> Last night, as I was going to bed,
> I got your charming cap;
> O could I wear it on my head,
> Reclin'd on your dear lap!
> This beauteous cap & you, my own,
> I'd envy none that wears a crown.[97]

I do not know the upshot of this *affaire*, but there seems to be some warrant for anticipating a repetition of the Methuen–Earle incident.[98]

The rupture of diplomatic relations between Britain and courts where we maintained both a diplomatic and a consular agent was normally followed by the withdrawal of the consuls. Thus both in 1727 and 1779 the British ambassador, on the eve of the rupture, gave orders to all consuls to quit Spain, although in 1727 one consul in fact retired adroitly into a convent and another took to his bed with gout. During the Anglo-Spanish War of 1739–48 at least two consuls retired from Spain but continued to send intelligence from Portugal.[99]

There is one peculiar difference between eighteenth-century consuls and diplomatists. No woman would have been considered for a moment for the diplomatic service, although Torrington at Brussels described his wife in a letter to the secretary of state as 'the soul of my office' and left her behind at Brussels on his return to England so that she could supervise the activity as *chargé*

---

[96] S.P. 89. 34.

[97] *Shenstone's Miscellany 1759–1763*, ed. I. A. Gordon, p. 95.

[98] There were also occasional conflicts between consuls and R.N. captains and the secretary of state in 1766 ruled that 'no captain of any of H.M.'s ships . . . can acknowledge a superior authority in his consul, or be obliged to apply through him for anything they might be entitled to by treaty' (*Cal. H.O. Papers 1766–69*, no. 216). It may partly have been to supply naval captains with the information required to enable them to act independently of consuls that *Extracts from the Several Treaties subsisting between Great Britain and other Kingdoms and States of such Articles as relate to the Duty and Conduct of the Commanders of His Majesty's Ships of War* was published and reissued from time to time (3rd ed., London, 1758). The treaties from which extracts were thus published include those with the Barbary states, Austrian Netherlands, Denmark, France, Portugal, Russia, Savoy, Spain, the States General, Sweden, and Turkey.

[99] S.P. 94. 133.

d'affaires of his youthful secretary.[1] But in the case of consuls the appointment of the widow of a consul is occasionally recommended to the secretary of state. Titley from Copenhagen on 25 January 1752 advised the appointment, on the death of her husband, of Mrs. Elizabeth Fenwick, 'a very notable woman', as consul in Denmark as long as she remained unmarried.[2] Still more remarkable, the secretary of state applied to the Treasury[3] for the usual consular allowance for management of the Tripoli consulate between the death of Consul White and the arrival of his successor to be paid to Mrs. White.

[1] F.O. 26. 13.   [2] S.P. 75. 95. One of her sons was appointed.
[3] *Cal. H.O. Papers 1766–69*, no. 713.

CHAPTER XIV

Diplomatists and Secret Agents

WHEN relations between two states are bad, it is almost inevitable that their diplomatic agents at each other's courts should be regarded as spies with credentials. When Lieutenant-Colonel Robert Campbell was sent to Stockholm on 'an abortive exploratory mission'[1] in 1757, he had to tell the secretary of state that he was looked upon by the Swedes as 'a spy under credentials'[2] and in the end he was not received as a public minister. About the same time French ambassadors at The Hague were expected to organize a group of spies in England, collect their reports, which sometimes came to Holland in the diplomatic bag of the Austrian ambassador at London, and forward them to Paris.[3] Similarly, Hanbury Williams wrote from St. Petersburg: 'The constant accusation of me to the Empress is that I am in the king of Prussia's interest, to which some people have added that Her Imperial Majesty ought to look upon me more as a Prussian spy than as an English ambassador.'[4]

With earlier cases of this kind in mind Callières remarked: 'The ambassador has sometimes been called an honourable spy because one of his principal occupations is to discover great secrets; and he fails in the discharge of his duty if he does not know how to lay out the necessary sums for this purpose.' If his master does not allow him sufficient cash 'he must be even prepared to do it at his own charges'.[5] Many British diplomatists claimed that they had acted upon this recommendation. Macartney said that during his mission to Russia he had 'spent above a thousand pounds of my own money for secret service. This I never mentioned before [to Pitt], nor do I intend to speak of it to the office, though, upon my honour, it is true.'[6] Sir R. M. Keith claimed 'that in the five-and-

[1] J. F. Chance in *B.D.R.*, p. 143.
[2] Quoted from copies of his correspondence in H.M. General Register House, Edinburgh.   [3] Thompson and Padover, *L'Espionnage politique*, pp. 151-7.
[4] S.P. 91. 65, dispatch of 22 Mar. 1757.
[5] Callières, *De la Manière de négocier avec les souverains*, ed. Whyte, p. 27.
[6] *Chatham Corresp.* iii. 18.

twenty years, during which I have had the honour of serving his Majesty in various foreign missions, I never charged a *single shilling* for secret service money to the account of Government'.[7]

Callières continued:

As there is no expense better designed, nor more necessary than that which is laid out upon a secret service, it would be inexcusable for a minister of state to neglect it.... Let an ambassador retrench all superfluous expense in order that he may have the funds at his disposal to maintain a secret service which will inform him of all that happens in the foreign country of his service.[8]

There were, of course, limits which diplomatists must observe.

It has been truly said that there is no service which a prince may not expect from good subjects and faithful ministers, but such obedience cannot be held to cover any action against the laws of God or of justice, which do not countenance for one moment attempts on the life of a prince, or against the security of the state, or any other unfriendly act committed under cover of the protecting title of ambassador. A good ambassador will always discourage plans of this kind, and if his master persists in them he may and should demand his recall and retire into obscurity, jealously guarding his sovereign's evil secret.

'But', he continues,

let me not be misunderstood. There is all the difference between the attempt to debauch the subjects of a sovereign prince in order to ensnare them in conspiracy against him, and the legitimate endeavour to use every opportunity for acquiring information. The latter practice has always been permissible, and indeed is a necessary part of diplomacy.[9]

Most of what Callières said on this subject had appeared also in Wicquefort and was repeated a generation later by Pecquet. The latter, however, held that the use of spies, even to procure information, was 'peu honorable', and, in view of the danger that it might recoil on his own head, argued that a diplomatist should employ spies only when all other means of obtaining information have failed.[10] The author of the *Observations on the Office of an*

[7] *Keith Memoir*, ii. 533.
[8] *Callières*, op. cit., pp. 26–27.   [9] Ibid., pp. 86–87.
[10] *Discours sur l'art de négocier*, pp. 91–92.

Ambassador remarked that 'a good intelligence is the life of all public negotiations, but that is most to be depended on which is purchased by the Minister's purse and industry; for, if an ambassador be too credulous, he will often be imposed upon'.[11]

British diplomatists were usually familiar with these works of reference and usually followed the advice given in them. There are, however, cases in which by excess of zeal they overstepped what the authorities in diplomacy regarded as legitimate intervention. It was believed in Stair's own lifetime that he had not limited his intelligence service to procuring 'the best intelligence of all the Pretender's motions of any public minister abroad', but had 'employed Ant. Hammond (now living within the Rules of the Fleet prison on account of debt) to assassinate the Pretender, which he was very near doing at Dunkirk'.[12] Hanbury Williams in 1750 was willing to 'undertake to find a Pole who will engage to seize upon his [the Pretender's] person in any part of Poland and carry him to any port in the North that his Majesty shall appoint. I have had offers of this sort already made me to which your Grace may be sure I gave no answer except thanking the persons for the zeal they shew'd for the King my master; but I am convinced that the thing is very practicable.' This caution was commendable because one of those who offered their services was 'in the greatest confidence', with both Marshal Saxe and Count Brühl, the Saxon Prime Minister.[13] It is not surprising that Newcastle found it necessary to warn his over-zealous subordinate to be very cautious in his dealings with spies.[14]

The moment an energetic British diplomatist arrived at a new court he set about collecting intelligence. Often it was not sufficient to have these informers placed in the capital of the state to whose sovereign the diplomatist was accredited. Wich, while Resident to the Hanse Towns, employed one Jacob Deiling to inform him of what was going on at Dresden and paid £60 a year for his services.[15] Stair and other ambassadors to France corresponded regularly with secret agents in other countries, e.g. with Wilkins in Spain in 1720.[16] While cases occur from time to time in which spies are directly in touch with the office of the secretary of

---

[11] Op. cit., p. 52.   [12] H.M.C., *Egmont Diary*, iii. 349.
[13] S.P. 88. 70, letters of 11 June and 11 Sept. 1749.
[14] S.P. 88. 70, dispatch of 20 Oct. 1750 (from Williams to Newcastle).
[15] S.P. 81. 177.
[16] S.P. 94. 90–91.

state, as a rule the ministers abroad were used to link these secret agents with London.

A great deal depended on the court to which the diplomatist was accredited. News was much easier to obtain at some than at others. As a rule it was easy to get reliable intelligence at a friendly court. Some, if not all, of the ministers and courtiers would be well disposed to Britain and it was the diplomatist's own fault if he did not soon live in a circle of friends able and willing to help him. Social contacts would quite naturally gain for him informal, reliable information. Even so, such informants often expected something in exchange—at the very least, good cheer at the ambassador's table. In other cases, presents and favours to show that their services were appreciated by the ambassador's master would be expected. Occasionally, substantial cash payments were openly demanded, not of course as bribes to influence conduct, but as rewards for giving the help they would have given in any case.

The venality of the Russian court was axiomatic to contemporaries. Hyndford found it necessary to distribute *largesse* to unimportant persons with a fairly lavish hand.[17] In addition, Chesterfield authorized him to 'lend' £5,000 to the Great Chancellor, with the promise of a further £5,000 when a convention was concluded. Bestuzhev was so angry at this shabby treatment that Hyndford had to explain to his government that at St. Petersburg a loan without interest was not looked upon as a reward. Through its agent at St. Petersburg, Baron Wolff, the British government then advanced 50,000 roubles to Bestuzhev, who executed a mortgage on his new house and invited fifty of the principal courtiers, 'enemies and all', to be witnesses to the deed. 'His politik [*sic*] in this', Hyndford believed, 'is to prevent the suspicion of his having had any part of this money as a present and to show his enemies that he is very poor, which he really is, and that the Empress may relieve him of this debt.'[18] Bestuzhev was soon demanding further sums from the British government and in 1756 Hanbury Williams paid him another £10,000.[19] In addition he would have liked an annual pension of £2,500 from the British government.[20] At the

---

[17] See his bill for extraordinaries in *E.H.R.* xliii (1928), 610–11.

[18] B.M. Add. MSS. 11383–4 (Hyndford Papers), especially 11384, fo. 421.

[19] Horn, *Williams and European Diplomacy*, p. 229.

[20] Ibid., p. 244.

same time Williams paid to the Great Duchess Catherine £10,000 on the understanding that it would be used for 'the King's service'.[21] This sum was described as a 'loan' and after Catherine became Tsaritsa she offered to repay 44,000 roubles to the British government,[22] which instructed its diplomatic representative at St. Petersburg 'to endeavour to avoid accepting the £10,000 offered you in repayment' on the ground that 'in itself it is not an object of consequence enough for her Majesty to be at all solicitous about repayment'.[23] Smaller sums continued to be paid from British secret-service funds during the War of American Independence.[24]

Another court at which considerable sums were paid as bribes was Stockholm, where the nobles who controlled the state were usually divided into a French party and a Russian party. Each party expected its foreign backer to contribute lavishly to party funds, if not also to the private finances of its members. Britain exerted what influence she possessed at Stockholm in favour of the pro-Russian 'caps' and against the Francophil 'hats'; and, especially in the reign of George III, Russia urged Britain to join with her in financing the 'caps'. In 1764 Sandwich, as secretary of state for the northern province, invited the Prime Minister, Grenville, to consider giving this financial support. He argued that if France were not effectively opposed at Stockholm she would be able to make use of the Swedish fleet for her own purposes in the Baltic.[25] In the following year Conway, deputizing for Grafton, who had succeeded Sandwich in the northern secretaryship, recommended sending to the British minister at Stockholm £2,000 or £3,000 at least to be spent at his discretion.[26] Doubts were later expressed by Rochford, when Russia was urging that the British government should again contribute to the common cause at Stockholm, over the way in which Goodricke had disposed of the money previously placed at his disposal.[27] Probably the most detailed

---

[21] Ibid., pp. 250-1.

[22] *Buckinghamshire Corresp.* ii. 164.

[23] Ibid. ii. 179-80.

[24] Isabel de Madariaga, 'The Use of British Secret Service Funds at St. Petersburg, 1777–1782', in *Slavonic and East European Review*, xxxii (1954), 464-74.

[25] *Grenville Papers*, ii. 434-5.

[26] *George III Corresp.* i. 178-9.

[27] Martens, *Recueil des Traités conclus par la Russie*, IX (X), *Angleterre*, under date 1772. Some information, perhaps not entirely accurate, about Goodricke's bribes in Thompson and Padover, *L'Espionnage politique*, pp. 157-62.

account in print of the secret-service activity of a British diplomatist in our period is that given by Professor Cobban of Malmesbury's mission to The Hague, where, although the money was spent in the United Provinces, the main object was to resist French control of the Netherlands. Substantial sums, on one occasion £20,000, passed through Harris's hands.[28]

A different situation arose at courts where Britain had few friends, and most of those she did have were afraid to incur the danger to their own position and prospects, of consorting openly with a British diplomatic agent. Harris made this point very clearly in the 1780's when he was contrasting his position at The Hague with that of his predecessors:

> The system which [then] prevailed was a favourable one, the machine was well wound up, and people found their account in doing what we wished. Now the direct contrary is true, and whoever espouses our cause shuts against himself every door to preferment, and there are very few indeed liberal or zealous enough to sacrifice their own interests to the support of a political system.[29]

Even at an unfriendly court there would probably be some persons who would supply information if absolute secrecy could be observed; but the main reliance would have to be placed on professional spies. The author of the *Observations on the Office of an Ambassador* remarked that 'a proper application of money is many times useful, and often necessary; but to conceal the channels through which it is conveyed is a secret of as much importance to the giver as to the receiver; and it is a nice part of the ministerial art to execute things of that nature with a good grace'.[30]

Spies did not always want money in return for information. An appreciable number of them were exiled Jacobites anxious to work their passage home. The Earl Marischal was an outstanding example of this class and he attained his objective by informing the British government betimes of the conclusion of the third Family Compact in 1761.[31] When Seignoret was spying for Trumbull, the secretary of state brought pressure to bear upon the bishop of London to admit Seignoret to Holy orders, though it is

---

[28] Cobban, *Ambassadors and Secret Agents*, especially pp. 110–16, 175.
[29] Ibid., pp. 111–12.   [30] Op. cit., p. 53.
[31] Another case, an Irishman this time, in S.P. 88. 71, dispatch of 17 Oct. 1750.

not clear whether this was intended as a reward for services rendered or as a means of enabling him to carry out more successfully his duties as a spy in the future.[32] We are told, too, that spies sent into Holland by Charles II during the Dutch wars 'do not seem to have received anything for their pains but only their expenses',[33] though I must add the comment that after the Glorious Revolution cases of such disinterested devotion to duty seem to be exceedingly rare, if indeed any exist.

Most of the spies, records of whom survive among the State Papers, were concerned with the national enemy *par excellence*, France. A great deal of the information supplied by them in peace-time would not now be classified as secret, but would be found in print in the *Army List* or Jane's *Fighting Ships* or some such publication. In war-time efforts were redoubled and a considerable mass of material accumulated in the offices of the secretaries of state. Much of this might be irrelevant or common knowledge; and of the remainder much was unreliable gossip, or else took so long to reach London that its usefulness was diminished or entirely lost. Often the functions of the diplomatic agents in this connexion were limited to arranging for the prompt and safe conveyance of information collected by secret-service agents over whom they had virtually no control[34] and of whose true identity they might well be unaware. Especially in war-time, merchants' addresses were often used in the hope of concealing from foreign post offices the nature of the correspondence. Ciphers or cant phrases, arranged in advance, were frequently used. Invisible ink was sometimes employed and messages written on newspapers might escape close inspection in the continental post offices.[35]

Some of these informants might themselves be diplomatic agents with credentials from other sovereigns. Not infrequently offers from foreign diplomatists to render this sort of information service to the British government have survived amongst the official papers. La Sarras, minister at The Hague from the Grisons, we hear 'is desirous to have his correspondence accepted by your lordship [Townshend] for a suitable gratuity'.[36] Bolingbroke made use of the Saxon resident at London, 'a vain and a lying Gascon',

[32] H.M.C., *Downshire MSS.* i. 909. [33] Fraser, *Intelligence*, p. 111.
[34] H.M.C., *Downshire MSS.* i. 732. [35] Ibid., pp. 597, 674.
[36] *Honest Diplomat*, p. 208.

who was paid £300 for his services in advance, to discover things of moment at Utrecht while the treaty was being negotiated and 'to penetrate as far as he is able into the intrigues of the Germans and others'.[37] Newcastle was for long on very close terms with both the Saxon minister Flemming and the Sardinian diplomatists at London. During Waldegrave's embassy to France he depended on various spies for information, one a former agent of the elector of Saxony, and another the then Swedish envoy to the French court, who passed on to Waldegrave what the French ministers said to him.[38] Malmesbury at The Hague depended greatly on the help of the Sardinian consul at Amsterdam.[39]

Obviously an official position, no matter how lowly, and a claim to diplomatic immunity were valuable assets to an informer; but few eighteenth-century under-cover men enjoyed these advantages. Often they were expatriates, Huguenot refugees or Jacobite Scots, living by their wits on the verge of starvation. Not many prospered as spies, although the notorious Sicilian abbots, Caracciolo and Platania, banished from Spain by Elizabeth Farnese, settled happily in Paris. Here they conducted a sort of private information service, which was utilized by France, Spain, and, above all, Britain. Basil Williams believed that 'no better defence can be found for Walpole's refusal to interfere actively in the Polish war than the masterly argument which they drew up in support of that policy'.[40]

Successive British diplomatists at the French court spent a great deal of time and a certain amount of money in trying to procure reliable information about the French court, army and navy, finances, &c. Lord Preston, when envoy to the French court under James II, was already employing several informers and spies;[41] but during the prolonged Jacobite succession crisis (when the courts were not actually at war) the number of such agents increased. In spite of attempts to check the traffic by passports and other means, secret agents of all sorts found it comparatively easy to slip across the Channel, while others found it easier, especially

---

[37] *Bolingbroke Corresp.* i. 394.
[38] Basil Williams, 'The Foreign Office of the first two Georges', in *Blackwood's Magazine*, vol. 181, p. 104.
[39] Cobban, *Ambassadors and Secret Agents*, p. 113.
[40] Basil Williams, op. cit., p. 103. Was there a third Sicilian abbot or did one of them write as the Abbé Paretti to Marchmont during the Congress of Cambrai? (*Marchmont Papers*, ii. 414.)   [41] H.M.C., *Report VII*, App., pp. 392 ff.

in time of actual war, to travel via the Low Countries. At one point Nottingham actually proposed to the King to send 'all the French Papists, merchants and others' out of the kingdom 'for they send intelligence of the sailing of our merchant ships and of all other matters, and carry on the trade with France. I have not evidence enough to convict them, but sufficient to persuade me of the truth of these practices by which they do us mischief, and I know no good we reap by their company here.'[42] One of the objections taken to the numerous chaplains maintained by the Roman Catholic ambassadors at London was that these men were often under-cover spies.

Smuggling and spying were often two aspects of a single enterprise. Shrewsbury, when secretary of state in 1695, was asked to decide 'whether the intelligence [Captain Peterson] can now bring from Brest will countervail the damage the nation may receive by their endeavouring to import some few French commodities'.[43] In 1695 one of Trumbull's spies proposed that the secretary should allow certain London merchants to buy a Danish ship, which could make seven or eight voyages a year to different French ports carrying two spies at each time, on condition that the goods on board are 'not to be surprised or visited by English officers, and they [the London merchants] shall not be liable to any penalties'.[44]

Formal instructions as well as passes were sometimes given to such spies, especially if it might prove necessary for them to get into touch directly with admirals of the royal navy.[45] Faked passes were already a commonplace. One of Nottingham's informants reported that 'a yacht with a pigeon and olive-branch at the stern, pretty handsomely set out' had been specially constructed at Amsterdam to the order of certain English merchants, who were now looking for an able and trustworthy captain well acquainted with the French coast. This vessel had 'a large cabin for passengers and some secret holes to hide something in'.[46]

Bishop Burnet blamed Nottingham for 'our want of intelligence of the motions of the French, while they seemed to know every thing that we either did or designed to do'; but the editor of Nottingham's papers in the Historical Manuscripts Commission Reports is fully justified in his conclusion

[42] H.M.C., *Finch MSS.* iii. 176–7.   [43] H.M.C., *Buccleuch MSS.* ii. 213.
[44] H.M.C., *Downshire MSS.* i. 485.   [45] H.M.C., *Finch MSS.* iii. 41.
[46] Ibid., pp. 146–7, 164.

that Nottingham was at pains not only to organize an effective intelligence service but to acquaint himself from every other available source—such as examinations of suspected persons, intercepted letters, and information voluntarily offered—both with what the French were doing or had in preparation on land or at sea and with the intrigues of the Jacobites who pinned their hopes on them in England and Scotland.[47]

The great importance attached to the Barbary states in the early part of our period was partly due to the need to secure early and accurate intelligence of the French fleet's movements in the Mediterranean.[48]

Trumbull and Shrewsbury continued to employ spies and intelligencers to provide information about France.[49] Bolingbroke thought highly of one of them named Mezière, whom he described as 'subtle and bold . . . a veteran, and as high as his conversation can reach, [he] will be extremely useful'.[50] Of the ambassadors to France, Waldegrave was perhaps the most energetic and successful in this part of his duties. He managed to obtain, from a clerk in the French secretary of state's office, ten ciphers; and he paid the clerk 100 louis for each.[51] He was also in close touch with the Sicilian abbots who served him well for a modest financial outlay. His greatest triumph was to secure the services of Bussy, one of the two *premiers commis* in the French Foreign Office, who was subsequently sent on diplomatic missions to England and Hanover. Although Bussy was paid £15,500 in five years, very little useful information was in the end obtained from him.[52]

During the wars between Britain and France in the middle years of the eighteenth century, spies and intelligencers abounded. After 1763 Alexander Scott is said to have obtained from Choiseul's apartment of business the marriage treaty between the Dauphin, later Louis XVI, and Marie Antoinette.[53] Partly as a counter-espionage measure, the clerks in both the British and the French Foreign Offices were forbidden to receive callers at their

---

[47] H.M.C., *Finch MSS.* iii. vi–vii.
[48] H.M.C., *Buccleuch MSS.* ii. 278.
[49] See H.M.C., *Downshire MSS.* i, index (under Chenailles and Seignoret).
[50] *Bolingbroke Corresp.* i. 395.
[51] Basil Williams, op. cit., p. 102.
[52] Ibid., pp. 104–5; cf. Coxe, *Walpole Memoirs*, iii. 268, 437, 451.
[53] L. M. Hawkins, *Memoirs*, i. 5.

offices in business hours. Nevertheless, Robert Ainslie succeeded in securing in the seventies anecdotes of the French court and copies of official dispatches, which were believed to be of great value.[54] On British spies against France during the War of American Independence there is much useful information in F. P. Renaut's book, *L'Espionnage naval au XVIIIᵉ siècle. Le Secret Service de l'Amirauté britannique au temps de la guerre d'Amérique, 1776–83*, published at Paris in 1936. Sir George Rodney, while visiting France in 1778, wrote to John Robinson, secretary to the Treasury, that 'during my stay here I shall make it my business to learn the destination of their squadrons, that his M[ajesty]'s Min[iste]rs may be informed, which I shall send by every safe conveyance'.[55] George III, on the other hand, felt impelled a year later to order 'a final stop to the intercourse between Dover and Calais. We can gain nothing by the communication and certainly it enables the disaffected to give much intelligence to our avowed enemies.'[56] In the next decade a father and son named Hake were employed: the father had previously been connected with the Wolters agency at Rotterdam.[57] Malmesbury believed that they were 'stupid, heavy and interested' and thought that their intention was 'not to get or give intelligence but to get money'.[58] Another agent employed about this time was St. Marc, who had been hired for three months at a salary of sixty guineas a month and then ceased to be employed since Hailes, our minister plenipotentiary at the French court, thought he was untrustworthy.[59] Information about other British secret-service activities against France in the eighties can be found in Professor Cobban's *Ambassadors and Secret Agents*.[60]

Probably France, in the period taken as a whole, employed more spies against Britain than we did against France. Early in the period Nottingham regarded the whole of the French colony settled in London as potential or actual spies; and a hundred years later Hailes wrote from Paris that 'every Frenchman of any condition that goes to England is more or less a spy, and brings back all the intelligence he can to ingratiate himself with the Minister. The Duke of Liancourt spied as well as he could in England and

[54] *Infra*, p. 275. [55] H.M.C., *Report X, App. 6*, p. 21.
[56] *George III Corresp.* iv. 379.
[57] *Infra*, p. 274. [58] *Malmesbury Diaries*, ii. 282.
[59] H.M.C., *Report XI, App. VII* (Leeds MSS.), p. 55.
[60] See Cobban, 'British Secret Service in France', in *E.H.R.* lxix (1954), 238–48.

got the *cordon bleu*. M. de Bombelles spied in Ireland and has got an embassy. They are *sinons* [*espions*?] all.'[61] Some justification for Hailes's suspicions is to be found in the extremely full reports of parliamentary debates, regularly transmitted by French diplomatic agents in London to their government,[62] and the close contacts some of them maintained with Opposition politicians. While some of these reports may have been derived directly or indirectly from the Parliamentary Opposition, others were certainly concocted by members of the embassy staff in concert with paid informers. As a security measure during the Seven Years War, a strict regulation was introduced

that nobody should be admitted to the House, unless introduced by a member of Parliament of his acquaintance, who has to apply to the Speaker for permission. A Marquis de St. Simon, who had served with the Prince de Condé and had been in Hanover with him in 1759, had been accused of having availed himself of the freedom of entry into the House, when he was here a year or two ago, to take notes of the speeches and transmit them to his court, probably by order. He had been removed therefore from the House when this was discovered.[63]

The government took a more serious view of spies who corresponded directly with France. In 1758 a certain Dr. Florence Hensey, who had been educated at Louis XIV's College at Paris and had afterwards taken a medical degree at Leyden, was tried and convicted of having carried on a correspondence with the enemy. Hensey, whose brother was one of the Spanish ambassador at London's chaplains, had volunteered to do this and received only about £100 a year for his services. His instructions and part of his correspondence were discovered among his papers. Even Hensey, although sentenced to death, was reprieved and in a few months pardoned.[64]

Messrs. Thompson and Padover believe that the French secret service in the Seven Years War against Britain was much inferior in efficiency to Pitt's organization against France, and that ultimately France relied solely on intelligence supplied by the Russian

---

[61] H.M.C., *Report XI, App. VII* (Leeds MSS.), pp. 54–55.

[62] P. J. Mantoux, 'French Reports of British Parliamentary Debates', in *A.H.R.* xii (1907), pp. 244–69, and *Comptes rendus des séances du Parlement anglais* (Paris, 1906).

[63] Count Frederick Kielmansegge, *Diary of a Journey to England* [1761–2] (London, 1902), p. 160.   [64] *Grenville Papers*, i. 238–9.

ambassador at London.[65] None the less, French espionage in England certainly continued after the end of the war. Gabriel Jahrs was sent to report on British industries:[66] other spies were concerned with the state of coastal defences. Prominent amongst the latter was Colonel Grant of Blairfindy, a Scots Jacobite who submitted to the French government elaborate plans for a French invasion of southern England, in which use would have been made of requisitioned French fishing boats. Once safely across the Channel, the French army would march straight on London, scattering like chaff the handful of regular troops and the few thousand militiamen which were all that the British government had available for the defence of the capital. These plans were apparently stolen from the French war department, but the French government was so impressed by them that they sent Grant of Blairfindy back again to England in 1768.[67] Frederick the Great's jest that the French king had twenty cooks and only one spy, while he (Frederick) had only one cook and twenty spies was not intended to be taken literally.

British secret-service activities were mainly concentrated against France, though agents were often stationed in neighbouring countries. When Holland joined our enemies during the War of American Independence, agents were sent to inquire into the condition of the Dutch fleet and send back intelligence about the state of affairs in the Low Countries.[68] Hugh Elliot, in his anxiety to discover the objects with which two *soi-disant* Americans had come to Berlin, encouraged one of his servants to burgle their apartments and bring him their papers. When he confessed his unintentional complicity in this outrage he was censured by his court 'which', according to the secretary of state, 'disdained and will ever disdain to trust the crooked paths of duplicity and treachery' and advised for the future to 'abstain from vivacities of language and to control and discourage so criminal an activity on the part of his dependants'.[69] Soon afterwards Elliot was recalled. Spies were sometimes employed at Stockholm and one of them,

[65] *L'Espionnage politique*, pp. 151–7.
[66] *Natural Philosophy through the Eighteenth Century*, ed. A. Ferguson, pp. 94–96.
[67] Details in Thompson and Padover, op. cit., pp. 163–7.
[68] *George III Corresp.* v. 224, vi. 339–40.
[69] *Elliot Memoir*, pp. 114–18. Cf. the highly coloured account of this incident in Thompson and Padover, op. cit., pp. 168–71.

Alexander Blackwell, was executed in 1747, probably on a trumped-up charge.[70]

An important part of secret-service work was the planting of spies in the 'families' of diplomatists from hostile states. An elaborate plan to put a French spy into Hanbury Williams's house at St. Petersburg was frustrated. The Emperor Francis I revealed the plot to Keith at Vienna and also sent a courier directly to St. Petersburg. The spy's name was Messonière and he was 'a native of Languedoc who is under the protection and much in the confidence of the family of Czartoryski; and . . . it is by their recommendation that it is proposed to bring this matter about, the Czartoryskis not having the smallest suspicion of this fellow's roguery'.[71] When Murray was ambassador at Constantinople, a French spy was successfully introduced into his household and for years all his correspondence and ciphers were known to the French government.[72]

A considerable number of these secret-service agents and informers were suspected of contacts with both the British and French governments. Thus, when Admiral Rooke sent to Shrewsbury the depositions of one John Saurin, Shrewsbury replied that Saurin's measures looked 'like a trick to get intelligence' and advised the Admiral 'to secure him and his vessel for so long time as may put it out of his power to give the enemy any information concerning the Fleet that may be of use to them; after which he may be discharged'.[73] In Anne's reign, at the time of the Greg scandal in the secretary of state's office, it was believed that Valière, who had been associated with Greg, 'was more in the enemy's interest than ours' and 'that it is dangerous to connive at persons going over from the coast to France'.[74] Horatio Walpole in 1738 warned Robert Trevor at The Hague that a letter which was sent by the 'canal' of one of his secret agents 'to our minister in Switzerland was seen deciphered afterward by Lord W[alde-gra]ve upon the Cardinal [Fleury]'s table; however I think this suspicion is so loose and uncertain that I should be inclined to trust him'.[75] Hanbury Williams at Berlin, when Prusso-British

[70] *Chambers's Encyclopaedia*, *sub* Blackwell.
[71] Add. MS. 35492, fo. 78b, Keith to Williams, 7 July 1755.
[72] Comte de Saint-Priest, *Mémoires*, pp. 131–2: A.É. *Correspondance politique Turquie*, vol. 154, Saint-Priest to Choiseul, 16 June 1770, no. 14.
[73] H.M.C., *Buccleuch MSS.* ii. 342.   [74] H.M.C., *Portland MSS.* iv. 482.
[75] H.M.C., *Report XIV, App. IX* (Buckinghamshire MSS.), p. 22.

relations were at their worst, hoped to obtain valuable information from an Irishman, who had been a Prussian spy in Russia for three years and was now left quite unprovided for. Consequently he was willing to betray all he knew to anyone who would give him bread, or so the optimistic British minister believed.[76] It seems to have been the case that a number of spies who offered their services to France during the Seven Years War were really British counter-espionage agents and that this contributed to the breakdown of the French secret service during the war.[77]

As a rule it was obviously desirable to keep the diplomatic and the secret-service activities of the secretaries of state as distinct as possible. Callières regarded it as normal practice to send abroad secret agents whose very existence was unknown to the ambassador and part of whose duties was to report on the behaviour of the diplomatic agents of France in the country to which they were sent;[78] but this never became British practice. Occasionally, when there was a marked divergence of view in the Cabinet, individual ministers secured the dispatch of separate secret agents primed with their own particular views, as when Shelburne sent one agent and Grafton another to General Paoli at the crisis of the Corsican question in 1768.[79] But when it was thought necessary to control the actions of a diplomatist, without actually superseding him, the agent selected for this awkward task was always given diplomatic status.

There are, however, quite a number of cases in which a diplomatic agent with full credentials became in fact more important as a secret service agent than as a negotiator. This was the case with Hanbury Williams at Petersburg after the Diplomatic Revolution. It was the position from the very beginning of Robert Campbell in his mission to Stockholm, while in the War of the Spanish Succession, Mitford Crowe, with credentials to Genoa, was really commissioned to watch the Catalan revolt and report enemy naval movements.

Perhaps the best example of this type of dual-purpose appointment was George Cressener, who, from at least 1745, sent intelligence to the British government from the Low Countries and who

[76] S.P. 88. 71, dispatch of 17 Oct. 1750.
[77] Thompson and Padover, op. cit., pp. 153–6.
[78] De la Manière de négocier avec les souverains, ed. Whyte, p. 239.
[79] Grafton, Autobiography, pp. 204–9; Fitzmaurice, Shelburne, ii. 141.

was appointed resident at Liège in 1747. Eight years later he was
transferred with credentials to Cologne and resided there until
expelled by the French in 1759. Then he removed to Maestricht
and 'no other way occurred of giving him a proper protection than
by a credential to the States-General'.[80] In January 1763 he was
again transferred to Ratisbon as minister to the Imperial Diet.
Finally 'the indefatigable Mr. Cressener', as Keith called him,[81]
served as minister plenipotentiary to Cologne and Mayence until
his death at Bonn in 1781. At least until the end of the Seven Years
War his most important business had been as head of a British
spy ring which collected information from France, and for part
of this time he was also a subordinate official in the French civil
service. For 'stealing intelligence by deputy' he received substantial sums;[82] and in the sixties he was still sending to the British
government information about the French army and finances.[83]

With Cressener during the Austrian Succession War were associated the Chevalier Guillaume Hetzler and Dr. Fauconnet. Hetzler's letters seem to be largely copied from the *Gazettes* and
Fauconnet, who dealt mainly with maritime affairs, was told that
his information was useless and his financial demands exorbitant.
Naturally enough, his letters then ended abruptly.[84] Much more
important was Richard Wolters, the king's 'agent' at Rotterdam,
who supplied the secretaries of state with shipping news, information about Jacobite conspiracies, and some intercepted correspondence. From 1750 he combined the posts of king's agent at
Rotterdam and Post Office agent at Helvoetsluys. These appointments afforded a useful front for his main business of supplying
information which he collected from his correspondents posted at
all important French, Spanish, Portuguese, and Belgian naval
bases. On his death in 1770 his widow took over, but the efficiency
of the organization declined and the secretary of state closed down
the correspondence in 1785.[85] Even while the Wolters's agency
was in its hey-day the British government used other spies, for

[80] S.P. 84. 491, dispatch of 10 Mar. 1761: *B.D.R.*, pp. 166–7.
[81] *Keith Memoir*, i. 444.
[82] Torrens, *History of Cabinets*, ii. 211–12.
[83] *George III Corresp.* ii. 25.   [84] S.P. 81. 125.
[85] Large quantities of Wolters's correspondence in S.P. Foreign. See also
H.M.C., *Report XI, App. VII* (Leeds MSS.), p. 47; K. Ellis, *The Post Office in the
Eighteenth Century*, pp. 61–62; Jucker, *Jenkinson Papers 1760–66*, especially
p. 196; and (from the French point of view) F. P. Renaut, *Le Secret Service de
l'Amirauté britannique 1776–1783*, pp. 52–90.

example one Irvine was posted in Flanders at the beginning of the Seven Years War to collect and transmit reports from other spies whom he dispatched into Normandy and to Dunkirk and elsewhere to find out all they could about the projected French invasion of Britain.[86]

Occasionally the government did not go the length of giving a credential to a secret agent, but entrusted him with a piece of official business which would serve to cloak his real object. A good example of this was Alexander Cunningham's mission to France in 1701,[87] while the post of commissary at Dunkirk was kept in nominal existence until 1741 partly with a view to procuring intelligence.[88] Sometimes, too, a commission as consul was used for this purpose. Captain John Deane was twice commissioned as consul in Russia although sent on secret political service.[89] When war broke out with Spain, British consuls occasionally crossed the Portuguese frontier and continued to send any information they could pick up about the Spanish war effort.

Apart from Cressener, a few diplomatists and consuls owed their appointments to a successful career in the secret service. These include Sir John Goodricke and Sir Robert Ainslie of Pilton, near Edinburgh, and Bordeaux, where he was brought up as a merchant. At the most critical stage in the Falkland Islands dispute he is said to have procured, out of the duc d'Aiguillon's office, copies of the French dispatches to the court of Madrid, which encouraged the British government to take a firm line with Spain in the dispute.[90] As a reward for this and other services,[91] he was in 1775 appointed to the Constantinople embassy, where he remained until 1793. It was apparently not felt at the time that the reasons for his appointment were at all discreditable and the story was published in Ainslie's lifetime. Captain James Jefferyes, who had been Robinson's private secretary and then served as a volunteer with Charles XII in his Russian campaign, sending back news to Robinson, was rewarded with the appointment of minister resident to Peter the Great, and, after the break between Britain and Russia, as resident at Danzig. A Scottish merchant named

[86] S.P. 77. 101.
[87] Cunningham, *History of Great Britain*, i. xiii. 238.
[88] S.P. 76. 1–8. [89] *B.D.R.*, p. 112.
[90] J. P. Wood, *Cramond*, p. 22; Douglas, *Baronage*, p. 302.
[91] Including his 'Anecdotes of the Court of France by Mr. Ainslie' which George III copied out in his own hand (*George III Corresp.* ii. 311–16).

Pringle, who had wormed himself into the confidence of the Spanish Jacobites, was believed in Spain to have been 'the first person to warn the English court' of the Jacobite invasion attempt of 1719. 'For this most valuable service he was given a consular patent . . . [and] protected by the intervention of the English court.'[92] William Augustus Miles, employed as a secret agent in the Low Countries, hoped that his service would be rewarded with the position of *chargé d'affaires* or resident at Liège.[93] There is at least one case on record in which an accredited diplomatist, Richard Oakes, who had been *chargé d'affaires* at Petersburg and held credentials as Minister Plenipotentiary at Warsaw, subsequently (during the American War) played an active part in secret-service activities. He brought intelligence from Paris and news about the Dutch fleet and also visited Ostend and Brest to gain information about the state of the French naval forces.[94]

It was, throughout the eighteenth century, a recognized duty of the secretaries of state to gain intelligence by means of the post office. They exercised the traditional prerogative power, confirmed in 1711 by the Post Office Act, of ordering the interception of mail. Their inspection became closer and more continuous after the accession of George I. Correspondence from or to named diplomatists resident in London was regularly intercepted, deciphered, and submitted to the secretaries. After 1765 successive secretaries of state issued general warrants which ordered the copying of all diplomatic correspondence passing through the London post office. In addition unofficial mail was often opened on suspicion, a necessary precaution in view of the general use of cover addresses for diplomatic correspondence entrusted to the Post Office.[95]

To deal with all this foreign correspondence the secretaries of state maintained a special office, often called 'the Secret Office', under an official known as 'the Foreign Secretary'. The staff of this office increased and a distinct 'Deciphering Branch' was organized. Under George III, if not earlier, there were specialist openers of letters, engravers of seals, decipherers, and translators. In addition the Foreign Secretary and his specialists 'prepared "plant"

---

[92] J. O. MacLachlan, *Trade and Peace with Old Spain*, p. 212.

[93] Cobban in *E.H.R.* lxix (1954), 247.

[94] *George III Corresp.* vi. 339–41. I assume that the secretary of state is unlikely to have employed two agents of the same name at approximately the same time, one for diplomatic and the other for secret service.

[95] Fraser, *Intelligence*, pp. 76–77.

letters for foreign courts or agents, searched suspected letters with special "liquors" for invisible ink, identified British reports to cover addresses, and occasionally facilitated contact between the government and enemy ministers. Channels of correspondence were closely watched, and advice or "cribs" passed to the Deciphering Branch.'[96]

Unlike the secret office, the deciphering branch was always controlled directly by the secretaries of state. At first the decipherers were part-time amateurs, usually university dons. The best-known seventeenth-century decipherer was Dr. John Wallis, professor of geometry at Oxford;[97] his grandson, William Blencowe, became in 1703, on the death of his grandfather, the first official decipherer. Nine years later Blencowe committed suicide. His successor, Dr. John Keill,[98] proved 'a failure, if not a booby' and in 1716 the Rev. Edward Willes was appointed as the (third) official decipherer. Until the abolition of the office of official decipherer in 1812 and of the deciphering branch in 1844, Willes and his descendants in the male line held the office and supplied most of the staff of the department. The modest official salary of the decipherer was supplemented by gifts of deaneries and bishoprics from a grateful government.[99]

Interceptions secured by the Hanoverian post office were made available to selected ministers and helped to fill gaps in the British interceptions. Particularly useful at the middle of the century was the correspondence between Paris and Stockholm which usually passed through the Hanoverian post office. From time to time efforts were made to extend this system to other post offices on the Continent. In the early 1720's, when relations with Russia had been broken off, Joshua Kenworthy, a merchant and the 'king's agent' at Danzig, was employed to open in the post and send on copies of the dispatches from the French agents in Russia. In 1722 he proposed to include in his service all dispatches passing through

---

[96] Quoted from Ellis, *Post Office*, p. 70. The preceding and following paragraphs are based on pp. 60–77 of this work. The volumes published by the Historical Manuscripts Commission contain a good deal of information about methods of intercepting and deciphering letters, especially *Downshire MSS.*, *Portland MSS.*, *Finch MSS.*, and *Bath MSS.*

[97] H.M.C., *Finch MSS.* ii. 233, 252, 355; H.M.C., *Downshire MSS.* i. 508, 552.

[98] See Atterbury's characteristic letter recommending a successor with 'a very good pen as well as a good head. His ability in deciphering might be tried before he is pitched upon' (H.M.C., *Portland MSS.* v. 217–18).

[99] Ellis, *Post Office*, appendix 1.

the Danzig post office. This he estimated would cost £1,590 per annum in bribes to the postmasters. When the British government demurred at the expense he tried to put pressure on them. Under-secretary Tilson, in a letter dated 12 February 1723, rapped him over the knuckles for letting letters pass to force compliance with his demands, as when he wrote that he had 'viewed every letter in the mail' and decided there was nothing worth sending. When Kenworthy failed to answer repeated instructions about opening letters he was forced to give up his commission as agent in 1723.[1] About the same time the celebrated spy John Macky, many letters from whom are scattered in the State Papers,[2] 'set on foot a correspondence betwixt me [Sir Robert Walpole] and Monsieur Jaupain, the Postmaster-General at Brussels, who has engaged to open and send me copies of all letters that come and go to the bishop [Atterbury] from all parts of Europe, and whatever else he may apprehend to be of consequence'.[3] This venture proved rather disappointing,[4] as did other attempts made subsequently from time to time at other important post towns on the Continent.

The main reliance continued to be placed on the London and Hanover interceptions where, in Mr. Ellis's opinion, 'a high level of efficiency was maintained, especially in the case of diplomatic correspondence, the seals being carefully engraved, special wax procured, and opening and closing being done without trace. Neither time nor trouble was spared, three hours being regularly spent on the King of Prussia's despatches in mid-century.'[5] Mr. Ellis adds that 'the best tribute to the standard of security came from foreign governments, diplomats and private correspondents, continually trusting the Post Office and providing the government with valuable intelligence'.[6] It should be observed that interceptions not only supplied information about the intentions of foreign governments and the activities of their avowed and secret agents, but enabled the British government to observe the conduct of their own diplomatists and spies.

The 'Secret Office' and the elaborate system of intercepting and

[1] S.P. 88. 21.   [2] Especially S.P. 77. 70–71.
[3] Coxe, *Walpole Memoirs*, ii. 284.   [4] Ibid. ii. 290
[5] Ellis, *Post Office*, pp. 75–76.
[6] *Post Office*, p. 77; cf. ibid., p. 72. One hundred volumes of intercepted correspondence between 1726 and 1766 remain at P.R.O. (M. A. Thomson, *Secretaries of State*, p. 155): there are others in B.M. Add. MSS., &c. (cf. K. L. Ellis in *Bull. Inst. Hist. Research*, xxxi (1958), 159, note 2).

deciphering diplomatic correspondence continued until 1844, when parliamentary restiveness forced Peel's government to abolish both the 'Secret Office' and the Deciphering Branch. During the parliamentary debates it was said that England 'does not stand in need of such expedients for her safety'. Palmerston certainly did not share this view; and 'the loss of foreign interceptions in 1844 helps to explain the contrast between previous successes and subsequent failures, illustrated for example by Palmerston's career'.[7] One reason for success earlier was certainly the strict limitation in the number of persons involved in working the system of interception[8] and the still more limited circulation of its results.[9]

Similar organizations for intercepting and deciphering diplomatic and other correspondence existed at the leading continental capitals. Stories are told of Sir R. M. Keith, while envoy at Vienna, complaining to Kaunitz that he sometimes received from the Imperial post office the intercepted copies and not the original dispatches sent to him from London. To which Kaunitz replied airily: 'How clumsy these people are.'[10] The corresponding organization at Paris has been fully described by M. Eugène Vaillé.[11] In 1698 Prior wrote indignantly from Paris: 'These people make no scruple of opening any letters whatsoever that come into their hands', to which James Vernon replied: 'One can't put a letter into their [French] hands, but they will be thrusting their nose and their eyes into it.'[12] When Bedford was ambassador at Paris at the end of the Seven Years War his friend Rigby thought that a letter sent 'by the common French post' might be less liable to interception in France than one sent by the French ambassador's courier; and he added: 'The practice of opening letters increases every day; scarce a letter now comes from Germany which is not read, and I should imagine a Paris correspondence at present would excite at least as much curiosity.'[13] Even some lesser courts copied the methods of the Great Powers in intercepting diplomatic correspondence.[14]

In spite of Mr. Ellis's high opinion of the security measures

[7] Ellis, *Post Office*, especially appendix 4.
[8] Estimated by Mr. Ellis at 30 (*Post Office*, p. 76).
[9] Ellis, *Post Office*, appendix 7.
[10] Thompson and Padover, op. cit., pp. 113–14.
[11] *Le Cabinet Noir*, especially chap. 8.
[12] H.M.C., *Bath MSS.* iii. 194, 198.
[13] *Bedford Corresp.* iii. 125.   [14] H.M.C., *Polwarth MSS.* i. 379.

taken by the secretaries of state, it is clear that the existence of the 'Secret Office' and the Deciphering Branch was known in 1771 to the French ambassador at London, when he protested successfully against a reduction in the number of his couriers and the use of the British Post Office in order to save money. He pointed out to his government that at London there was a bishop whose job it was to decipher all dispatches sent by post to and from foreign ministers. This bishop, he added, was able to find the key to any cipher, no matter how difficult. It is even alleged that French diplomatic agents occasionally sent through the British Post Office a fake ciphered dispatch, such as the one in which Fox was praised as an ideal secretary of state, with the intention that it should be intercepted, deciphered, and taken at its face value by the British Foreign Secretary.[15]

In the Restoration period the secretaries of state had also had close contacts with the compilers of foreign gazettes and news-letters. Official British newsletters containing confidential information were regularly sent to certain unofficial correspondents abroad as well as to British diplomatic and consular agents. Not unreasonably the latter sometimes protested against this practice, which continued well into the eighteenth century. In exchange, the secretaries expected their correspondents to supply them with confidential information which could not be obtained from the printed *Gazettes*.[16] Later on the *London Gazette* was compiled largely from foreign newsletters, dispatches, and gazettes received from abroad by the secretaries' office. They had constantly to bully reluctant diplomatists and consuls to supply them promptly with news from their respective posts suitable for insertion in the *London Gazette*. Often in sending to a favoured diplomatist the official newsletter the under-secretary of state would add something by way of comment and explanation in his own hand-writing.[17] Holdernesse, while secretary of state, made a large collection of foreign newsletters;[18] and Jenkinson as late as 1779 thought it worth while to propose to the secretary to the Treasury 'that a small pension be given to the Abbé Jeaurinvilliers as it is important to engage the writers of foreign gazettes'.[19]

[15] Vaillé, op. cit., pp. 185-6.
[16] Fraser, *Intelligence*, especially pp. 26-32, 39-43, 72-75.
[17] e.g. H.M.C., *Polwarth MSS., passim.*
[18] H.M.C., *Report XI, App. VII*, p. 52.
[19] H.M.C., *Report X, App. VI* (Abergavenny MSS.), p. 25.

Use was also made in war-time by the secretaries of state of the letters sent to prisoners of war in England. During the Spanish Succession War 'the comptroller of the foreign posts gathers all the letters he can discover to be for any French prisoner under what cover soever they come and sends them to one of the Secretary's offices'.[20]

In view of the prominence of the female spy in twentieth-century fiction and fact, it may be worth while to point out that they were few and far between in the eighteenth-century British secret service. Mrs. Aphra Behn, 'the first Englishwoman to make a living by her pen',[21] was sent in 1666 by Arlington on a secret mission to Holland, but found it so unprofitable that she was reduced to pawning her rings.[22] Madame Wolters took over control of her late husband's spy-ring[23] in 1770; but she is hardly likely to have borne any resemblance to the *femme fatale* of twentieth-century fact and fiction. Torrington's wife, after her husband's departure from Brussels in 1789, may well have been involved with British secret agents in the Low Countries.

Nevertheless, Pecquet warned diplomatists that sobriety and continence were necessary to a good diplomatist; and he considered that on the whole women were worse than wine, especially if the diplomatist suffered from 'un attachement de cœur'.[24] Similar views were expressed later on by experienced British diplomatists. There was need for these warnings, since Frenchwomen seem to have been more frequently used as spies than their English sisters. The French Foreign Secretary, Torcy, apparently introduced Bolingbroke to the later Madame de Tencin with the intention (which was achieved) of obtaining access to important state papers.[25] It was similarly believed of several British ambassadors to France that their liaisons with court ladies, opera and ballet stars, and whole-time ladies of the town damaged the interests of their country. Sometimes these liaisons led to the accidental divulging of secret information to the French government. Even when this did not happen public scandal was caused, as when the duke of Dorset, during his embassy to France, allowed Madame Bacelli to dance in his Garter ribbon at the Paris opera. When a

[20] H.M.C., *Portland MSS.* iv. 475.
[21] G. N. Clark, *Later Stuarts*, p. 401.
[22] Fraser, *Intelligence*, pp. 111–12.   [23] *Supra*, p. 274.
[24] Pecquet, *Discours sur l'art de négocier*, pp. 33–37.
[25] Eves, *Prior*, p. 265.

diplomatist employed as his servants natives of the country to which he was accredited he was warned that they would probably be spies,[26] and sometimes women were included among these servants.

It would be difficult to estimate the total annual expenditure of the British government on secret service. Each secretary of state received a substantial sum for this purpose. From 1707 this allowance was fixed at £3,000 a year each and it came to be regarded rather as an addition to salary than as a fund for rewarding spies and intelligencers. From time to time, however, additional sums were issued to the secretaries for secret service or, less often, paid directly by the Treasury to the agents employed by the secretaries.[27] Mr. Fraser calculates that in Charles II's reign 'whereas in peace-time the secretaries could no doubt easily manage on their allowance of £2,500, in war-time they must have exceeded that sum'.[28] A century later the secretary of state for the Home department paid, between 13 July 1782 and 21 March 1783, £3,281. 4s. 6½d. for foreign secret service. His colleague at the newly created Foreign Office during a few months in 1782 disbursed no less than £18,115. 14s. 6d. for this purpose.[29] According to Professor Cobban's calculations, based on the returns made under the Act of 1782, 'the joint expenditure of the two principal secretaries of state, in which the share of the Secretary for Foreign Affairs was by far the greater, remained between £15,000 and £35,000 up to 1786'.[30] Not all the expenditure before 1782 passed through the hands of the secretaries of state.

On the whole I believe that the extent and importance of the British secret service organization in the eighteenth century has been exaggerated. It may be that this is because most of its records have been destroyed. Certainly recipients of secret intelligence were often adjured[31] to burn the letter or return the original by some sure channel to the sender. Great care was also taken to pre-

---

[26] Callières, *De la Manière de négocier avec les souverains*, ed. Whyte, p. 181.
[27] Thomson, *Secretaries of State*, p. 150.
[28] Fraser, *Intelligence*, p. 113.
[29] *George III Corresp.* vi. 339–44.
[30] Cobban, *Ambassadors and Secret Agents*, p. 111: details for 1784–92 in *E.H.R.* lxix (1954), 233–7. See *infra*, Appendix A, for a statement of expenditure on foreign secret service covering the years 1783–9, which suggests that foreign secret service accounted for nearly a quarter of the total cost to the public of conducting British foreign policy in the eighties.
[31] H.M.C., *Downshire MSS.* i. 515.

vent secret intelligence, especially information about post office interceptions, leaking out from the narrow circle of Ministers and technicians who necessarily had access to these state secrets. As a rule, although not invariably, such information was excluded from the office files and some secretaries of state treated reports from spies, &c., as private documents and took them away at the end of their period of office. On the other hand, a considerable bulk of secret intelligence has in fact survived amongst the state papers and elsewhere. Admittedly it is difficult to appreciate the true value of a secret correspondence which has survived, as most of them have, in a fragmentary or at least incomplete form. Also, a shrewd secretary could no doubt derive additional information by reading between the lines, calculating the probable significance of omissions, and comparing one agent's reports with those of another which have since disappeared. But after making every allowance, it cannot be said that the quality of the surviving material is high.

Even if we attempt to distinguish between mere purveyors of confidential or advance information about foreign courts in time of peace, and the inner core of professional spies who tried to reap a rich harvest in time of war, this generalization would seem to be justified by the available evidence, much of it in print. It was a stock complaint in the secretary of state's office that an intelligencer copied most of his information from the foreign gazettes, while spies filled their letters with demands for expenses and gave very little in return.

Jacobitism and the linking of internal and foreign politics had given an artificial stimulus to the development of the secret service, both by intensifying the need for it and supplying ready-made material for spies and intelligencers of all sorts. After the final collapse of Jacobitism, the secretaries of state paid less attention to the need for secret intelligence from abroad, at least in time of peace. When war came they usually found themselves ill prepared. Stormont in 1779 warned George III that 'there is at present a want of regular, immediate, secret intelligence that is highly prejudicial to your Majesty's service'.[32] But once again many of those employed as intelligencers and spies during the War of American Independence proved unsatisfactory and were discharged.[33]

[32] *George III Corresp.* iv. 518.   [33] e.g. ibid. v. 255.

CHAPTER XV

Diplomacy and Authorship

DIPLOMATISTS made a substantial contribution to the published literature of the eighteenth century, though it could not be said of many of them that 'while he was effectually serving his country as a minister, he justly acquired the reputation of a scholar'.[1] Often such publication was a mere accident, as when Villiers's letters to Frederick the Great were published and aroused the unfavourable notice of Horace Walpole.[2] On the other hand, if the dramatist, Richard Cumberland, had not been sent on a mission to Spain in 1780, he would probably not have published in 1782 *Anecdotes of Eminent Painters in Spain during the Sixteenth and Seventeenth Centuries.*

Few of the men listed in my volume on *British Diplomatic Representatives 1689–1789* could be described, as Sir George Clark describes William Aglionby, as 'diplomat and author'.[3] Macky said of him that he 'understands most of the modern [European] languages well'[4] and on at least one occasion he was accused of speaking French too well to be an Englishman.[5] His first publication seems to have been *The Art of Chymistry*, a translation from the French (1668). In 1669 he published *The Present State of the United Provinces of the Low Countries*, and a few years later turned his knowledge to practical account as secretary to Sir William Temple when ambassador to the United Provinces. In 1686 he published *Painting illustrated in three Dialogues containing Observations upon the Art, together with the Lives of the Most Eminent Painters*, based partly on Vasari's *Lives*.[6] This was soon followed by another translation, *The Opinion of Padre Paolo given to the Lords the Inquisitors of State, in what Manner the Republic of Venice ought to govern themselves* (1689).

---

[1] Sir W. Jones of Sir James Porter, quoted in Larpent, i. 14.
[2] *Letters*, ed. Toynbee, under date 26 Dec. 1748.
[3] *Notes and Queries*, 12th series, ix. 141.
[4] Macky's 'characters', *sub* Aglionby, in *Memoirs of Secret Services*.
[5] H.M.C., *Downshire MSS.* i. 215.
[6] See Tancred Borenius's article in *Burlington Magazine*, xxxix (1921), 188 ff.

Aglionby's Francophobe views made him *persona grata* to William III's government and he published in 1690 a pamphlet, *Quelques considérations sur la nécessité d'interdire le commerce des lettres avec la France*, in which he wrote: 'La France est si absolue que, tant qu'il y aura de l'argent, elle en trouvera.'[7] He was one of the very few Englishmen regularly employed abroad by William III and his diplomatic career continued in the first years of Anne's reign, when he died in 1705. Before the Revolution he had been given an appointment in the Post Office, which he retained, and several of his missions abroad were concerned with postal negotiations.

But the object of this chapter is not to compile an exhaustive list of eighteenth-century diplomatists who had any of their writings published, still less to prepare a *catalogue raisonné* of all their literary works. I wish merely to show in a general way the rather tenuous connexion between diplomacy and authorship and to indicate the main fields in which diplomatists made a significant contribution during the eighteenth century.

It may be stated at the outset that while few authors were diplomatists, all diplomatists were authors. The composition of dispatches to be sent at frequent intervals to the secretary of state was a universal obligation incumbent upon all diplomatists.[8] Indeed it was often explicitly mentioned in the formal instructions which each received on setting out for his place of residence: if not so included, it was tacitly understood and cases where the diplomatic agent neglected to furnish such reports at regular intervals are exceedingly rare. Yet the writing of dispatches, or even of more elaborate characters of the leading ministers at the court to which our diplomatists were accredited, would hardly justify their description as authors; and actual publication of such literary efforts was much rarer in the eighteenth than it is now in the twentieth century, when British diplomatists who have held important posts abroad often contrive, in spite of the Official Secrets Act, to publish accounts of their missions soon after their return home; while others write chatty books about their experiences with titles such as 'Twenty Years in the Foreign Service'. Such

---

[7] G. N. Clark, *War and Society in the Seventeenth Century*, p. 64.

[8] Newcastle (for example) warned Holdernesse, when the latter was ambassador at The Hague, that Laurenzi sometimes sent earlier accounts of what passed at The Hague than Holdernesse did. 'That', he added, 'is taken notice of' (Add. MS. 32820, fo. 263).

practices were virtually unknown in the eighteenth century. There was nothing like the Official Secrets Act; but one or two notorious cases of such publication in the late seventeenth century had established a definite and well-observed tradition that such accounts should not be published, at least until the passage of time had rendered them politically innocuous.

The first and best known of these exceptional cases of publication was perpetrated by Robert Molesworth, later first Viscount Molesworth, who had served as envoy to Denmark from 1689 to 1692. Molesworth has been depicted by Professor Caroline Robbins as the leader of a group of Whig extremists who were dissatisfied with the practical results of the Glorious Revolution. They wished to secure 'a federal system in the British Isles, an amendment of parliament, a diminution of ministerial prerogative, an increased toleration and some modification of mercantilist regulations'.[9] Although Molesworth had quarrelled with the Danish court, when he published anonymously in December 1693[10] his *Account of Denmark as it was in the Year 1692*, his attention was more directed to the British Isles than to Denmark. He was anxious that the development of absolute monarchy which had happened in Denmark should not occur also in England; and his book was 'at least as much an attack on the short-comings of the English as on those of the Danish government', as the Danish diplomatic agent at London pointed out to William III at the time.[11]

His animadversions started off a lively pamphlet warfare. Dr. William King, Student of Christ Church, Oxford, speedily attacked Molesworth's book in his *Animadversions on a Pretended Account of Denmark*. Jodocus Crull joined in the fray with his *Denmark Vindicated* and other pamphlets followed. Later on, Molesworth's book was translated into French and German and also reprinted.[12] Nearly a century later it was still in repute as a travel book: Boswell, writing to a friend about his own book on Corsica, remarked in 1768:[13] 'Ah, do you rank your Boswell with Molesworth and Stanyan?'[14]

[9] Robbins, *The Eighteenth-Century Commonwealth Man*, p. 6. Chapter 4 of this work gives an admirable account of Molesworth's life, ideas, and friends.
[10] Ibid., p. 93.   [11] Ibid., p. 99.
[12] Ibid., pp. 393–4.
[13] *Letters*, ed. Tinker, p. 154.
[14] *Infra*, p. 290.

In his preface Molesworth made his intentions quite clear: 'For although a man', he wrote,

may see too frequently the misery of such as are deprived of health without quitting his own country, yet (thanks to Providence) he must go out of these kingdoms who would know experimentally the want of *Publick Liberty*. He that travels into a climate infected with this disease (and he can find few that are not) does not only see, but in some measure feel the grievances occasioned by it in several inconveniences of living, in some proportion with the natives so as to relish better upon his return . . . the freedom and ease of his own home Constitution.[15]

Later he explained that 'the more polished and delicious countries of France, Spain or Italy are not the places where this observation may be made to greatest advantage' since most travellers are dazzled by the goodness of the air and diet, the magnificence of the buildings, pleasantness of the gardens, &c., which cast a disguise upon the slavery of those parts. 'But in the *Northern Kingdoms* and *Provinces* there appears little or nothing to divert the mind from contemplating slavery in its own colours without any of its ornaments.'[16] Starting from these premises, it is not surprising that he concluded that 'the ancient love of liberty seems to be quite extinct in the North'.[17] For this and other reasons Molesworth believed the present state of Denmark 'is fixed and durable; and that the people with great difficulty may perhaps change their masters, but never their condition'.[18]

The inevitable Danish protests failed to secure the banning of the book,[19] but it is true that Molesworth was not again employed by William III. Molesworth's Whiggish, if not Republican, principles later appeared in his translation of Hotman's *Franco-Gallia*, which came out in 1711. His preface to this work was reprinted in 1775 under the new title, *Principles of a real Whig*.[20]

No doubt it was the success of Molesworth's work on Denmark that induced the same publisher to issue a few months later, in 1694, the Rev. John Robinson's *Account of Sueden*. Unlike the *Account of Denmark*, this publication was entirely unauthorized.

[15] Preface to edition of 1694, not paged.
[16] Ibid.
[18] Ibid., p. 271.
[19] Hatton, 'John Robinson and the *Account of Sueden*', in *Bull. Inst. Hist. Research*, xxviii (1955), 140.
[20] Robbins, op. cit., p. 394.

It was even more embarrassing, since Robinson was still employed in an official capacity at Stockholm. Though Robinson's anonymity was preserved, the publisher gave a hint when he stated in his preface that the work, which was already circulating in manuscript, was 'written some few years ago by a very able and learned gentleman'.[21] While Robinson's work was not a polemical piece of propaganda of the Molesworth variety, it made various reflections upon the Swedish system of government and the aggressive foreign policy which Sweden had pursued, which were bound to be offensive to the reigning sovereign, Charles XI. To make things worse, he suggested that Sweden's achievement was not so much due to 'its native strength, as to foreign assistance of Germans, French, English and especially Scots, of whom they have used great numbers in all their wars'.[22]

On the other hand, most of the work consisted of a factual account of the history, topography, institutions, and social condition of Sweden; and Robinson, unlike Molesworth, found things to praise as well as to criticize. No official protest seems to have been lodged against this publication by the Swedish government at this time and no steps were taken at London to suppress it.[23] For a time, however, Robinson was greatly concerned lest publication should prevent his promotion from *chargé d'affaires* to an established post at Stockholm; as late as 1711, when a reissue of his work produced an official Swedish protest and request for the suppression of the new edition, Robinson 'spoke feelingly . . . of the danger in which diplomats would live if reports meant for the eyes of their superiors alone should habitually find their way into print without their knowledge and consent'.[24] Partly by chance and partly by deliberate dissimulation, Robinson's own diplomatic career did not suffer, but until his death he did his best to disclaim responsibility for his own published work. Editions of his *Account of Sueden* continued to be published, the fourth appearing in 1738, and there were also translations into French and Dutch.[25]

Another work of the same type was Abraham Stanyan's *Account of Switzerland*, published by Tonson in 1714, the year

[21] Preface unpaged: Dr. Hatton in reproducing this phrase omits 'able and', which certainly appears in the edition of 1694 from which I quote.

[22] P. 126.   [23] R. Hatton, op. cit., p. 151.

[24] Ibid., p. 155.

[25] Ibid., pp. 140–1, 153–8.

in which Stanyan gave up the Berne mission.[26] A brief geographical and historical survey was followed by rather more detailed accounts of the actual government and institutions of Switzerland. Stanyan then discussed the qualities of the Swiss people, who were universally, he said, allowed to be men of valour, though their reputation 'for wit runs so low in the world, that whoever undertakes to defend them upon that head, is in danger of being thought to have a very little share of it himself'.[27] This opinion Stanyan tried to discredit by attributing it mainly to the French.[28] The peasants were 'honest, robust and laborious' and often prospered. The lot of the gentry who did not enjoy the privilege of citizenship of the capital of any canton was less happy, since they were thereby excluded from all employments at home and driven 'to seek their fortune in some foreign service, whereof there are but few that succeed'. The citizens in turn he divided into three classes: (1) Tradesmen and merchants 'who are generally esteemed to be proud and lazy'. (2) The pen-men, i.e. those who had neither served as soldiers abroad nor exercised a trade at home. They were entirely immersed in politics and eager to secure offices under the government. (3) The military men who either served abroad all their working lives or returned home after a time to compete for offices with the pen-men.[29]

Stanyan did indeed censure the corrupt administration of justice by officials,[30] and insisted upon the bigotry of the Catholics, while explaining the political reasons for the lack of toleration in the Protestant cantons of Protestant dissenters.[31] In discussing trade, Stanyan pointed to the exclusive privileges granted to natives of the capital cities as the main obstacle to the development of local manufactures.[32] After rejecting the United Provinces as a suitable organization for comparison with the Helvetic body, Stanyan instituted an elaborate analogy between ancient Greece and modern Switzerland and concluded that, provided they avoid the

[26] This work, often attributed to Temple Stanyan, must be by Abraham, since the author states in the preface that 'the duty of my employment obliged me to be inquisitive; and a residence of above eight years has afforded me sufficient opportunities of informing myself fully about it'—conditions fulfilled by Abraham but not by Temple. See also A. Zeerleder, 'Die politische und literarische Mission des englischen Gesandten Abraham Stanyan in der Schweiz 1705–13', in *Berner Zeitschrift für Geschichte und Heimatkunde* for 1942.

[27] P. 134.   [28] P. 137.
[29] Pp. 137–43.   [30] P. 151.
[31] P. 167.   [32] Pp. 180–1.

snares of France, 'the Switzers may preserve their liberty, as the Grecians did, between two great princes [France and Austria], till such a resistless power, as that of the Romans, arise again, and overrun all Europe with its conquests'.[33]

Obviously there was little in this work to arouse vehement protests from the Swiss government. Stanyan's *Account* was occasionally reprinted, once as late as 1756 at Edinburgh, and continued to be used by intelligent travellers.[34] Publication had no perceptible influence upon Stanyan's later career in diplomacy. He was appointed, three years after the original publication of his book, as ambassador at Constantinople.

Closer to Robinson than to Molesworth on the one side or to Stanyan on the other was the earlier work of Paul Rycaut on the Turks. Rycaut had served as secretary to the earl of Winchilsea's embassy to Constantinople and *The Present State of the Ottoman Empire* was published in 1668 with a dedication to Lord Arlington, one of the secretaries of state, while Winchilsea was still resident at Constantinople.[35] It was subsequently translated into French, Polish, and German. Much later, Rycaut dedicated to William III and published in 1700 *The History of the Turks beginning with the Year 1679*. Parts of this were also combined with the earlier work of Richard Knolles (originally published in 1603), *The Generall History of the Turks*.

Although Rycaut's contributions to an understanding in western Europe of the Turks are often criticized in detail, he was usually regarded, for most of the eighteenth century, as the best western authority on Turkey[36] until a later ambassador at Constantinople, Sir James Porter, published in 1768 his *Observations on the Religion, Law, Government and Manners of the Turks*. This was the mature fruit of sixteen years at Constantinople and received the commendation of the eminent historian, William Robertson, who remarked that it was the work of a man who had observed the government of the Turks with attention and described it with ability.[37] Whereas Rycaut's career as consul at Smyrna and diplomatic agent to the Hanse Towns followed upon the publication of *The Present State of the Ottoman Empire* and may have contributed to it, Porter had retired on a pension three

[33] P. 216.   [34] *Supra*, p. 286.
[35] See the *Epistle Dedicatory*.
[36] See, e.g., E. Pears writing in *E.H.R.* xi. 168.   [37] Larpent, i. 1.

years before his *Observations* were published. Rycaut gave as one of his reasons for dedicating his *History of the Turks* to William III that it had been 'compiled by me at my leisure hours during my ten years' attendance on your Majesty's service at Hamburg'[38] and 'doth of right belong to your Majesty'. Rycaut was also connected with other literary ventures, including Platina's *Lives of the Popes* and Garcilaso de la Vega's *Royal Commentaries of Peru*.

A third writer on the Turks, Aaron Hill, who published in 1709 his *Full Account of the Ottoman Empire*, had a more slender connexion with diplomacy, being related to and for a time resident with Lord Paget, who was ambassador at Constantinople from 1692 to 1702. He himself is said to have been ashamed of this youthful work in later life:[39] it was certainly less esteemed than those of his rivals, Rycaut and Porter.

Several works about Russia by British diplomatic agents were published in the eighteenth century. Charles Whitworth's *Account of Russia as it was in the Year 1710* was not printed until 1758,[40] long after it had become a merely historical document; but Sir George Macartney's *Account of Russia 1767* was printed at London in the following year, a mere twelve months after his departure from St. Petersburg. On the other hand, W. Richardson, who had been in Russia as tutor to a later ambassador's children, did not publish his *Anecdotes of the Russian Empire in a Series of Letters written a few years ago* until 1784, twelve years after the termination of his employer's embassy. Letters written in the 1730's by the wife of the British resident at St. Petersburg, Claudius Rondeau, were not published until 1775 and then anonymously under the title *Letters from Russia*.

Almost the only publication of this kind concerning Spain was the *Letters concerning the Spanish Nation written at Madrid during the years 1760 and 1761* and published in 1763. The author was the Rev. Edward Clarke, who states explicitly in his preface to the work that he had been chaplain to the British ambassador at Madrid, the earl of Bristol. This work was less political in content than most of the others so far mentioned in this chapter, but,

---

[38] While at Hamburg he is said to have discovered the uses of the eiderdown and sent specimens home to his friends (Margery Lane in the *Nineteenth Century*, cii (1927), 562).   [39] *D.N.B. sub* Hill.

[40] By Horace Walpole at Strawberry Hill.

even so, its publication aroused some criticism. Similarly, James Vernon, who had served as envoy to Denmark from 1702 to 1706, allowed his companion, de Vrigny, to publish, only a year after the end of his mission, *Travels through Denmark and some parts of Germany by way of Journal in the Retinue of the English Envoy*.

Although down to 1789 comparatively few accounts by diplomatic agents of the country and court to which they had been accredited had been published, many more existed in manuscript. One factor which contributed to this was the practice, dating back at least to the reign of Charles II, that each diplomatic agent's instructions included a clause ordering him to prepare an exact narrative of his negotiation, the state of the court at which he had resided, and the characters of the ministers and principal persons at that court. This was probably copied from the diplomatic practice of Louis XIV, but in England it seems never to have been regularly enforced and soon became a dead letter, though the instruction continued to be given to most diplomatic agents on appointment. Many such papers were therefore conscientiously prepared by British diplomatists and are now to be found amongst the State Papers Foreign and Foreign Office Papers at the Public Record Office, or occasionally in the British Museum and elsewhere.

Some of these have been published by nineteenth- and twentieth-century historians, such as George Stepney's *Account of the Imperial Court* (October 1693)[41] and William Duncombe's *Summary Report* on Sweden in 1692.[42] Others, although they were not yet published, circulated in manuscript and won reputation for their authors. Such were the account of the Imperial court prepared by Sir Charles Hanbury Williams in 1753 to explain the failure of his special mission to Vienna,[43] Edward Finch's accounts

---

[41] H.M.C., *Bath MSS*. iii. 8–14.

[42] *E.H.R.* xxxix. 571.

[43] Coxe, *Pelham Administration*, ii. 469–82. Joseph Yorke wrote (of this paper) from The Hague to his father, Lord Hardwicke: '[Williams] *was very communicative of his productions and indeed they greatly amused me; his description of the Court of Vienna is apparently wrote to please two persons who will see it but I a little wonder at him for being so free in shewing it here* for the turn of it is very free and all our friends here are not in the same way of thinking about the Court of Vienna as he is and think too that as they have lived there longer they know it better. I think however you will be entertained with the perusal of it . . .' (Add. MS. 35356, fo. 171).

of the revolutions of 1740 and 1741 in Russia,[44] Robert Keith's account of the deposition of Peter III of Russia in 1762,[45] and Sir William Hamilton's observations on the Kingdom of Naples, 1774.[46] But the great bulk of such documents were unobtrusively filed in the secretary of state's office and have reposed there undisturbed ever since. This category presumably includes Henry Davenant's long description of his mission to certain Italian courts[47] and the Hon. Henry Grenville's account of the Ottoman Empire.[48]

These examples are sufficient to show that the diplomatists of the eighteenth century were chiefly tempted to indulge in compositions about the country of their residence; but a few of them used their special knowledge to try to influence the foreign policy of their own country. The elder Horatio Walpole and his friend Stephen Poyntz wrote several pamphlets of this sort.[49] George Stepney, the best-known career diplomat of William III's reign, took part in the pamphlet warfare which contributed to bring England into the War of the Spanish Succession. His pamphlet, *An Essay upon the present Interest of England* (2nd ed. 1701), advocated intervention by England with her allies to expel the French completely from America by arranging an advantageous neutrality for the Spanish possessions there on condition that the Spanish colonies would trade freely with England. Similarly, Lord Townshend, the negotiator of the Barrier Treaty of 1709 with the Dutch, is sometimes credited with the authorship of *The Barrier Treaty Vindicated*, published in 1712. And Joseph Ewart, envoy to Prussia from 1788 to 1791, had his *Observations on the nature of the connection which has hitherto subsisted between Great Britain and Russia* privately printed at the height of the anti-Russian Ochakov incident in 1791.[50]

In one or two cases a man already known as a political pamphleteer, such as William Eden, was given a diplomatic appointment, partly as a reward for political services. Similarly, David Hartley, selected to negotiate peace with the American colonists, was known for his pamphlets on the state of the nation and *Letters on the American War*. Occasionally the diplomatist tried in a

[44] B.M. Stowe MS. 253.   [45] Ibid.
[46] Ibid. 307, fo. 230.   [47] S.P. 79. 14 (19 Nov. 1722).
[48] Mentioned H.M.C. iii. 134.
[49] e.g. the one mentioned in H.M.C., *Egmont Diary*, i. 125.
[50] H.M.C., *Fortescue MSS*. ii. 44–49.

pamphlet to justify his behaviour after his mission was over—
the best-known example of this is the earl of Peterborough under
Queen Anne. His defence, written by Dr. Freind, sparked off a
lively pamphlet warfare.

A few diplomatic agents were more interested in history than
in politics. Thus Christian Cole, who had been secretary to the
duke of Manchester's embassies to Venice and France, compiled
from his master's papers a magnificent folio with the resounding
title *Historical and Political Memoirs, containing Letters written
by Sovereign Princes, State Ministers, Admirals and General
Officers, etc. from almost all the Courts in Europe beginning with
1697 to the End of 1708*. This he published by subscription in 1735
with a dedication to George II in which he claimed that

it not only relates great actions, and the springs of them, many of
which have been hitherto hid; but it refers to that particular time, in
which the great assertor of that British Liberty, which your Majesty
most gloriously maintains and improves, opened the way to the happy
succession of your royal family to the throne of these kingdoms.[51]

Cole's views on history are set forth in the introduction to the
volume: 'no writers have deserved more of the public, than those
who have given us plain, true and faithful accounts of those
transactions, in which they were themselves employed, and of
which they had a certain knowledge'. After comparing these to
'*French* Memoirs, which give us accounts of the amours and feats
of private men and of ladies, and ought to be looked upon as a
kind of romances', he proceeded:

It were to be wished that Ministers of State, Admirals, Generals and
others who have the conduct of grand affairs, would leave to their
posterity some authentic memoirs, out of which those who are masters
of style and method might gather and compile true histories of what
has passed before their time, and on which they might make such
remarks as would be useful, instructing and diverting to all readers;
but more particularly to princes and ministers of state in the following ages by showing them as in a glass all that has happened, and
what ought to be imitated, and what steps should be avoided.[52]

He justified the study of contemporary or near-contemporary history on the ground that 'the nearer the times are the more they
concern us, and the more they are therefore worth our notice'.[53] On

[51] P. iv.   [52] P. ix.   [53] P. x.

the other hand, he was a strong advocate of history written from official documents and avoids giving characters of persons such as were so popular in the seventeenth century, concluding ''Tis the actions of men, rather than their characters, the public is concerned in; and of these we may have a certain knowledge when a great deal of the other is nothing but conjecture'.[54]

Perhaps more interesting than Cole was his contemporary Alexander Cunningham, a member of a family which specialized so much in tutoring the sons of noble houses on continental tours that it was believed in Germany that 'Cunningham' was English for a travelling tutor.[55] During Anne's reign he was closely associated with Harley in the collection of books and manuscripts, but in politics he was a sound Whig. As early as 1697 he had served as tutor to the great duke of Argyll; and in 1715, while Oxford was in the Tower, his Whig friends secured his appointment as resident at Venice. On his way to take up this appointment, he visited the University of Padua for the fifth time, as he himself stated when he signed the visitors' book kept by that university.[56] After four years' service at Venice he came home, 'passed barrister in London and was much employed as a chamber counsel [and] died 1739'.[57] He had, however, sufficient leisure to compile in Latin a *History of Great Britain from the Revolution of 1688 to the Accession of George the First*—the last Latin work of the kind known to me—which was (long after the author's death) translated and published in English in 1787. The two massive volumes are introduced by an account of the author and his writings, contributed by Dr. William Thomson, the continuator of Watson's *History of Spain*.

Thomas Lediard, who had acted as private secretary to Sir Cyril Wich at Hamburg for many years, and is said by the *Dictionary of National Biography* to have managed the Hamburg Opera in the pecuniary interests of his master, returned to England, and published in rapid succession a whole series of historical works. The first of these, published in 1735, is his *Naval History of England in all its branches* [1066–1734] which gives him a claim to be 'the first important naval historian of British birth'.[58] This was

54 P. xii.
55 Cunningham, *History of Great Britain*, i. xxxviii.
56 H. F. Brown, *Inglesi e Scozzesi all' Università di Padova*, no. 1485.
57 Thomas Murray, *Biographical Annals of the Parish of Colinton*, p. 26.
58 Medley and Pargellis, *Bibliography of British History 1714–1789*, p. 188.

followed by his *Life of Marlborough*, to whom he had acted for some time during the War of the Spanish Succession in a secretarial capacity, and a more ambitious but less successful work, the *History of the Reigns of William III and Mary and Anne*.

Yet another diplomatist to dabble in contemporary history, although his approach is not historical but polemical, was Matthew Prior, author of a *History of his own Time*. This title seems to have been given to the work by Prior's executor: it is more correctly entitled *An History of the Negotiations of Matthew Prior Esq.* and consists largely of official dispatches, instructions, treaties, &c. When this work breaks off in 1713 the story is taken up by *Mr. Prior's Journal at the Court of France*. After his return to England and arrest by order of the House of Commons, Prior gives his own account of his examination before a Committee of the Privy Council and also his answer to the Report of the Committee of Secrecy appointed by order of the House of Commons. It need hardly be said that his aim throughout is to justify his conduct as a diplomatic agent, not to give a history of his own time.[59]

There are traces of journalistic ventures from time to time. Boswell tried to secure an essay by Robert Keith for inclusion in a volume to be published in favour of the brave Corsicans,[60] but apparently without result. On the other hand, Malmesbury, while ambassador at The Hague and much in the public eye, is said to have published an Introduction to the *History of the Dutch Republic*.[61]

But the two names which appear on the roll of diplomatists and are still remembered as historians are Lord Bolingbroke and David Hume. It is odd to think that Bolingbroke's one foreign mission was designed, according to his rival Oxford, to compensate him for not being created an earl and it seems on the whole unlikely that this experience contributed much to his eminence as an historian in the early Hanoverian period. Nor is it easy to trace the influence upon Hume's historical works of his appearances, in minor roles, on the stage of diplomacy. Perhaps the most that can be said is that they presumably strengthened the French

---

[59] All the papers mentioned in this paragraph are printed in *Miscellaneous Works of his late Excellency Matthew Prior, Esq.*, vol. i (London, 1740).
[60] Boswell's *Letters*, ed. Tinker, i. 157.   [61] *Chatham Corresp.* iv. 67 n.

influences on Hume's work which have led, in spite of his own protests, to his being classed by some historiographers amongst the school of Voltaire. Apart from this conjectural effect, the influence of his diplomatic career may perhaps be seen in the realistic approach which he displays to contemporary political and economic problems in some of his Essays.[62]

To this list of diplomat-historians should be added perhaps Lewis Dutens, since he alone among the diplomatic host became an English historiographer royal; but his voluminous published works cannot be classed as history, even as the genre was understood in the eighteenth century. His *Itinéraire des routes les plus fréquentées de l'Europe* (1786) was obviously a by-product of his diplomatic and other travels. It was intended for the use of travelling milords, supplying them with advice and information on distances, posts, foods, hotels, and what to see in western Europe. Dutens himself measured some of the distances by means of an odometer attached to the wheels of a carriage. His final publication, *Mémoires d'un voyageur qui se repose* (1806), may best be classed as contemporary history or journalism; but he is remembered, if at all, for his edition of Leibniz's *Opera Omnia* (Geneva, 1768).

In view of Dr. Johnson's opinion of the connexion between history and poetry we may consider the poets next. 'Great abilities', Dr. Johnson wrote, 'are not requisite for an historian; for in historical composition all the greatest powers of the mind are quiescent. He has the facts ready to his hand; so there is no exercise of invention. Imagination is not required in any high degree; only about as much as is used in the lower kinds of poetry.' Judged by this contemporary standard the diplomat-poets are even less remarkable than the diplomat-historians, and again the link between a career in diplomacy and the publication of verse is a tenuous one. The best example of a concurrent exercise of talent as poet and diplomatist is certainly Matthew Prior:

> While with labour assid'ous due pleasure I mix,
> And in one day atone for the bus'ness of six,
> In a little Dutch-chaise on a Saturday night,
> On my left hand my HORACE, a NYMPH on my right.

[62] The edition of Hume's letters edited by Klibansky and Mossner includes his dispatches from Paris and attempts an estimate of his achievement as a diplomatist.

No Memoire to compose, and no Post-Boy to move,
That on Sunday may hinder the softness of love;

. . . .

When good VANDERGOES, and his provident VROUGH,
As they gaze on my triumph, do freely allow,
That search all the province, you'd find no man there is
So bless'd as the *Englishen Heer* SECRETARIS.[63]

Another writer of *vers de société*, Sir Charles Hanbury Williams, had made his reputation before securing a diplomatic appointment, and much of his verse was really political pamphleteering, and therefore ephemeral. Sir George Etherege, whose diplomatic career ended under James II, and Richard Cumberland are dimly remembered dramatists who had a brief connexion with diplomacy, while Thomas Crawfurd, who served as Stair's secretary of embassy at Paris from 1715 to 1720, is still remembered as the author of the familiar song 'The Bush aboon Traquair'.

Nor are the diplomatic men of letters who wrote in prose more outstanding. Joseph Addison heads the list in virtue of his brief membership of a complimentary mission, headed by Lord Halifax, to the Electress Sophia in 1706. Lord Chesterfield is still remembered, largely for his letters to his son, Philip Stanhope, who also appears on the roll of British diplomatists. Horace St. Paul, who had fought on the Austrian side in the Seven Years War, left behind him a *Journal of the First Two Campaigns of the Seven Years' War*, published under the editorship of G. G. Butler in 1914 by the Cambridge University Press. William Fullarton, after a spell as secretary of embassy at Paris, went out to India and published *A view of the English interests in India and an account of the military operations in the southern parts of the Peninsula during . . . 1782–84*. Onslow Burrish, long before his entry into diplomacy, had published *Batavia Illustrata* and dedicated it to Sir Robert Walpole. Bubb Dodington's *Diary* is still a valuable source for anyone interested in the seamier side of eighteenth-century politics, but owes nothing to its author's brief mission to Spain after the treaty of Utrecht. On the other hand, some of the most interesting of Lady Mary Wortley Montagu's letters are due to the fact that she accompanied her husband on his embassy to Constantinople.

[63] *Miscellaneous Works*, ii. 21–24.

Nor are the links between diplomacy and scholarship much closer than between diplomacy and literature. It is true that Walter Titley, while at Copenhagen in the diplomatic service, had ample time for such pursuits. He wrote Latin verse and translated Horace, while his learned works were admired by Bentley. Alexander Cunningham, already mentioned as an historian, was also a scholar of repute in his own day, as was Henry Newton, the author of at least two Latin works, who, after service for a few years in Italy, under Queen Anne, returned to England and became a judge of the High Court of Admiralty. Lord Cardross, who was named as secretary of the Madrid embassy early in George III's reign, though in the end he did not take up the appointment, is still remembered for his services to Scottish scholarship, especially for the part he took in the foundation of the Society of Antiquaries of Scotland. Hugh Elliot's secretary at Copenhagen, the Rev. James Johnstone, published in 1786 *Antiquitates Celto-Normannicae*. Robert Daniel, *chargé d'affaires* at Brussels, composed a Latin ode on the death of George I. Jezreel Jones, a protégé of Paul Methuen's, who was sent on a mission to the Barbary states, was also a traveller and collector for the Royal Society and from 1698 to 1701 had acted as its clerk.[64] Sir William Hamilton, while envoy at Naples, filled his dispatches with scientific material, while his publications included *Observations on Mount Vesuvius, Mount Etna and other Volcanoes* (1772) and a *Collection of Engravings from Ancient Vases* (in five volumes).

Possibly of greater practical importance were the contributions made by other diplomatists to the agrarian revolution, notably by Townshend in his retirement. Robert Molesworth wrote and published at Dublin in 1723 *Some Considerations for the promoting of agriculture and employing the poor*. Here he advocated the establishment of practical schools of husbandry.[65] Nathaniel Kent, who served abroad as Sir James Porter's secretary at Brussels, later published in 1775 *Hints to gentlemen of landed property*.[66]

Only in one case, but a very important one, is there any evidence of direct conflict between official duty as a diplomatist and the claims of authorship. It concerns John Locke, who served abroad in the Restoration period and was more than once after 1688 pressed to accept another diplomatic commission. Locke, according to his own statements to a foreign correspondent, would have accompanied Lord Pembroke on his embassy to the United Provinces in 1689 had he not been detained in England by imperative business. His latest biographer conjectures that this business was the publication of his *Essay* and *Treatises*.[67] The impartial observer must admit that if this is so the gain to humanity and humane studies greatly exceeded the loss to diplomacy. It may well be, however, that Locke never intended to go on such a mission and was merely excusing himself civilly to his friends abroad.

In conclusion some near misses may be briefly recorded. On 21 August 1708 Erasmus Lewis wrote to Robert Harley: 'The author of the *Tale of a Tub* goes Queen's Secretary to Vienna',[68] but this did not happen. Would Swift have found exile in the foreign service more tolerable than rusting in Ireland? And when Smollett, a few months before his death at Leghorn, had to go to Italy for his health, it is said that his friends tried to get him a job as consul. About the same time, in 1759, Edmund Burke was anxious to secure appointment to the vacant post of consul general at Madrid.[69] If Addison really was appointed secretary of state as a reward for writing a poem on Blenheim,[70] there does not seem to be any parallel by which a literary work indisputably won for its author an appointment in the diplomatic service.

[67] R. Cranston, *John Locke*, p. 323.   [68] H.M.C., *Portland MSS*. iv. 502.
[69] *Chatham Corresp.* i. 431–3.
[70] Thomson, *Secretaries of State*, p. 132.

Estimate of the Cost to the Public of conducting British Foreign Policy (1783–9)[1]

	The year ending						
	5/4/84	5/1/85	5/1/86	5/1/87	5/1/88	5/1/89	5/1/90
	£	£	£	£	£	£	£
1. Salaries of diplomatic agents and consuls abroad	62,757	70,332	75,543	75,266	72,286	81,323	86,733
2. Equipage for foreign ministers	5,800	1,800	200	1,800	2,500	2,500	2,100
3. Extra extraordinaries to foreign ministers	1,620	1,448	1,401	2,293	5,582	552	1,556
4. H.M. messengers to enable them to perform foreign journeys		12,256	10,000	16,000	7,000	19,000	18,000
5. Foreign Secret Service	27,196	27,006	31,878	25,727	39,844	21,508	32,154
6. Presents to foreign diplomatists accredited to Court of St. James	1,710	1,639	767	1,262	471	3,434	2,017
7. Salary of one Secretary of State	5,680	5,680	5,680	5,680	5,680	5,680	5,680
8. Master of the Ceremonies	300	300	300	300	300	300	300
Assistant and Marshal of the Ceremonies	222	222	221	221	221	221	221
9. Salary of the Under Secretary	500	500	500	500[2]	500	500	500
10. Salaries of 16 messengers at £60 a year say[3]	960	960	960	960	960	960	960
11. Rent of the Secretary of State's office	311	311	311	311	429	429	429[4]
12. Stationery and incidents for Foreign Secretary of State's Office	..	..	..	2,955	5,888	1,359	3,388
	£107,056	£122,454	£127,761	£133,275	£141,661	£137,766	£154,038

[1] The figures given here are no doubt neither complete nor entirely accurate, but are intended to provide a first approximation to the actual cost, so far as met out of public funds. It should be noted that a substantial part of the cost was met from fees and perquisites payable to Foreign Office clerks, consuls, &c., by individuals, which are not included in this table. Chief clerks depended entirely on fees and gratuities: other clerks received salaries not from the state but from the secretary of state (ibid., p. 142). The actual emoluments of the under secretary and clerks for 1784 will be found listed in F.O. 83. 10.

[2] M. A. Thomson, *Secretaries of State*, p. 142.

[3] Plus board wages of £2. 12s. 6d. a week while in waiting (F.O. 366. 542).

[4] Cf. Appendix C, showing rent and taxes at £657. 12s. 2d.

APPENDIX B

Whole Cost of the Establishment in 1782–3 excluding Contingencies[1]

	£	s.	d.
Secretary of State's Salary	5,680	–	–
Profit of *Gazette*	282	–	–
Fees	2,186	–	–
Two Under Secretaries @ £500	1,000	–	–
Fees	1,419	6	8
Allowance by Act of 1769	750	–	–
Fees of First Clerk	851	–	–
Salaries of Clerks and Tradesmen's Bills . . .	1,510	–	–
Franking	500	–	–
	£14,178	6	8

[1] Quoted from Tilley and Gaselee, *Foreign Office*, p. 30.

APPENDIX C

Explanation of the Contingent Account for the Foreign Department in the year 1795[1]

	£	s.	d.
Couriers sent by His Majesty's Ministers abroad to this and Foreign Courts; Travelling Expences, and Sundry Disbursements, allowed to Ministers, and other Persons employed on His Majesty's Service	5,385	11	4
Extra Messengers attending the Office when the Established Messengers were employed on Foreign Service	819	15	10
Allowance to Clerks retired from Office . . .	1,075	–	–
Rent and Taxes of the Office	657	12	2
Interpreter to the Turkish Ambassador . . .	200	–	–
New Cyphers	150	–	–
Writing and Sending notices of Parliamentary Business	100	–	–
Translating Papers	206	4	6
Bills for Porterage	221	1	–
Tradesmen's Bills	344	14	1½
Christmas Boxes, Expresses and sundry small Payments	758	13	3
	£9,918	12	2½

[1] F.O. 95.591.

APPENDIX D

Law Officers Reports, Great Britain and General 1764–1839 (F.O. 83, 2279). Report dated 6th May 1776 from James Marriott to Lord Suffolk, Secretary of State for the Northern Department

THE extent of the powers or rather of the functions of any consul depends upon the terms of his commission. But the exercise of them executively and *to any effect* depends on the *permission* and *aid* of the Sovereign local authority in that country where the commission and person bearing it are received and allowed. Because in many countries where a Minister is received a consul is sometimes refused. It has been so in our own country in several instances; and it is a matter of grace and favour to allow a consul where a consul has not been usual, as in the case of the present consul from Russia. The commission of a consul from England runs in very general *indefinite* terms '*to do all things which appertain to the duty of a consul*'. The King's Minister [Sir W. Gordon] therefore seems to be greatly mistaken in supposing that what a consul does is to be supported by 'his *political* character', if by that he means some character which is to raise him above being amenable to any civil judicature in that country where a consul resides. A consul has no such *political* character independent of his civil. Ambassadors themselves (privileged as *they* are from any arrests) are yet amenable to courts of justice every where. When cited, they must appear or take the consequences of their contumacy, and they must answer to a charge. It is true they may appear under protest; and they may answer in bar, or by plea loco responsi dilatorie, as the civilians and foreign lawyers call it—quia differt litem, which plea is *instead of an answer*, and *gives the go by* to the demand by a previous question viz. they may appear first under protest; [and] they may extend that protest into a plea of *privilege* by way of answer. The corps diplomatique of ambassadors disavow all privileges of consuls as derogatory to the rights of their body. Even *they* must answer, therefore much more must consuls answer, being cited before the magistrate in cases of any mercantile property of third parties; for consuls have only a mercantile public character, being the centre of union of the mercantile interests of their countrymen wherever they reside. They are agents for the trading affairs of the subjects of that crown which authorizes them to *consult* and to *be consulted* with: to represent their wants or complaints to both courts reciprocally by a proper medium: they are to take care of wrecks belonging to those subjects: to settle, as in a sort of *forum domesticum*, matters of salvage, damages, wages of seamen and arbitrations, to receive evidences and protests, and to register acts of the body of merchants and to preserve effects from being embezzled in cases of absences, deaths or other accidents of owners, and to act as the chief merchant of every factory in favour of the whole and their privileges, by a sort of general consent of those who choose to apply to them and by public commission of the Prince and to prosecute all general and particular affairs committed to them, either by the Sovereign, or their constituents and principals, relative to all trading concerns—but, having not any *strictly political* character, they are to call in the aid of the public accredited Minister, if there is one upon the spot; and where any local force is wanted to support their mandates, they must apply through his medium at the foreign court for the assistance of the Sovereign Power or they must apply for aid to the tribunals in the ordinary course of regular justice, because otherwise they have not any means in themselves of supporting their authority, if not submitted to voluntarily, by their countrymen. . . .

INDEX

13–14; his view of The Hague mission, 18; keeps a good table, 62; early career of, 94–95; combines diplomacy with politics, 100, 104, 108; gives advice to a would-be placeman, 104; his accomplishments, 137; is responsible for many diplomatic appointments, 152; tries to secure promotion of Titley, 169; sent to Paris to rival Schaub, 171; relations of, with Finch, 172; Hervey's description of, 180; and the conclusion of an alliance with France without the Dutch, 184; censures association between foreign diplomatists at London and the Opposition, 193–4; verses attacking, 201; and spies, 272; writes pamphlets, 293.

Walpole, Horace, 4th earl of Orford: pays tribute to Fox as foreign secretary, 8; accuses foreign ministers in London of smuggling and stockjobbing, 56, 59; and difficulty of filling the Madrid embassy (1766), 87; and Hanbury Williams's claims to Turin mission, 105; on appointment of Scots to diplomatic posts, 118–19, 121; reports unusual method of selecting a Lord of the Admiralty, 154; accuses Mansfield of trying to make an alliance with France (1774), 196; and publication of Villiers's letters, 284; published Whitworth's *Account of Russia*, 291 n.

Walpole, Sir Robert, 1st earl of Orford: suspects George II of writing secretly to Robinson, 3; objects to missions of compliment, 79; and diplomatic appointments, 86, 88, 104, 152–4, 166, 171–2; and Wortley-Montagu, 93; his relations with Harrington, 103; believed to be aiming at making his brother secretary of state, 108; disappearance of Scots from diplomatic service under, 117; pamphlet dedicated to, 126; diplomatists advised to cultivate his good graces, 151; said to use his brother as a 'treaty-dictionary', 180; Austrian minister tries to undermine his position, 193; fall of, linked with attacks on Keene, 200; attempts to injure, by attacking Leheup, 201–2; and the 'Sicilian abbots', 266; and intercepted letters, 278; *Batavia Illustrata* dedicated to, 298.

Walsingham, Thomas de Grey, 2nd baron, 87.

Walton, John, 28.

Warren, Sir Peter, 154.

Warsaw mission: origins of, 14–15; linked with Dresden, 25; history of, 35; extra allowance for travel given to heads of, 51; competition for headship of, 129; attempt to obtain information about instructions given to head of, 195.

Watkins, Henry, 150.

Wedgwood, Josiah, 252 n.

Welsh in the diplomatic service, 122.

Wentworth, Lieut.-General Thomas, 39.

West, Gilbert, 132.

Wesley, John, 121.

Westminster election, 176.

Weymouth, Thomas Thynne, 3rd viscount, 161, 203.

Wharton, Thomas, 1st earl of, 198–9.

White, Robert, consul, 258; wife of, 258.

Whitworth, Charles, 1st baron, 21, 46 n., 137, 171–2, 291.

Whitworth, Charles, 1st earl, 155 n., 190.

Wich, Sir Cyril, 39, 295.

Wich, John, 70, 261.

Wicquefort, Abraham, 42 n., 123–4, 134, 192, 238, 260.

Wilkes, John, 93, 120.

Wilkins, J., British spy, 261.

Willes, Rev. Edward, 277.

William III, king of Great Britain: position of secretaries of state under, 4, 106; does not maintain separate Scottish diplomatic service, 8–9; recognized as king by Louis XIV, 14–15; resumes diplomatic relations with Russia in 1699, 21; leaves vacant the Ratisbon mission, 24; mediates between Austria and the Turks, 33; dispenses with the Warsaw mission, 35; recognizes Manchester as Dutch agent at court of Louis XIV, 37; gives credentials to foreigners, 38, 112; diplomatic service of, 43–45; and payments to diplomatists, 51 n., 78; inadequacy of his civil list, 68–69; and diplomatic appointments, 76, 102, 144–5, 157; tries to economize on diplomatic service, 77–78; sends Portland into honourable banishment, 87; despises English ministers' knowledge of foreign affairs, 144; expels Spanish ambassador from London, 193; his views on packet-boats, 228; employs Aglionby, 285; and Molesworth's *Account of Denmark*, 286–7; Rycaut's *History* dedicated to, 291.

William V, of Orange, 4, 60.